Merger Control in the EU

Merger Control in the EU

A survey of European Competition Laws

Prepared by

Nauta Dutilh
Binder Grösswang & Partner
Lett, Vilstrup & Partners
Slaughter and May
Roschier-Holmberg & Waselius
   Attorneys Ltd.
Moquet Borde et Associés
Boesebeck Droste
G.S. Kostakopoulos & Associates
Studio Legale De Berti, Jacchia,
   Perno & Associati
McCann Fitzgerald
Morais Leitão & J. Galvão Teles
Gomez-Acebo & Pombo
Mannheimer Swartling

Peter Verloop (ed.)

Third revised edition, 1999

KLUWER LAW INTERNATIONAL
THE HAGUE – LONDON – BOSTON

Published by Kluwer Law International
P.O. Box 85889
2508 CN The Hague, Netherlands

Sold and distributed in North, Central and South America by
Kluwer Law International
675 Massachusetts Avenue
Cambridge, MA 02139, USA

Sold and distributed in all other countries by
Kluwer Law International
Distribution Centre
P.O. Box 322
3300 AH Dordrecht, The Netherlands

Library of Congress Cataloging-in-Publication Data

    Merger control in the EU : a survey of European competition laws /
    prepared by Nauta Dutilh . . . [et al.]. – – 3rd rev. ed. / Peter
    Verloop.
        p.   cm.
    ISBN 9041112324 (alk. paper)
        1. Consolidation and merger of corporations – – Law and legislation –
  – European Economic Community countries. 2. Antitrust law – – European
  Economic Community countries. I. Verloop, Peter. II. Nauta
  Dutilh. III. Merger control in the EEC.
    KJE6467.M49 1999
    346.4'06626 – – dc21

Printed on acid-free paper

ISBN: 90 411 1232 4

3rd revised edition

© 1999 Kluwer Law International

Kluwer Law International incorporates the publishing programmes of Graham & Trotman Ltd, Kluwer Law and Taxation Publishers and Martinus Nijhoff Publishers.

This publication is protected by international copyright law.
All rights reserved. No part of this publication may be reproduced, stored in a retrieval system, or transmitted in any form or by any means, electronic, mechanical, photocopying, recording or otherwise, without the prior permission of the publisher.

Table of contents

Introduction by the editor xvii

European Union 1
Introduction 3
I. Concept of concentration 5
    1. Three situations 5
    2. Sole control 6
    3. Joint control 6
    4. Creation of joint ventures 7
    5. Ancillary restraints 8
II. Jurisdictional issues 9
    1. Community dimension 9
    2. Exceptions to the one-stop shop principle 11
    3. Applicability of Articles 85 and 86 post-Merger Regulation 13
    4. The EU and the rest of the world 14
III. Procedure 15
    1. Notification 15
    2. "First phase" procedure 17
    3. "Second phase" procedure 18
    4. Time-limits 19
    5. Powers of the Commission 20
    6. Third parties 20
    7. Judicial review 21
IV. Substantive issues 22
    1. Dominance 22
    2. Relevant market 23
    3. Factors relevant for establishing the existence of a dominant position 25
    4. Defences and undertakings 27
    Notes 28

Austria 33
1. Introduction 35
2. Definition of concentrations 36
    2.1. General 36
    2.2. Acquisition of a business 37
    2.3. Acquisition of rights over another's business 38
    2.4. Acquisition of shares 38

- 2.5. Interlocking boards 39
- 2.6. Catch-all clause 39
- 3. Concentrative joint ventures 40
- 4. Notification thresholds 41
  - 4.1. General 41
  - 4.2. Large concentrations 43
  - 4.3. Medium-sized concentrations 43
  - 4.4. Specific provisions for certain sectors of the economy 43
  - 4.5. Exemption from any notification requirement 46
  - 4.6. Foreign-to-foreign concentrations 47
- 5. Notification and sanctions 48
  - 5.1. General 48
  - 5.2. Large concentrations 49
  - 5.3. Medium-sized concentrations 50
- 6. Time-limits for notification 50
  - 6.1. Large concentrations 50
  - 6.2. Medium-sized concentrations 51
- 7. Procedural time-frame and suspension requirements 51
  - 7.1. Large concentrations 51
  - 7.2. Medium-sized concentrations 54
  - 7.3. Figures and background 54
- 8. Substantive test for clearance and political intervention possibilities 56
  - 8.1. Test of dominance 56
  - 8.2. Balancing clause 57
- 9. Competent authorities 57
  - 9.1. General 57
  - 9.2. The Cartel Court and the Superior Cartel Court 58
  - 9.3. The Official Parties and the Joint Committee for Cartel Matters 58
  - 9.4. The Criminal Courts 59
  - 9.5. The Competition Authority with the Federal Ministry of Commerce 59
- 10. Summary 60
  - 10.1. Definition of concentrations 60
  - 10.2. Joint ventures 60
  - 10.3. Notification thresholds 61
  - 10.4. Notification and sanctions 63
  - 10.5. Time-limits for notification 63
  - 10.6. Procedural time-frame and suspension requirements 64
  - 10.7. Substantive test for clearance and political intervention possibilities 65
  - 10.8. Competent authorities 65
  - Notes 66

Belgium 71
I. Introduction: An outline of Belgian competition law 73
   1. Outline of the substantive provisions of the Act 73
   2. The Belgian competition authorities 74
   3. Sanctions 74
   4. Outline of Belgian Merger Control 75
II. The concept of a concentration 76
   1. Undertakings 76
   2. The concept of control 77
   3. Types of concentrations 77
III. Jurisdictional thresholds 80
   1. The turnover threshold 80
   2. The market share threshold 82
   3. Jurisdictional thresholds: conclusion 88
IV. The substantive appraisal of concentrations 89
   1. Legislative provisions 89
   2. General comments on the Competition Council's case law 89
   3. Criteria for the assessment of concentrations 91
   4. Conditional clearance 94
   5. The prohibition decisions so far 96
V. Ancillary restrictions 98
VI. Procedural matters 98
   1. The notification 98
   2. First phase proceedings 101
   3. Second phase proceedings 103
   4. Sanctions for infringements of the Competition Act 104
   5. Appeals 104
VII. Amendments introduced by the Acts of 26 April 1999 105
   1. The new competition authorities 105
   2. The concept of a concentration 106
   3. Jurisdictional thresholds 106
   4. The substantive appraisal of concentrations 107
   5. Procedural matters 108
VIII. Conclusion 110
   Notes 111

Denmark 117
I. Introduction 119
II. Rules governing mergers, acquisitions and amalgamations 121
   A. The notification obligation 121

         B. Joint ventures 124
         C. Jurisdiction 125
         D. Sanctions 126
    III. Other regulatory issues 127
    IV. Conclusions 127
         Notes 128

Finland 131
    1. Introduction 133
    2. Relevant legislation and authorities 133
    3. Definition of a concentration 133
         3.1. Acquisition of control of a business, or a merger 134
         3.2. Joint ventures 134
         3.3. Acquisitions by financial institutions 135
    4. Which concentrations are caught 136
         4.1. Turnover thresholds 136
         4.2. Transactions between foreign companies 137
    5. Timing of the notification 138
    6. Preparation of the notification 138
         6.1. Notification form 138
         6.2. Pre-notification meeting 139
    7. Time-limits and procedure 140
         7.1. Time-limits 140
         7.2. Procedure 140
         7.3. Insurance companies 141
    8. Suspension 142
    9. Substantive test for clearance 143
         9.1. Dominance 143
         9.2. Ancillary restraints 144
         9.3. Conditions 144
    10. Judicial review 145

France 147
    1. Introduction 149
    2. The definition of concentration 153
         2.1. Concentration by way of a transfer of assets, rights and obligations 153
         2.2. Concentration by acquiring a "decisive influence" over one
              or several undertakings 154
    3. Control thresholds 160

3.1. The definition of "economically-linked" undertakings 161
3.2. Pre-tax turnover threshold 162
3.3. Market share threshold 163
4. Procedure 167
4.1. Benefits and disadvantages of a notification 168
4.2. Notification procedure 169
4.3. Opinion of the Competition Council 172
4.4. Relationship between the French authorities and the
European Commission 173
5. Criteria used for determining whether a concentration is admissible 174
5.1. First step of the analysis: Consequences of the concentration
on the competitive market situation 175
5.2. Second step of the analysis: Economic benefits/disadvantages
analysis 178
6. Final decision of the Minister of the Economy 181
Notes 184

Germany 189
Introduction 192
1. Definition of concentration 193
1.1. Overview 193
1.2. General: merger control applies to "enterprises" only 194
1.3. Merger by acquisition of assets 194
1.4. Merger by acquisition of shares 195
1.5. Merger by acquisition of control 197
1.6. Merger by exercise of influence which is substantial as regards
competition 198
1.7. Exceptions 200
2. Joint Ventures 201
3. Notification thresholds/jurisdiction issues 202
3.1. Basic turnover thresholds for German merger control to apply 202
3.2. Effect of mergers in Germany, in particular: Foreign-to-foreign
mergers 202
3.3. De minimis thresholds for exceptions from German merger control 203
3.4. Specific thresholds for newspaper/magazine publishing and
broadcasting 203
3.5. Reasons for changes of relevant turnover thresholds 204
3.6. Method of calculating turnover 205
4. Notification/sanctions 206
4.1. Mandatory pre-merger notification without official form 206

MERGER CONTROL IN THE EU

- 4.2. Content of notification 206
- 4.3. Exception from notification requirement: Referral by European Commission 207
- 4.4. Sanctions 208
- 5. No time-limits for notifications 209
- 6. Procedure 210
  - 6.1. Time-frame and standstill obligation 210
  - 6.2. Imposition of conditions/undertakings by clearance decision 211
  - 6.3. Fees charged by the BKartA 211
  - 6.4. Written statement of reasons: increased transparency 212
  - 6.5. Third party rights 212
- 7. Substantive test: dominance 213
  - 7.1. General rule: Prohibition of dominant positions/possibility to override anti-competitive effects of merger 213
  - 7.2. Creation of market dominance or strengthening of an already existing position of market dominance 214
  - 7.3. Presumption of market dominance 217
  - 7.4. Possibility to override: Balancing clause 218
- 8. Competent authorities 219
  - 8.1. Federal Cartel Office (Bundeskartellamt, BKartA) 219
  - 8.2. Approval by Federal Minister of Economics 219
  - 8.3. Judicial review 220
- Summary 221
- Annex 1 224
- Annex 2 232
  - Notes 235

Greece 241

- 1. Introduction 243
  - 1.1. Development of the law 243
  - 1.2. First and second amendment of Act 703/1977 by Acts 1934/1991, 2000/1991 244
- 2. Legislation of the merger control rules: Current position 245
  - 2.1. Definition of concentration 246
  - 2.2. Obligation to notify 251
  - 2.3. Obligation to pre-notify 253
  - 2.4. Preventive control of concentrations: Main procedure 256
  - 2.5. Suspension of concentrations 259
- 3. Competent authorities 259
  - Notes 261

… TABLE OF CONTENTS

Ireland ... 263

1. Introduction ... 266
   1.1. The Mergers and Take-overs (Control) Act, 1978 (as amended) ... 266
   1.2. The Competition Act, 1991 (as amended) ... 266
   1.3. Other relevant legislation ... 267
2. Transactions to which the Mergers Act's notification obligation applies ... 267
   2.1. The notification obligation ... 267
   2.2. Asset acquisitions ... 270
   2.3. Thresholds ... 271
   2.4. Newspaper transactions ... 272
   2.5. Non-application of the Mergers Act ... 272
3. Joint ventures ... 273
   3.1. The Mergers Act ... 273
   3.2. The 1991 Competition Act ... 273
4. Notification of mergers and take-overs under the Mergers Act ... 274
   4.1. Notification by the parties ... 274
5. Procedure under the Mergers Act ... 274
   5.1. The two-stage procedure ... 274
   5.2. First stage: Clearance without reference to the Competition Authority ... 275
   5.3. Second stage: Reference to the Competition Authority ... 276
   5.4. The Minister's decision ... 276
   5.5. Appeals ... 277
6. The substantive criteria applied in the review of mergers and take-overs ... 277
   6.1. Legislative framework for the substantive criteria ... 277
   6.2. The Section 8 criteria ... 278
   6.3. Practical application of the substantive criteria ... 278
7. Mandatory nature of filing ... 279
   7.1. Obligation to notify ... 279
   7.2. Criminal consequence ... 279
   7.3. Title to shares or assets ... 280
8. The application of the Mergers Act to transactions involving non-Irish parties ... 280
   8.1. Lack of precision in thresholds ... 280
   8.2. Practice in relation to non-Irish transactions ... 281
9. Other procedural issues under the Mergers Act ... 281
   9.1. Protection of business secrets and confidentiality ... 281
   9.2. Publicity, complaints and interveners ... 281
10. The Competition Act ... 282
    10.1. Application of the Competition Act to mergers and take-overs ... 282
    10.2. The Competition Act's prohibitions ... 282

MERGER CONTROL IN THE EU

    10.3. Procedure under the Competition Act 283
    10.4. The Competition Authority's view on the application of the
         Competition Act to mergers and take-overs. 284
    10.5. The substantive analysis of mergers and take-overs in the
         Authority's notice 285
11. Proposals for reform 289
    11.1. Expert group 289
    11.2. Recommendations 289
12. Regulation of acquisitions in the banking and financial services sectors 290
    12.1. The Central Bank Act, 1989 290
    12.2. Notification under the Central Bank Act, 1989 290
    12.3. Notification under the Investment Intermediaries Act, 1995
         and the Stock Exchange Act, 1995 291
    12.4. Notification under the Non-Life Insurance Framework
         Regulations, 1994 and the Life Assurance Framework
         Regulations, 1994 292
13. Other clearances 293
    13.1. IFSC companies 293
    13.2. Companies in receipt of incentives 294
Annex 1 295
Annex 2 297
    Notes 298

Italy 301

1. The Italian merger control system 303
2. The Italian Antitrust Authority 304
3. Relationship between the Authority and the European Commission
    and other authorities 305
4. Definition of concentration 306
5. Operations which do not constitute a concentration 307
6. Filing a notification: Thresholds, deadlines 309
7. The clearance procedure 311
8. Implementation prior to clearance 313
9. Powers of the Authority 314
10. The rights of parties involved in the investigation 316
11. Publicity and confidentiality 316
12. Substantive tests for clearance 317
13. Oligopolistic dominance 319
14. Remedies 320

15. Behavioural remedies	321
16. Structural remedies	322
17. Operations forbidden by the Authority	322
18. Clearance or prohibition due to national economic interest	324
19. Judicial review and redress	324
20. Special sectors	326
21. Conclusion	327
Notes	328

The Netherlands 333

I. Introduction	335
II. The Netherlands Competition Authority	335
Undertaking	336
III. Consequences of an infringement of the NCA	337
IV. Legal Protection	337
V. Merger Control	337
Compulsory notification of concentrations	337
Concentration	338
Creeping mergers	339
Exception for credit institutions and insurance companies	339
Jurisdictional thresholds	340
The notification procedure and the notification form	342
Exceptions	343
The licence procedure	344
Confidential information	345
Ancillary restrictions	345
Conditions attached to a licence	346
Request to the Minister	347
Practical issues	348
Practice of the Competition Authority	348
Notes	350

Portugal 351

I. Introduction	353
II. General outline and procedure	354
III. Scope of the law	359
1. Territorial	359
2. Material	360
IV. Definition of concentration	361
1. Control	362

2. Turnover 363
V. The substantive test 363
VI. Sanctions 364
      Notes 365

Spain 367
1. Introduction 369
2. Merger control in Spain: Law 16/1989, of 17 July, on the Defence of
    Competition 369
      2.1. Competition authorities 370
      2.2. Definition of "concentration" 370
      2.3. Scope of Chapter II of Law 16/1989 on the Control of Concentrations .. 376
      2.4. Notification 383
      2.5. Procedure 385
3. Special Provisions regulating Concentrations carried out through
    Public Bids: Royal Decree 1197/1991, of 26 July 394
      3.1. Voluntary notification by the bidder 395
      3.2. Referral of the operation to the Service for the Defence of
          Competition by the National Stock Exchange Commission 397
      3.3. Publicity 397
4. Requests and referrals to the European Commission under the
    EC Merger Regulation 398
      4.1. Referrals under Article 9 of the EC Merger Regulation 398
      4.2. Requests under Article 22(3) of the EC Merger Regulation 398
5. Setting proposals for a future reform 399
6. Summary 399
Addendum 401
The New Merger Control Procedure in Spain 403
      Notes 405

Sweden 409
1. Introduction 411
2. The substantive rules 412
      2.1. Criteria for application: Existing rules 412
      2.2. Criteria for application: Expected amendments 418
      2.3. Test for clearance: Existing rules 420
      2.4. Test for clearance: Expected amendments 424
3. The procedural rules 424
      3.1. Notification matters 424
      3.2. Enforcement agencies and adjucative bodies 427

3.3. Confidentiality, trade secrets and disclosure 429
3.4. Expected amendments to the procedural rules 429
4. Special rules 430
   Notes 430

United Kingdom 435
1. Introduction 437
2. The institutions 439
   2.1. Director General of Fair Trading 439
   2.2. Secretary of State for Trade and Industry 440
   2.3. Competition Commission 441
3. Law 441
   3.1. Qualifying merger 441
   3.2. "Enterprise" 442
   3.3. "Ceasing to be distinct" 442
   3.4. The "assets" test 445
   3.5. The "share of supply" test 445
   3.6. Time limits for reference 447
   3.7. Competition Act 1998 448
4. Merger Reference Policy 449
5. Procedure 450
   5.1. "Standard" OFT clearance procedure 452
   5.2. Merger Notice procedure 454
   5.3. Confidential guidance 455
   5.4. Undertakings in lieu of reference to the CC 457
   5.5. Merger fees 459
6. Reference to the CC 460
   6.1. Interim measures 460
   6.2. Period of reference 462
   6.3. CC procedure 462
   6.4. Powers of the CC to compel evidence 463
   6.5. Confidentiality 463
   6.6. Assessment criteria 464
7. Remedies 464
   Notes 467

Survey of mergers and acquisitions 471

Addresses of contributors 495

Introduction by the editor

Since the publication of the second edition of *Merger Control in the EC* in 1993, the European Commission's Merger Task Force has rendered a broad range of decisions pursuant to the Council Regulation on the control of concentrations between undertakings, commonly referred to as the Merger Regulation. The last six years have also witnessed the enactment of laws setting up a system of merger control in all Member States of the European Union which had not done so previously, except Luxembourg. Generally, these laws are preventive in nature, providing for the compulsory notification of proposed mergers meeting certain conditions. In the United Kingdom, France and Spain, whose merger control laws were already in place in 1993, there is no general pre-merger notification obligation. Preventive merger control is effected on the initiative of the authorities or upon a complaint by interested parties.

This book contains a concise description of both the laws of the European Union with regard to mergers and acquisitions at Community level and the relevant national laws and regulations. The national rules on merger control will certainly, in co-existence with the rules of the European Union, continue to play an important role in the maintenance of effective competition.

The Merger Regulation provides for exceptions to the general rule that the Commission has exclusive jurisdiction over concentrations with a Community dimension. Where a concentration with a Community dimension threatens to create or strengthen a dominant position in one Member State, on a market which is distinct from other geographical markets, the Commission may refer the case to the competent national authorities. This exception is generally known as the "German clause". Conversely, a Member State may ask the Commission to review a concentration without a Community dimension which creates or strengthens a dominant position on the territory of such Member State. This clause is generally known as the "Dutch clause". Although it is envisaged that the Dutch clause will be applied less often in the future, now that all Member States except Luxembourg have effective merger control in place in their own legislation, the clause may continue to play a role in the interaction between the Merger Task Force and the national competition authorities.

In general, it should be noted that, with the enlargement of the European Union, the Commission will wish to continue its efforts to decentralise the enforcement of the rules for the protection of effective competition within the

European Union by engaging the national competition authorities and the national courts in this enforcement. The Commission's White Paper of 28 April 1999, proposing a fundamental reform of the system for enforcing EU competition rules, reveals a two-pronged approach: opening up effective decentralisation, while maintaining an adequate level of legal security and consistent application of the rules. Although the White Paper deals only with the application of Articles 85 and 86 of the EC Treaty and therefore not directly with the Merger Regulation, it certainly sets a trend for the approach of the Commission in the future.

Practitioners may still find opportunities for some "forum shopping". National rules will continue to differ in many respects. For example, where two or more undertakings jointly acquire control over another undertaking, or together set up a joint venture, the question whether the acquisition of control or the creation of the joint venture falls within the scope of the Merger Regulation will be determined by, among other factors, the turnover figures of the undertakings acquiring control. Under the rules of the Merger Regulation, joint control exists where two or more parent companies have equal voting rights in the controlled undertaking, or exercise their voting rights jointly. The presence of minority shareholders with veto rights that do not go beyond the rights normally accorded to minority shareholders in order to protect their financial interests as investors is not interpreted as joint control. Joint control may, however, exist where one of the shareholders has a majority of the votes but the other shareholder has rights which allow him to veto decisions which are essential for the strategic commercial behaviour of the joint venture. These veto rights may be set out in the statute of the joint venture, or conferred by an agreement between its parent companies. Thus, the turnover figures of one of the joint venture partners may or may not be relevant for the determination of whether or not the thresholds of the Merger Regulation have been reached, depending upon the precise contents of the joint venture agreement. Clearly, the parties to a joint venture may wish to influence the competence of either the Merger Task Force, or one or more of the national competition authorities, when drafting the agreement between the parent companies in this respect.

This book introduces the reader to the issues of merger control which are relevant when preparing an acquisition within the European Union. Without answering all the questions, it is aimed at providing insight into the problem areas.

European Union

Marc van der Woude

Aymeric Dumas-Eymard

Contents

Introduction 3
I. Concept of concentration 5
    1. Three situations 5
    2. Sole control 6
    3. Joint control 6
    4. Creation of joint ventures 7
    5. Ancillary restraints 8
II. Jurisdictional issues 9
    1. Community dimension 9
    2. Exceptions to the one-stop shop principle 11
    3. Applicability of Articles 85 and 86 post-Merger Regulation 13
    4. The EU and the rest of the world 14
III. Procedure 15
    1. Notification 15
    2. "First phase" procedure 17
    3. "Second phase" procedure 18
    4. Time-limits 19
    5. Powers of the Commission 20
    6. Third parties 20
    7. Judicial review 21
IV. Substantive issues 22
    1. Dominance 22
    2. Relevant market 23
    3. Factors relevant for establishing the existence of a dominant position 25
    4. Defences and undertakings 27
    Notes 28

Introduction

In the absence of specific provisions on merger control in the Treaty of Rome, concentrations with a potential adverse effect on competition within the common market were appraised to a limited extent under Articles 85 and 86 of the Treaty until 1990. On 21 December 1989, the Council of the European Communities adopted a merger control regulation, Regulation No. 4064/89 EEC, which came into effect on 21 September 1990. This regulation was recently amended by Regulation No. 1310/97 EC which was adopted on 30 June 1997 and came into force on 1 March 1998.

Under Regulation No. 4064/89, the Commission has the power to review concentrations with "a Community dimension", in other words concentrations which meet the thresholds laid down in Article 1 of the Regulation. The application of these thresholds is subject to a number of provisos and exceptions[1]. As a rule, undertakings should examine whether the conditions of Article 1 are met as soon as the aggregate world-wide turnover of all the undertakings concerned is more than € 2.5 billion.

Through the use of the notion of "concentration with a Community dimension", the Regulation determines the scope of the respective jurisdictions of the Commission and the national authorities in the field of merger control. The Commission has almost exclusive jurisdiction to review concentrations having such a dimension, while Member States' competition authorities are free to exercise their jurisdiction over concentrations which fall below the thresholds.[2]

Decisions on the compatibility of a concentration with Regulation No. 4064/89 are taken either by the Commission as a college or by an individual Commissioner to whom the college of Commissioners have delegated the authority to make such a decision. However, the appraisal of concentrations under the Regulation is primarily entrusted to Directorate B of the Commission's Directorate-General for Competition (DG IV): the Merger Task Force[3].

In exercising its task under the Regulation, the Commission is assisted by national authorities. Article 19 provides for a mutual duty to exchange information. Furthermore, under Article 11, "the Commission may obtain all necessary information from the Governments and competent authorities of the Member States". Finally, Articles 12 and 13 call for co-operation between the Commission and national authorities for investigation purposes.

Regulation No. 4064/89 has created a body of substantive and procedural rules designed to enable the Commission to control concentrations which could potentially affect competition within the Community. Under the Regulation, a concentration with a Community dimension must be notified to the Commission[4] and must be suspended until it has been approved[5]. Within a month of notification[6], the Commission must decide whether or not the concentration gives rise to competition concerns. If it does, then the Commission must initiate second phase proceedings[7]. The duration of these proceedings must not exceed four months[8]. During these four months, the Commission must determine whether the concentration creates or strengthens a dominant position as a result of which effective competition would be significantly impeded in the common market or in a substantial part of it[9]. If it does then the Commission must declare it incompatible with the common market[10].

A decision of compatibility adopted on completion of either first phase or second phase proceedings may be the result of a commitment on the part of the undertakings concerned to modify the original concentration plan so as to ensure the compatibility of the concentration with the common market. In that case the Commission's decision may require these undertakings to fulfil certain conditions and obligations[11]. If they fail to do so, the Commission is entitled to revoke the declaration of compatibility[12]. Such a decision may also be revoked where the Commission finds that it was based on incorrect information for the undertaking responsible[13].

Finally if a concentration has already been implemented when the Commission adopts a prohibition decision pursuant to Article 8(3), the Commission may "require the undertakings or assets brought together to be separated or the cessation of joint control or any other action that may be appropriate in order to restore conditions of effective competition."[14]

Information concerning the application of the Regulation and the policy of the European Community in matters of merger control is available from a large number of sources such as:
- the Official Journal of the European Communities
- the home page of the Directorate-General for Competition (DG IV) on the Internet: http://www.europa.eu.int/comm/dg04
- the Commission's annual report on competition policy
- DG IV's EC competition policy newsletter, published three times a year
- non-official sources such as reviews and textbooks with an interest in Community law.

I. Concept of concentration

1. Three situations

A concentration within the meaning of Regulation No. 4064/89 arises in three situations:
   (i) where two previously independent undertakings merge[15]; or
   (ii) where one or more persons already controlling at least one undertaking acquire direct or indirect control of the whole or parts of one or more other undertakings[16]; or
   (iii) where one or more undertakings already controlling at least one undertaking acquire direct or indirect control of the whole or parts of one or more other undertakings[17].

All three situations correspond to a similar occurrence, namely a change in control over an undertaking. Therefore "control" is the essential criterion to establish whether a transaction amounts to a concentration within the meaning of the Regulation.

Although the Regulation is commonly referred to as the "Merger Regulation", the term "merger" is used therein exclusively to refer to the first situation, whereas the phrase "acquisition of control" relates to the other two. The Regulation does not define what constitutes a "merger" within the meaning of Article 3(1)(a). In its 1998 Notice on the Concept of Concentration[18], the Commission has shed some light on its understanding of that term. The Notice identifies two types of "mergers"; legal mergers and *de facto* amalgamations. A legal merger arises either when two or more undertakings amalgamate into a new undertaking and cease to exist as separate legal entities or when an undertaking is absorbed by another, the latter retaining its legal identity while the former ceases to exist as a legal entity. By contrast, a *de facto* amalgamation does not affect the legal personality of the parties. It occurs when the activities of previously independent undertakings are combined to form a single economic unit. The Notice makes it clear that "a prerequisite for the determination of a single economic unit is the existence of a permanent, single economic management."[19]

Indications of what will amount to an "acquisition of control" within the meaning of Article 3(1)(b) can be found in the Regulation itself and in the

1998 Notice on the Concept of Concentration. According to Article 3(3) of the Regulation, control is constituted by rights, contracts or any other means which confer the possibility of exercising decisive influence on an undertaking. Since control is defined as the mere possibility of exercising influence, there is no doubt that it exists even where this influence is not actually exercised. Article 3(3) provides two examples of what may confer decisive influence: (a) ownership or the right to use all or part of the assets of an undertaking; and (b) rights or contracts which confer decisive influence on the composition, voting or decisions of the organs of an undertaking. Although it is not expressly stated in the Regulation, options to acquire shares will not normally be regarded as conferring decisive influence[20].

2. Sole control

Control can be held either solely or jointly. In the aforementioned Notice, the Commission provided useful guidance as to what will amount to sole control. The Commission took the view that sole control is normally acquired on a legal basis where an undertaking acquires a majority of the voting rights in a company. It accepted that sole control may also result from the acquisition of a "qualified minority" of the share capital[21]. This may be established on a legal basis where specific rights are attached to the minority shareholding, thus conferring on the minority shareholder either a majority of the voting rights or the power to appoint more than half the members of the supervisory board or the board of directors. It may also be established on a *de facto* basis where the minority shareholder is highly likely to obtain a majority at the shareholders' meeting. This may occur where the remaining shares are widely dispersed and it is thus improbable that all the smaller shareholders will attend the meeting. Finally, sole control may also arise where a minority shareholder has acquired the right to manage the activities of the company and to determine its business policy.

3. Joint control

The Notice has provided similar guidance in relation to joint control. It states that the Commission will find joint control to exist where two or more undertakings or persons have the possibility of exercising decisive influence over another undertaking because they have the power to oppose strategic decisions concerning the controlled undertaking. Section 2 of the Notice lists three situations where this will be the case. The first situation is where there are only two parent companies which share equally the voting rights in the controlled undertaking or have the right to appoint an equal number of members to its decision-making bodies. The second situation arises either where there are two parent companies which do not enjoy equal rights or where there are more than two parent companies. If in both cases the minority shareholders have the right to veto essential strategic decisions, then joint control may exist. The third and last situation is where there are two or more parent companies which, even in the absence of specific veto rights, exercise their voting rights jointly.

The significance of the distinction between joint control and sole control is particularly obvious where a transaction leads to a change in the structure of control of an undertaking. Indeed, such a transaction may amount to a concentration within the meaning of Regulation No. 4064/89. Thus a passage from joint control to sole control or a change in the share-holding in an existing joint venture are operations which may constitute notifiable concentrations[22].

4. Creation of joint ventures

Another essential feature of merger control at the EC level is that joint ventures occupy a special position within the scheme. In its original form, Article 3(2) of Regulation No. 4064/89 introduced a distinction between co-operative joint ventures and concentrative joint ventures. Joint ventures which had as their object or effect the co-ordination of the competitive behaviour of undertakings (the parent companies) which remained independent fell into the former category. Joint ventures performing on a lasting basis all the functions of an autonomous economic entity, which did not give rise to co-ordination of the competitive behaviour amongst themselves or between them and the joint venture, fell into the latter. All co-operative joint ventures fell outside the scope of the Regulation. Regulation No. 1310/97, which entered into force on 1 March 1998, has changed this situation by collapsing the strict distinction between co-operative and concentrative joint ventures. Some co-operative joint ventures are now included within the notion of concentrative joint ventures. This results from amendments to Article 3(2) of Regulation No. 4064/89 and from the insertion of a new paragraph 4 in Article 2 which states that full-function joint ventures which have as their object or effect the co-ordination of the competitive behaviour of the parent companies constitute concentrations within the meaning of Article 3. The effect of these changes is that the question determining the application of the Regulation to joint ventures is not so much whether the joint venture is concentrative or co-operative as it is whether or not the joint venture is a full-function joint venture. A full-function joint venture is one which performs on a lasting basis all the functions of an autonomous economic entity. In order to do so, the joint venture must have a management dedicated to its day-to-day operations as well as sufficient financial and human resources and assets [23]. A joint venture that only performs one of the business activities of the parent companies, such as research and development, production or distribution, is not a full-function joint venture [24].

As already mentioned full-function joint ventures which have as their object or effect the co-ordination of the competitive behaviour of the parent companies now constitute concentrations within the meaning of Article 3 (as amended by Regulation No. 1310/97). Article 2(4) provides that the co-operative aspects of such joint ventures are to be assessed within the same procedure as the concentration. However the criteria in accordance with which their compatibility with the common market will be assessed are primarily the criteria of Article 85(1) and (3) of the Treaty [25].

5. Ancillary restraints

The successful implementation of a concentration usually requires the undertakings concerned to accept a certain amount of restrictions on their freedom of action in the market. Articles 6(1)(b) and 8(2) of Regulation No. 4064/89 provides that a decision of the Commission declaring a concentration compatible with the common market must clear such restrictions in so far as they are directly related and necessary to the implementation of the concentration [26].

In its "Notice regarding restrictions ancillary to concentrations" of 14 August 1990 [27], the Commission indicated that restrictions would be considered "necessary" where "in their absence the concentration could not be implemented or could only be implemented under more uncertain conditions, at substantially higher cost, over an appreciably longer period or with considerably less probability of success" [28]. As to the phrase "directly related" the Commission understands it to mean that the restrictions should be "subordinate in importance to the main object of the concentration" and not wholly different in nature to the restrictions which result from the concentration itself[29]. The most commonly encountered type of restrictions are non-competition clauses. For instance, where the concentration is in the form of an acquisition of sole control over an undertaking, the seller may agree to refrain to a certain extent from competing with the acquirer. The Notice states that such a prohibition on competition is justified only when its duration, its geographical field of application, its subject matter and the persons subject to it do not exceed what is reasonably necessary to that end[30]. The Commission takes the view that an acceptable duration for such a restriction is five years where the transfer of the undertaking includes the goodwill accumulated by the vendor and the know-how he has developed[31]. If the transfer of the undertaking includes only the goodwill, then a period of two years will be acceptable[32]. However, the Commission is free to depart from these rules when particular circumstances so require.

Where the concentration is in the form of a joint venture, the parent companies may enter into an agreement not to compete with their joint venture. Such a restriction "will be recognised as an integral part of the concentration"[33] and will be assessed together with it[34].

Other types of restriction which may be regarded as ancillary if they are necessary and directly related to the implementation of the concentration include licences of industrial and intellectual property rights and know-how, purchase and supply agreements.

II. Jurisdictional issues

1. Community dimension

Regulation No. 4064/89 intended to introduce a mechanism of merger control at the Community level which would obviate the need for multiple filings of concentrations[35]. In order to give effect to this "one-stop shop" principle, the Regulation was drafted in such a way as to remove the risk of an overlap between the respective jurisdictions of the Commission and the competent national authorities. As already mentioned, the allocation of jurisdiction between these two sources of control under the Regulation depends on the concept of a "concentration with a Community dimension". The general rule, embodied in Article 21(2) of Regulation No. 4064/89, is that "[n]o Member

State shall apply its national legislation to any concentration that has a Community dimension". This provision has the effect of conferring upon the Commission quasi-exclusive jurisdiction over such concentrations.

Whether a concentration has a Community dimension depends on whether it meets the threshold requirements laid down in Article 1 of the Regulation. Article 1(2) of the Regulation states that:

"a concentration has a Community dimension where:
(a) the combined aggregate world-wide turnover of all the undertakings concerned is more than €5000 million; and
(b) the aggregate Community-wide turnover of each of at least two of the undertakings concerned is more than €250 million,

unless each of the undertakings concerned achieves more than two thirds of its aggregate Community-wide turnover within one and the same Member State."

In the years that followed the entry into force of the Regulation, businesses expressed concern over these thresholds. Many felt that they were too high, as a result of which too many concentrations remained subject to control in the various Member States. They argued that this defeated one of the aims of the Regulation, which was to avoid multiple filings. The Community legislator was receptive to this argument. Response came in the form of a new Article 1(3) of the Regulation[36] which introduced lower additional thresholds. The provision states that:

"a concentration that does not meet the thresholds laid down in Article 1(2) has a Community dimension where:
(a) the combined aggregate world-wide turnover of all the undertakings concerned is more than €2500 million;
(b) in each of at least three Member States, the combined aggregate turnover of all the undertakings concerned is more than €100 million;
(c) in each of at least three Member States included for the purpose of point (b), the aggregate turnover of each of at least two of the undertakings concerned is more than €25 million; and
(d) the aggregate Community-wide turnover of each of at least two of the undertakings concerned is more than €100 million,

unless each of the undertakings concerned achieves more than two thirds of its aggregate Community-wide turnover within one and the same Member State."

A recurring notion in Article 1 and throughout the Regulation is that of "undertakings concerned". This notion was clarified by a Commission Notice[37] issued in 1994. A definition of this phrase can be found in paragraph 3 of the introduction: "From the point of view of determining jurisdiction, the undertakings concerned are, broadly speaking, the actors in the transaction in so far as they are the merging, or acquiring and acquired parties."

According to Article 5(1) of the Regulation, the aggregate turnover of an undertaking comprises the amounts derived by the undertakings concerned in the preceding financial year from the sale of products and the provision of services falling within the undertakings' ordinary activities after deduction of sales rebates and of VAT and other taxes directly related to turnover. It excludes the sale of products or the provision of services between the undertakings concerned, those undertakings over which they have direct or indirect control and those undertakings which have direct or indirect control over them. As to the geographical allocation of turnover, Article 5(1) §2 provides that the location of turnover is determined by the location of the customer at the time of the transaction.

Paragraphs 3 and 4 of Article 5 lay down special rules for the application of the thresholds to financial institutions and insurance undertakings. As far as financial institutions are concerned, the figure to be used in lieu of turnover is the sum total of interest income and similar income, income from securities, commissions receivable, net profit on financial operations and other operating income. As far as insurance undertakings are concerned, the figure to be used is the value of gross premiums written.

By contrast, the Regulation contains no special rules concerning public undertakings. Recital 12 stresses that the principle of non-discrimination between the public and private sectors must be respected. It states that, in the public sector, calculation of the turnover of an undertaking concerned in a concentration needs to take account of undertakings making up an economic unit with an independent power of decision, irrespective of the way in which their capital is held or of the rules of administrative supervision applicable to them. A concentration between public undertakings governed by the same public agency may have to be notified[38].

2. Exceptions to the one-stop shop principle

In some situations, the provisions of the Regulation derogate from the one-stop shop principle described above. Thus, as already mentioned, there are exceptions to the general rule according to which the Commission has exclusive jurisdiction over concentrations with a Community dimension. The first exception concerns concentrations which threaten to create or strengthen a dominant position as a result of which competition would be significantly impeded on a market, within a Member State, which presents all the characteristics of a distinct market[39]. In that case, Article 9 provides that the Commission may refer the case, in its entirety or partially, to the competent national authorities and allow them to exercise their jurisdiction over the concentration in question in lieu of itself.

Conversely, under Article 22(3) of the Regulation, a Member State or group of Member States may ask the Commission to review a concentration which does not have a Community dimension in so far as it affects trade between Member States. If the Commission then finds that this concentration creates or strengthens a dominant position capable of significantly impeding competition on the territory of this Member State, it may adopt one of the decisions provided for in Article 8 paragraphs (2), (3) and (4)[40].

The second exception to the exclusive jurisdiction of the Commission to review concentrations with a Community dimension relates to the situation where a Member State raises concerns over the protection of its legitimate interests. Article 21(3) allows Member States to take appropriate measures to ensure this protection. It lists three interests which will always be regarded as legitimate: public security, plurality of the media and prudential rules[41]. Other public interests may be accepted as legitimate interests by the Commission if it regards them as compatible with Community law. For the Commission to make a determination on compatibility, all such public interests must be notified to it before the Member State concerned can rely on them to adopt appropriate measures.

The third exception stems from Article 223(1)(b) of the EC Treaty. This provides that a Member State may take such measures as are considered "necessary for the protection of the essential interests of its security which are connected with the production or trade in arms, munitions and war material". Under this provision, Member States may decide that undertakings operating within their jurisdiction should not notify their transaction to the Commission. However, notification remains compulsory for "dual use goods" and the purely civil aspects of the transaction[42].

3. Applicability of Articles 85 and 86 post-Merger Regulation

One important issue which arose from the adoption and entry into force of Regulation No. 4064/89 is the extent to which Articles 85 and 86 EC remain available as instruments for the control of concentrations by the Commission. There is little doubt that the Commission will no longer resort to either Article to appraise concentrations with a Community dimension. This would go against the purpose of the Regulation, which was to become the only instrument for the control of concentrations from the point of view of their effect on competition in the Community[43]. Moreover, Article 22(2) of the Regulation has made Regulation No. 17/62 inapplicable to all concentrations, with the exception of joint ventures that do not have a Community dimension and which have a co-operative object or effect.

Thus the powers which the Commission would require to successfully apply Articles 85 and 86 to such concentrations have been taken away from it. In fact the latter point is also true in relation to concentrations which do not have a Community dimension since the disapplication of Regulation No. 17/62 concerns all types of concentrations. Furthermore, the Commission's express policy is not to apply Articles 85 and 86 to concentrations which fall below the thresholds.

The issue of the continuing applicability of Articles 85 and 86 EC after the entry into force of Regulation No. 4064/89 also arises in relation to national authorities and national courts. In theory, since both provisions have direct effect, it should remain possible for the latter to enforce them. However, the enforcement of Article 85 by national authorities or courts has become problematic, since the Commission no longer has the power to grant exemptions under Article 85(3) for concentrations which could have been caught by Article 85(1). This is because Article 22(2) of Regulation No. 4064/89 has made Regulation No. 17/62 inapplicable to concentrations. By contrast, Regulation No. 4064/89 does not preclude national courts from applying Article 86 to concentrations. However, where the concentration has a Community dimension, the Regulation will apply. The application by the Commission of Article 2 thereof should then make it unnecessary for a national court to apply Article 86 EC to the same transaction since the essence of the tests included in these two provisions is essentially the same. Where the concentration does not have a Community dimension, nothing prevents the application of Article 86 by national courts. However, in practice, this will rarely occur.

4. The EU and the rest of the world

Important jurisdictional issues also arise from the geographical scope of Regulation No. 4064/89. The Regulation applies to the territory of the European Economic Area (EEA). This trade area was created by the "EEA Agreement", which entered into force in January 1994. It now includes the 15 Member States of the European Union and three out of the four members of the European Free Trade Area (EFTA), namely Iceland, Liechtenstein and Norway. The Commission has exclusive jurisdiction within the entire territory of the EEA to appraise concentrations which meet the threshold requirements set out in Article 1 of the Regulation. However, if the thresholds are only met within the territory of the EFTA, then it will be for the EFTA's own competition authority, the Surveillance Authority, to exercise its jurisdiction. This will not affect the right of EU Member States' competition authorities to exercise their own jurisdiction over the same transaction if it contravenes with their national competition rules.

The fact that a concentration takes place outside of the EEA territory does not prevent the application of Regulation No. 4064/89. Recital 11 states that "a concentration with a Community dimension exists … where the concentrations are affected by undertakings which do not have their principal fields of activities in the Community but which have substantial operations there". An oft-cited example of a decision giving effect to this understanding of the geographical scope of the Regulation is the decision of the Commission concerning the Boeing/McDonnell-Douglas merger[44]. Although both undertakings are active mainly in the United States, their Community turnovers made the Regulation applicable to this transaction.

As an increasing number of transactions have effects which extend far beyond the boundaries of a particular state, continent or trade area, there is a growing need for international co-operation in competition matters. This has led the Community to conclude agreements with the United States for co-operation and co-ordination of US and EU competition policies, first in 1991[45] and then in 1998[46]. The 1991 Agreement places the parties under a duty to exchange relevant information[47], to assist each other[48], to co-operate in the enforcement of their respective competition rules (positive comity)[49] and to refrain from enforcing these rules in a manner which would harm important interests of the other party (traditional comity)[50]. The 1991 Agreement contains specific provisions concerning merger control. In particular, it states that where a merger is notified to one party's authorities and one or more of the undertakings concerned are incorporated or organised under the laws of the other party, these authorities are to notify the other party's authorities if their enforcement activities may affect the other party's interests. The 1998 Agreement has reinforced the positive comity mechanism of the 1991 Agreement; it provides that the competition authorities of either party may request the competition authorities of the other party "to investigate and, if warranted, to remedy anti-competitive activities in accordance with the Requested Party's competition rules."[51] The Agreement also contains, *inter alia*, provisions concerning the use of information exchanged (with due regard for its potentially confidential nature)[52], as well as provisions for the deferral or suspension of investigations or enforcement activities by one party when enforcement activities of the other party are still pending[53]. A co-operation agreement has also been concluded between the European Community and Canada.

III. Procedure

1. Notification

Concentrations with a Community dimension must be notified to the Commission. Notification is to take place no more than 1 week after the conclusion of the agreement, the announcement of the public bid or the acquisition of a controlling interest. That week begins when the first of these events occurs.

If the concentration consists of a merger within the meaning of Article 3(1)(a) or an acquisition of joint control within the meaning of Article 3(1)(b) then it is to be notified jointly by the parties to the merger or by the undertakings acquiring joint control. In all other cases, the concentration must be notified by the person or undertaking acquiring control of the whole or parts of one or more undertakings.

Notification of concentrations to the Community must be made by means of a special form called "Form CO". The current version of the form is to be found in Regulation No. 447/98. Form CO specifies the information that must be provided by any person or undertaking notifying a concentration to the Commission, and the format in which that information is to be laid out. The information to be provided consists of:

- (a) information on the notifying parties and their representatives (Section 1)
- (b) the nature of the concentration; a list of the economic sectors involved; details of the turnover of the undertakings concerned (Section 2)
- (c) for each of the parties, a list of all undertakings belonging to the same group (Section 3)
- (d) details of financial and personal links between these groups and other undertakings operating on the affected relevant product markets; details of recent acquisitions of undertakings active on these affected markets by the aforementioned groups (Section 4)
- (e) information on the affected markets (Section 7)
- (f) information on the general conditions within these markets (Section 8)
- (g) general market information and information on other general matters (Section 9 and 11)
- (h) where the concentration is a joint venture, information on any co-operative effects it may have (Section 10)
- (i) a standard declaration signed by the notifying parties or their representatives guaranteeing in particular the completeness and accuracy of the information they have provided (Section 12).

The notification of a concentration is therefore a burdensome process, especially in view of the fact that supporting documentation must be provided for most of the aforementioned information. However, where a joint venture has no, or *de minimis*, activities within the territory of the EEA, notification can be effected by means of short form[54], as a result of which the notifying parties need not provide all the information normally required by Form CO.

Notifications which do not provide all relevant information may be declared incomplete.[55] This implies that the Commission is not prepared to review and hence to approve the concentration. In order to avoid such problems, it is recommended to contact the DG IV case team to discuss which information of Form CO is actually required. However, DG IV will only be prepared to accept such pre-notification meetings if it is adequately briefed in advance.[56]

Failure to notify a concentration may lead to sanctions being imposed by the Commission in the form of fines[57]. Any information provided by the notifying parties in the course of notification which amounts to a business secret must not be made public by the Commission[58].

The Commission may sometimes find that an operation which has been notified does not constitute a concentration within the meaning of Article 3 of Regulation No. 4064/89. If the parties so request, the Commission may then treat the notification as an application or notification under Regulation No. 17/62 or one of the other Regulations made pursuant to Article 87 EC. This is known as the "conversion of notifications"[59].

Concentrations with a Community dimension are not to go ahead until they have been notified and they must be suspended until they have been declared compatible with the common market[60]. Article 7(4) of the Regulation provides that the Commission may, on request, grant a derogation from this requirement where serious damage would be caused to one of the undertakings concerned if the transaction were postponed. A request for a derogation must be reasoned.

2. "First phase" procedure

During this initial period of examination, the Commission verifies that the notification is complete and issues requests for any information which the parties have failed to provide. It publishes a notice in the Official Journal calling upon interested third parties to make representations in relation to the concentration.

Article 6 of the Regulation provides that once the Commission has examined a notification, it may reach any one of three conclusions. The type of decision which the Commission is to take in each case is predetermined by the Regulation:
  (a) where the Commission finds that the concentration does not fall within the scope of the Regulation, it must adopt a decision recording that finding (Article 6(1)(a));
  (b) where it finds that the concentration does fall within the scope of the Regulation but does not raise serious doubts as to its compatibility with the common market, it must adopt a decision declaring that the concentration is indeed compatible (Article 6(1)(b)). Such an outcome may obtain where the undertakings have committed themselves to modifying the concentration plan in such a way that the transaction no longer poses a threat to competition (Article 6(1a));
  (c) where it finds that the concentration not only falls within the scope of the Regulation but also raises serious doubts as to its compatibility

with the common market, then it must decide to initiate proceedings (Article 6(1)(c)).

All three types of decision must be notified to the undertakings concerned and the competent authorities of the Member States.

3. "Second phase" procedure

This second phase begins when the Commission adopts a decision under Article 6(1)(c). It then carries out a more detailed investigation of the concentration. If following that investigation it is satisfied that the relevant operation is in fact compatible with the common market, then it may adopt a decision under Article 8(2) declaring the concentration to be compatible with the common market. In some cases, this outcome is achieved thanks to a modification by the undertakings concerned of the concentration plan which cancels the potentially harmful effects of the concentration on the structure of competition in the Community. The Commission may then attach to its decision any condition or obligation which its deems necessary to ensure that the undertakings fulfil their commitments.

Where the Commission takes the view that the concentration's adverse effects on competition have not been cancelled by a modification of the concentration plan, a written statement of objections is issued to the parties[61]. The latter are then given the opportunity to respond to these objections in writing and/or exceptionally, by way of an oral hearing. For this purpose they are given access to all parts of the file which do not contain confidential information. They may still at this stage enter into commitments *vis-à-vis* the Commission. If they fail nonetheless to convince the Commission that the concentration does not significantly impede competition in the common market, then the Commission shall issue a decision under Article 8(3) of the Regulation declaring that the concentration is incompatible with the common market. A particular situation arises where a concentration which is incompatible with the common market has already been implemented. The Commission may then order the concentration to be brought to an end. Such a decision can be included within a decision adopted pursuant to Article 8(3)[62] or can be adopted as a separate decision[63].

Article 19 of Regulation No. 4064/89 created an Advisory Committee consisting of representatives of the national authorities (one or two per Member

State). Before the Commission can adopt a decision pursuant to Article 8(2) declaring a concentration to be compatible with the common market, regardless of whether or not this declaration is made subject to the type of conditions or obligations envisaged by Article 8(2) § 2, the Commission must consult the Advisory Committee. Consultation takes place at a joint meeting chaired by the Commission. The opinion which the Committee delivers is appended to the Commission's draft decision. The Commission is required to take the utmost account of this opinion and to inform the Committee of the manner in which it has been taken into account.

4. Time-limits

Time-limits play an important part in the unfolding of the procedure described above. As was already stated, notification of a concentration with a Community dimension must take place no more than one week after the conclusion of the agreement, or the announcement of the public bid, or the acquisition of a controlling interest. That week begins to run when the first of these events occurs. Fines may be imposed for failure to comply with this time-limit.

Article 10 of the Regulation sets out the time-limits for the Commission to initiate proceedings and adopt decisions. The Commission's decisions adopted pursuant to Article 6(1), which determine whether or not to initiate second phase proceedings must be adopted within one month which begins to run either the day after notification is received or, if the information provided is incomplete, on the day following that of the receipt of the complete information. It is possible to extend this period to six weeks, in particular where the undertakings concerned submit commitments pursuant to Article 6(1a) which are intended by the parties to form the basis for a decision pursuant to Article 6(1)(b).[64]

Decisions pursuant to Article 8(2) declaring a concentration to be compatible with the common market "must be taken as soon as it appears that the serious doubts referred to in Article 6(1)(c) have been removed" and no more than four months after the initiation of second phase proceedings[65].

Decisions pursuant to Article 8(3) declaring a concentration to be incompatible with the common market must be taken within not more than four months of the date on which second phase proceedings were initiated[66]. This is subject to one exception; where the Commission exercises its power to revoke a decision of compatibility adopted pursuant to Article 8(2) and decides to substitute a decision of incompatibility under Article 8(3) for its original decision, it is not bound by the four-month time-limit[67].

If the Commission fails to adopt a decision under Article 6(1)(b) or (c) or Article 8(2) or (3) within the prescribed time-limits, then the concentration is deemed to have been declared compatible with the common market.

5. Powers of the Commission

In carrying out its duties under Regulation No. 4064/89, the Commission has at its disposal a wide range of procedural powers. The investigative powers conferred upon it by Article 13 are virtually identical to those which it has under Article 14 of Regulation No. 17/62; they include the right to examine books, to ask for oral explanations on the spot, to enter premises, and so on. Article 11 of Regulation No. 4064/89 mirrors Article 11 of Regulation No. 17/62. It permits the Commission, when it is carrying out its duties under the Regulation, to obtain all necessary information from the governments and competent authorities of the Member States, as well as from undertakings and associations of undertakings.

The powers of the Commission also include powers of a punitive nature. Article 14 entitles it to impose fines on persons or undertakings in a variety of situations: where they fail to notify a concentration; supply incorrect or misleading information; produce incomplete books or business records; refuse to submit to an investigation; put into effect a concentration which should remain suspended; put into effect a concentration which has been held incompatible with the common market; fail to comply with an obligation imposed by the Commission under Article 7(4) or 8(2). The Commission can also impose periodic penalty payments in order to compel the persons or undertakings concerned to: comply with a request for information; submit to an investigation; comply with an obligation imposed by the Commission when it granted a derogation from the requirement of suspension of a concentration or when it issued a decision pursuant to Article 8(2) declaring a concentration to be compatible with the common market.

6. Third parties

Regulation No. 4064/89 provides for the involvement of third parties at various stages in the control procedure. The first opportunity for third parties to make their views known arises when the Commission publishes a notice in the Official Journal whenever a concentration is notified to it. Unlike Regulation No. 17/62, Regulation No. 4064/89 did not expressly provide for a procedure entitling third parties to file formal complaints to the Commission. However, in practice, third parties' comments on the Commission's notices in the Official Journal may sometimes convince the Commission to pursue its proceedings further than it would otherwise have done. Thus it is not entirely inappropriate to speak of "complainants" in the context of merger control at the EC level.

Of course, a notice in the Official Journal only gives limited publicity to a concentration. Where comments by third parties are too scarce, the Commission will occasionally use its Article 11 powers to seek more information from third parties. Furthermore Article 18(4) states that the Commission may, in so far as it deems it necessary, hear any third party it sees fit. It places the Commission under a duty to hear third parties that can demonstrate a sufficient interest, "especially members of the administrative or management bodies of the undertakings concerned or the recognised representatives of their employees". Article 11(c) of Regulation No. 447/98 provides that customers, suppliers and competitors of the undertakings concerned are also to be regarded as parties having a sufficient interest and therefore entitled to be heard.

In order to exercise their right to be heard pursuant to Article 18(4) of the Regulation, interested third parties must apply to the Commission. On receipt of such an application, the Commission must inform the applicants of the nature and subject matter of the procedure and fix a time-limit within which to make their views known in writing[68]. It may also invite them to an oral hearing[69].

7. Judicial review

Although the Commission is the key player in the merger control procedure, its decisions under the Regulation are subject to review by the Court of First Instance and the European Court of Justice[70]. Article 16 of the Regulation and Article 172 EC confers upon the Court (ECJ and CFI) unlimited jurisdiction to review decisions of the Commission imposing a fine or periodic penalty payment pursuant to the relevant Articles. The CFI and the ECJ have it in their power to increase, reduce, or cancel the amount of the latter. All the other types of decision envisaged by the Regulation which have been referred to above, in particular decisions adopted pursuant to Articles 6 and 8 of the

Regulation, can be challenged on the basis of Article 173 EC. The four grounds of appeal listed in this provision are: lack of competence; infringement of an essential procedural requirement; infringement of the Treaty or of any rule of law relating to its application; misuse of powers. Such an appeal can be initiated not only by the addressees of the decisions but also by third parties where they can demonstrate that the decision is of direct and individual concern to them. Finally, proceedings can be initiated against the Commission under Article 175 EC if it fails to act although the Regulation prescribed that it should.

IV. Substantive issues

1. Dominance

EC concentration control relies on a dominance test. Article 2 (3) of Regulation No. 4064/89 provides in this respect that a concentration shall be declared incompatible with the common market if it creates or strengthens a dominant position as a result of which effective competition would be significantly impeded in that market. Although this provision seems to impose an additional qualification to the dominance test, the Commission does not actually examine whether or not the dominant position significantly impedes competition. The mere existence of a dominant position suffices to trigger a prohibition.

The concept of dominant position corresponds to the notion used in Article 86 EC. This notion has been interpreted by the European Court of Justice as a position where a firm or group of firms is able to behave to an appreciable extent independently of its competitors, its customers and ultimately of its consumers [71]. However, even if the concept of dominance under Regulation No. 4064/89 corresponds to the notion used in Article 86, the analysis is different. Article 86 concerns the control of behaviour in the past. It is retrospective in nature, whereas *a priori* concentration control is forward looking. Under Regulation No. 4064/89 the Commission has to assess the future effects of a concentration. This means that the Commission cannot rely on a static market analysis. It has to take account of the evolution of the market. For example, in *Mannesmann/Hoechst*[72] the Commission decided not to oppose a merger of two steel tube producers, even if this merger led in the short term to a dominant position in Germany. The Commission considered, *inter alia*, that the German market would open up in view of the adoption of harmonised technical standards and the entry into force of public procurement directives.

The dominance test relies in the first place on the position held by a single firm; i.e. the dominant position of the merged entity or the joint venture which results from the notified concentration. However, it also applies to dominant positions held collectively by the entity produced by the merger and a third undertaking[73]. This means that a concentration may be prohibited, even if it does not give rise by itself to a dominant position. However, before concluding that a concentration gives rise to a collective dominant position, the Commission should establish the existence of an economic and/or legal relationship between the merged entity and the third undertaking. In particular, it should establish the links which explain why the undertakings in question are likely to co-ordinate their market conduct; e.g. the existence of distribution agreements, minority share-holdings, joint ventures[74].

Moreover, the prohibition of Article 2(3) of Regulation No. 4064/89 may also apply to concentrations which do not lead to the creation or strengthening of individual or collective dominant positions. This may occur in situations where the concentration leads to duopolistic or oligopolistic dominance[75]. The Commission established this principle in the *Nestlé/Perrier* case[76] where the acquisition of Perrier by Nestlé would lead to a situation where only two undertakings, BSN and Nestlé, would together hold 94% of the relevant market for mineral water in France. However, it noted that the mere creation or reinforcement of a duopoly or oligopoly does not suffice to justify a prohibition. Additional factors should indicate why the remaining market operators have an economic interest to behave in a parallel manner and/or not to actively compete. These factors may relate, *inter alia*, to the symmetric nature of the duopoly, brand loyalty, similar cost structures, market transparency, inelastic demand, market maturity, product homogeneity and high barriers to entry[77].

Finally, it should be noted that joint ventures which lead to the co-ordination of competitive behaviour of the parent undertakings shall be appraised in accordance with the criteria of Article 85(1) and (3) EC[78].

2. Relevant market

In order to assess whether or not a concentration creates or reinforces a dominant position, the Commission should define the market on which the effects of a concentration can be measured. Such a relevant market is two-dimensional; it includes a product market and a geographic market. The Commission has provided guidance as to how it applies these concepts in a Notice issued in 1997[79].

The Commission usually feels able, on the basis of the preliminary information available to it, to form an opinion on what are the possible relevant markets. If it is then satisfied that the operation does not raise competition concerns under these alternative market definitions, it will not seek to arrive at a precise market definition before clearing the concentration. If, on the contrary, doubts remain as to the compatibility of the concentration with the common market, then the Commission will need to reach a definitive conclusion on the precise product and geographic markets.

The Notice lists the basic principles which the Commission resorts to in the process of defining a relevant market. Demand substitution is the main yard stick; the extent to which the customers of the undertakings concerned would switch to substitutes in response to a small but permanent relative price increase in the products being considered, thus making the price increase unprofitable. Therefore, the analysis starts from the type of products which the undertakings concerned sell [80] and then adds to these "all those products ... which are regarded as interchangeable or substitutable by the consumer, by reason of the products' characteristics, their prices and their intended use."[81]

Supply substitution is only taken into account for the purposes of defining the relevant market if other suppliers are able to switch production to the relevant products and market them in the short term without incurring significant additional costs, in response to small and permanent changes in relative prices. In other words, supply substitution only matters "in those situations in which its effects are equivalent to those of demand substitution in terms of effectiveness and immediacy."

The definition of the relevant geographic market follows a similar pattern to that of the product market. Here again, demand substitution is the main criterion.

The Notice on the definition of the relevant market also deals with the type of evidence which the Commission relies on in this connection. It states that "[t]he Commission does not follow a rigid hierarchy of different sources of information or types of evidence."[82] The Commission regards the following categories of evidence as relevant in order to determine whether two products are demand substitutes: evidence of substitution in the recent past; quantitative tests specifically designed for the purpose of delineating markets (e.g. tests for the measurement of own-price and cross-price elasticities); the views of the consumers and competitors on the boundaries of the product market; consumer preferences, as expressed in marketing studies, consumer surveys and so on; barriers and costs associated with switching demand to potential substitutes; the existence of distinct groups of consumers which could be subject to price discrimination. As regards the definition of the relevant geographic market, the Commission relies on the following categories of evidence: past evidence of diversion of orders to other areas; basic demand characteristics (e.g. national preferences, language, culture and life style, the need for a local presence); the views of customers and competitors on the boundaries of the geographic market; the current geographic pattern of purchases; trade flows and pattern of shipments; barriers and switching costs associated with diverting orders to companies located in other areas.

3. Factors relevant for establishing the existence of a dominant position

In order to assess the competition effects of a transaction, Article 2(1) of Regulation No. 4064/89 provides that the Commission shall take into account:
"(a) the need to maintain and develop effective competition within the Common Market in view of, among other things, the structure of all the markets concerned and the actual and potential competition from undertakings located either within or without the Community;
(b) the market position of the undertakings concerned and their economic and financial power, the alternatives available to suppliers and users, their access to suppliers and markets, any legal or other barriers to entry, supply and demand trends for the relevant goods and services, the interests of the intermediate and ultimate consumers, and the development of technical and economic progress provided that it is to consumer's advantage and does not form an obstacle to competition."

The Commission's application of these criteria usually starts within the assessment of the position of the merged entity on the relevant market and in particular of its share of that market. If this share is lower than 25%, the transaction is presumed to be compatible with the common market.[83] By contrast, if the market share exceeds 40%, the Commission is likely to examine the transaction in greater detail. Whether or not such a share gives rise to a dominant position will depend to a large extent on the structure of supply; what is the strength of the remaining competitors. In addition, it will examine how this market share has evolved over time; does it reveal an upward or down trend ?

Although market shares provide a useful *prima facie* indication of the relative strength of an undertaking, they are not conclusive by themselves. The Commission also attaches importance to other factors to measure this strength, e.g. financial power, technological advantages, brand image, economies of scale, long term supply contracts, product range and structural links with other market operators. In addition, a relatively strong position of the merged entity at the supply side may be offset by countervailing forces at the demand side. If demand is concentrated, the merged entity will probably not be in a position to act independently *vis-à-vis* its customers [84].

Finally, the Commission's analysis should be dynamic and include potential competition. At this stage, the Commission takes account of supply side substitutability originating from producers of neighbouring producers and/or from producers in adjacent geographical markets. In this respect, it should identify possible barriers to entry, such the necessity to invest in high sunk costs, the over capacity of established suppliers, regulatory barriers, distribution agreements and brand loyalty.

When carrying out this analysis, the Commission not only examines the horizontal aspects of the concentration, but also its vertical impact. In fact, foreclosure effects have been the main reasons to vet a series of joint ventures in the television and media sector [85]. These joint venture involved undertakings which had dominant or very strong positions in adjacent markets. For example, *RTL/Veronica/Endemol* concerned a joint venture regrouping the two main providers of commercial television in the Netherlands together with, Endemol, the main producer of Dutch commercial television programmes. In consequence, Endemol would have preferential access to the main outlet for Dutch television programmes, hence foreclosing access for its competitors.

Moreover, even in the absence of clear horizontal or vertical effects, concentrations may in certain specific circumstances cause competition concerns. These circumstances could be classified as conglomerate or range effects. For example, in *Guinness/Grand Metropolitan* [86] the Commission expressed concern about the combination of a series of prestigious brands which could give rise to "portfolio" brand or the ability for the merged entity to make the sale of one brand conditional upon the sale of another. Similarly, in *Boeing/McDonnell Douglas*[87], the Commission paid attention to the fact that Boeing could offer a family of various aircraft to its customers. Another specific circumstance occurred in *PTTPost/TNT-GD Express Worldwide*[88] which raised a problem of cross-subsidies between the postal and telecommunications activities for which PTT Post held exclusive concession rights and the free market for express mail delivery.

Once the Commission has established in this manner that a concentration has either created or reinforced a dominant position, it must decide whether this dominant position constitutes a significant impediment of competition in the common market. In practice, this part of the process of appraisal has become confounded with the dominance test. Even so, the significant impediment test might offer a reason to approve concentrations which by themselves create or reinforce dominant positions. For example, in *Coca-Cola Entreprises/Amalgamated Beverages*[89] the Commission decided not to oppose the acquisition of the British bottler of Coca-Cola and Schweppes (CCSB) by a subsidiary of The Coca-Cola Company (TCCC) did not appreciably alter competitive conditions, since it would not significantly change CCSB's pre-existing dominant position on the British cola market.

4. Defences and undertakings

In some cases the Commission's appraisal of a concentration is not terminated by its finding that the concentration gives rise to a dominant position as a result of which competition is significantly impeded. Indeed, parties may raise defensive arguments to justify their transaction. For example, they my argue that their concentration ensures the development of technical and economic progress and does so to the consumers' advantage without forming an obstacle to competition[90]. This "efficiencies defence" has met with little success to this day.

By contrast, the Commission and the Court of Justice accepted the principle of a "failing firm" defence. In *Kali und Salz/MdK/Treuhand*[91], the parties relied on this defence because they demonstrated that: (a) the acquired company would have been forced out of business had it not been acquired; (b) the acquiring company would have taken over the market share thus left vacant; (c) there was no other less anti-competitive option. The Court ruled that under such conditions there is no causal link between the concentration and the deterioration of competitive conditions.

Finally, parties may try to avoid a negative decision by offering undertakings under Article 6(1)a and 8(2) of Regulation No. 4064/89. Since the reasons for a prohibition will in most cases result from an aggregation of market shares, the most frequent undertaking relates to a commitment to dispose of a part of the newly acquired market share. Such partial divestment may, for example, be achieved by selling subsidiaries, assets, trademarks, technology or shares[92]. These type of undertakings are seen as structural remedies, because they affect the number of players on the market. They correspond to the objective of a priori concentration control which is to preserve sound market structures.

However, in some cases the Commission has been increasingly prepared to accept conduct remedies which do not relate to market structure, but which determine market behaviour of the merged entity. The majority of the behavioural remedies accepted so far relates to the conclusion or termination of distribution or technology transfer agreements; grant of technology licenses in *DuPont/ICI*[93] and in *Boeing/McDonnell Douglas*, conclusion of supply agreements in *Elf Aquitaine-Thyssen/Minol*[94], termination of distribution agreement in *KNP/BT/VRG*[95], *Unilever France/Ortiz-Miko* and in *The Coca Cola Company/Carlsberg*[96], termination of long term supply agreements in *Boeing/McDonnell Douglas*. In fact, in the latter case conduct remedies were the only means which enabled the Commission and the US authorities to prevent a deadlock; apart from the conduct remedies already mentioned, Boeing also undertook to separate ("ring fence") its military and civilian activities.

Notes

1   Cf. *infra*.
2   For the exceptions to the Commission's exclusive jurisdiction, cf. *infra*.
3   Address: Commission of the European Communities
                  Directorate-General for Competition (DG IV)
                  Merger Task Force
                  150 avenue de Cortenberg/Kortenberglaan 150
                  B-1049 Bruxelles/Brussel
                  Belgium
                  Telefax: (00 32-[0]2) 296 4301 / 296 7244
   DG IV's e-mail address for general enquiries: Info4@dg4.cec.be

4   Article 4.
5   Article 7(1).
6   Article 10(1).
7   Article 6(1)(c).
8   Article 10(3).
9   Article 2(3).
10 Article 8(2).
11 Article 6(1a) and Article 8(2) § 2.
12 Article 6(1b)(b) and Article 8(5)(b).
13 Article 6(1b)(a) and Article 8(5)(a).
14 Article 8(4), Regulation No. 4064/89.
15 Article 3(1)(a).
16 Article 3(1)(b).
17 Article 3(1)(b).
18 1998 O.J. C 66/5.
19 Recital 7.
20 Recital 15.
21 For an application of this principle, see *Anglo-American Corporation/Lonrho*, 23.04.97, IV/M.754. There, the Commission found that the acquisition of a qualified majority of 27.5% of the share capital sufficed to acquire sole control. See also *Mannesmann/Vallourec/Ilva*, 31.1.94, IV/M.315, 1994 O.J. L102/15.
22 See the Commission's Notice on the Notion of Undertakings Concerned, 1994 O.J. C 385/12.
23 Commission Notice on the Concept of Full-function Joint Ventures, 1998 O.J. C 66/01, recital 12; see also *ENW/Eastern*, 15.10.98, IV/M.1315.
24 *Ibid.*, recital 13. See *Generali/Unicredito*, 25.3.96, IV/M.711, , 1996 O.J. C 44; this decision has been challenged before the Court of First Instance (Case T-87/96) but the case is still pending.
25 See the Notice on the Concept of Full-function Joint Ventures, 1998 O.J. C 66/01.
26 If ancillary restrictions are not directly related and necessary for the concentration, they may be assessed separately under Article 85 EC, see e.g. *Coca-Cola Enterprises/Amalgamated Beverages*, 22.1.97, IV/M.794, 1997 O.J. L 218.
27 1990 O.J. C 203.
28 Part II, Recital 5.
29 Part II, Recital 4.
30 Part III, Section A, Recital 1.
31 Part III, Section A, Recital 2.
32 *Ibid*.
33 Part V, Section A.
34 Paragraph 16, Commission Notice on the concept of full-function joint ventures, 1998 O.J. C 66/01.
35 This idea is expressed in recital 7 of the Regulation, which states that the Regulation is to be the only instrument applicable to concentrations from the point of view of their effect on the structure of competition in the Community.
36 Introduced by Regulation No. 1310/97.

37 Commission Notice on the notion of undertakings concerned 1994 O.J. C 385/12.
38 See *CEA Industrie/France Télécom/SGS-Thomson*, 22.2.93, IV/M.216, 1993 O.J. C 68/6.
39 For example, activities with heavy transport costs (see *Tarmac/Steetley* (bricks), IP/92/104; see also *Holdecim/Cedest* (concrete), in XXIVth Competition Report, 1994, point 332); networks (see *RWE/Thyssengas*, in XXVIth Comp. Rep., 1996, point 154); retail or wholesale (see *GEHE/Lloyds Chemist*, in XXVIth Comp. Rep., 1996, point 153; see also *Promodes/Casino*, IP/97/937).
40 See *Kesko/Tuko*, 20.11.96, IV/M.784; see also *Blokker/Toys 'R' Us*, 26.6.97, IV/M.890.
41 See *IBM France/CGI*, 19.5.93, IV/M.336, 1993 O.J. C 151/5. See also *Newspaper Publishing*, 14.3.94, IV/M.423 and *Lyonnaise des Eaux/Northumbria Water*, 21.12.95, IV/M.657.
42 See *British Aerospace/ VSEL*, 24.11.94, IV/M.528, O.J. C 384.
43 Recital 7.
44 Decision of 30.7.97, IV/M.877, O.J. L 336. See also *British Telecom/MCI*, 14.5.97, IV/M.856 and *Worldcom/MCI*, 8.7.98, IV/M.1069.
45 1991 O.J. L 131/38. Note: It was not until 1995 that the 1991 Agreement was finally adopted by the Council and the Commission after the Agreement had been nullified by the ECJ.
46 1998 O.J. L 173.
47 Article III.
48 Article IV.
49 Article V.
50 Article VI.
51 Article III.
52 Article V.
53 Article IV.
54 Cf. Part C of Form CO.
55 Article 4(2), Regulation No. 447/98.
56 See the Best Practice Guidelines prepared by the European Competition Law Forum Committee and posted on DG IV's website.
57 Article 14, Regulation No. 4064/89. See *Samsung/AST*, IP/98/166.
58 Article 17, Regulation No. 4064/89.
59 Article 5, Regulation No. 447/98.
60 Article 7(1), Regulation No. 4064/89.
61 Article 13, Regulation No. 447/98.
62 See *Blokker/Toys 'R' Us*, 26.6.97, IV/M.890.
63 See *Kesko/Tuko*, 19.2.97, IV/M.784, 1997 O.J. L 174.
64 Another situation where the period can be extended to six weeks is where, pursuant to Article 9(2), a Member State has expressed concerns that the concentration notified to the Commission might impede competition on a distinct market within that Member State.
65 Article 10 paragraphs 2 and 3.
66 Article 10 paragraph 3.
67 Article 10 paragraph 6.
68 Article 16(1) and (2), Regulation No. 447/98.
69 Article 16(2), Regulation No. 447/98.

70 Article 21, Regulation No. 4064/89.
71 Case 85/76 *Hoffman-La Roche v. Commission* [1979] ECR 461.
72 Decision of 12.11.92, IV/M.222, O.J. C 114.
73 See Cases C-68/94 and C-30/95 *France v. Commission*, [1998] ECR I-1375.
74 See also *Pilkington-Techint/SIV*, 21.12.93, IV/M.358.
75 The distinction between collective dominance and oligopolistic dominance was collapsed by the judgment of the Court of First Instance in case T-102/96 *Gencor Ltd v. Commission* (25 March 1999).
76 Decision of 22.7.92, IV/M.190, 1992 O.J. L 356/1.
77 See also *Mannesmann/Vallourec/Ilva*, 31.1.94, IV/M.315, 1994 O.J. L102/15; *Unilever France/ Ortiz-Miko*, 15.3.94, IV/M.422; *Gencor/Lonrho*, 24.4.96, IV/M.619.
78 See *Telia/Telenor/Schibsted*, JV.1, 27 May 1998.
79 Notice on the definition of relevant market for the purposes of Community competition law 1997 O.J. C 372/03.
80 Recital 16.
81 Cited in recital 7.
82 Recital 25.
83 Recital 15.
84 See *Electrolux/AEG*, 21.6.94, IV/M.458; see also *Orkla/Volvo*, 20.9.95, IV/M.582, O.J. L 66.
85 See *RTL/Veronica/Endemol*, 17.7.96, IV/M.553; see also *MSG Media Service*, 9.11.94, IV/M.469; see also *Nordic Satellite*, 19.7.95, IV/M 490.
86 Decision of 15.10.97, IV/M.938.
87 Decision of 30.7.97, IV/M.877, O.J. L 336.
88 Decision of 22.7.96, IV/M.787, O.J. C 360.
89 Decision of 22.1.97, IV/M.794, 1997 O.J. L 218.
90 According to Article 2(1)(b) of Regulation No. 4064/89, this is a factor which the Commission must take into account when assessing a concentration.
91 Decision of 15.12.93, IV/M.308.
92 See respectively *Nestlé/Perrier*, 22.7.92, IV/M.190, 1992 O.J. L 356/1; *Accor/Wagon-Lits*, 28.4.92, IV/M.126; *Kimberley-Clark/Scott Paper*,16.1.96, IV/M.623; *Shell/Montecatini*, 8.6.94, IV/M.269; *Anglo-American/Lonrho* 23.04.97, IV/M.754.
93 Decision of 30.9.92, IV/M.214.
94 Decision of 4.9.92, IV/M.235.
95 Decision of 4.5.93, IV/M.291.
96 Decision of 11.9.97, IV/M.833.

Austria

Michael Kutschera

Johannes Barbist

Contents

1. Introduction 35
2. Definition of concentrations 36
   2.1. General 36
   2.2. Acquisition of a business 37
   2.3. Acquisition of rights over another's business 38
   2.4. Acquisition of shares 38
   2.5. Interlocking boards 39
   2.6. Catch-all clause 39
3. Concentrative joint ventures 40
4. Notification thresholds 41
   4.1. General 41
   4.2. Large concentrations 43
   4.3. Medium-sized concentrations 43
   4.4. Specific provisions for certain sectors of the economy 43
   4.5. Exemption from any notification requirement 46
   4.6. Foreign-to-foreign concentrations 47
5. Notification and sanctions 48
   5.1. General 48
   5.2. Large concentrations 49
   5.3. Medium-sized concentrations 50
6. Time-limits for notification 50
   6.1. Large concentrations 50
   6.2. Medium-sized concentrations 51
7. Procedural time-frame and suspension requirements 51
   7.1. Large concentrations 51
   7.2. Medium-sized concentrations 54
   7.3. Figures and background 54
8. Substantive test for clearance and political intervention possibilities 56
   8.1. Test of dominance 56
   8.2. Balancing clause 57
9. Competent authorities 57
   9.1. General 57
   9.2. The Cartel Court and the Superior Cartel Court 58
   9.3. The Official Parties and the Joint Committee for Cartel Matters ... 58

9.4. The Criminal Courts 59
9.5. The Competition Authority with the Federal Ministry of
    Commerce 59
10. Summary... 60
   10.1. Definition of concentrations 60
   10.2. Joint ventures 60
   10.3. Notification thresholds 61
   10.4. Notification and sanctions 63
   10.5. Time-limits for notification 63
   10.6. Procedural time-frame and suspension requirements................. 64
   10.7. Substantive test for clearance and political intervention
        possibilities 65
   10.8. Competent authorities.. 65
   Notes 66

1. Introduction

Concentrations between or among previously independent undertakings have been subject to a genuine merger control in Austria[1] since the entry into force of the Austrian Cartel Act Amendment 1993 (*Kartellgesetznovelle 1993*)[2] on 1 November 1993. Since then, large concentrations must be notified to the Cartel Court prior to their implementation (pre-merger notification) and shall not be put into effect before clearance by the Cartel Court or the Superior Cartel Court (the "Cartel Courts"). In contrast, medium-sized concentrations may be carried out immediately but are subject to mandatory post-merger notification within one month from their being carried out.

Prior to 1993, the Austrian rules on concentrations contained a mere post-merger notification requirement for all, save *de minimis*, concentrations. This requirement was introduced by the Austrian Cartel Act (*Österreichisches Kartellgesetz*) 1972[3], implementing Austria's international obligations under the Free Trade Association Agreements with the European Communities, and was maintained by the Austrian Cartel Act 1988. The Cartel Courts were, however, neither granted any right to undertake an in-depth analysis of a notified concentration nor the power to prohibit it in case effects detrimental to the Austrian market structure had to be expected. The concentration was only registered with the Cartel Register and could only be scrutinised according to the rules on the abuse of dominance at a later stage.

Finally, the Austrian Cartel Act Amendment 1993 introduced a mandatory pre-merger clearance requirement for large concentrations[4]. In contrast to, for example, the *Bundeskartellamt* in Germany or the Competition Directorate of the European Commission, the key authority in the Austrian clearance proceedings is not the independent Cartel Court (or the Superior Cartel Court) but such function is shared with the so-called Official Parties, i.e. organisations which have been established to represent the interest of employers, employees and the agricultural sector (the "Social Partners") and the Republic of Austria represented by its Federal Law Office (*Finanzprokuratur*). Only upon their request the Cartel Court is allowed and obliged to initiate investigation proceedings in respect of a concentration whereupon the envisaged transaction will be examined pursuant to the test of dominance. The post-merger notification requirement – previously relevant for all but *de minimis* concentrations – was made applicable to medium-sized concentrations only, while small (*de minimis*) concentrations are still exempt from any notification obligation.

With Austria's accession to the European Union on 1 January 1995, the EC Merger Control Regulation[5] became directly applicable in Austria. Consequently, only those concentrations continue to fall within the scope of the Austrian merger control regime which are not subject to EC merger control ("one stop-shop principle"[6]).

On June 16, 1999 the Austrian Parliament adopted the Austrian Cartel Act Amendment 1999 ("99 Amendment"). As regards concentrations, the 99 Amendment abolishes the notification requirement for medium-sized concentrations and considerably amends the turnover thresholds for large concentrations. It will enter into force on 1 January 2000.

2. Definition of concentrations

2.1. General

In contrast to the EC Merger Control Regulation, the Austrian Cartel Act 1988 as amended (the *KartG*)[7][8] does not expressly adhere to the concept of "acquisition of control" but contains a broader definition of concentrations, namely

- the acquisition of an entire business or a major part thereof by another undertaking (asset deal),
- the acquisition of rights over the business of another undertaking by means of agreements providing for the management of such business or the use of its resources by the aquiror,
- the acquisition of shares of an undertaking by another undertaking (share deal), if thereby an interest of either 25% or 50% is reached or exceeded,
- the creation of interlocking boards,
- all transactions that confer upon one undertaking the power to exercise dominating influence over another undertaking (catch-all clause), and
- concentrative joint ventures.

The statute covers concentrations between or among independent undertakings (*Unternehmer*). Undertakings are corporations, partnerships, other legal entities and physical persons which through their businesses (*Unternehmen*) perform commercial activities[9]. Even natural persons who do not directly operate a business may qualify as undertaking if they are – owing to their position (e.g. as majority shareholder of a corporation[10]) – commercially active, i.e. possess management powers in respect of the business, and (may) adopt the fundamental business decisions.[11]

2.2. Acquisition of a business

The acquisition of a business – or a major part thereof – by another undertaking constitutes a concentration irrespective of the chosen form. Pursuant to the relevant statutory provision such acquisition may in addition to regular asset deals take the form of a merger (*Verschmelzung*) or a change of corporate form (*Umwandlung*) as well.

The term "merger" is identical to the one used in the Austrian Corporation Act (*Aktiengesetz*) and the Austrian Companies Act (*GmbH-Gesetz*) and embraces both the consolidation (two or more independent undertakings are replaced by a single new undertaking) and the amalgamation (one undertaking being merged into another independent undertaking).

A change of corporate form is considered to be a concentration only in case of a change of identity by formation (e.g. two GmbHs are merged into a newly founded AG) or by merger (e.g. a GmbH is merged into an existing AG). A mere conversion of form (e.g. a GmbH turns into an AG) does not qualify.

According to the statutory definition also the acquisition of a major part of a business is deemed a concentration. The meaning of the term "major part" is not entirely clear; it covers, however, the acquisition of a permanent establishment (*Betriebsstätte*) or the majority of the assets of an undertaking. In addition, the acquisition of a separable part of a business qualifies if thereby the position of the acquiror on the relevant market may, *in abstracto*, be strengthened.[12]

2.3. Acquisition of rights over another's business

A concentration is deemed present if an undertaking acquires rights over the business of another undertaking – or a major part thereof – by means of agreements providing for the latter's management (*Betriebsüberlassungsverträge, Betriebsführungsverträge*).

The most prominent example is the lease of a business.

2.4. Acquisition of shares

The acquisition of shares is, in practice, the most frequent type of concentrations and covers the direct or indirect acquisition of shares of an undertaking (e.g. a corporation, a private limited company or a partnership) by another undertaking if thereby an interest of 25%, or one of 50% is reached or exceeded. Shares already held by an acquiring undertaking have to be included in the calculation. Both thresholds are independent from each other and have to be applied strictly, as the table opposite shows.

In case the percentage of capital shares does not correspond to the percentage of voting rights (e.g. in case of non-voting preference shares), a concentration is deemed to arise if the shares in the capital alone reach the 25% threshold. Whether this applies *vice versa*, i.e. the voting rights reach the threshold but not the shares in the capital, is unclear as yet[14].

The direct acquisition of a shareholding of 25% qualifies as a concentration irrespective of whether such minority shareholding confers upon the acquiror a dominant influence over the target. Whether the same applies in case of an "indirect" acquisition is in dispute[15].

For example: If M holds 25% in A, and A acquires 25% in B, a concentration within the meaning of the *KartG* is effected as between A and B (direct acquisition). What about the relationship between M and B (indirect acquisition)? According to the Cartel Court[16] and the majority of legal treatises[17]

% of share-holding prior to acquisition	% of shares acquired	% of aggregate shareholding	concentration within the meaning of the *KartG*
0	24,9	24,9	no
20	4	24	no
24,9	0,1	25	yes
26	23,9	49,9	no/yes[13] (see 2.6. *infra*)
49,9	0,1	50	yes

the existence of a dominating influence is required for every indirect acquisition. Consequently, the indirect acquisition of 25% in B would be sufficient to qualify as a concentration only if M may exercise a decisive influence over (i.e. controls) A.

2.5. Interlocking boards

A concentration is also deemed present if at least half of the members of the executive or supervisory boards of two or more undertakings are caused to be identical. The involved undertakings exercise reciprocal control through these personal identities without being formally connected to each other. There is no need for identical persons to be appointed to the corresponding functional bodies of the involved undertakings[18]. For example, if half of the members of the management board of corporation A and half of the members of the supervisory board of corporation B are identical, that would be considered a concentration.

2.6. Catch-all clause

This situation embraces all deals which confer upon one undertaking the power to exercise dominating influence over another undertaking. An influence is considered to be dominating if an undertaking is able to enforce its intent on another dependent undertaking, irrespective of whether the dependent undertaking agrees to such intent or not. This catch-all clause is designed to cover legal constructions which try to circumvent the above types of concentrations.

For example: A, B and C are shareholders of D. A holds 30%, B holds 10% and C holds 15% in D. A has concluded a syndication agreement with B (including duties on the part of B to vote in line with A's requests). The shareholder C sells his entire shareholding to A, who now owns 45% in D and, by means of the syndication agreement, may exercise a dominating influence over B. Such situation might – depending on the circumstances – thus be covered by the catch-all clause.

3. Concentrative joint ventures

The creation of a joint venture (i.e. an undertaking under joint control of at least two partners) constitutes a concentration if it:
- performs on a lasting basis all functions of an autonomous economic entity, and
- does not give rise to co-ordination of the competitive behaviour of the founding undertakings between themselves or among themselves and the joint venture.

This definition corresponds to the one given in the EC Merger Control Regulation and raises similar questions in particular, whether a joint venture is regarded as being concentrative or co-operative.

It is important to note that the *KartG* does not provide for an automatic assessment of the notified activity both under the merger control provisions and the cartel provisions. If a joint venture of a co-operative nature is (wrongly) notified as a concentration, the Cartel Court will have to render an order declaring such transaction not to constitute a concentration. Depending on the nature of the joint venture in question, the parties may be obliged to initiate proceedings according to the cartel provisions of the *KartG* (e.g. in case of intentional cartels (*Absichtskartelle*) such as purchase pools). If the co-operative joint venture qualifies as intentional cartel, such joint venture may not be implemented prior to its approval by the (Superior) Cartel Court ("prohibition principle"). In contrast to the merger control provisions, the Cartel Court is –

with respect to the application of the cartel provisions – not time-constrained, must apply different assessment criteria and may only approve the co-operative joint venture for a certain period of time.

4. Notification thresholds

4.1. General

The legal consequences of a concentration depend to a large extent on the aggregate turnover (in certain instances the balance sheet total or the premium incomes) derived by the respective undertakings on the Austrian market (see 4.6. *infra*) in the preceding financial year.

Aggregate turnover of the involved undertakings shall comprise the typical net proceeds derived by the undertakings concerned from the sale (or the surrender of the use and benefit) of goods of whatever nature and the provision of services falling within the undertakings' ordinary activities[19].

Whether an undertaking is deemed to be involved in the respective concentration depends on the respective type of concentration at issue[20]:

- In case of an acquisition of a business (or a major part thereof), the acquiror and the target (or the parts which are the subject of the transaction respectively) are the involved parties whose turnovers have to be taken into consideration. The turnover of the seller (or those parts which are not the subject of the transaction respectively) will not be taken into account save the latter remains connected to the target by way of one of the types described under 2 *supra*.
- In case of an acquisition of rights over another's business, the turnovers of the acquiror and of the target have to be taken into account.
- In case of an acquisition of shares, the turnovers of the acquiror and of the target have to be taken into consideration. Subject to the following, the turnover of the seller will not be taken into account unless the latter remains connected to the target by way of one of the types described under 2 *supra*. In case such connection is constituted by a shareholding of 25% or more but less than 50%, it is unclear as of yet whether the turnover of the seller has to be included in the calculation[21].
- In case of a creation of interlocking boards, the turnovers of those companies which are under identical control must be taken into account.
- In case of a creation of a joint venture, the turnovers of the parent companies have to be included in the calculation.

Once the undertakings directly involved in the concentration have been determined, the consolidated turnovers of all group companies connected to them in one of the manners described under 2 *supra* shall be included in the calculation[22]. Intra-group turnover has to be deducted.

For example: A is the purchaser of all shares of another undertaking. The following group companies of A will, in general, have to be included in the calculation of A's turnover:
- each parent company of A which has a shareholding in A of at least 25%;
- each grandparent (etc.) company of A which has a shareholding in a parent company of A of at least 25% and such parent company has the power to exercise dominating influence over A;
- each grandparent (etc.) company of A which can exercise a dominating influence over any of A's parent companies, if the latter has a shareholding in A of at least 25%[23];
- the sister companies of A if they are connected to a parent or grandparent company of A in one of the above manners and the turnover of such parent or grandparent company has to be included pursuant to the above principles [24];
- each subsidiary of A in which A has a shareholding of at least 25%;
- each sub-subsidiary (etc.) of A provided A has the power to (directly or indirectly) exercise dominating influence over the parent company of such sub-subsidiary in question and the former has a shareholding in such sub-subsidiary of at least 25%;
- each sub-subsidiary (etc.) of A provided A (directly or through a company over which it has controlling influence) has a shareholding of at least 25% in a direct or indirect parent company of such sub-subsidiary and such parent company can (directly or indirectly) exercise dominating influence over such sub-subsidiary[25].

Specific provisions for the calculation of turnover apply in the media, the banking and the insurance sectors (see 4.4 *infra*).

Depending on the respective aggregate (consolidated) group turnover derived in Austria, the parties to the concentration shall submit a pre-merger notification (in case of a large concentration) or a post-merger notification (in case of a medium-sized concentration).

Certain acquisitions of shares by banks and investment funds are exempted from any notification requirement altogether (see 4.5 *infra*).

4.2. Large concentrations

These are concentrations where, in the preceding financial year:
- the aggregate (consolidated) group turnover of all involved undertakings is at least ATS 3,500 million (approx. € 254.4 million), and
- the turnover of at least two of the involved undertakings reaches or exceeds ATS 5 million (approx. € 0.4 million)

Such concentrations require a pre-merger notification to, and a clearance by, the Cartel Court prior to their implementation.

The 99 Amendment provides for the following thresholds for large concentrations:
- the aggregate (consolidated) world-wide group turnover of all involved undertakings is at least ATS 4,200 million (€ 300 million),
- the aggregate (consolidated) group turnover of all involved undertakings in Austria is at least ATS 210 million (€ 15 million), and
- the world-wide turnover of at least two of the involved undertakings reaches or exceeds ATS 28 million (€ 2 million).

4.3. Medium-sized concentrations

These are defined where the aggregate (consoldiated) group turnover of all involved undertakings in the preceding financial year reaches or exceeds ATS 150 million (approx. € 10.9 million) without reaching all the turnover thresholds for large concentrations as defined above.

Such concentrations require a post-merger notification within one month of their implementation without being subject to any suspension requirement.

According to the 99 Amendment, the post-merger notification requirement for such concentrations is repealed.

4.4. Specific provisions for certain sectors of the economy

The *KartG* embraces specific provisions with respect to the calculation of turnover
- for banks or building and loan associations,
- in the media sector, and
- for insurance undertakings.

4.4.1. Banks or building and loan associations[26]

In order to acknowledge the distinct character of the financing and credit business, in particular the enormous turnover achieved therein, the *KartG* provides for a different method of how to measure the significance of a concentration.

If banks or building and loan associations are involved undertakings, for the purposes of examining the ATS 3.5 billion and the ATS 150 million thresholds, their turnover shall be replaced by 5% of their (trade) balance sheet total. However, for the purpose of examining the ATS 5 million threshold their turnover shall be replaced by 0.05% of the respective balance sheet total.

In case of a concentration between two banks (alone), the respective thresholds would therefore be as follows:
- for large concentrations: (i) an aggregate balance sheet total of at least ATS 70 billion (approx. € 5.09 billion), and (ii) a balance sheet total of at least two of the undertakings concerned of at least ATS 10 billion (approx. € 726.7 million) in the preceding financial year.
- for medium-sized concentrations: an aggregate balance sheet total of at least ATS 3 billion (approx. € 218 million).

In case of concentrations involving corporate groups consisting of banks which hold controlling interests in other undertakings or vice versa, the respective relevant turnover must be calculated as follows:
- the relevant percentage of the balance sheet total of the involved banks (calculated after eliminating from the balance sheet such positions as reflect shareholdings in non-bank undertakings, if any) plus
- the turnover of the controlled other undertakings.

The 99 Amendment replaces the turnover of banks and building and loan associations by their revenues. The normal notification thresholds pursuant to the 99 Amendment shall apply (see 4.2. *supra*).

4.4.2. Media sector

Given the fact that, at the beginning of the 1990s, strong concentration movements occurred in the Austrian media sector, the legislators felt the need to introduce more stringent provisions for concentrations in this sector of the

AUSTRIA

economy. One set of these specific rules relates to the calculation of turnover in case of media concentrations while the other set introduced an additional legal basis for the prohibition of large concentrations (the impairment of media diversity).

The *KartG* provides for a narrow definition of media concentrations, using those terms already defined in the Media Act (*Mediengesetz*)[27].

Therefore, a medium is deemed to be any means suitable for mass circulation of information or presentations of an intellectual content to a large group of persons. The information or presentation must be expressed either in words (oral or written), sound or pictures, i.e. newspapers, magazines, books, as well as radio and television broadcasts.

A media concentration is a concentration if at least two of the involved undertakings or businesses belong to one of the following categories:
- production, and circulation, e.g. publishing houses, radio and television broadcasting companies),
- media service (i.e. an undertaking supplying media businesses with contributions in written or oral form, sound or pictures on a regular basis, e.g. news or press agencies),
- media support undertaking (i.e. publishers, provided that they are not media undertakings, printers and businesses which procure advertising orders or which distribute media on a large scale), or
- undertakings that individually or jointly, directly or indirectly, hold a 25% interest in a media undertaking, media service, or media support undertaking ("media parent").

In addition, a concentration will be deemed a media concentration if only one of the involved undertakings belongs to the undertakings enumerated above and one or several media undertakings, media services, or media support undertakings directly or indirectly hold an interest of at least 25% in at least one other undertaking concerned by the concentration ("media subsidiary").

In order to apply a tighter pre-merger control in this sector, the turnover proceeds of media undertakings and media services shall be multiplied by 200, the turnover proceeds of so-called media support undertakings by 20 upon determination of whether or not the notification thresholds are met. As a consequence, concentrations of medium-size or even small media undertakings with an aggregate (consolidated) group turnover of the parties of ATS 17.5 million (approx. € 1.27 million) or ATS 175 million (approx. € 12.7 million) respectively will, in most cases, be subject to pre-merger control.

According to the 99 Amendment, the turnover proceeds of media undertakings and media services are multiplied by 200, the turnover proceeds of so-called media support undertakings by 20 upon determination of whether or not the ATS 4,200 million and ATS 210 million thresholds are met. These thresholds drop, in case of media undertakings and media services to ATS 21 million (€ 1.5 million) and ATS 1.05 million (€ 0.075 million) respectively; in case of media support undertakings to ATS 210 million (€ 15 million) and ATS 10.5 million (€ 0.75 million) respectively.

4.4.3. Insurance undertakings

In this sector of the economy, the turnover proceeds shall be replaced by the premium incomes of the insurance undertakings.

4.5. Exemption from any notification requirement

The *KartG* provides for three exemptions in which the acquisition of shares by banks and investment funds will not be subject to any notification requirement irrespective of the turnover achieved, namely if
- a bank acquires the shares in a business for the purpose of reselling them (resale acquisition),
- a bank acquires the shares for the purpose of reorganising the company (restoring its financial soundness) or to securing its claims against the respective company (reorganisation/securing acquisition), or if
- the shares are acquired by an undertaking in the course of its capital investment or capital fund business or such other business, the only purpose of which is the acquisition, administration and disposal of the shareholdings, without the intent to actually engage in the business of the target undertaking.

In case such concentration would normally require a pre-merger notification, the acquiror of the shares (i) shall not exercise voting rights in respect to the shares in question for the purpose of determining the competitive behavior of that undertaking and (ii) shall exercise voting rights only for the purpose of preserving the full value of the investment and of preparing the disposal of all or parts of the shares of the undertaking or the disposal of the entirety or of parts of the business or its assets; any such disposal must take place within one year of the date of acquisition (extension possible) and the completion of the reorganisation/securing purpose respectively.

If such acquiror does not comply with these obligations, the Cartel Court shall – upon prior warning – submit a decision to terminate such infringement and may even impose fines.

4.6. Foreign-to-foreign concentrations

The *KartG* does not expressly define its scope of application, neither according to quantitative thresholds (e.g. domestic market shares[28]), nor according to the geographical area of activity of the undertakings concerned (e.g. Austria), nor according to a general criterion referring to a concentration having an appreciable effect in Austria.

The Austrian merger control provisions do not – although referring to the turnover of the undertakings concerned – define the geographical area on which this turnover must be derived. Until 1996, both the treatises and the Cartel Courts considered the world-wide turnover as being the relevant figure for the calculation of turnover.

Such approach, however, became untenable in case of foreign-to-foreign concentrations. For example: A Brazilian-based business is merged with a US-based business. Both parties (including group companies) do not have any business establishment in Austria and do not perform any business activities in Austria. While they do not generate any turnover in Austria, their joint world-wide turnover would easily meet the thresholds of the *KartG*. Thus, there was a need to limit the territorial scope of the *KartG* to concentrations "with an Austrian element" ("principle of territoriality" under public international law).

The legal treatises have adopted various theories thereto, ranging from an analogous application of the "effects" doctrine, i.e. basing jurisdiction on the economic repercussions within Austria of conduct irrespective of the place of its origin, to the requirement of a business establishment in Austria or even Austrian market shares[29].

The Superior Cartel Court – although never confronted with the problem of a foreign-to-foreign concentration – stated in two landmark decisions of 1996[30] and 1997[31] respectively, that the calculation of turnover should focus on the turnover achieved in Austria. The Court reasoned that since (i) the purpose of the *KartG* was to maintain a competitive Austrian market, (ii) the *KartG* did not provide for any domestic turnover threshold comparable to the EC Merger Control Regulation, and (iii) an (Austrian) market share criterion was foreseen by the *KartG* prior to its amendment in 1993, only the turnover achieved in Austria should be used in the calculation as it was the Austrian turnover which had an impact on the Austrian market.[32] These court decisions obviously led to a significant drop in the number of pre-merger notifications (from 276 in 1996 to 132 in 1997)[33].

This shift in the practice of the Superior Cartel Court did not render the criterion of "structural connection" (*strukturelle Verankerung*) to Austria – adopted by the Cartel Court in some earlier decisions[34] – inapplicable for sure.

The 99 Amendment resolves the above issues and expressly determines the territories within which the turnovers must be achieved (see 4.2.*supra*) thereby removing the above uncertainties.

5. Notification and sanctions

5.1. General

Depending on the amount of the aggregate group turnover of the involved undertakings, concentrations will be subject to a mandatory pre-merger (in case of large concentrations) or mandatory post-merger (in case of medium-sized concentrations) notification obligation or no such obligation at all (in case of *de minimis* concentrations).

Unlike the EC Merger Control Regulation, the Austrian merger control regime does not require the use of a specific standard form. In addition, the Cartel Courts have not issued any guidelines in this respect.

Each of the undertakings concerned is entitled to submit a notification and is responsible for the contents of such notification.

Any notification shall include the following information[35]:
- name, registered office, address (and registration number) of the parties,
- mode of business,
- connected undertakings,
- Austrian turnover of all involved undertakings in the preceding financial year,

AUSTRIA

- mode of concentration, and
- date of implementation (in case of medium-sized concentrations only).

A pre-merger notification must, in addition, provide details on the following[36]:
- the ownership of all undertakings connected to the parties with related information on voting rights and share interests held,
- total consolidated turnover (or balance sheet total and premium incomes respectively) of the undertakings concerned for the preceding financial year shown separately for each undertaking and by product and service type,
- the parties' market shares within Austria together with a description of the general market structure in Austria of those markets on which the parties are active[37] (in particular information as to actual and potential competitors), and
- the parties' assessment as to whether the transaction is likely to create or strengthen a dominant position on the different markets.

The 99 Amendment provides for an abolishment of the post-merger notification requirement for medium-sized concentrations.

5.2. Large concentrations

The parties to a large concentration shall submit a pre-merger notification thereof to the Cartel Court prior to its implementation. Any agreement on large concentrations is invalid (null and void) and may not be implemented until the issuance of a clearance decision by the (Superior) Cartel Court. This provisional invalidity, however, is limited to the extent necessary for the enforcement of the Austrian merger control provisions. In other words, an agreement covering various concentrations will only be provisionally void with respect to such concentrations as fall within the jurisdiction of the Cartel Courts.

An involved undertaking which renders materially incorrect or incomplete information upon notification to the Cartel Court, implements a concentration in a prohibited way (i.e. prior to its clearance), or thwarts the effect of such implementation prohibition, commits a serious criminal offence triggering fines of up to 360 daily rates (one daily rate amounts to between ATS 30 (approx. € 2) and ATS 4,500 (approx. € 325)).

To the extent involved undertakings are conducted in the form of corporations or similar entities, criminal responsibility is on the part of those who, pursuant to statute or the constituent documents of the respective undertakings are entrusted with their outside representation (e.g. the managing directors or the management board members).

The criminal courts may, upon application of the public prosecutor, in addition, impose penalties on the respective undertakings of up to ATS 1 million (approx. € 70,000), and in severe cases, of up to ATS 10 million (approx. € 700,000) in order to prevent any unjustified enrichment of the respective party.

5.3. Medium-sized concentrations

A medium-sized concentration shall be notified to the Cartel Court within a period of one month from its implementation. In case, the parties to such concentrations fail to submit a post-merger notification in time, or make incorrect or incomplete statements therein, the Cartel Court shall, *ex officio* or upon application of the Social Partners, impose fines on undertakings or associations of between ATS 50,000 (approx. € 3,630) and ATS 500,000 (approx. € 36,300).

The 99 Amendment abolishes the above sanctions.

6. Time-limits for notification

6.1. Large concentrations

A specific time-limit for the notification of large concentrations is not foreseen and, in fact, superfluous, as the parties to a large concentration will endeavour to notify at the earliest possible date so as to ensure that such concentration may be implemented at the envisaged date (i.e. as soon as possible after the date of receipt of the clearance decision of the (Superior) Cartel Court).

The notification of a mere concentration plan is sufficient provided that the parties thereto prove their sincere intent to effect the concentration in the near future, in particular by way of enclosing an agreement – which already embraces the exact structure of the envisaged concentration – and a time schedule for its carrying out.[38]

6.2. Medium-sized concentrations

Any medium-sized concentration must be notified to the Cartel Court within one month of its implementation, i.e. the transfer of economic control or influence to the acquiring party. The time-limit starts at
- the date at which the acquiring undertaking is able to use its dominant influence over the target undertaking for the first time, or
- the date of the formation of the joint venture, or
- the date of acceptance of the appointment by the officers in case of the establishment of interlocking boards.

The 99 Amendment abolishes such notification requirement.

7. Procedural time-frame and suspension requirements

7.1. Large concentrations

The *KartG* provides for a two phase procedure similar to the one under the EC Merger Control Regulation, with slightly longer time-limits. Most of the pre-merger notifications are cleared in this first phase which, in general, extends to no more than six weeks from notification to receipt of the confirmation. The second phase (if applicable) extends to approximately 15 weeks. The entire procedure before the Cartel Court shall be terminated within five months of the date on which proceedings are initiated (receipt of the notification).

Appellate proceedings before the Superior Cartel Court may however, not last longer than two months (from the receipt of the appeal until the rendering of the final decision), so that the maximum aggregate period for final clearance or prohibition is approximately eight months from the receipt of a complete notification by the Cartel Court.

7.1.1. First phase: Preliminary investigation procedure

The Cartel Court publicly announces the notification in the Austrian Official Gazette (*Wiener Zeitung*) disclosing the names of the undertakings and businesses concerned and the type of concentration envisaged. Copies of the notification are sent to the Social Partners and the Joint Committee for Cartel

Matters. Within four weeks of receipt of the notification, any of the Social Partners may request an examination of the concentration. Competitors of the parties have no standing to request such investigation.[39] Thus, it is the Social Partners which have the sole power to decide whether or not the concentration shall be examined in detail by the Cartel Court.

If none of the Social Partners submits (and maintains) a request for investigation, the Cartel Court shall issue a formal written confirmation stating that none of the Social Partners has requested an examination of the concentration or that all such requests have been withdrawn. Upon receipt of such confirmation the concentration is finally cleared and the parties may implement it, regardless of whether it meets the other substantial conditions of the *KartG*.

The 99 Amendment grants to the Cartel Court the right to initiate the second phase investigation procedure upon its own initiative, if said investigation is considered to be in the public interest. In addition, any third party undertaking concerned by the notified concentration is entitled to submit written observations within two weeks from the announcement of said notification.

7.1.2. Second phase: Investigation procedure

In case, the Social Partners submit an application for investigation, the Cartel Court is obliged to initiate an investigation procedure by requesting the Joint Committee for Cartel Matters to submit an expert opinion on whether or not the conditions for the prohibition of a concentration are fulfilled. Here again, the Social Partners are represented and play a decisive role in the proceedings. Upon receipt of the expert opinion the Cartel Court has to assess the concentration in accordance with the principles set out under 8 *infra*.

The Cartel Court will then issue a decision (i) clearing the respective concentration and, if necessary, imposing restrictions or setting conditions thereto, or (ii) prohibiting such concentration.

Only if the Official Parties have requested an investigation of a concentration which in fact does not qualify as such according to the statutory definition of concentrations, the Cartel Court shall render a decision to that end and terminate the proceedings without any further investigation.

Finally, the proceedings must be terminated if the Cartel Court fails to render a decision within five months from the receipt of the notification. In such case, the Cartel Court is obliged to issue a confirmation to such effect whereupon the concentration is cleared.

According to publicly available sources, no concentration has ever been prohibited in Austria.[40]

7.1.3. Appellate proceedings

If, after the completion of the investigation procedure, the Cartel Court issues a decision clearing the respective concentration, the Official Parties are entitled to lodge an appeal against such clearance decision within a period of four weeks from the receipt of the decision.

If, on the other hand, the investigation procedure ends with a decision prohibiting the concentration, an appeal may be submitted within the same period of time.

Upon receipt of the appeal, the Superior Cartel Court must provide for the service of such appeal to the other parties involved who may reply within a further period of four weeks from its receipt.

The Superior Cartel Court must render a decision within two months from its receipt of the appeal. If it fails to render a decision within such period of time, it is unclear whether the Superior Cartel Court or the Cartel Court will have to issue a confirmation to that end (not provided for in the *KartG*), or whether the concentration is deemed to be cleared at once and may thus be implemented.[41]

7.1.4. Suspension requirement

A large concentration shall not be put into effect until cleared by the merger proceedings. Such suspension will not terminate upon the expiration of a certain period of time, but only upon either the receipt or the becoming final of one of the following orders of the (Superior) Cartel Court:
- confirmation of the Cartel Court stating that none of the Official Parties has requested an examination of the concentration (implementation permitted upon receipt);
- confirmation of the Cartel Court stating that all requests of the Official Parties for investigation have been withdrawn (implementation permitted upon receipt);
- confirmation of the Cartel Court stating that the five-month period for the

rendering of a decision has elapsed without a decision having been taken (implementation permitted upon receipt);
- clearance decision of the Cartel Court becoming final (implementation permitted upon expiration of the appeal period provided no appeal is taken); or
- clearance decision of the Superior Cartel Court (implementation permitted upon receipt).

So far, most of the concentration proceedings have been terminated by the issuance of a confirmation stating that none of the Official Parties has requested an examination or all such requests have been withdrawn. Such confirmation will, in general, be issued within six weeks from receipt of the notification.

According to the 99 Amendment, the suspension terminates, *inter alia*, upon receipt of a confirmation of the Cartel Court that no second phase investigation proceedings have been opened or such opened proceedings have been discontinued.

7.2. Medium-sized concentrations

With respect to medium-sized concentrations, the *KartG* provides for a mandatory post-merger notification without any power of the Cartel Court to instigate an in-depth analysis of the respective concentration. The Social Partners and the Joint Committee for Cartel Matters are informed of the notification by service of a copy thereof. There is no possibility to prohibit such transactions even if harmful to competition. The concentration will – upon decision of the Cartel Court – be registered in the Cartel Register. The parties to the concentration receive a copy of such order.

No time-frame for the post-merger notification procedure is laid down in the *KartG*; in general, the entire procedure (date of notification until service of the Court order) will last for approximately four to six weeks.

The 99 Amendment abolishes said notification requirement.

7.3. Figures and background

From the introduction of the pre-merger control in Austria in November 1993 until September 1997, 998 concentrations have been notified to the Cartel Court. Towards the end of 1996, the number of notified concentrations increased significantly. In 1997, owing to the decision of the Superior Cartel Court stating that only the Austrian turnover of the involved undertakings shall be decisive in the calculation of turnover (see 4.6 *supra*), the number of notified concentrations decreased significantly, as the following table shows[42]:

Period	Number of notified concentrations
11/1993-12/1994	238
1995	267
1996	316
1/1997-9/1997	177

The above decision also had an effect on the ratio of post-merger/pre-merger notifications: while until end 1996 the respective ratio was about 1:2, there was a considerable shift in favour of post-merger notifications in 1997.[43]

Between 1994 and June 1995, the Official Parties submitted only two requests for investigation which, however, did not lead to negative decisions of the Cartel Court. In fact, according to the public sources available, no concentration has yet been prohibited in Austria.[44] The main reasons therefore are the "noble modesty" of the Official Parties to submit requests for investigation and the "generous" treatment of concentrations by the Austrian cartel authorities.[45] For example, the Cartel Court cleared (with restrictions however) the majority take-over of two construction undertakings (STUAG and STRABAG) by the Bau Holding AG which created the biggest construction group in Austria, four times as big (in terms of turnover) than the second biggest, Porr AG, and with a market share of 43% of the road construction sector.[46]

Recently (end of 1998), in the case of REWE/MEINL, a major concentration in the food retail business, the Austrian Minister for Economic Affairs vigorously attempted to bring the respective concentration under the jurisdiction of the Austrian Cartel Courts for the professed purpose of prohibiting it. The case was, however, dealt with by the Competition Directorate of the European Commission and finally cleared upon imposition of very stringent restrictions and conditions[47] – Austrian cartel authorities would most probably not have arrived at such a severe result.

8. Substantive test for clearance and political intervention possibilities

8.1. Test of dominance

In general, the concentration will be prohibited if a dominant position on the Austrian market will be created or strengthened (test of dominance). The *KartG* provides for certain situations in which it considers an undertaking to have a dominating market position, namely if the undertaking:
- is not exposed to any, or only insignificant, competition; or
- is exposed to competition by at most two undertakings and has a share of the entire domestic market of more than 5%; or
- is one of the four largest undertakings that together have a share of the entire domestic market of at least 80%, provided that it has a share of the entire domestic market of more than 5% itself; or
- has, in relation to the other competitors, a very superior market position (taking into account, in particular, its financial strength, its relationship to other undertakings, its access capacities to supply on sales markets as well as any circumstances limiting market access for other undertakings); or
- has, in relation to its customers or suppliers, a very superior market position (in particular, if its customers or suppliers are dependent on the maintenance of the business relationship with the respective undertaking in order to avoid severe disadvantages to their businesses).

A media concentration shall also be prohibited if it is expected that media diversity will be impaired through the respective concentration unless it is necessary to maintain or improve the international competitiveness of the businesses involved and is justified from a national economic perspective (see also 8.2 *infra*).

The 99 Amendment alters the test of dominance in two ways: First, the above quantitative (market share) criteria only raise a rebuttable presumption of dominance. Secondly, an undertaking reaching a share of 30% on the entire domestic market or another geographically defined market, are, rebuttably, considered market-dominant.

8.2. Balancing clause

The *KartG* provides for two exemptions where the court must hold an envisaged concentration admissible even if it creates a dominant market position. These exemptions arise where:
- it is expected that through the concentration, improvements in competition will also occur that outweigh the disadvantages of market domination, or if
- the concentration is indispensable in order to maintain or improve the international competitiveness of the participating undertakings and is furthermore justified from a national economic point of view.

In case the prerequisites for authorisation do not otherwise exist, the Cartel Court may link the statement of non-prohibition with adequate restrictions or conditions. These restrictions or conditions have to be of such kind that through compliance with them:
- the concentration is not expected to create or strengthen a dominant market position; or
- at least one of the situations mentioned above is fulfilled.

In case such restrictions or conditions take the form of continued or repeated obligations, the Cartel Court may, upon application, modify or revoke them if the situation changes.

While restrictions have been imposed and conditions set in very few notified concentrations, the (Superior) Cartel Court has, according to publicly available sources, never prohibited any concentration.

9. Competent authorities

9.1. General

In Austria slightly more than 30 persons (excluding clerical staff) are entrusted with tasks related to the enforcement of the *KartG*[48], in particular the Cartel Courts and the Official Parties. In addition, the Criminal Courts and the Competition Authority with the Federal Ministry of Commerce play a (very minor) role in Austrian antitrust law.

9.2. The Cartel Court and the Superior Cartel Court

The main cartel authorities in Austria are the Cartel Court as court of first instance and the Superior Cartel Court as court of second instance and last resort. The three panels of the Cartel Court, when exercising cartel jurisdiction, consist of one judge as presiding judge and two lay judges. The ordinary panels of the Superior Cartel Court, when exercising cartel jurisdiction, consist of one judge as presiding judge and four expert lay judges. The full panels of the Superior Cartel Court, however, consist of seven judges and four lay judges.

The lay judges are nominated by the Social Partners and – upon the proposal of the Federal Government – appointed by the President of the Republic of Austria. In each panel, one half of the lay judges must have been nominated by the Austrian Chamber of Commerce and the other half by the Federal Chamber of Labour.

The Cartel Court is a specialised department of the Vienna Court of Appeals with jurisdiction for all of Austria in cartel matters. There is thus no special authority or agency which deals with cartel matters, comparable to the *Bundeskartellamt* in Germany or the *FTC* in the US. In particular, the Cartel Court does not pursue a competition policy comparable to Directorate-General IV of the European Commission and is neither entitled (i) to *sua sponte* examinations of anti-competitive behaviour or concentrations nor (ii) to deal with complaints of competitors independently[49]. These duties are upon the Social Partners, which, however, act on their own discretion.

The 99 Amendment provides for the possibility of the Cartel Court to open second phase investigation proceedings on its own initiative, if it considers such investigation to be in the public interest.

9.3. The Official Parties and the Joint Committee for Cartel Matters

The Social Partners, i.e. the Federal Chamber of Labour, the Austrian Chamber of Commerce and the Presidential Conference of the Austrian Chambers of Agriculture, together with the Republic of Austria represented by the *Finanzprokuratur*,[50] have standing in most cartel proceedings even if they are not directly involved as applicants and are thus called Official Parties. In the merger proceedings they play a decisive role as only upon application of at least one Official Party the Cartel Court may initiate (second phase) investigation proceedings.

The Social Partners, in addition, nominate the lay judges with the (Superior) Cartel Court as well as the eight members of the Joint Committee for Cartel Matters which are finally appointed by the President of the Republic of Austria upon proposal of the Federal Government.

The Official Parties altogether employ about 10 persons who are directly responsible for tasks related to antitrust policy and if required additional human resources of these institutions may be – and are in fact – called in for support.[51]

The Joint Committee for Cartel Matters gives expert opinion on any premerger notification once the second phase procedure has been opened. These expert opinions describe the relevant circumstances concerning a possible prohibition of the concentration and, in general, form the basis for any order of the Cartel Court. In the performance of their duties, the members are not bound by instructions of the Social Partners.

9.4. The Criminal Courts

The Criminal Courts have jurisdiction to hear serious violations against certain provisions of the *KartG* which are treated as criminal offences (see 5.2 *supra*). As such violations qualify as criminal offences, the prosecution authorities (including the police, public prosecutor) may also exercise their legal powers in antitrust matters. These powers exceed those of the European Commission by far and embrace, *inter alia*, the right to search private property and persons, to confiscate deeds or other objects, to arrest an accused person pending further investigations or the right to telephone surveillance.

9.5. The Competition Authority with the Federal Ministry of Commerce

In 1993, the Competition Authority, a department in the Federal Ministry of Commerce, was set up to perform the rights and obligations of the Federal Ministry of Commerce with respect to the implementation of the European competition rules (for the year 1994 the EEA rules, from 1995 onwards the EC rules) in Austria[52].

The Competition Authority is the national authority for Austria pursuant to EC antitrust law (e.g. Section 19 EC Merger Control Regulation) and thus obliged to assist the European Commission in any competition proceedings (e.g. with respect to investigations at the premises of undertakings). The Authority also represents Austria in the Advisory Committee for the control of concentrations which must be consulted prior to any important decision.

The Competition Authority is, however, also involved in the implementation of the *KartG*.

10. Summary

10.1. Definition of concentrations

The Austrian merger control regime is based on a statutory definition of concentrations. The core thereof are:
- the acquisition of an entire business or a major part thereof by another undertaking (asset deals); and
- the acquisition of shares of an undertaking by another undertaking if thereby an interest (not necessarily voting rights) of either 25% or 50% is reached or exceeded (share deals).

Further, the creation of interlocking boards, the acquisition of rights over the business of another undertaking by means of agreements providing for the management of such business by the acquiror, transactions that confer upon one undertaking the power to exercise dominating influence over another undertaking, and the formation of concentrative joint ventures, constitute concentrations within the meaning of the *KartG*.

10.2. Joint ventures

The formation of a joint venture constitutes a concentration if it performs on a lasting basis all functions of an autonomous economic entity and does not give rise to co-ordination of the competitive behaviour of the parties between themselves or among themselves and the joint venture.

Therefore, only concentrative joint ventures fall within the scope of the Austrian merger control rules while co-operative joint ventures are subject to the antitrust provisions dealing with restraints on competition other than concentrations.

A parallel application of such antitrust provisions and the rules on concentrations is excluded. In contrast to the EC Merger Control Regulation, the *KartG* does not contain an automatic (*ex officio*) assessment of the notified transaction both under merger control and the respective other antitrust provisions: in case a co-operative joint venture is (wrongly) notified as a concentration, the Cartel Court will have to render an order declaring such transaction not to constitute a concentration. Depending on the nature of the co-operative joint venture in question the parties thereto will have to comply with the relevant provisions which may include the initiation of other proceedings before the Cartel Court.

10.3. Notification thresholds

The relevance of concentrations is determined according to the turnover (in certain instances the balance sheet total or the premium incomes) of the involved undertakings (normally the acquiror and the target or the partners to, and, possibly, the vehicle of, a concentrative joint venture) in the financial year preceding the concentration.

The turnover of group companies (upstream and downstream) will be included in the calculation if connected in one of the manners described in 10.1. *supra*. Companies so connected are deemed one involved undertaking for purposes of Austrian merger control.

Intra-group turnover has to be deducted and, according to two landmark decisions of the Superior Cartel Court, only such turnover shall be taken into account as is derived on the Austrian market.

Depending on the relevance of the respective turnover there are three types of concentrations:
- *large concentrations*, i.e. concentrations where (i) the aggregate (consolidated) group turnover of all involved undertakings is at least ATS 3,500 million (approx. € 254.4 million), and (ii) the turnover of at least two of the involved undertakings reaches or exceeds ATS 5 million (approx. € 0.4 million),
- *medium-sized concentrations*, i.e. concentrations between or among undertakings with an aggregate (consolidated) group turnover of at least ATS 150 million (approx. € 10.9 million), and

- de minimis *concentrations*, i.e. concentrations which do not meet any of the above thresholds.

If banks or building and loan associations are involved undertakings in a concentration, their turnover is generally replaced by 5% of their balance sheet total. However, the relevant factor for the ATS 5 million (approx. € 0.4 million) threshold for large concentrations is 0.05% of the respective balance sheet total.

Certain acquisitions of shares by banks and investment funds are exempt from all notification requirements even if they reach the above thresholds.

In the media sector, the turnover of media undertakings and media services shall be multiplied by 200, the turnover for so-called media support undertakings by 20 upon determination of whether or not the thresholds met, which results in tighter merger control in this area.

The turnover of insurance companies is calculated according to the premium incomes.

Foreign-to-foreign concentrations are subject to Austrian merger control only if the involved undertakings (including their relevant group companies) generate Austrian turnover which reaches or exceeds the thresholds mentioned above. Pursuant to the two landmark decisions of the Superior Cartel Court in 1996 and 1997, no additional criterion is required in order to apply Austrian merger control to such foreign-to-foreign concentrations.

The 99 Amendment not only expressly determines the territories within which the respective turnovers must be achieved; it also abolishes the post-merger notification requirement and alters the only remaining thresholds for large concentrations as follows:
- the aggregate (consolidated) world-wide group turnover of all involved undertakings is at least ATS 4,200 million (€ 300 million),
- the aggregate (consolidated) group turnover of all involved undertakings in Austria is at least ATS 210 million (€ 15 million), and
- the world-wide turnover of at least two of the involved undertakings is at least ATS 28 million (€ 2 million).

In addition, the 99 Amendment replaces the turnovers of banks and building and loan associations by their revenues. Finally, the above-mentioned specific provisions on the calculation of the turnovers of media concentrations apply in regard to the ATS 4,200 million and the ATS 210 million thresholds.

10.4. Notification and sanctions

There is a mandatory pre-merger notification requirement for large concentrations and a mandatory post-notification requirement for medium-sized concentrations. There is neither a notification requirement nor optional notification for *de minimis* concentrations.

Not only the mere failure to notify a large concentration but its carrying out by the involved undertakings prior to clearance (see 10.6 *infra*) is forbidden and constitutes a criminal offence. The same applies if materially incorrect or incomplete information is rendered upon notification of concentrations to the Cartel Court. Such criminal offences trigger fines of up to 360 daily rates (one daily rate amounts to between ATS 30 (approx. € 2) and ATS 4,500 (approx. € 325)). In addition, penalties of up to ATS 1 million (approx. € 70,000) or, in very serious cases, up to ATS 10 million (approx.€ 700,000) may be imposed on involved undertakings by the Criminal Courts upon application of the public prosecutor. To the extent involved undertakings are conducted in the form of corporations or similar entities, criminal responsibility is on the part of those who, pursuant to statute or the constituent documents of the involved undertakings in question, are entrusted with the outside representation thereof.

Any agreements with respect to large concentrations are provisionally invalid until cleared by the (Superior) Cartel Court.

The violation of the obligation for timely notification of a medium-sized concentration will trigger (administrative) fines of between ATS 50,000 (approx. € 3,630) and ATS 500,000 (approx. € 36,300).

The 99 Amendment abolishes the post-merger notification requirement and any sanctions relating thereto.

10.5. Time-limits for notification

Large concentrations have to be notified prior to their carrying out. The notification of a mere concentration plan is qualified as being sufficient provided that the parties prove their sincere intent to effect the envisaged concentration in the near future.

Medium-sized concentrations have to be notified within one month from their implementation, i.e. the passing of economic control to the acquiror (post-merger notification).

The 99 Amendment abolishes the notification requirement for medium-sized concentrations.

10.6. Procedural time-frame and suspension requirements

10.6.1. Large concentrations

Large concentrations must not be carried out until cleared by the (Superior) Cartel Court. The sanctions for a violation of such prohibition are set out under 10.4 *supra*.

After the filing of the respective notification, the Cartel Court has it published in abbreviated form and served in full upon the Official Parties. Within four weeks from receipt of service, the Official Parties may request an investigation of the notified concentration. If none of them does so (or all requests are withdrawn) the Cartel Court issues a written confirmation to such effect whereupon the concentration is cleared and may be carried out. From the initial filing to publication and service upon the Official Parties and from the expiration of the four-week time period to the issuance of the confirmation, normally one week elapses in each case, which results in an aggregate time period of approximately six weeks from filing to clearance if no investigation request is made.

If an investigation is requested, the Cartel Court must render its decision within five months from its receipt of the original notice. If no decision is rendered within such period it must issue a confirmation to such effect whereupon the concentration is cleared. If it renders a favourable decision the concentration is cleared upon the expiration of the four-weeks appeal period, provided no appeal is taken (in particular by any Official Party).

If the Cartel Court renders a decision prohibiting the concentration and an appeal is taken, the Superior Cartel Court (as final instance) must rule within two months from its receipt of the appeal.

The above periods start to run upon submission of a complete and proper notification or a correction to such effect only.

The 99 Amendment grants to the Cartel Court the right to open a second phase investigation procedure upon its own initiative and also grants to the concerned third party undertakings the right to submit written observations to the notified concentration.

10.6.2. Medium-sized concentrations

Medium-sized concentrations are not subject to any suspension requirement and may be carried out immediately. The involved undertakings must, however, submit a post-merger notification within one month from the carrying out of the concentration.

The 99 Amendment abolishes said notification requirement.

10.7. Substantive test for clearance and political intervention possibilities

If any Official Party requests the investigation of a large concentration, the Cartel Court will have to examine whether or not to prohibit this concentration if thereby the creation or strengthening of a dominant position on the Austrian market is to be expected (test of dominance).

In case of media concentrations, the Cartel Court will also examine whether or not an impairment of media diversity is to be expected from the concentration, and, if so, has to prohibit the notified concentration.

A balancing clause provides for an exceptional admission of large concentrations which create a dominant market position (i) where it is expected that the envisaged improvements in competition outweigh the disadvantages of market domination or (ii) where the concentration is indispensable in order to maintain or improve the international competitiveness of the involved undertakings and is furthermore justified from a national economic point of view (the latter criterion may even justify the impairment of media diversity in case of media concentrations).

To date, no large concentration has ever been prohibited in Austria.

The 99 Amendment partly alters the test of dominance.

10.8. Competent authorities

The main authorities involved in Austrian merger control are the Cartel Court, i.e. the Appellate Court Vienna) and the Superior Cartel Court (i.e. the Austrian Supreme Court) together with the Official Parties and the Joint Committee for Cartel Matters. Notifications have to be filed and are processed and resolved upon by the Cartel Court, the Superior Cartel Court serving as court of appeal.

The Official Parties act primarily as participants and applicants in the clearing procedure of large concentrations and the Joint Committee for Cartel Matters opines on relevant issues in such procedure.

Minor duties are performed by the Criminal Courts and the Competition Authority with the Federal Ministry of Commerce.

Notes

1 For a more detailed reading on this subject, see, in particular, W. Barfuß, H. Wollmann, R. Tahedl, *Österreichisches Kartellrecht* (Wien, Manz, 1996); H. Koppensteiner, *Österreichisches und europäisches Wettbewerbsrecht* (Wien, Orac, 1997); K. Wessely, *Das Recht der Fusionskontrolle und Medienfusionskontrolle* (Wien, Manz, 1995); N. Gugerbauer, *Handbuch der Fusionskontrolle* (Wien, Orac, 1995); N. Gugerbauer, *Kommentar zum Kartellgesetz* (Wien, Springer, 1994); R. Roniger, W. Punz, *Das österreichische Kartellrecht* (Wien, Orac, 1996); D. Duursma, *Fusionskontrolle bei Banken* (Wien, Orac, 1999). See also in English language: Groehs-Polak, Austrian Competition Law, 1996.
2 See Federal Law Gazette 1993/693.
3 Federal Act of 22 November 1972 concerning provisions on cartels and on the maintenance of free competition, Federal Law Gazette 1972/460.
4 As defined in 4.1. *infra*.
5 Council Regulation No. 4064/89 of 21 December 1989 on the control of concentrations between undertakings, corrigendum published in OJ 1990 L 257/14, as amended by the Council Regulation No. 1310/97 of 30 June 1997, OJ 1997 L 180/1.
6 As regards the relationship of the *KartG* to EC merger control, Art. 21 para 2 of the EC Merger Control Regulation states that the Member States shall not apply their rules to concentrations with a community-wide dimension. This rule was applied by the Superior Cartel Court, for example, in its Decision of 9 December 1996 (16 OK 1/95), partly published in (1997) *Österreichische Blätter*, at p. 185.
7 Federal Act of 19 October 1988, Federal Law Gazette 1988/600, on Cartels and Other Restrictive Trade Practices, as amended by the Federal Law Gazettes 1993/693, 1995/520 and 1998/143. An English version of this Act is available on internet at: http://www.bmwa.gv.at/wettbew/carta.htm.
8 All provisions quoted in this contribution without indicating a particular code are provisions of the *KartG* as amended.
9 See e.g. H. Koppensteiner, *Österreichisches und europäisches Wettbewerbsrecht* (Wien, Orac, 1997), pp. 93-98, 254-256; K. Wessely, *Das Recht der Fusionskontrolle und Medienfusionskontrolle* (Wien, Manz, 1995), pp. 35-40.
10 See e.g. H. Koppensteiner, *Österreichisches und europäisches Wettbewerbsrecht* (Wien, Orac, 1997), pp. 254-255; K. Wessely, *Das Recht der Fusionskontrolle und Medienfusionskontrolle* (Wien, Manz, 1995), pp. 37-38.

11 See e.g. decision of the Superior Cartel Court of 23 June 1997 (16 Ok 2/97), partly published in (1997) *Wirtschaftsrechtliche Blätter*, at p. 396.
12 See further K. Wessely, *Das Recht der Fusionskontrolle und Medienfusionskontrolle* (Wien, Manz, 1995), p. 41 *et seq*.
13 This situation might, however, fall within the catch-all clause of Sec. 41 para 2 no. 5 *KartG* (see *infra*).
14 See e.g. K. Wessely, *Das Recht der Fusionskontrolle und Medienfusionskontrolle* (Wien, Manz, 1995), pp. 52; H. Koppensteiner, *Österreichisches und europäisches Wettbewerbsrecht* (Wien, Orac, 1997), p. 258 (footnote 60);.
15 See e.g. K. Wessely, *Das Recht der Fusionskontrolle und Medienfusionskontrolle* (Wien, Manz, 1995), pp. 61-63; H. Koppensteiner, *Österreichisches und europäisches Wettbewerbsrecht* (Wien, Orac, 1997), p. 259; W. Barfuß, H. Wollmann, R. Tahedl, *Österreichisches Kartellrecht* (Wien, Manz, 1996), p. 116.
16 Decision of the Cartel Court of 13 November 1996 (25 Kt 435/96), partly published in (1997) *ecolex*, pp. 272 with comments of R. Tahedl.
17 See, in particular, pp. 61-63; H. Koppensteiner, *Österreichisches und europäisches Wettbewerbsrecht* (Wien, Orac, 1997), p. 259; W. Barfuß, H. Wollmann, R. Tahedl, *Österreichisches Kartellrecht* (Wien, Manz, 1996), p. 116.
18 K. Wessely, *Das Recht der Fusionskontrolle und Medienfusionskontrolle* (Wien, Manz, 1995), pp. 66-67; H. Koppensteiner, *Österreichisches und europäisches Wettbewerbsrecht* (Wien, Orac, 1997), pp. 260-261.
19 See e.g. H. Koppensteiner, *Österreichisches und europäisches Wettbewerbsrecht* (Wien, Orac, 1997), pp. 264-265; N. Gugerbauer, *Handbuch der Fusionskontrolle* (Wien: Orac, 1995), pp. 33-36.
20 See further e.g. K. Wessely, *Das Recht der Fusionskontrolle und Medienfusionskontrolle* (Wien, Manz, 1995), pp. 104-106; W. Barfuß, H. Wollmann, R. Tahedl, *Österreichisches Kartellrecht* (Wien, Manz, 1996), pp. 120-122.
21 See further Fellner, *"Beteiligte Unternehmen" und Umsatzberechnung beim Zusammenschluß gemäß § 41 Abs 1 Z 3 KartG (Anteilserwerb)*, (1998) *Recht der Wirtschaft*, at p. 660.
22 See further as regards the limits of such inclusion: Decision of the Superior Cartel Court of 13 November 1996 (25 Kt 435/96), note 12 *supra*, and K. Wessely, *Das Recht der Fusionskontrolle und Medienfusionskontrolle* (Wien, Manz, 1995), pp. 108-113.
23 This was confirmed by the Decision of the Superior Cartel Court of 13 November 1996 (25 Kt 435/96), note 12 *supra*. A chain of minority shareholdings (e.g. A has 25% in B, B has 25% in C, C has 25% in D, etc) is, therefore, not sufficient for the purposes of the inclusion of the respective grandparent (etc.) and sub-subsidiaries (etc.) respectively in the calculation of turnover.
24 K. Wessely, *Das Recht der Fusionskontrolle und Medienfusionskontrolle* (Wien, Manz, 1995), p. 113. The Cartel Courts have not yet been confronted with such problem.
25 See K. Wessely, *Das Recht der Fusionskontrolle und Medienfusionskontrolle* (Wien, Manz, 1995), p. 113; D. Duursma, *Fusionskontrolle bei Banken* (Wien, Orac, 1999), p. 40.
26 See, in particular, D. Duursma, *Fusionskontrolle bei Banken* (Wien, Orac, 1999), pp. 48-50.
27 Federal Law Gazette 1981/314 as amended.
28 The *KartG* in its original version provided for a domestic market share threshold of 5% on

the Austrian market of all involved undertakings in the concentration. See e.g. W. Barfuß, G. Auer, *Kartellrecht samt EWG-Kartellrecht* (Wien, Manz, 1989), p. 72.
29 See e.g. H. Koppensteiner, *Österreichisches und europäisches Wettbewerbsrecht* (Wien, Orac, 1997), p. 252; W. Barfuß, H. Wollmann, R. Tahedl, *Österreichisches Kartellrecht* (Wien, Manz, 1996), p. 24; K. Wessely, *Das Recht der Fusionskontrolle und Medienfusionskontrolle* (Wien, Manz, 1995), p. 29.
30 Decision of 9 December 1996 (16 OK 1/95), partly published in (1997) *Österreichische Blätter*, at p.185. See comments of H. Wollmann, "Paradigmenwechsel in der Fusionskontrolle" (1997) *ecolex*, at p. 171, and glossary of Mayr, JAP 1996/97, 254.
31 Decision of 23 June 1997 (16 OK 12/97), partly published in (1997) *Recht der Wirtschaft*, at p. 453. See comments of H. Wollmann, (1997) *ecolex*, at p. 859.
32 This reasoning is not entirely convincing. See further to this criticism K. Wessely, "Aufgriffsschwellen der Fusionskontrolle: Einbeziehung von Auslandsumsätzen?" (1997) *Recht der Wirtschaft*, at p. 123.
33 See V. Thurnher, "Plädoyer für ein österreichisches Kartellamt" (1998) *Wirtschaftsrechtliche Blätter*, at p. 191.
34 See, for example, Decision of 11 July 1996 (25 Kt 253/96) and Decision of 28 March 1996 (1 Kt 54/95-6). This concept means that a concentration must, apart from generating effects on the Austrian market, be structurally connected to Austria, namely at least one of the involved undertakings (or undertakings connected to them) needs to be located in Austria.
35 See e.g. N. Gugerbauer, *Handbuch der Fusionskontrolle* (Wien, Orac, 1995), p. 33; Barfuß, H. Wollmann, R. Tahedl, *Österreichisches Kartellrecht* (Wien, Manz, 1996), pp. 123-124.
36 The contents of a pre-merger notification is determined by S. 68a para 1 *KartG*.
37 It is on these overlapping markets where a dominant position may be created or strengthened.
38 See e.g. Decision of the Superior Cartel Court of 23 June 1997 (16 Ok 4/97), and K. Wessely, "Aufgriffsschwellen der Fusionskontrolle: Einbeziehung von Auslandsumsätzen?" (1997) *Recht der Wirtschaft*, at p. 125.
39 See, for example, Decision of the Superior Cartel Court of 23 June 1997 (16 Ok 6-8/97). If the legal or economic interests of competitors are affected by the concentration, such competitors have a right of application (i) in order to determine whether a concentration was implemented illegally (Sec. 42a para 5) or (ii) in the field of the control of abusive practices (Sec. 35).
40 See e.g. V. Thurnher, "Plädoyer für ein österreichisches Kartellamt", (1998) *Wirtschaftsrechtliche Blätter*, at pp. 185-187.
41 See W. Barfuß, H. Wollmann, R. Tahedl, *Österreichisches Kartellrecht* (Wien, Manz, 1996), p. 129.
42 The numbers were taken from the Annual Report on Competition Policy in Austria 1995, internet address: http://www.bmwa.gv.at/wettbew/wettb95.htm; Annual Report on Competition Policy in Austria (1995/1996), internet address: http://www.bmwa.gv.at/wettbew/oecd_e.htm; Competition Law Report Austria 1996/1997, internet address: http://www.bmwa.gv.at/positionen/wbbe.htm.
43 See further Competition Law Report Austria 1996/1997, internet address: http://www.bmwa.gv.at/positionen/wbbe.htm.

44 See e.g. V. Thurnher, "Plädoyer für ein österreichisches Kartellamt", (1998) *Wirtschaftsrechtliche Blätter*, at pp. 185-187.
45 D. Duursma, *Fusionskontrolle bei Banken* (Wien, Orac, 1999), p. 8.
46 See D. Duursma, *Fusionskontrolle bei Banken* (Wien, Orac, 1999), p. 8.
47 Decision of February 3, 1999 (No. IV/M.1221).
48 See further Competition Law Report Austria 1996/1997, internet address: http://www.bmwa.gv.at/positionen/wbbe.htm.
49 See further V. Thurnher, "Plädoyer für ein österreichisches Kartellamt", (1998) *Wirtschaftsrechtliche Blätter*, at p. 191.
50 That is the Republic of Austria represented by the Federal Law Office as the attorney of the Federal Government acting by order of the Department for Competition at the Federal Ministry of Commerce.
51 See Competition Law Report Austria 1996/1997, internet address: http://www.bmwa.gv.at/positionen/wbbe.htm.
52 See further Federal Law concerning the implementation of the Competition Rules of the European Union, Federal Law Gazette 1993/125 as amended.

Belgium

Thomas Chellingsworth

Marc van der Woude

Contents

I. Introduction: An outline of Belgian competition law 73
    1. Outline of the substantive provisions of the Act 73
    2. The Belgian competition authorities 74
    3. Sanctions 74
    4. Outline of Belgian Merger Control 75
II. The concept of a concentration 76
    1. Undertakings 76
    2. The concept of control 77
    3. Types of concentrations 77
III. Jurisdictional thresholds 80
    1. The turnover threshold 80
    2. The market share threshold 82
    3. Jurisdictional thresholds: conclusion 88
IV. The substantive appraisal of concentrations 89
    1. Legislative provisions 89
    2. General comments on the Competition Council's case law 89
    3. Criteria for the assessment of concentrations 91
    4. Conditional clearance 94
    5. The prohibition decisions so far 96
V. Ancillary restrictions 98
VI. Procedural matters 98
    1. The notification 98
    2. First phase proceedings 101
    3. Second phase proceedings 103
    4. Sanctions for infringements of the Competition Act 104
    5. Appeals 104
VII. Amendments introduced by the Acts of 26 April 1999 105
    1. The new competition authorities 105
    2. The concept of a concentration 106
    3. Jurisdictional thresholds 106
    4. The substantive appraisal of concentrations 107
    5. Procedural matters 108
VIII. Conclusion 110
    Notes 111

I. Introduction: An outline of Belgian competition law

The Belgian competition rules are contained in the Act of August 5, 1991 on the protection of economic competition[1] (hereafter "the Act" or "the Competition Act"). This provides for a European-style system, centred essentially on a prohibition of restrictive agreements, a prohibition of abuses of a dominant position and compulsory pre-notification and control of concentrations. The Act entered into force on 1 April 1993.

In contrast to the European rules, the Act attempts to codify all aspects of the competition regime in a single legislative text. As a result, this contains not only substantive rules, but also institutional provisions, procedural rules, and sanctions for infringement of the substantive and procedural rules. The following paragraphs will give a brief outline of the various provisions of the Act.

Just as this book was going to press, two Acts were passed introducing far-reaching amendments to the Competition Act[1bis]. Certain provisions of these Acts, in particular the merger notification thresholds, have already entered into force. Others are to enter into effect at a date yet to be decided, but in any event no later than October 1, 1999. Sections 1 to VI of this contribution set out the existing merger control rules. Section VII gives an overview of recently introduced amendments.

1. Outline of the substantive provisions of the Act

Article 2 of the Act essentially prohibits anti-competitive agreements, decisions and concerted practices. With the exception of the requirement that trade between EU member states be affected, Article 2 of the Act closely, indeed almost literally follows the wording of Article 85(1) of the EC Treaty. As under the European rules, individual and group exemptions are possible. Article 3 of the Act prohibits abuses of a dominant position, also in terms closely following Article 86 of the EC Treaty. Both prohibitions are subject to a national *de minimis* rule.

The Belgian merger control rules are contained in Articles 9 to 11 of the Act. These provide, essentially, for a system of compulsory pre-notification and control of concentrations similar to that provided for by the EC Merger Regulation[2]. A brief outline of the merger regime is given under section 4 below.

2. The Belgian competition authorities

The Act provides for three distinct Belgian competition authorities: the Competition Council, the Competition Service and the Competition Commission.

The Competition Council is the main decision-making body charged with the enforcement of the Competition Act. It has the status of an administrative tribunal, and consists of twelve working members, six of whom are members of the judiciary, and twelve substitutes, six of whom are likewise members of the judiciary. Besides its functions as a decision-making body, it also has broad investigative powers. Article 19, § 2 of the Act provides, in very broad terms, that it may "proceed (…) to all useful investigations", including the appointment of experts and the hearing of witnesses. Finally, the Competition Council may advise the Minister of Economic Affairs on general questions of competition policy, either on its own initiative or at the Minister's request.

The Competition Service is a specialised department within the Ministry of Economic Affairs, and is essentially an investigative body. For the purpose of its investigations, the Service has wide-ranging powers similar to those of the European Commission under Regulation 17.

The Competition Commission is essentially an advisory committee at policy level. It gives advice on draft Royal Decrees, implementing the Competition Act on general questions of competition policy, and on proposed group exemptions. However, it does not have any powers of enforcement.

It is a widely held view that the functioning of the Competition Council and Service is inadequate, and that the main reason for this is the shortage of personnel. As a result of this shortage, the Belgian competition authorities have until now been confined almost exclusively to handling merger notifications, and have not been able effectively to combat cartels and abuses of a dominant position.

3. Sanctions

The Competition Act provides for fines and penalty payments for infringements of the prohibitions. As under EC competition law, the maximum fine for breaches of the substantive provisions of the Act is set at ten percent of the turnover of the undertakings concerned.

4. Outline of Belgian Merger Control

The Act provides for compulsory pre-notification of all concentrations which exceed the national jurisdictional thresholds, but do not have a Community dimension.

These thresholds are twofold. Assuming it does not have a Community dimension, a concentration is subject to Belgian merger control if the undertakings involved, firstly, have a combined world-wide turnover of more than *three billion Belgian francs* and, secondly, have a combined *market share of more than 25 percent*.

Concentrations which are subject to the Act must be notified to the Competition Service, and are examined in a two-phase procedure similar to that of the EC Merger Regulation. During the first phase, the Competition Service conducts an initial investigation, and the Competition Council rules on whether the concentration, firstly, falls within the scope of the Act and, secondly, raises serious doubts as to its admissibility. Where a concentration is found to raise serious doubts, the Council will open the second phase procedure. During this second-phase procedure the Service again investigates the operation, and the Council finally rules on its admissibility. The Act provides for strict time limits. Where no decision is issued within these time limits, the notified concentration is deemed to have been approved.

The substantive assessment is based primarily on a market dominance test. In accordance with Article 10, § 2 of the Act, concentrations may only be permitted if they do not lead to the creation or strengthening of dominant position which appreciably restricts effective competition in the Belgian market concerned, or a substantial part thereof. However, Article 10, § 3 provides for a secondary test based on certain other considerations of an economic nature. Concentrations which do not satisfy the primary test may thus be permitted under the secondary test.

In the following, the concept of a concentration will first be described. Secondly, the jurisdictional thresholds which trigger the obligation to notify will be explored. Thirdly, the rules governing the substantive assessment of concentrations will be examined. Finally, the merger control procedure will be briefly considered.

II. The concept of a concentration

The concept of a concentration, as defined in Article 9 of the Act, mirrors the definition under the European Merger Regulation. However, the Act has not (yet) been amended in line with Regulation 1310/97. The Act is thus no longer fully in step with the Merger Regulation, particularly as regards joint ventures.

Article 9 of the Act defines four distinct types of concentration. Common to all is the requirement that the operation involve a change in the *control* over one or more *undertakings*. Both these concepts are defined in accordance with the Merger Regulation.

1. Undertakings

An *undertaking* is defined in Article 1 of the Act as "all natural or legal persons which durably pursue an economic objective". This definition, inspired by the case law of the European Court of Justice, represents a significant departure from the traditional concept of a "tradesman" (*commerçant/handelaar*) familiar from Belgian commercial law. The concept of an undertaking, being functional rather than formal, and based on the broad notion of an economic objective, is generally considered to be more in line with present-day commercial realities.

Merger control, like the other provisions of the Act, applies to undertakings from all sectors of the economy, including public undertakings and undertakings granted special or exclusive rights by the authorities. However, Article 47 of the Act provides that these two categories of undertakings are subject to the provisions of the Act only insofar as the application thereof does not obstruct the performance, in fact or in law, of the particular task assigned to them by or on the basis of the law.

The Act does not specify whether or not parent companies and subsidiaries are to be considered as a single undertaking. This question is therefore to be resolved using the criteria developed by the European Court of Justice. Where a subsidiary enjoys economic independence from its parent, it is to be considered as a separate undertaking; where this is not the case, the parent and the subsidiary will be part of one and the same group of undertakings.

In the case of intra-group transactions, the question of whether or not a subsidiary constitutes a separate undertaking is closely entwined with the question of whether or not the transaction entails a change in control. This was apparent in *Eugen O. Butz/Ieper Industries*[3]. In this case, the notified operation was conducted in two stages, the first of which was an intra-group transaction. The Competition Council held that this first stage did not constitute a concentration. The reason given, however, was not that the various members of the group constituted a single undertaking, but that the first stage did not involve a change in the *control* over the subsidiary in question.

2. The concept of control

The definition of *control*, given in Article 9, §§ 3-4 of the Act, closely follows the corresponding definition in Article 3(3) of the Merger Regulation. Control may be constituted either by rights, or by contracts, or by any other means which, either separately or in combination, and having regard to the considerations of fact or of law involved, confer the possibility of exercising decisive influence on an undertaking. These rights and agreements include not only ownership of, but also the right to use all or part of the assets of an undertaking, and rights or agreements conferring decisive influence on the composition, the voting or the decisions of the organs of an undertaking.

Certain forms of control do not give rise to a concentration. This is the case, subject to certain conditions, for the temporary holding of assets by credit institutions, other financial institutions and insurance companies. Likewise, control obtained by a judicial or public office holder in the context of compulsory liquidation will not give rise to a concentration.

3. Types of concentrations

Article 9, §§ 1-2, of the Act lists four types of concentration, namely mergers, the acquisition of securities, the acquisition of assets and the creation of a so-called full-function concentrative joint venture.

a. Mergers and acquisitions

The Competition Council has had to examine only a limited number of mergers. The acquisition of shares, on the other hand, is clearly the most common type transaction which the Council has had to consider. Such operations will constitute a concentration where the shares acquired (in combination with other rights, agreements or other circumstances, as the case may be) allow the acquirer to exercise control over an undertaking.

The Competition Council has on a number of occasions examined transfers of assets. In this respect, the question arises when the transferred assets will be sufficient for the operation to constitute a concentration. The "bottom limit" of what will be sufficient has not yet been tested. However, it is clear from the case law that an asset transfer will constitute a concentration at least where the purchased assets form a "business unit, to which a certain turnover may be attributed"[4]. This is in accordance with the European Commission's notice on the concept of concentration under the Merger Regulation[5].

b. Joint ventures

Joint ventures are the subject of Article 9, § 2, of the Act. This Article, which is practically identical to Article 3(2) of the Merger Regulation before it was amended by Regulation 1310/97, provides that *concentrative* full-function joint ventures do constitute a concentration, but that *co-operative* joint ventures do not.

The Competition Council's case law pursuant to Article 9, § 2, broadly follows the European Commission's notice on the distinction between concentrative and co-operative joint ventures[6]. *Office National Ducroire/COBAC/SFAC* is particularly revealing in this respect[7]. The Council found, firstly, that the operation in question led to joint control by the two parents. This finding was based not only on the parent undertakings' respective shareholdings, but also on the agreement governing their conduct as parents of the joint undertaking. The Council observed, secondly, that "COBAC [the joint venture] is capable of durably accomplishing all functions of an autonomous economic entity acting as an economic operator in the market; that it indeed possesses the human and financial means necessary to play such a role; (…); that COBAC SA will be able to conduct its own commercial policy." Thirdly and finally, the Council pointed out that the operation would not lead to co-ordination of competitive conduct either between the parents, or between the parents and the joint venture, since there was no overlap between the two parents' activities or between the activities of either parent and the joint venture[8].

The Competition Council has held that, where the parent companies withdraw from the markets on which the joint venture is to be active, there can be no question of co-ordination, and the joint venture will thus be of a concentrative nature[9].

However, the Competition Council appears not to follow entirely the European Commission notice on the distinction between concentrative and co-operative joint ventures[10]. In *Maas International*/Lekkerland, the Council held that the operation in question constituted a concentration since "there [could] be no question of co-ordinated conduct, either between the founding undertakings, or between the founding undertakings and the joint venture"[11]. Likewise in *Telenet Vlaanderen*[12], the Council held that the joint venture in question constituted a concentration since "co-ordination of the competitive conduct of US West, one of the parent companies, with Telenet, the joint venture [was] improbable". In *Mechelse Veilingen*[13], the Council observed that "V.M.S. [the joint venture] will be active in a different market from the parent undertakings, with the result that co-ordination of their competitive conduct must be considered improbable". The Competition Council thus appears to lend weight to the question whether or not the transaction may lead to co-ordination between the parents on the one hand, and the joint venture on the other[14]. In contrast to this view, the Commission notice on the distinction between concentrative and co-operative joint ventures makes it clear that co-ordination between the parents and the joint venture is in itself irrelevant: such co-ordination is only significant insofar as it is an instrument for co-ordination between the parents.

A particular question arises in the event of certain two-stage concentrations, namely where the transaction involves joint control at a first stage, but provides for a call and/or put option leaving open the possibility of sole control at a later stage. In this case, the question arises whether the entire operation (i.e. the first and second stage) is to be considered as a single operation which may be examined as a whole, or whether each stage constitutes a separate concentration.

In *Serpos/Linguatech*[15] the Council was confronted with such a two-stage operation. The concentration in question consisted of the purchase of 45% of the shares in two target companies, resulting in joint control by the seller and the purchaser. However, the agreement provided for call and put options on the remaining shares, which could lead to the purchaser acquiring sole control over the target companies at a later stage. The notifying parties requested the Competition Council to rule on the admissibility of the entire transaction (i.e. including the "second stage" call and put options). In response, the Council decision stated: "The Council cannot entertain this request because every concentration is to be examined in function of the concrete market circumstances".

The circumstances were somewhat different in *IMS/PMSI*[15bis]. This case concerned the acquisition by IMS of a number of subsidiaries of PMSI. However, the parties contended that there was no concentration in Belgium since the share purchase agreement provided only for a call option on the PMSI's Belgian subsidiaries. Until this option was exercised, the purchaser had no stake in these targets. The Competition Council rejected this view, pointing out, firstly, that IMS had already declared its intention to exercise the option, secondly that if the options were not exercised, the two Belgian target companies would disappear, thirdly that the option prevented PMSI from negotiating with other potential purchasers, fourthly that the option effectively prevented PMSI's Belgian subsidiaries from taking strategic decisions without regard for IMS' wishes, and finally that IMS already exercised *de facto* control over PMSI. In the Council's view, the option itself constituted a concentration. This decision may have been influenced by the fact that the option in question had to be exercised within the very short time limit of three months.

It appears to follow that, at least where the acquisition of sole control is uncertain or is not immediate, call and put options will not be treated as part of the original concentration, and may have to be notified separately where they are exercised. On the other hand, where the exercise of an option is both probable and imminent, as in *IMS/PMSI*, that option may in itself constitute a concentration.

III. Jurisdictional thresholds

Belgian concentration control is at present greatly complicated by the fact that, unlike the Merger Regulation, the Competition Act provides not only for a turnover threshold, but also for a market share threshold.

1. The turnover threshold

The turnover threshold was originally set at one billion Belgian francs. This was increased to three billion Belgian francs by Royal Decree[16]. Where an undertaking's turnover is expressed in a currency other than Belgian francs, the conversion rate used is the average exchange rate, as calculated by the National Bank of Belgium, for the year in which the turnover was achieved.

Article 46, § 1, of the Act provides that the relevant figure, for each undertaking, is the total turnover achieved during the previous financial year *in Belgium and abroad*, i.e. world-wide turnover. Turnover is to be understood within the meaning of the legislation on the annual accounts of undertakings, i.e. excluding VAT. It follows from Article 11 of the Act that the turnover figures for the various parties to the concentration must be added together.

Where the concentration consists of the acquisition of only *parts* of another undertaking or group of undertakings, the relevant figure, as regards the seller, is the turnover achieved by the parts which are the object of the transaction (Article 46, § 2). This admittedly ambiguous provision only applies to the seller: the acquiring party's turnover is not to be excluded[17]. Where two or more such partial acquisitions take place within a two-year period, they are to be treated as a single concentration taking place on the date of the last transaction (Article 46, § 2).

For banks, credit institutions and other financial institutions, turnover is replaced by a figure equal to one tenth of the balance total. For insurance undertakings, the relevant figure is the value of the gross premiums written, comprising all amounts received and receivable in respect of insurance contracts issued by or on behalf of the insurance undertakings, including outgoing reinsurance premiums, and after deduction of taxes and parafiscal levies charged on the basis of the premiums or the total thereof (Article 46, § 3)[17bis].

Where a party to a concentration is part of a group of undertakings, the turnover figure to be taken into account is the sum of the turnover figures for all undertakings forming part of the same group (Article 46, § 4).

For public undertakings and undertakings granted special or exclusive rights by the public authorities, the relevant figure is the turnover achieved by "all undertakings forming an economic whole with autonomous decision-making power, regardless of who may hold the capital and whatever rules of administrative supervision may apply" (Article 46, § 5).

The turnover threshold has given rise to few disputes but to much dissatisfaction[18]. The fact that the threshold is based on *world-wide* turnover has indeed led to a large number of concentrations having to be notified merely on the basis of their international dimension and despite their limited significance for the Belgian market. Under the Bill currently before Parliament, the world-wide turnover threshold would be replaced by a national turnover threshold.

2. The market share threshold

Whereas the turnover threshold is relatively straightforward, the market share threshold has given rise to considerable uncertainty and dispute, particularly between the Competition Service and the Competition Council. This threshold was originally set at 20%, but was increased to 25% by the Royal Decree of March 31, 1995.

In order to establish whether a concentration has to be notified, the parties must determine whether their joint market share exceeds 25% of the "market concerned". In order to calculate this market share, they will first have to define the *relevant product markets* and *relevant geographic markets* .Then they will have to decide which of these markets are "markets concerned". The calculation is not simplified by the use of a fourth concept, that of the "affected market".

These concepts have not been used at all consistently in the Competition Council's case law. Particularly the distinction between the concepts of "market concerned" and "affected market" is not altogether clear.

a. Relevant product markets

The notification form for concentrations (form CONC-C/C-1) defines the "market for goods affected" as comprising "all goods or services regarded by the consumer as interchangeable or which may be substituted one for the other given their characteristics, price and the purpose for which they are intended (…)."

The basic criterion for market definition is demand-side and, to a lesser extent, supply-side substitutability. In *Bekaert/Tréfileurope* the Competition Council defined these concepts as follows[19]: "There is supply-side substitutability where the products in question are considered by the user as similar on the basis of their qualities, their price and their use. There is supply-side substitutability were an undertaking, in determining its competitive conduct, has to take into account the possibility that another undertaking might enter the market concerned".

On a few occasions the Competition Council has proceeded to detailed market analysis in order to define the relevant markets. In *Kinepolis*[20] the Council examined the Belgian cinema markets in considerable detail, and was able to state with confidence that "it can be deduced from the increase in cinema admissions during the last ten years that the increase in the sale of videocassettes and broadcasting rights for television has not caused a fall in the sale of cinema tickets", and that the relevant market thus included cinema film showings, but excluded other forms of film showings. In *Mattel/Tyco Toys*[21] the notifying parties submitted a market study concerning the market for dolls. On the basis of various indicators, including price elasticity, diversion ratios and the evolution in sales, it was demonstrated that "fashion dolls" and other dolls were substitutes. The Competition Council followed the findings of this study, and held that "fashion dolls" did not constitute a separate product market.

Both in *Kinepolis* and in *Mattel/Tyco Toys* the Competition Council had the benefit of reliable figures allowing detailed market analysis. However, these decisions are very much the exception. In most cases, with little market information available, the Competition Council gives either very limited and often uninformative reasons for its market definition, or no reasons at all. Where reasons are given, demand-side substitutability remains the central criterion.

A regular feature of the Council's reasoning are references to answers from competitors and customers to questions posed by the competition authorities. Thus in *Henkel/Loctite*[22] the Competition Council held that the markets for two distinct types of glue "must be considered as separate markets since these [types of glue] are not substitutable with other glues. This position is contested by the notifying party, but the Council follows the Service regarding the separate delimitation of these markets on the basis of an answer to a question given by a competitor and a customer". Another frequent source of inspiration are decisions or other documents issued by international or foreign authorities[23]. Thus in *Procter & Gamble/Tambrands*[24], the Competition Council found that sanitary towels and tampons constituted distinct product markets, and justified this finding entirely by reference to the European Commission's decision in *Procter & Gamble/Schickedanz*[25], and to a report by the UK Monopolies and Mergers Commission.

As an example of odd reasoning, the decision in *Johnson/Schmalbach* deserves particular mention[26]. After finding that "there is no outspoken consensus on a clear and well-delineated definition of the relevant markets", the Competition Council stated: "The market definition as offered by the notifying parties is as good as any which was obtained, and can be accepted".

Although the definition of the relevant product market is often hotly disputed in proceedings before the Belgian competition authorities, these disputes are, on the whole, not reflected in the case law. The Competition Council's decisions are, with few exceptions, very brief, even laconic. This is true particularly as regards market definition. As a result, it remains difficult to give general guidelines on how the market will be defined in any particular instance.

b. Relevant geographical markets

The notification form for concentrations defines the "geographical market affected" as comprising "the area within Belgium in which the businesses concerned are involved in the supply and demand of goods and services (...)."

For the purpose of Belgian merger control, the relevant geographical market is a peculiarly ambiguous concept, since it serves a double purpose. Under EC competition law, market shares (and therefore the definition of the relevant geographic market) are part of the substantive appraisal of a concentration. Under the Belgian merger control rules, however, market shares are important not only for the *substantive* assessment, but particularly for the *jurisdictional* question of whether or not the 25% market share threshold is exceeded.

For *jurisdictional* purposes, the relevant geographical market is never wider than the Belgian territory: what matters is whether or not the parties to the concentration have a market share over 25% *in Belgium*. As it has been rightly observed, if this were not the case, neither of the jurisdictional thresholds would constitute a territorial criterion[27]. The turnover threshold already explicitly refers to *world-wide* turnover. If the market share threshold likewise referred to market shares outside Belgium, numerous concentrations would come within the scope of the Act even though none of the parties had any activities in Belgium.

In *Regla Beheer Nederland/Glaceries de Saint Roch*[28] the notifying parties contended that the European Union should be considered as the relevant geographic market. The Competition Council rejected this view, stating that concentrations are to be examined in relation to the Belgian market.

Although the relevant geographic market is never wider than Belgium, it may be more limited. In *Kinepolis*, for example, the markets for film showings in cinemas were found to be more limited than the national territory since "the distance which the majority of users is prepared to travel for a cinema visit, is limited"[29]. Somewhat puzzling was the finding in *Telenet Vlaanderen*[30] that the relevant geographic market coincided with the Flemish Region. Since the European Commission has consistently observed a tendency towards telecommunications markets of European dimension, it is surprising that a national competition authority should instead find a regional telecommunications market.

In certain cases there will be no relevant geographic market at all in Belgium. In *Eugen O. Butz/Ieper Industries*[31] the Competition Council found that the products in question (luggage systems for motor vehicles) were used by a number of vehicle assembly plants in Belgium. However, the Council held that "supply and demand do not meet in Belgium, since the car producers, who have only assembly units in Belgium, enter into direct contact with the producers of luggage systems via their [= the car producers'] headquarters, not situated in Belgium. (…) There thus appears to be no Belgian market for luggage systems". In other words, although luggage systems may physically be installed in Belgium, no purchasing decisions are taken in this country. The Council accordingly decided that the notified operation fell outside the scope of the Act.

Whilst the geographic market defined for the *jurisdictional* purpose of the market share threshold is never wider than Belgium, the *substantive* appraisal takes into account the "real extent" of the market.

This peculiarity has lead the Competition Council to make such seemingly contradictory statements as the following in *Henkel/Loctite*[32]: "The relevant geographic market for this concentration is Belgium. However, the international nature of the market should be taken into account."

c. The "market concerned"

Once the relevant product and geographic markets have been defined, the question must be answered as to which of these various markets are "markets concerned" within the meaning of Article 11 of the Act, and thus have to be taken into account for the purpose of the market share threshold.

The Competition Council has defined the concept of "market concerned" as "the national product market for which the concentration may have consequences, however small"[33].

It is well established that, where the acquiring undertaking and the acquired undertaking are active on the same market (horizontal relationship), this market will be taken into account for the purpose of the market threshold test, and thus constitute a "market concerned". Likewise, if there is a vertical relationship between the acquiring and the acquired party, the markets which are the subject of this vertical relationship will be a "market concerned".

If the parties are active not in the same market, but in "neighbouring markets" ("neighbouring relationships"), these markets will also be taken into account. Two markets are considered to be "neighbouring markets" where one may influence the other, e.g. in the case of complementary products[34]. However, the case law is not always clear on the notion of "neighbouring markets". In *Procter & Gamble/Tambrands*[35], the Competition Council held that the markets for sanitary towels and for tampons were distinct product markets. Nevertheless, the Council immediately added that "these separate markets are, however, neighbouring markets, and it is not a priori excluded that one market might influence the other, albeit marginally, by reason of the use of the different products." In consequence, the parties' market share on these neighbouring markets had to be taken into account. Since the market share threshold was apparently exceeded on at least one of these neighbouring markets (the decision is not explicit on this point), the operation had to be notified. Why the two markets were to be considered as "neighbouring markets" was not explained in the decision.

The case law becomes less clear where there is neither a horizontal, nor a neighbouring, nor a vertical relationship between the acquiring and the acquired undertaking, and the concentration is thus essentially of a conglomerate nature. Precisely this point has been the subject of dispute between the Competition Council and Service[36], and it has rightly been claimed that the concept of "market concerned" has been interpreted with a certain measure of "poetic licence"[37].

Whether or not a market is a "market concerned" appears to depend essentially on whether or not the concentration in question may *influence* that market. The absence of horizontal, vertical or neighbouring relations between the parties is not decisive in this respect. For a fuller understanding of the case law, the reader is referred to the various detailed analyses of the Competition Council's case law[38]. Suffice it for the present purpose to cite two decisions regarding conglomerate concentrations.

In *Amoco/Albemarble*[39], the acquiring undertaking (Amoco) was not present in any of the relevant product markets in Belgium, and thus had a zero market share. The acquired undertaking (certain of Albemarble's assets), on the other hand, was found to have a market share in excess of 25%. This fact alone was sufficient for the Competition Council to hold that the market share threshold was exceeded. On the basis of this decision, one might assume that, as soon as either the acquiring undertaking or the acquired undertaking controls more than 25% of any market in Belgium, the jurisdictional threshold will be exceeded even if this market has no connection whatsoever with the market in which the acquired undertaking is active. Such an extensive interpretation has been the subject of criticism[40].

In *Isolde/BASF*, the acquiring party (the Kohap group) was likewise not present in any of the affected markets. However, unlike in *Amoco/Albemarble*, the Competition Council found that "there is neither a horizontal, nor a vertical relationship between the markets in which the notifying parties are active. (…) There is only an essentially conglomerate relation. The notified operation has no effect on the existing competitive relations in Belgium." The Council went on to state: "The scope of the Belgian concentration control regime is within the Belgian market. Take-overs which neither have nor can have any influence on the Belgian market, even though the undertakings concerned might, jointly or individually, have a market share in excess of 25 %, do not fall under the Act"[41].

It is clear that this test, based on the notion of "influence" or "effect", requires detailed analysis on a case by case basis, and is by no means conducive to legal certainty.

d. The calculation of market shares

The Competition Act does not specify how market shares should be calculated. In practice, shares appear most frequently to be calculated on the basis of turnover. However, this is by no means a universal rule, and the Competition Council has on occasions used other criteria. In *TIP Trailer Rentals*[42], for instance, market shares were calculated on the basis of the total number of trailers available for rental (i.e. capacity), and this calculation was justified by the fact that capacity utilisation did not differ greatly between competitors. In *Kinepolis*, the Council offered three alternative sets of market share figures for the Belgian cinema market, the first based on the number of halls, the second based on the number of seats and the third based on the number of admissions.

In practice, the method for calculating market shares is to a large extent dictated by the figures available.

e. The difficulty of calculating market shares

It will be clear from the preceding paragraphs that the market share threshold is far from satisfactory. Not only does such a threshold require in-depth market analysis merely to discover whether or not a concentration need be notified, it also creates considerable legal uncertainty. Firstly, the information necessary to calculate the market share will often be difficult, if not impossible to obtain. Secondly, the Competition Council's case law is unclear in several respects, with the result that it is sometimes doubtful which markets should or should not be taken into account.

As a result, it is not surprising that a considerable number of concentrations are notified merely by way of precaution, and that the Competition Council has on many occasions found that a notified concentration falls outside the scope of the Competition Act and is thus not subject to notification. In fact, the Council has more than once opened second phase proceedings, only to decide afterwards that the concentration in question need never have been notified[43, 44].

In the event of genuine uncertainty, there exists an assumption that the market share threshold is not exceeded. In *Recticel/Folio*[45] the Competition Council found that the market share figures offered by the Competition Service did not include all relevant sales, and could not therefore be accepted. Consequently, the Council stated that "it does not appear as proven that the 25% market share is exceeded", and declared that the concentration fell outside the scope of the Act. The decision in *Maas International Europe/Lekkerland EZ Holding*[46] likewise stated: "Taking into account these corrections of the figures adopted by the Competition Service, one therefore arrives at a market share of approximately (...)[deleted in the published version]. In any case it is not proven that the 25% market share threshold was achieved".

3. Jurisdictional thresholds: conclusion

Both the turnover threshold and the market share threshold have given rise to considerable dissatisfaction. Moreover, the market share threshold has given rise to a considerable measure of confusion and legal uncertainty.

It is therefore not surprising that the Bill currently before Parliament contains significant changes in this respect. If the Bill is passed, the existing thresholds will be replaced by a *double turnover threshold*. On the basis of the text available at the time of writing, a concentration will have to be notified if, firstly, the undertakings involved have a combined turnover *in Belgium* of more than 400 million francs, *and* at least two of those undertakings have a turnover *in Belgium* of at least 200 million francs each. It is still arguable that these figures are too low. However, the proposed change would considerably reduce legal uncertainty, whilst also providing a better measure of a concentration's relevance to the Belgian market.

IV. The substantive appraisal of concentrations

1. Legislative provisions

The principal test for the substantive appraisal of concentrations is contained in Article 10, § 2, of the Competition Act, which provides as follows: "Only those concentrations which do not have as a consequence that a dominant position is acquired or strengthened which noticeably restricts effective competition in the Belgian market concerned or a substantial part thereof, may be permitted."

A dominant position is defined in Article 1(b) of the Act as "the position which enables an undertaking to prevent the maintenance of effective competition and allows it to act, to a high degree, independently of its competitors, customers or suppliers." Belgian merger control is thus primarily based on a market dominance test, rather than a broader public interest test. This principle is weakened somewhat by Article 10, § 3, which provides that a concentration which does not satisfy the primary test may nevertheless be permitted if its contribution to the improvement of production or distribution, of technical or economic progress or of the competition structure within the market overrides the resulting restriction of competition. Article 10, § 3, thus allows for a broader *general economic interest* test, but without going so far as a general *public* interest test. The appraisal of concentrations is therefore essentially an economic assessment.

2. General comments on the Competition Council's case law

Certain decisions – including the few prohibition decisions so far – give a detailed and closely reasoned assessment of the notified concentration. These are, however, very much the exception. The striking feature about the Competition Council's case law is that its decisions are, with few exceptions, remarkably short.

A good representative example in this respect is the decision in *Henkel/Loctite*[47], in which the Council reasoned its approval of the notified concentration as follows:

"(…) the Council decides not to oppose the concentration:
1. the undertakings concerned have no production units in Belgium;
2. the markets where the highest market shares are achieved have a limited turnover in Belgium;
3. the markets concerned are to be seen in a European or world-wide context and there appear to be plenty of suppliers present abroad and on other continents;
4. there are no barriers to access (capital, technology, brand reputation, transport costs, …)
5. the purpose is to acquire an important position in the American market;
6. the Bundeskartellamt has not opposed the concentration;
7. the undertakings which were questioned have all stated that there are enough alternatives abroad;
8. Loctite Corporation's customers are multinational undertakings with a strong negotiating position."

Not only is this a clear example of the very short reasoning given in many Competition Council decisions, it also gives a representative picture of the various types of criteria used to asses concentrations. Firstly, it includes a number of criteria which are now familiar from the European Commission's practice, such as the presence or absence of market entry barriers, the presence of potential competitors and the existence of countervailing buyer power. Secondly, it includes criteria which appear to be more typically Belgian, e.g. the observation that customers and/or competitors have not expressed any objections, and that a foreign competition authority has decided not to oppose the concentration. Thirdly, by referring to the strengthening the undertakings' position in America as an argument in favour of the concentration, the Competition Council fails to distinguish between market dominance criteria (Article 10, § 2) on the one hand, and arguments touching on the broader economic interest (Article 10, § 3) on the other.

The next section briefly examines the criteria most commonly used by the Competition Council in its assessment of concentrations.

3. Criteria for the assessment of concentrations

a. A European or international market dimension

It was emphasised above that, for jurisdictional purposes, the relevant geographic market is never wider than the Belgian territory. For the purpose of the substantive assessment, on the other hand, the European or international nature of a market is fully taken into account. The Competition Council does not, however, attempt to define a second geographic market within which the concentration is to be assessed. The international dimension is, rather, seen as one among many criteria for the substantive assessment of a concentration[48].

b. Market shares

Compared to European Commission practice, market shares play a rather limited role in the Competition Council's case law. Indeed, the Council very rarely gives precise market shares in its decisions, preferring instead such expressions as "considerable market shares"[49], "a strong position"[50] or "rather small [market] shares"[51].

Noticeable exceptions to this tendency were the conditional clearance decision in *Kinepolis*, in which the Council was able to calculate that the new entity's market share as 46,74 %[52], and the prohibition decisions in *Callebaut/ Barry I*[53] (the precise figure being deleted in the published version, replaced with the words "situated between 75% and 85%") and *Parfumerie Douglas/ Compartilux*[54] (in which the market share figures were likewise deleted in the published version).

c. No change or limited change in market shares

Where the concentration does not lead to a change in the parties' market shares, this will count in favour of the notified operation[55]. This may be the case in the event of vertical integration, i.e. where an undertaking merely takes over its existing distributor[56].

The same is true where the concentration leads only to a limited increase in market share[57].

d. Access to the Belgian market

The Competition Council has on many occasions considered the absence of barriers to entry into the Belgian market as an argument in favour of a notified concentration[58].

In this respect, the case law makes regular reference to the duration of contracts between buyers and sellers in the market. Where these are of short duration, this is considered to facilitate market entry, and to reduce the risk of a dominant position[59].

e. Countervailing buyer power

The Competition Council regularly refers to the bargaining power (*pouvoir de négociation*) wielded by customers, or their ability to switch between competing suppliers[60]. In the prohibition decision in *Callebaut/Barry I*[61], the Council stated that "the negotiating power of the numerous and dispersed customers confronted with the new entity, is weak (…) even the negotiating power of the large customers which form part of multinationals is weakened as a result of the concentration, since they do not in the short run have sufficient alternative sources of supply (…)"

f. One of the undertakings is not active in Belgium

Where one of the undertakings involved in the concentration was not active in Belgium, the Council has, in certain cases, found that the concentration had no effect on any market in this country, that there was therefore no "market concerned" in which the jurisdictional market share threshold could be exceeded, and that the operation was accordingly not notifiable[62].

In other cases, the Council has held that an operation could have an effect on a market in Belgium even though one of the parties was not present in this country. Assuming the jurisdictional thresholds are exceeded, the operation will thus have to be notified. However, the fact that one party is absent from the Belgian market (although this is not sufficient to avoid notification) will clearly be of importance for the substantive appraisal of the concentration[63].

g. The small size of the relevant market in Belgium

On several occasions the Competition Council has counted the small size of the relevant market in Belgium as a factor in favour of a notified concentration[64].

h. The presence of competitors and potential competitors

The Competition Council regularly refers to the existence of competitors (both actual and potential, and particularly internationally active competitors), capable of preventing the entity resulting from the concentration from exercising market power[65].

i. Competitors' opinions

As part of the concentration control procedure, the Competition Service systematically contacts the notifying parties' competitors and customers. Where these third parties have no objections to the notified operation, this is regularly cited in the Competition Council's decision as a reason why the concentration will not lead to the creation of a dominant position[66]. In *Promedia/BDS*, the Council noted that the questioned undertakings actually presented arguments in favour of the notified transaction[67]. The decision in *Fresenius/Pharmacia/Upjohn* explicitly stated[68]: "(…) the Council deplores the lack of co-operation on the part of the majority of the parties questioned, who either do not answer at all, or do so incompletely."

j. Foreign decisions

Decisions issued by foreign competition authorities or by the European Commission appear to carry considerable weight with the Competition Council, not only as regards market definition, but also as regards the substantive appraisal[69]. In *Fresenius/Upjohn/Pharmacia*[70], the Council listed the countries in which the concentration had been notified, but stated "so far no national authority has taken a decision".

k. Article 10, § 3: Broader considerations of general economic interest

On several occasions the Competition Council has observed that the notified operation would not affect consumers' interests, in particular because these would be able to obtain the same products and marketing and distribution services after the concentration[71]. This argument is clearly part, not so much of a market dominant test, as of a broader general economic interest test within the meaning of Article 10, § 3, of the Act. The fact that a concentration will improve Belgian undertakings' abilities to compete with foreign undertakings[72], is likewise an "Article 10, § 3, argument". In most cases, the Council does not make a clear distinction between "dominant position"-considerations and considerations touching upon the general economic interest.

Two notable exceptions to this tendency were *Promedia/BDS* and *Kinepolis*. In *Promedia/BDS*[73] the two operators on the market for the publication of telephone directories were to merge, with the result that they would in the future publish a single set of telephone directories, as opposed to two competing series as before. The Competition Council found that the operation would lead to a dominant position, but listed numerous "Article 10, § 3-reasons" in favour of the concentration. These included the benefits for advertisers (who would no longer have to place advertisements in two publications), environmental considerations (less paper, and thus less waste), the fact that, in a liberalised market, private competitors might enter the market and, interestingly, the general dissatisfaction among the public at the appearance in 1994 of a second telephone directory. The Council went on to state that these benefits outweighed the disadvantages of the dominant position.

In *Kinepolis*[74], the Council likewise found that the concentration would result in a dominant position. However, it pointed out, firstly, that the notified transaction would improve the resulting group's chances of development at European level and meeting international competition, and, secondly, that the concentration could contribute to the progress of audiovisual technology, which would be of benefit to consumers. Moreover, the group's increased competitiveness at international level could, in the Council's view, improve the equilibrium in the Belgium market. These considerations were sufficient to outweigh the dominant position to which the concentration would give rise, and the concentration was accordingly cleared, albeit subject to conditions.

4. Conditional clearance

Article 33, § 1, of the Competition Act provides as follows: "Where the investigation relates to a concentration, the Competition Council may by reasoned decision determine that: (1) a concentration is admissible; this decision may include conditions and obligations where Article 10, § 3, is applied. (...)"

It follows from the text of the Act that, where a concentration is permitted on the basis of the "general economic interest" test (Article 10, § 3), a decision declaring the operation admissible may be made subject to conditions and obligations, but that, where a transaction is cleared on the basis of the market dominance test (Article 10, § 2), no conditions or obligations may be imposed.

In *VUM/Het Volk*[75], the concentration consisted of the acquisition by one newspaper publisher (VUM) of another (Het Volk). The concentration gave rise to concern. In particular, the Competition Council feared that the purchasing of advertising space in newspapers from one group might be made conditional on the purchase of space in newspapers from the other. The transaction was therefore cleared subject to the condition that the new entity should refrain from such forms of "tying". Despite the wording of Article 33, § 1, of the Competition Act, the concentration was clearly approved pursuant to Article 10, § 2 of the Act (the market dominance test), and not Article 10, § 3 (the general economic interest test). Unless one accepts an extensive interpretation *contra legem* of Article 33, § 1, the decision in *VUM/Het Volk* thus appears to be in breach of the Act.

In *Kinepolis*[76], the Competition Council found that the concentration created a dominant position, but that this was counteracted by certain considerations of general economic interest. Nevertheless, in order to limit the effects of the transaction on the Belgian market, the Council imposed a series of conditions, initially offered by the notifying parties as voluntary undertakings. These included one structural condition and a number of conditions relating to the group's conduct. The structural condition was a broad prohibition preventing the group from establishing, taking over, expanding, renovating or replacing new cinema complexes without prior permission from the Competition Council. The various "conduct conditions" included a prohibition on requesting or requiring exclusivity from film distributors, and a prohibition on reserving the group's own films for its own cinema's.

Although the Competition Act is silent on this point, the Competition Council has held that conditions and obligations may be imposed only in second phase proceedings[77].

5. The prohibition decisions so far

To date the Competition Council has prohibited only *three* concentrations. In contrast to the general tendency, both prohibition decisions contain extensive reasons, and thus deserve more detailed examination.

a. *Parfumerie Douglas/Compartilux*

In *Parfumerie Douglas/Compartilux*[78], the Competition Council had to rule on a concentration in the Belgian market for the selective distribution of perfumes.

The substantive assessment first examines the notifying parties' market shares. The exact figure is deleted in the published version, but it is stated that the entity resulting from the operation would have a market share five times that of its nearest competitor. The Council apparently considered this figure to be in itself an indication of a dominant position.

The Council further pointed out the strong economic and financial position which the new entity would enjoy, the high barriers to market access (in particular the cost of the investments required, and the risk of failure) and the fact that the producers were not in a position to exercise countervailing market power restricting that of their selective distributors. Particular attention was paid to the fact that the undertakings involved had in the past already driven a number of competitors out of the market by means of predatory pricing.

In view of these objections, the Council declared the concentration inadmissible.

b. *Callebaut/Barry*

In *Callebaut/Barry I*[79] the Competition Council had to examine the planned acquisition by the chocolate producer Callebaut of Barry, also active in the chocolate industry. After first describing the product, the production process and the regulatory framework, the Council analysed the Belgian chocolate market in considerable detail. Its strongly reasoned appraisal of the notified transaction may be summarised as follows.

The new entity would have achieved a market share of between 75% and 85% (the exact figure being deleted in the published decision). Moreover, the nearest competitor would have been eliminated. The new group would have had a far broader product range than any competitor, and five times the number of production lines of its competitors. The chocolate market was found to be a mature one, in which acquired positions were difficult to challenge. High barriers to market access, including high transport costs and customer loyalty, made market entry difficult. As a result, foreign competitors were found to exercise little competitive pressure. Customers were likewise not strong enough to exercise pressure on the new group. Demand was considered to be inelastic, partly due to the level of customer loyalty, allowing the new entity to increase prices with impunity. On the basis of these findings, the Competition Council held that the concentration would strengthen a dominant position.

As far as Article 10, § 3, was concerned, the claim that the concentration could improve the undertakings' competitiveness at international level was considered not to be proven.

The Council accordingly declared the concentration inadmissible.

This decision was annulled on appeal for reasons explained below. The same concentration was subsequently re-notified, and again prohibited by the Competition Council. This second prohibition was also annulled on appeal[80].

c. *IMS/PMSI*

In *IMS/PMSI*[80bis] the Competition Council had to decide on a concentration in the Belgian market for market studies in the pharmaceutical sector. The Council distinguished two relevant markets, that for "quantitative studies" and that for "qualitative studies".

The Council found that the purchaser, IMS, already held a dominant position, and that the Concentration would strengthen this. The finding that IMS already had a dominant position was based firstly on the opinion of certain of its customers. The Council also pointed out that the market was stable and mature, that IMS had "for more than twenty years (...) occupied a monopoly position as regards quantitative studies", and that the barriers to market access were considerable. The concentration was found to strengthen IMS' dominant position, firstly, because it would expand IMS' range of products. Secondly, IMS' current product range and that of the target companies were found to be complementary, with the risk that the concentration might lead to tying practices. As a result of this expansion of its product range and the "necessary complementarity" IMS would have become an inevitable partner for the pharmaceutical industry.

The concentration was accordingly prohibited, and IMS was required to divest the target company which it had already acquired through the exercise of the option.

V. Ancillary restrictions

On the subject of restrictions ancillary to concentrations, the Competition Act is silent. The merger notification form does not request any information on such restrictions either. In the past this led to doubts as to whether or not ancillary restrictions were to be judged as part of the concentration, and could thus benefit from the strict procedural time limits[81]. As recently as 1997 the matter was still somewhat doubtful[82].

However, this matter now appears to have been settled. In *Johnson/Schmalbach*[83], the Competition Council stated: "(…) the take-over contract provides for a non-competition clause stipulating that Johnson Controls will not enter the market which it has left during the first five years after the realisation of the concentration, which appears acceptable".

It is therefore clear that ancillary restrictions are indeed to be treated as part of the concentration in question. Although there is as yet little case law on this matter, it may be assumed that the Competition Council will follow European Commission practice in this respect.

VI. Procedural matters

1. The notification

a. The term for notification

Article 12, § 1, of the Competition Act provides that concentrations which are subject to Belgian merger control must be notified within one week after the conclusion of the agreement, the publication of the bid or the acquisition of control, whichever takes place first.

The conclusion of an agreement (e.g. a share purchase or asset purchase agreement) is by far the most common event triggering the obligation to notify. In this case, the term for notification starts only when a *binding* agreement has been concluded. Mere letters of intent, and other documents which are not binding on the parties, do not constitute an agreement within the meaning of Article 12, and do not trigger the one week period[84]. Where such agreements are nevertheless notified, the Competition Council will refuse to issue a decision[85].

Where the contract provides for one or more suspensive conditions, these may delay the start of the one week term for notification[86]. Whether this will be the case depends, essentially, on whether or not the parties are *bound* to proceed with the concentration. Thus in *Groenwoudt/Compartilux*, the Competition Council held that

> "The purchase agreement of April 17, 1996 contains a series of suspensive conditions which must be fulfilled within a certain time limit after execution of the agreement.
>
> It appears that none of these conditions gives either of the notifying parties the right to decide to complete or not to complete the concentration operation according to his own wishes.
>
> The conditions will only have to be fulfilled after the Council's first phase decision term has lapsed.
>
> However, on the date of the present decision the obligation to achieve the concentration under the conditions provided for in the agreement, is binding upon parties.
>
> The concentration is therefore notifiable"[87].

A common suspensive condition provides that the closing shall be delayed until all necessary regulatory approvals, including those of the competent competition authorities, have been obtained. The fulfilment of this condition is not dependent on the parties, who remain bound by the agreement, and concentrations which are subject to such conditions will be notifiable[88].

A concentration may be brought about by a series of agreements. A first "framework" agreement between parent companies may provide for the general terms of the concentration, and impose on the parents an obligation to arrange the transfer of their subsidiaries. The terms of the transfer of these subsidiaries are then agreed in a series of contracts, e.g. one for each jurisdiction involved. In such cases, the agreement at the parent company level, provided it is binding as regards the concentration, will be notifiable and thus subject to the one week time limit[89].

Where a concentration is not notified within the one week time limit, Article 37, § 2 of the Competition Act provides for fines of between 20,000 and 1,000,000 francs. A fine may be imposed even where the concentration in question is subsequently found to be admissible.

In *Westimex/Dalgety Holland* a fine of 100,000 francs was imposed for late notification[90]. In *De Post/Hagefin*, the Competition Council again imposed a fine of 100,000 francs, stating that:

"The concentration was not notified within the time limit prescribed by article 12 of the Competition Act and the notification was filed only after the Competition Service had, of its own movement, contacted The Post by telephone and in writing"[91].

However, these two decisions are very much the exception. Although late notifications are very common, the Competition Council has only rarely imposed fines. Its case law contains frequent references to specific circumstances justifying the decision not to impose fines. Such circumstances may include the difficulty and delays in obtaining the necessary information[92], doubts as to whether the operation is notifiable[93], the lack of co-operation on the part of seller[94] and the fact that a concentration was notified to the European Commission in error[95]. Sometimes the Council's decision makes no reference at all to the fact that a concentration was notified outside the statutory time limit[96]. In order to avoid penalties in the event of late notification, it appears important to inform the Competition Service in good time of the concentration and of the intention to notify[97].

The sanction for late notification should not be confused with the sanction for implementing a concentration without awaiting the Competition Council's decision. This will be examined in point 4 under VI below.

b. The notification form

Notifications must be made using the form "CONC-C/C-1" issued as an annex to the Royal Decree of 23 March 1993[98]. This document, which is similar to the EC merger notification form, requires a vast amount of information which is often difficult and sometimes impossible to obtain, particularly within the one week time limit. This alone frequently makes it difficult to notify on time. However, provided the Competition Service is informed in good time of the concentration and of the intention to notify, and provided the notifying parties are seen to be acting in good faith, a reasonable delay in order to gather the required information may be expected not to result in a fine.

Moreover, Article 5, § 4, of the Royal Decree of 23 March 1993 on the notification of concentrations provides that the Competition Service may grant a waiver where it considers that certain information is not necessary for its investigation. Such a waiver does not prevent the Service or the Council from requesting the information at a later stage.

Where a notification is found to be incomplete in any material respect, the Competition Service must inform the notifying parties thereof, and specifies a time limit within which the missing information must be supplied.

The concentration control procedure is subject to the Act of 18 July 1966 on the use of languages in administrative matters[99]. The notification should therefore be filed in the language of the linguistic region in which the central office of the undertakings in question is established. Thus in *Douglas/ Compartilux* a concentration was notified in French, but had to be re-notified in Dutch since the relevant office was in Antwerp[100]. Where none of the undertakings has a central office in Belgium, the notification form should be in one of the national languages.

c. Notifying parties

Article 12, § 2 of the Act provides that, where a concentration is brought about by an agreement, the notification must be filed jointly by the parties concerned. In other cases, i.e. where the concentration is the result of a unilateral act of a single party, the concentration must be notified by that party.

2. First phase proceedings

Upon receipt of the notification, the Competition Service immediately conducts an investigation into the planned concentration. In contrast to the European merger regime, the Act does not provide for publication of the fact that the concentration has been notified. However, as part of its investigation, the Service puts a number of questions to the customers and competitors of the notifying parties, who are thus informed of the notification. In accordance with Article 24, § 3, of the Act, the Competition Service has to hear the notifying parties in the course of its investigation.

Upon conclusion of its investigation, the Service files its report with the Council, which sends a copy to the notifying parties.

Before issuing its decision, the Council must, in accordance with Article 27, § 2 of the Act, hear at least the notifying parties. If it considers this to be necessary, it may also hear one or more third parties. Any natural or legal person with a sufficient interest is entitled to be heard at his request. Moreover, before taking its decision, the Council may request the Service (Article 27, § 2, *in fine*) or any other body[101] to conduct further investigations.

The first phase procedure is, in principle, concluded by a decision of the Competition Council. In this respect, Article 33, § 2, of the Act provides for three types of decision. The Council may, firstly, find that the concentration falls outside the scope of the Act (Article 33, § 2.2.a). Secondly, the Council may find that, although the notified concentration falls within the scope of the Act, it does not raise any serious doubts as to its admissibility (Article 33, § 2.2.b). In this case, the Council must declare the concentration admissible. Thirdly, if the concentration is found to raise serious doubts, the Council must open second phase proceedings (Article 33, § 2.2.c).

Under the terms of Article 33, § 2.3, these decisions must include reasons, and must be given within one month after receipt of the notification. Where the initial notification is found to be incomplete, this one month period starts on the date following that on which the complete information was received.

If the Competition Council fails to issue a decision within the one month period, the concentration is deemed to be admissible (Article 33, § 2.4 of the Act). The Council has recently made increasing use of this provision. Where a concentration raises no serious doubts, and the Competition Service recommends its approval, it is not uncommon for the Council to send the notifying parties an informal letter stating that, in its opinion, no formal hearing is required, and that it will therefore let the one month period lapse without issuing a decision. In 1997, over half the concentration notifications led to such "implicit approvals"[102].

In contrast to the EC merger regime, the Competition Council cannot give conditional approval in a first phase decision. In *De Post/Hagefin*[103], the Competition Service recommended that the Council should approve the notified concentration subject to conditions. The Council rejected this recommendation, stating:

> "- either the Council comes to the conclusion that no serious doubt exists as to the admissibility of the concentration, and in that case it has to decide not to oppose it, without being able to impose conditions (article 33, § 2.2.b of the Competition Act);
> - or the Council invokes serious doubts as to the admissibility of the concentration and then it has to decide to start the [second phase procedure] (article 33, § 2.2.c of the Competition Act)."

3. Second phase proceedings

If the Competition Council decides to initiate second phase proceedings, it refers the concentration back to the Competition Service for an additional investigation, and sets a time limit within which the Service's report is to be submitted. During this investigation, the parties are once again heard by the Competition Service. Upon conclusion of its second phase investigation, the Service submits its second report to the Council, which sends the parties a copy. The notifying parties, and, as the case may be, third parties, are again heard at a hearing before the Competition Council.

Within seventy-five days after its decision to open second phase proceedings, the Competition Council must issue its final decision on the notified concentration. Where the Council fails to take a decision within this time limit, it is deemed to have approved the concentration.

This seventy-five day time limit was the subject of debate in *Callebaut/ Barry I*, one of the few prohibitions so far. In this case, the decision to open second phase proceedings was taken on September 6, 1996. The final decision, dated December 19, 1996, was issued well outside the seventy-five day limit, but made reference to "the notifying parties' agreement to extend the time limit for a decision, fixed by article 33 of the Act, until December 23, 1996". As discussed above[104], the Competition Council declared the concentration inadmissible. This decision was appealed, the notifying parties contending that the Council's decision had been taken outside the statutory time limit, and should therefore be quashed. The Court of Appeal agreed, stating that:

> "it is not for the notifying parties, nor for the Competition Council to take the legislator's place and to modify a time limit which the legislator has fixed (…) article 33, § 3.3 of the Competition Act, fixing the 75 day limit, must be considered as touching upon the 'ordre public';
> (…) consequently, the notifying parties could not renounce this term and agree to an extension (…)"[105].

The Court of Appeal accordingly annulled the Competition Council's prohibition decision, and the concentration was declared to be admissible in the absence of a decision within the statutory time limit.

After the prohibition decision in *Callebaut/Barry I*, but before the judgement on appeal, the same concentration was re-notified, with some modifications. Nevertheless, despite the undertakings offered by the parties, the Council still held that the operation was inadmissible[106]. This second prohibition decision was also appealed. The Court of Appeal held that, by not issuing a decision within the statutory time limit in *Callebaut/Barry I*, the Competition Council had exhausted its powers with regard to the concentration, and, by issuing a second decision on the same operation in the context of a re-notification, had exceeded its powers[107].

Article 33, § 4, of the Competition Act provides that, where the Council declares a concentration to be inadmissible, it must order the divestiture of the grouped undertakings, the termination of joint control, or any other appropriate measure in order to restore effective competition[108].

4. Sanctions for infringements of the Competition Act

The Competition Act provides several mechanisms for sanctioning infringements of its provisions on concentration control.

The sanction in the event of late notification was discussed above[109]. The same penalty, a fine of 20,000 to 1,000,000 francs, may also be imposed where the parties proceed with a concentration without notifying it at all (Article 37, § 2), and where the parties, deliberately or negligently, provide incorrect, distorted or incomplete information, provide information outside the set time limit, or obstruct the investigation (Article 37, § 1). The power to impose these fines lies with the Competition Council.

In addition, Article 38 of the Act provides that the Council may impose a fine not exceeding ten percent of the turnover of the undertakings concerned in the event that parties take measures rendering the concentration irreversible before the Council has issued its decision. In this case, periodic penalty payments not exceeding 250,000 francs per day may be imposed in order to enforce the decision.

5. Appeals

Decisions of the Competition Council may be appealed to the Brussels Court of Appeal. The term for appeal is thirty days, counting from the publication of the decision in the State Gazette (Article 43). This appeal involves a full re-examination of the concentration. Unlike under the EC merger regulation, the Court's powers are not limited to judicial review of the competition authority's decision.

The appeal does not suspend the effect of the Competition Council's decision. However, the Court of Appeal may, on request, suspend the obligation to pay the fines and penalty payments.

VII. Amendments introduced by the Acts of 26 April 1999

On 26 April 1999, two Acts were passed introducing far-reaching amendments to the existing Competition Act. The fact that two separate Acts were required, is explained by the Belgian constitutional rules regarding the powers of the Senate. Whilst certain amendments to the Competition Act required the Senate's approval (the so-called "bi-cameral procedure"), others were only subject to delay by the Senate, with the Chamber of Representatives having the final word (the so-called "partly bi-cameral procedure").

The result is two Acts. The first or "bi-cameral" amending Act[110] substantially changes the composition of the Competition Council, and contains some modifications to the rules on appeals against this body's decisions. Although this Act entered into force on 27 April 1999, the new Competition Council has not yet been put in place.

The second or "partly bi-cameral" amending Act[111] contains amendments to the substantive and procedural provisions of the Competition Act, and also introduces a new investigative body, the "Reporter Corps". This Act is to enter into force on a date to be determined by Royal Decree, but no later than October 1, 1999. At the time of going to press, a Royal Decree had been published, bringing the new merger notification thresholds into effect as of July 1, 1999[112].

This section briefly describes the principal changes brought about by both Acts.

1. The new competition authorities

a. The Reporter Corps

The second amending Act introduces the Reporter Corps. This body consists of independent reporters entrusted with leading and organising investigations into restrictive practices and concentrations. For the purpose of their investigations, the reporters may instruct the Competition Service to take specific investigative measures. After completion of their investigations, the reporters file a report with the Competition Council (Article 14 of the amended Competition Act).

The role of the Reporter Corps in concentration proceedings is discussed in more detail below.

b. The Competition Council

In future, the Competition Council will consist of twenty members instead of the present twelve. Of these, the president, the vice-president and at least four other members must be recruited from among the judiciary. In the past, membership of the Competition Council was a part-time occupation. Under the amended Competition Act, the president, the vice-president and at least two other members are to be appointed as salaried full-time members (Article 17 of the amended Competition Act).

2. The concept of a concentration

The second amending Act modifies the definition of a concentration as regards joint ventures. Whereas in the past a *concentrative* full-function joint venture constituted a concentration but a *co-operative* joint venture did not, in future all full-function joint ventures will fall within the definition of a concentration (Article 9 as amended). This modification brings the Belgian Competition Act into line with the Merger Regulation as amended by Regulation 1310/97.

3. Jurisdictional thresholds

Perhaps the single most important amendment to the Competition Act are the new notification thresholds. In future, concentrations must be notified if, firstly, the undertakings involved have a combined turnover *in Belgium* of more than one billion Belgian francs and, secondly, at least two of the undertakings concerned each achieve a turnover *in Belgium* of at least four hundred million Belgian francs (Article 11, § 1, as amended).

The new notification thresholds entered into force on 1 July 1999[113].

These thresholds represent a twofold change. Firstly, world-wide turnover is replaced by national turnover. Secondly, the market share notification threshold is abandoned in favour of a second turnover threshold. Particularly the abandonment of the market share threshold will considerably increase legal security. No longer will parties first have to perform the delicate and sometimes arbitrary exercise of defining the relevant market and market concerned, and then calculating their market share, in order to determine whether or not a concentration is notifiable.

4. The substantive appraisal of concentrations

a. The market share threshold reinstated

Whilst market share is abandoned as a notification threshold, it is reinstated for the purpose of the substantive appraisal of concentrations. Pursuant to Article 33, § 2.1.a) of the Competition Act, as amended, "where the undertakings concerned together control less than 25% of the market concerned, the concentration shall be declared admissible". It is surprising that this "substantive market share threshold" is contained in Article 33, which deals with procedures, rather than in Article 10, which deals with the substantive appraisal of concentrations.

b. The "public interest" test

The amended Competition Act maintains a substantive test which, despite changes to the wording, is based essentially on the concept of market dominance. In the past, this principle was weakened somewhat by Article 10, § 3, which provided for a secondary test based on certain considerations of general economic interest.

The "Article 10, § 3"-test is now replaced with a broader secondary test. Under Article 10, § 6, of the amended Competition Act, "where the public interest so justifies, the Cabinet may, of its own movement or at the parties' request, permit the formation of a concentration which has been declared inadmissible by the Competition Council pursuant to the rules contained in Article 34bis." Unlike the former Article 10, § 3, Article 10, § 6, does not limit the appraisal to considerations of an economic nature, but allows broader questions of public interest to be examined. This secondary test is no longer to be applied by the Competition Council, but by the Cabinet, i.e. the Government Ministers acting collectively, in what may be termed a "third phase procedure".

c. The appraisal of co-operative full-function joint ventures

It was pointed out above that the second amending Act brings co-operative full-function joint ventures within the definition of a concentration. As under the Merger Regulation, such joint-ventures will not be not subject to the principal substantive test based on market dominance. Instead, the appraisal will be based on Article 2 of the Competition Act, which prohibits restrictive agreements and closely mirrors Article 81(1) of the EC Treaty (Article 10, § 5, of the amended Competition Act).

5. Procedural matters

a. The notification

An amendment of major practical importance, is the extension of the term for notification from one week to one month. In future, concentrations will have to be notified within one month after conclusion of the agreement, publication of the bid or acquisition of joint control, whichever takes place first (Article 12, § 1, first indent, as amended).

A useful innovation is the fact that, pursuant to the new Article 12, § 1, second indent, the parties to a concentration will be able to notify a draft agreement, provided they explicitly declare their intention to conclude an agreement which, as far as all competition aspects are concerned, is not noticeably different from the notified draft.

Under the amended Competition Act, concentrations will be notified to the Competition Council instead of the Competition Service (Article 12, § 1, first indent, as amended). An extract of each notification must be published in the Belgian State Gazette (Article 41, § 1, as amended).

b. First phase proceedings

Upon receipt of a notification, the Competition Council will transfer it to the Reporter Corps. This will appoint a reporter to examine the matter and draw up a report. The reporter will submit both the file and his report to the Competition Council. At least fifteen days before the hearing of the Competition Council at which the concentration in question is to be examined, the reporter must send a copy of his report to the parties (Article 32bis of the amended Competition Act).

The second amending Act extends the time limit for first phase proceedings from one month to forty-five days after notification, or after completion of an incomplete notification (Article 33, § 2, 2, first indent). Where the Competition Council fails to issue a decision within forty-five days, the concentration in question is deemed to have been declared admissible.

However, this time limit may be extended in the following circumstances. In the course of his investigation, the reporter may issue a request for information. Where the addressee fails to provide the requested information, the Reporter Corps may issue a reasoned decision requiring the addressee to provide the specified information within a set time limit. If the addressee is a party to the concentration, the issuing of such a decision will suspend the forty-five day term either until the required information is forthcoming, or until the time limit set in the decision has passed (Article 23, § 2.3, second indent).

Article 32ter of the amended Competition Act regulates the question of access to confidential documents. Under this clause, the President of the Competition Council may, of his own movement or at the request of the interested party, refuse access to confidential documents. Alternatively, the President may decide to allow access where he is of the view that the document in question is necessary for the Council's decision, and that access thereto will be less detrimental than the restriction of competition. The President may request the parties or the reporters to produce a non-confidential version of the documents in question. Documents to which access has been refused must not form the basis of the Competition Council's decision on the merits of the case.

c. Second phase proceedings

Where the Competition Council decides to open second phase proceedings, the reporter will submit a second report, a copy of which is sent to the parties. The Competition Council must issue its final decision within sixty days after the decision to open second phase proceedings.

In *Callebaut/Barry I*, the Court of Appeal held that the time limit for second phase proceedings could not be extended even with the parties' consent[114]. Article 34, § 3, of the amended Competition Act changes this, providing that "the time limit [for a second phase decision] cannot be extended except at the parties' explicit request and at most for the duration proposed by them."

d. "Third phase proceedings"

Where the Competition Council has prohibited a concentration, the Cabinet may nevertheless permit it for reasons of public interest outweighing the competition concerns. Such a decision must be taken within thirty days after notification of the prohibition decision. If the Cabinet fails to issue a decision within thirty days, it is deemed not to have permitted the concentration (Article 34bis of the amended Competition Act).

e. Appeal

Decisions of the Competition Council may be appealed to the Court of Appeal in Brussels. This appeal must be lodged within thirty days. In the past, this term was counted from the date of publication of the decision in the State Gazette.

Pursuant to Article 34bis of the amended Competition Act, the notifying parties will in future have to appeal within thirty days after they have been given notice of the decision of the Competition Council. As far as third parties are concerned, the term for appeal will still be counted as from the date of publication in the State Gazette.

VIII. Conclusion

The Belgian merger control regime was, in the past, a clear example of the difference which may exist between the law in the books and the law in practice.

On paper, Belgian merger control rules are remarkably similar to their EC counterparts as regards both the substantive provisions and the procedure. In practice, however, the persistent lack of resources, and differences between the Competition Council and Service, have led to a competition policy which is widely felt to be inadequate. Firstly, a large number of concentrations have to be notified despite their limited significance for the Belgian market. It is debatable whether the new notification thresholds will change this. Secondly, in contrast to the European Commission's practice, the Competition Council's decisions are, with few exceptions, fairly brief, with little detailed market analysis.

It should in fairness be added that, in the last year, the Competition Council has been showing signs of becoming more assertive, and of investigating

BELGIUM

concentrations more closely than before. However, in view of the still limited number of concentrations prohibited so far -together with the fact that the prohibition decisions in *Callebaut/Barry* were subsequently annulled, it is not surprising that Belgian merger control is at times felt to be something of a "paper tiger".

Notes

1   State Gazette, October 11, 1991.
1bis Act of April 26, 1999 amending the Act of August 5, 1991 on the protection of economic competition, State Gazette, April 27, 1999 ; Act of April 26, 1999, amending certain articles of the Act of August 5, 1991, on the protection of economic competition, State Gazette, April 27, 1991.
2   Regulation 4064/89 of 21 December 1989 on the control of concentrations between undertakings, OJ L 385 of 31 December 1989, p 1, erratum OJ L 257 of 21 September 1990, p 13, as last amended by Regulation 1310/97 of 30 June 1997, L 180 of 9 July 1997, p 1.
3   Competition Council Decision of July 2, 1993, no 93-c/c-3, State Gazette, July 27, 1993.
4   Competition Council Decision of February 7, 1997, no 97/c/c-3, *Johnson/Schmalbach*, State Gazette, April 19, 197.
5   Commission notice on the concept of concentration under Council Regulation (EEC) No 4064/89 on the control of concentrations between undertakings, OJ C 66 of March 2, 1998, p 5.
6   Commission notice on the distinction between concentrative and co-operative joint ventures under Council Regulation (EEC) No 4064/89 of 21 December 1989 on the control of concentrations between undertakings, OJ 1994 C 385/1.
7   Competition Council Decision of June 23 1993, no 93-c/c-2, *L'Office National Ducroire/ COBAC/SFAC*, State Gazette, July 24, 1993.
8   See also Competition Council Decision of March 11, 1997, no 97-c/c-6, *SAIT-Radio Holland/Antwerp Marine Radio Company/INES*, State Gazette, April 4, 1997.
9   Competition Council Decision, August 11, 1997, no 97-c/c-17,*Maas International Europe/ Lekkerland EZ Holding*, State Gazette, November 29, 1997.
10 Commission notice on the distinction between concentrative and co-operative joint ventures under Council Regulation (EEC) No 4064/89 of 21 December 1989 on the control of concentrations between undertakings, OJ C 385v of December 31, 1994 , p 1.
11 Competition Council Decision of August 11, 1997, no 97-c/c-17, *Maas International/ Lekkerland*, State Gazette, November, 29, 1997; see also Competition Council Decision of August 9, 1995, no 95-c/c-30 ,*Huron Valley Steel Corporation*, State Gazette, October 3, 1995.
12 Competition Council Decision of July 9, 1996, no 94-c/c-12, *US West International, GIMV e.a.*, State Gazette, August 29, 1996.

13 Competition Council Decision of September 9, 1996, no 96-c/c-19, *Vennootschap Mechelse Veilingen, Veiling der Kempen & Limburgse Tuinbouwveiling*, State Gazette, October 3, 1996.
14 Wijckmans, F., Vanderelst, A. and Steenlant, J., "De aanmeldingspraktijk in het licht an één jaar toepassing W.B.E.M.", in *Wet tot bescherming van de economische mededinging. Haar werking*", *T.B.H.-Dossier nr. 1-94*, 1994, 12; Vandermeesch, D., *De mededingingswet*, p 181; De Vroede, P., *De wet tot bescherming van de economische mededinging*, Ghent, Mys & Breesch, 1997, p 159; *contra*: Steenbergen, J., "Drie jaar Belgische Wet Mededinging", *S.E.W.*, 1996, 324.
15 Competition Council Decision of October 28, 1997, no 97-c/c-24, *Serpos/Linguatech*, State Gazette December 2, 1997
15bis Competition Council Decision of December 14, 1998, no 98-c/c-16, *IMS/PMSI*, not yet published.
16 Royal Decree of March 31, 1995, State Gazette, April 28, 1995.
17 Competition Council Decision of December 15, 1993, no 93-c/c-23, *Reed Elsevier/Official Airlines/OAG Travel Marketing Services*, State Gazette, January 1, 1994.
17bis See in this respect the European Commission notice on calculation of turnover under Council Regulation (EEC) No 4064/89 of 21 December 1989 on the control of concentrations between undertakings, OJ C 385 of December 31, 1994, p 21.
18 Vandermeesch, D., *o.c.*, 181; De Vroede, P., *o.c.*, p 159 & 164.
19 Competition Council Decision of December 1, 1995, no 95-c/c-43, *Bekaert/Tréfileurope*, State Gazette, January 4, 1996.
20 Competition Council Decision of November 17, 1997, no 97-c/c-25, *Kinepolis*, State Gazette, February 5, 1998.
21 Competition Council Decision of April 30, 1997, no 97-c/c-11, *Mattel/Truck Acquisition/ Tyco Toys*, State Gazette, June 14, 1997.
22 Competition Council Decision of January 7, 1997, no 97-c/c-1, *Henkel/Loctite*, State Gazette, February 6, 1997; see also *IMS/PMSI*, footnote 15bis.
23 E.g. Competition Council Decision of May 18, 1994, no 94-c/c-14, *Parfumerie Douglas/ Compartilux*, State Gazette, July 12, 1994, in which the Council based its definition of the relevant markets for perfume on European Commission practice.
24 Competition Council Decision of May 23, 1997, no 97-c/c-12, *Procter & Gamble/ Tambrands*, State Gazette, August 6, 1997.
25 Commission Decision of 21 June 1994, IV/M.430, *Procter & Gamble/VP Schickedanz (II)*, OJ L 354/32 of December 31, 1994.
26 Competition Council Decision of February 4, 1997, no 97-c/c-3, *Johnson/Schmalbach*, State Gazette, April 19, 1997.
27 Stuyck, J., "Concentratiecontrole", in X., *De nieuwe wet van 5 augustus 1991 tot bescherming van de economische mededinging/La nouvelle loi du 5 août 1991 sur la protection de la concurrence économique*, Brugge, die Keure, 1993, 88; DE VROEDE, P., *o.c.*, 181.
28 Competition Council Decision of April 20, 1995, no 95-c/c-10, *Regla Beheer/Glaceries Saint Roch*, State Gazette, September 15, 1995.
29 See footnote 20.
30 Competition Council Decision of November 5, 1996, no 96-c/c-25, *Concentra Holding/ Katholieke Propaganda*, State Gazette, December 3, 1996.

31 See footnote 4.
32 See footnote 22.
33 Competition Council, First Annual Report 1993-1994, p 51.
34 Competition Council Decision, March 3, 1997, no 97-c/c-5, *Imperial Tobacco/UBS Capital*, State Gazette, June 14, 1997.
35 See footnote 25.
36 Competition Council Decision of July 12, 1993, no 93-c/c-5, *Sara Lee/SmithKlineBeecham*, State Gazette, August 12, 1993 ; Competition Council Decision of December 6, 1993, no 93-c/c-22, *Johnson & Johnson/LV MH*, State Gazette, January 5, 1994.
37 Ysewyn, J., "Overzicht van rechtspraak van de Raad voor de Mededinging in 1997", *T.B.H.*, 1998, 734.
38 Ysewyn, J., "Overzicht van de rechtspraak van de Raad voor de Mededinging in 1995", *T.B.H.*, 1996, 580-582; YSEWYN, J., "Overzicht van de rechtspraak van de Raad voor de Mededinging in 1996", *T.B.H.*, 1997, 538-540; DE VROEDE, P., *o.c.*, 170-180; YSEWYN, J., "Overzicht van de rechtspraak van de Raad voor de Mededinging", *T.B.H.*, 1998, 734-735.
39 Competition Council Decision of April 2, 1996, no 96-c/c-4, *Amoco/Albemarble*, State Gazette, May 21, 1996.
40 Ysewyn, J., "Overzicht van rechtspraak van de Raad voor de Mededinging in 1996
41 Competition Council Decision of February 4, 1997, no 97-c/c-2, *BASF/Isolde*, State Gazette, March 12, 1997.
42 Competition Council Decision of October 13, 1994, no 94-c/c-34, *TIP Trailer Rentals*, State Gazette, November 19, 1994.
43 *Mattel/Tyco Toys*, footnote 21.
44 *Reed Elsevier/OAG*, footnote 17.
45 Competition Council Decision of March 16, 1998, no 98-c/c-5, *Recticel/Folio*, State Gazette, May 5, 1998.
46 Competition Council Decision of August 11 , 1997, no 97-c/c-17,*Maas International Europe/Lekkerland EZ Holding*, State Gazette, November 29, 1997.
47 Footnote 22.
48 See e.g. *Henkel/Loctite*, footnote 22; Competition Council Decision of April 1, 1997, no 97-c/c-9 ,*Electrolux/Zanker*, State Gazette July 18, 1997 ; Competition Council Decision of January 6, 1998, no 98-c/c-1, *Friswit/Rentokil*, State Gazette, February 5, 1998.
49 *Electrolux/Zanker*, see footnote 48.
50 *Friswit/Rentokil*, see footnote 48.
51 Competition Council Decision of September 15, 1997, no 97-c/c-20, *De Post/Hagefin*, State Gazette, October 22, 1997.
52 See footnote 20.
53 Competition Council Decision of December 19, 1996, no 96-c/c-29, *Callebaut/Barry I*, State Gazette, February 21, 1997.
54 Competition Council Decision of May 18, 1994, no 94-c/c-14, *Parfumerie Douglas/ Compartilux*, State Gazette, June 12, 1994.
55 Competition Council Decision of July 16, 1996, no 96-c/c-13, *Fisher-Rosemount/Senpro*, State Gazette, August 20, 1996 ; Competition Council Decision of November 29, 1993, *Colgate-Palmolive/SC Johnson*, State Gazette, December 24, 1993.

56 Competition Council Decision of March 17, 1995, no 95-c/c-6, *Glaceries de Saint Roch*, State Gazette, May 3, 1995; Competition Council Decision of August 11, 1993, no 93-c/c-8, *Sega Europe/Adsum/Atoll*, State Gazette, September 3 , 1993.
57 *Serpos/Linguatech*, see footnote 15 ; Competition Council Decision of November 25, 1994, no 94-c/c-38, *Perstorp/Vynckier/Vyncolit*, State Gazette, December 16, 1994.
58 See e.g. *Friswit/Rentokil*, footnote 48 ;*Amoco/Albemarble*, footnote 39.
59 See e.g. Competition Council Decision of January 22, 1996, no 96-c/c-2,*Hydro Aluminium/ Gottschall Alcuilux*, State Gazette, February 28, 1996 ; Competition Council Decision of May 10, 1996, no 96-c/c-7, *Virgin European Airways/Eurobelgian Airways*, State Gazette, September 26, 1996 ; Competition Council Decision of February 24, 1995, no 95-c/c-5, *Galaxy Sunshine/Gardner Merchant*, State Gazette, April 27 , 1995.
60 *Johnson/Schmalbach*, footnote 5; *Electrolux/Zanker*, footnote 48;*Henkel/Loctite*, see footnote 22; Competition Council decision of May 31, 1995, no 95-c/c-16, *Group 4 Securitas/AviaPartner*, State Gazette, September 15, 1995; Competition Council Decision of November 8, 1993, no 93-c/c-18, *Rockwool/Grodan/Fisons*, State Gazette, December 15, 1993.
61 See footnote 53.
62 *BASF/Isolde*, see footnote 41. ;
63 *Amoco/Albemarble* (acquiring undertaking not active in Belgium), see footnote 39.
64 Competition Council Decision of November 5, 1996, no 96-c/c-24, *Philips/*GIMV, State Gazette, December 3, 1996; *Fisher Rosemount/Senpro*, see footnote 55; Competition Council Decision of November 24, 1994, no 94-c/c-38, *Perstorp/Vynckier/Vincolit*, State Gazette, December 16, 1994 ; Competition Council Decision of August 25, 1994, no 94-c/c-26, *Marvel/Panini*, State Gazette, September 17, 1994.
65 *Friswit /Rentokil* see footnote 48; Competition Council Decision of August 11, 1997, no 97-c/c-18, *Wimael/Ronald Fick*, State Gazette, November 21, 1997 ; Competition Council Decision of June 10, 1997, no 97-c/c-16, *BASF/Dow* Benelux, State Gazette, August 15, 1997; *Electrolux/Zanker*, footnote 48; *Henkel/Loctite*, footnote 22; *Johnson/Schmalbach*, footnote 5.
66 Competition Council Decision of September 9, 1998, no 98-c/c-14*Fresenius/Pharmacia/ Upjohn*, State Gazette, October 7, 1998 ;*Serpos/Linguatech*, footnote 15; Competition Council Decision of March 11, 1997, no 97-c/c-6, *SAIT-Radio Holland*, State Gazette, April 22, 1997 ; Henke*l/Loctite*, footnote 22; Competition Council Decision of June 25, 1996, no 96-c/c-10, *Cobelal*, State Gazette, July 24, 1996.
67 Competition Council Decision of August 24, 1998, no 98-c/c-13 ,*Promedia/Belgacom Directory Services*, State Gazette, November 26, 1998.
68 Competition Council Decision of September 9, 1998, no 98-c/c-14, *Fresenius/Pharmacia/ Upjohn*, State Gazette, October 10, 1998.
69 *Henkel/Loctite*, footnote 22; *Procter & Gamble/Tambrands*, footnote 25.
70 See footnote 66.
71 Competition Council Decision of December 20, 1995, no 98-c/c-45, *Bayer/Monsanto*, State Gazette February 6, 1996; *Colgate/Palmolive/Johnson*, footnote 55; *Hydro Aluminium/Gottschol*, footnote 59.
72 *Serpos/Linguatech*, footnote 15; *SAIT-Radio Holland*, footnote 9; Henkel/*Loctite*, footnote 22; *Cobelal*, see footnote 66; Competition Council Decision of April 14, 1994, no 94-c/c-

8, *Bekaert,* State Gazette June 3, 1994 ; Competition Council Decision of October 19, 1993, no 93-c/c-15, *Vennootschap Mechelse Veilingen,* State Gazette, December 3, 1993
73 See footnote 67.
74 See footnote 20.
75 Competition Council Decision of December 12, 1994, no 94-c/c-41,*VUM/Het Volk,* State Gazette, January 28, 1995
76 See footnote 20.
77 Competition Council Decision of September 15, 1997, no 97-c/c-20,*De Post/Hagefin,* State Gazette, October 22, 1997.
78 Competition Council Decision of May 18, 1994, no 94-c/c-14, *Parfumerie Douglas/ Compartilux,* State Gazette, July 12, 1994.
79 See footnote 53.
80 See section 3 under VI.
80bis See footnote 15bis.
81 Stuyck, J., *l.c.,* 106.
82 De Vroede, P. , 108.
83 See footnote 5.
84 Competition Council Decision of August 25, 1994, no 94-c/c-26, *Marvel/Panini,* State Gazette, September 17, 1994.
85 Competition Council Decision of July 28, 1998, no 98-c/c-11, *Promedia/Belgacom Directory Services,* State Gazette, September 18, 1998.
86 Competition Council Decision of May 13, 1996, no 96-c/c-08, *Betz/Grace,* State Gazette, July 6, 1996.
87 Competition Council Decision of May 31, 1996, no 96-c/c-9, *Groenwoudt/Compartilux,* State Gazette, July 6, 1996.
88 Competition Council Decision of November 5, 1996, no 96-c/c-24, *Philips et al.,* State Gazette December 3, 1996.
89 Competition Council Decision of July 8, 1993, no 93-c/c-4, *OSi Specialities Benelux/ Union Carbide Benelux,* State Gazette, July 27, 1993; *Johnson/Schmalbach,* see footnote 5.
90 Competition Council Decision of September 29, 1994, 94-c/c-31, *Westimex/Dalgety Holland,* State Gazette, November 19, 1994.
91 Competition Council Decision of September 15, 1997, no 97-c/c-20, *De Post/Hagefin,* State Gazette, October 22, 1997.
92 Competition Council decision of November 20, 1995, no 95-c/c-41, *Hexel/Ciba-Geigy,* State Gazette, December 9, 1995.
93 *Procter & Gamble/Tambrands,* see footnote 24.
94 *Henkel/Loctite,* see footnote 22.
95 Competition Council decision of July 19, 1995, no 95-c/c-25, *Ingersoll-Rand/Clark Equipment,* State Gazette, October 4, 1995.
96 E.g. *Johnson/Schmalbach,* see footnote 5.
97 E.g. *Henkel/Loctite,* see footnote 22; SAIT-*Radio Holland,* see footnote 9.
98 Royal Decree of March 23, 1993 on the notification of concentrations within the meaning of Article 12 of the Act of August 5, 1991 on the protection of economic competition, State Gazette, March 31, 1993.

99 State Gazette, August 2, 1966.
100 See footnote 81.
101 Competition Council Decision of December 19, 1996, no 96-c/c-29, *Barry/Callebaut*, State Gazette, February 21, 1997.
102 For statistics in this respect see YSEWYN, J., "Overzicht van rechtspraak van de Raad voor de Mededinging in 1997", *T.B.H.*, 1998, 726.
103 See footnote 51.
104 See section 5 b) under IV.
105 Brussels Court of Appeal, June 25, 1997, *Jaarboek Handelspraktijken en Mededinging 1997*, 1998, 719.
106 Competition Council Decision of June 3, 1997, no 97-c/c-14, *Callebaut/Barry II*, State Gazette, July 24, 1997.
107 Brussels Court of Appeal, January 15, 1998, *T.B.H.*, 1998, 202.
108 *Callebaut/Barry II*, see footnote 106, annulled by the Court of Appeal, see footnote 107; *IMS/PMSI*, see footnote 22.
109 Section 1 a) under VI.
110 Act of April 26, 1999, amending certain articles of the Act of August 5, 1991 on protection of economic competition, State Gazette, April 27, 1999.
111 Act of April 26, 1999, amending the Act of August 5, 1991 on protection of economic competition, State Gazette, April 27, 1999.
112 Royal Decree of May 7, 1999, regarding the entry into force of Article 6 of the Act of April 26, 1999, amending the Act of August 5, 1991 on protection of economic competition, State Gazette, July 1, 1999.
113 Royal Decree of 7 May, 1999, regarding the entry into force of Article 6 of the Act of April 26, 1999, amending the Act of August 5, 1991 on protection of economic competition, State Gazette, July 1, 1999.
114 See footnote 105.

Denmark

Jan Holgersen

Contents

I. Introduction 119
II. Rules governing mergers, acquisitions and amalgamations 121
    A. The notification obligation 121
    B. Joint ventures 124
    C. Jurisdiction 125
    D. Sanctions 126
III. Other regulatory issues 127
IV. Conclusions 127
    Notes 128

I. Introduction

The Danish competition rules have recently been subject to a thorough overhaul, resulting in the adoption of an entirely new Competition Act (the "Competition Act") in June 1997.[1] The overall importance of the new Danish Competition Act which entered into force on 1 January 1998 is that it ensures that Denmark now has become a member of the club of EU Member States, having put their national competition rules as regards anticompetitive agreements and the abuse of a dominant position into line with those applicable at EU level.

However, the Danish authorities have gone further than this in that the new Act also introduces rules governing mergers and acquisitions. While this represents a novelty in Danish competition law – since the previous competition rules did not contain provisions specifically applicable to mergers and acquisitions – it is important to emphasise that the new rules in this area do not amount to a proper merger control. The relevant rules provide for a mere duty to notify qualifying transactions without, however, including any sort of control procedure. In essence, the legal situation of mergers and acquisitions has therefore not undergone any substantial change in Denmark.

As regards the rules on anticompetitive agreements and the abuse of a dominant position, the relevant provisions in the Competition Act are – with the adaptations necessary for national application – essentially the same as Articles 85 and 86 of the EC Treaty.[2] The Danish rules in this respect are also to be interpreted on the basis of the relevant case-law, developed by the European Court of Justice and the European Commission.

This is very helpful for the authorities and market players who have to interpret the new rules, in particular in view of the fact that the new rules represent a rather drastic change of principle, compared to the previous rules in Danish competition law. The best illustration of this is that according to the Danish rules applicable previously, the intervention of the authorities would normally take place only after the implementation of an anticompetitive agreement.[3] The new rules – which basically force companies to draft their agreements in compliance with the competition rules – therefore introduce an entirely new approach for complying with the competition rules in Denmark.

As regards the new rules dealing with mergers and acquisitions, their mere existence do, as mentioned above, also represent another important change in Danish competition law.[4] However, as the new rules consist of a mere duty to notify, they are of a procedural nature only. No prior or subsequent review and/or approval has to be undertaken or given by the competent authorities in order for the transaction to legally proceed and a notification once filed cannot form the basis of legal intervention aimed at the transaction at a later point in time.[5] Denmark does not therefore have any merger control. The fact that the notification must be filed only after the notifiable transaction has been completed serves to underline this circumstance.[6]

The desire of the Danish authorities was not to introduce merger control. Rather the thinking behind the new rules was that the competition authorities should be provided with sufficient information to enable them to monitor the development of various market sectors. As a task complementary hereto, the competition authorities are also to estimate – on the basis of the information collected in respect of large-scale concentrations – whether there may be a need for surveying the future market behaviour of such large companies in particular. This supervision is based on the fact that, although the concentration itself cannot be hindered, a dominant position obtained by one of the participating companies by virtue of the merger or acquisition may nonetheless – later on – constitute part of the basis for being caught by the provisions on the abuse of a dominant position.

The fact that the Danish authorities have not gone the whole way and taken over the total set of EU rules in combination with the stated principle that the thrust of the Danish rules are to be interpreted in accordance with Community practice, does give rise to certain interpretation problems in practice. In the field of mergers and acquisitions such interpretation problems arise in respect of the treatment of joint ventures, which on EU level is governed by both EC Treaty Article 85 as well as the EC Merger Control Regulation.[7] In Denmark the lack of a merger control means that joint ventures cannot be treated in the same manner under the Danish rules as on EU level. The question then arises to which extent and how the EU principles governing this area are applicable in Denmark.

The following first describes in detail the scope of the notification obligation applicable to mergers, acquisitions and amalgamations, the thresholds and any ancillary rules, such as time limits and confidentiality provisions (Section II, A). This is followed by a section dealing specifically with the treatment of joint ventures (Section II, B). Then the rules concerning jurisdiction and sanctions are briefly described (Section II, C-D), and to finalise this chapter on Denmark is a brief description of other regulatory issues, such as merger control applicable to the financial sector (Section III).

II. Rules governing mergers, acquisitions and amalgamations

A. The notification obligation

Section 12 of the Competition Act provides for a duty to notify mergers, acquisitions and amalgamations. The thrust of the rules in this area are, however, laid down in an implementing decree, Royal Decree No. 461 (the "Merger Decree"), which also sets out the thresholds above which the duty to notify applies.[8]

As for the rest of the Competition Act, the rules on the duty to notify mergers, acquisitions and amalgamations are applicable to any kind of commercial activity.[9]

1. Definition of mergers, acquisitions and amalgamations

For purposes of the Competition Act a *merger* between limited companies and/or private companies is defined by reference to the definition given hereof in the Danish Companies Act.[10] According hereto a merger is deemed to exist when:
- a company is wound up (but not liquidated) by the transfer of the assets and liabilities as a whole to another limited or private limited company; and
- two limited or private limited companies are merged into a new limited or private limited company.

An ***acquisition*** is defined as the acquisition of all or part of the share capital or voting rights of a company to an extent which is sufficient to provide the acquiror with a decisive influence on the management of the acquired company.[11] Decisive influence is determined by reference to the Companies Act and is deemed to exist when a company:[12]
- owns the majority of the voting rights in a limited company or a private limited company;
- is a shareholder in a limited company or a private limited company and is entitled to appoint or dismiss the majority of the board members, or, where a private limited company does not have a board of directors, the management;

- is a shareholder in a limited or private limited company and has the right to exercise a decisive influence on the company by virtue of the Articles of Association or an agreement;
- is a shareholder in a limited or private limited company and – on the basis of an agreement with other shareholders – may dispose of the majority of the voting rights in the company; or
- owns shares in a limited company or private limited company and exercises a decisive influence in such company.

Amalgamations is a concept to cover all other concentrations which are not covered by the definition of a merger as set out in the Companies Act, or which do not qualify as a typical acquisition. An example hereof is the merger between two co-operative societies.[13]

2. Thresholds

Only mergers, acquisitions and amalgamations between companies meeting a certain turnover threshold must be notified. According to Merger Decree mergers, acquisitions and amalgamations must be notified where the combined annual turnover of the participating companies is in excess of DKr 50 million (approx. € 6.7 million).[14] An exception to this rule provides that where the annual turnover of only one of the participating companies is above DKr 10 million (approx. € 1.3 million) but where the remaining participants each has a turnover which is below this threshold, no notification needs to be filed.[15]

Intra-group mergers, acquisitions and amalgamations are not subject to the duty to notify.[16] Intra-group transactions are deemed to exist where the merger, acquisition or amalgamation is between a parent and a subsidiary or between two subsidiaries in the same group. Such transactions will not bring about any changes in the effective market shares held by the companies and are therefore exempt from notification.

3. Time-limits, form and responsibility for notification

The notification must be filed within four weeks after the merger, acquisition or amalgamation has been completed. According to the Companies Act a merger is considered completed at the point in time a decision to merge has been taken in all of the merging companies.[17] Although there is no statutory basis for this, it seems safe to say that acquisitions and amalgamations are considered to be completed – at a similar point in time – when the competent (corporate) bodies have taken a decision to go through with the transaction.[18]

While the "Competition Council" is the official body established to enforce the Competition Act, notifications must be filed with the "Competition Authority" which is a public, administrative body, functioning as a secretariat to the Competition Council and which is also the body in charge of the daily administrative tasks related to the enforcement of the Competition Act.[19]

Mergers, acquisitions and amalgamations must be filed on a specific form, referred to as "K2".[20] The completion of the K2 form requires that the participating companies indicate their market shares as regards products and/ or services in respect of which their market share exceeds 20%. This is the type of information to be used by the competition authorities for purposes of identifying the creation of large market players.

Apart from also having to provide information on turnover in the preceding financial year as well as the share capital of the participating companies, the completion of the K2 form also requires the indication of the nationality as well as information on the number of employees employed in the preceding financial year by the participating companies. If the transaction has been the subject of a filing submitted pursuant to the EC Merger Regulation, then this must also be indicated.

The responsibility for the duty to notify lies with the ongoing or acquiring company in the merger, acquisition or amalgamation.[21]

4. Business secrets

The fact that the form for notifying mergers, acquisitions and amalgamations does not require the companies involved to submit much information in respect of their business means that the issue of business secrets is hardly an issue. However, should the form contain certain information which may be considered sensitive, the only manner in which the competition authority may possibly convey such information (originating in a notification of a merger, acquisition or amalgamation) is by including it in the reports issued according to Section 13(3) of the Competition Act on the activities of the Competition Council. In this regard Section 13(4) of the Competition Act provides that business secrets and information on technical issues, including research and methods of production which are of significant financial importance to the individual or company in question, are exempt from publication.[22]

B. Joint ventures

Joint ventures in whatever form or size are not covered by the notification duty applicable to mergers, acquisitions and amalgamations. They are covered by the provision in the Competition Act governing anticompetitive agreements, namely Section 6.

This way of dealing with joint ventures is reminiscent of the "pre-merger regulation" days on EU level where the absence of an alternative to assessing joint ventures under Article 85 lead to the development of assessing certain "co-operative" joint ventures under Article 85 as opposed to those joint ventures which brought about a structural change, the so-called "concentrative" joint ventures which were to be considered under Article 86.

However, it is important to note that the Danish authorities have not opted for this solution either. All joint ventures – of no matter what type – are to be subsumed under Section 6 of the Competition Act. However, during the preceding discussions in Committees to the Danish Parliament, the fears of the business community were calmed, as it was pointed out that the assessment of joint ventures pursuant to Section 6 of the Competition Act was to be an evaluation of whether there would be elements restrictive of competition in the joint venture agreement – as opposed to being an assessment of the joint venture agreement itself (i.e. the agreement establishing the joint venture).[23]

This seems to leave the Danish business community free to enter into whatever joint venture they may favour without being worried about whether their potential business partner is a competitor or not – at least for the sake of the immediate deal.[24] As long as it is ensured that there are no separate anticompetitive clauses incorporated in the deal, joint ventures can be entered into without being subject to control.

It is not that simple, however. The approach outlined above leaves open a number of questions, such as how anticompetitive clauses are identified and, once identified, how evaluated.

At the EU level, the evaluation of whether the joint venture contains separate anticompetitive agreements depends on whether the provisions in question may qualify as ancillary restraints. According to the notices issued by the Commission concerning concentrative joint ventures and co-operative joint ventures, restrictions in the joint venture agreements are ancillary if they are directly related to and necessary for the establishment of the joint venture.[25] Restrictions which qualify as ancillary restraints will follow the assessment of the joint venture. Put in other words, if the joint venture is assessed under the EC Merger Regulation and is approved, so are the ancillary restraints, or if the joint venture falls within the scope of Article 85(1), so do the ancillary restraints and so on.

Recalling that the principle on which the Competition Act is based is that the Act is to be interpreted on the basis of the Commission's and the European Court of Justice's case-law, it is not clear how this principle will be adhered to in this context.

First of all, there are two Commission notices concerning ancillary restraints, one concerning co-operative joint ventures and one linked to the EC Merger Regulation on concentrative joint ventures.[26] It is not clear which one of these should be used for purposes of the Danish Competition Act. If both may be used it is still not clear whether – in order to determine which one of the notices should be applied in the concrete case – one would have to go through the exercise of determining whether the joint venture is co-operative or concentrative on the basis of the Commission's distinction in this regard.

Another issue is that under the Danish rules there will be no prior assessment of the joint venture agreement itself. This means that there is no assessment of the joint venture which the evaluation of the additional restrictions, qualifying as ancillary, can follow. The fate of ancillary restraints under Danish law is therefore uncertain. There are no rules which state that once it has been determined that the additional restrictions are ancillary, notification is not necessary. This in combination with the well-known principle that "if in doubt, you'd better notify" means that in many cases one may end up notifying.[27] The ancillary restraints exercise may therefore seem somewhat unnecessary.

The answers to the questions raised above will remain open until the Danish competition authorities have had a chance to develop a practice regarding this still fairly recent law.[28]

C. Jurisdiction

While the jurisdictional reach of the Danish rules corresponding to EC Treaty Articles 85 and 86 depends on the well-known – though not always easy to predict – "effect principle", the application of the duty to notify mergers, acquisitions and amalgamations requires that at least one of the participating companies is situated in Denmark.[29] The use of the term "participating" company also covers an acquired company.

In the event the merger, acquisition or amalgamation subject to a duty to notify involves companies with a combined turnover exceeding the thresholds set out in the EC Merger Regulation, notification must still be filed in Denmark. In other words, there may be situations where the legal advisors to a transaction must prepare double filings, one under the EU merger rules and one under the national Danish rules.[30]

There is one exception to the above-mentioned rule on jurisdiction which concerns joint ventures – which, as mentioned above, are subsumed under Section 6 of the Competition Act concerning anticompetitive agreements. Just as at EU level, the jurisdictional rule of Section 6 is the "effect principle", that is, the prohibition in Section 6 is applicable to agreements, decisions or concerted practices which are deemed to have an effect within the Danish territory – whether or not all participants may be established there.

Transferred to joint ventures, this means that whether or not the joint venture is established by companies located and registered in Denmark, anticompetitve agreements in the joint venture agreement may, in principle, still be subject to the prohibition in Section 6 if the relevant provisions have an effect within the Danish territory. How far the Danish competition authorities will go in reaching out and claiming jurisdiction in respect of joint ventures involving foreign participants remains to be seen but the legal basis is potentially there.

At this point it must be mentioned that Section 7 of the Competition Act exempts agreements of minor importance from the prohibition on anti-competitive agreements in Section 6. The very generous criteria in Section 7 allow anticompetitive agreements between companies with a combined turnover of up to DKr 1 billion (approximately € 130 million) and a market share below 10% in the relevant market, to escape the control of the Competition Act.[31] In fact, the turnover criterion is well above the level at which mergers, acquisitions and amalgamations have to notify, i.e., companies with a turnover in excess of DKr 50 million (approximately € 6.7 million).

D. Sanctions

Although the duty to notify is of a procedural nature only, it is to be taken seriously as the failure to comply with it is a criminal offence and potentially subject to the imposition of a fine.[32] According to Section 23(3) of the

Competition Act in combination with Section 9 in Merger Decree, even legal persons may be prosecuted for committing the offence.

III. Other regulatory issues

As also indicated in the introduction, the fact that there are no merger controls in Denmark, does not mean that the abuse of a dominant position by the merged, acquiring or amalgamated companies may not be subject Section 11 of the Competition Act on the prohibition of the abuse of a dominant position. The information collected by the competition authorities in respect of the merged, acquiring or amalgamated companies holding significant market shares will serve as background knowledge in connection with a subsequent case concerning the alleged abuse of a dominant position of the companies in question.

As regards the financial sector, the Consolidated Bank and Savings Act No. 730 of 8 June 1996 provides that mergers and acquisitions between banks are subject to the prior approval by the Ministry of Economic Affairs. The rules originate not only in the wish to protect the funds of clients but are also of a political nature in that the Minister of Economic Affairs should be able to hinder mergers or acquisitions between banks if they are undesirable from the point of view of the public.

According to the Consolidated Insurance Companies Act No. 746 of 8 June 1996 mergers and acquisitions between insurance companies are subject to the approval of the "Finanstilsynet", i.e., the Danish Supervisory Authority of Financial Affairs. The supervision is aimed at looking after the interests of the customers of the merging insurance companies. Similar approval requirements are applicable to mergers and acquisitions between companies operating in other fields of the financial business sector.

IV. Conclusions

The Competition Act has been in force for about a year now, and so far there has been no initiative to introduce tighter control on mergers and acquisitions. The Danish politicians probably want to see whether and to what extent the competition authorities are watching over the developments in the transactions which have been notified before considering introducing any real merger regulation.

Notes

1 Law No. 384 of 10 June 1997. The commentary to the law of 20 February 1997 contains the observations made upon the submission of the law to the Danish Parliament and is referred to in the following as the "Commentary".
2 Section 6 of the Competition Act prohibits anticompetitive agreements, decisions and concerted practices between companies, and Section 11 prohibits the abuse of a dominant position. Section 7 concerns anticompetitive agreements of minor importance and Section 8 provides for the possibility of obtaining individual exemptions from the prohibition in Section 6.
3 Section 5 of the previous Danish Competition Act, Law No. 370 of 7 June 1989, imposed a duty to notify agreements and decisions which enabled the parties to exercise a dominant influence. The notification had to be completed within 14 days after the conclusion of the agreement or decision in question. In practice, this meant that the potentially illegal practices (originating in an agreement or decision) would normally already be implemented by the parties by the time the duty to notify was triggered.
4 Prior to the entry into force of the Competition Act, mergers and acquisitions were also subject to the general provision in Section 5 of the previous Danish 1989 Competition Act, note 3, above, if the agreement would provide the parties the ability to exert a dominant influence. However, there were no specific rules governing mergers and acquisitions.
5 The Commentary at p. 9.
6 See further Section II, A, 3 on Time-limits, form and responsibility for notification, below.
7 This refers to the Commission's practice of distinguishing between co-operative and concentrative joint ventures, including the guidelines which is laid down in the Commission's notice on the concept of autonomous joint ventures, O.J. (1998) C 66/1.
8 Royal Decree No. 461 of 23 June 1998 (which replaces Royal Decree No. 1031 of 17 December 1997) on the notification of mergers, acquisitions and amalgamations between companies.
9 Section 2 of the Competition Act.
10 Companies Act, consolidated Act No. 545 of 20 June 1996 in Chapter 15 which concerns, *inter alia*, mergers. The reference to a "private limited company" covers companies which, in comparison to a limited company, require a smaller minimum share capital, allow for a simpler organisational structure and the deviation of a number of otherwise mandatory rules. In essence this company form is used by small or medium-sized enterprises. The definition of a merger has now been incorporated in Section 3 of Merger Decree, note 8, above.
11 Section 4 of Merger Decree, note 8, above.
12 Section 6 of Merger Decree, note 8, above, in combination with Section 2 of the Companies Act, note 10, above.
13 Section 5 of Merger Decree, note 8, above and the Commentary at p. 31.
14 Section 2 of Merger Decree, note 8, above. Figures given in euro are based on the exchange rates applicable on 27 January 1999.
15 This exception was introduced on the basis of Swedish experience. Under the Swedish Competition Act (which also provides for a notification obligation on mergers and

acquisitions), large companies had to notify numerous acquisitions of small insignificant businesses. As a consequence the Swedish authorities introduced a specific provision aimed at exempting such transactions from notification.

However, one may question whether an exception to this extent – without also being dependent on a market share threshold – does not open the door for the creation of monopolies. Larger companies could use the exception to buy up smaller companies active in the same market in stages, thereby slowly building up a monopoly in the relevant market.

16 Section 12(1) of the Competition Act and Section 1(2) of Merger Decree, note 8, above.
17 Section 134(h) of the Companies Act, note 10, above.
18 This point of view is expressed in "Konkurrenceloven" Jurist- og Økonomforbundets Forlag (1998) by Kirsten Levinsen, at p. 232, which is an annotated edition of the Competition Act. The author is head of unit of the Competition Authority.
19 Section 14(2) of the Competition Act. Section 15 and implementing rules in Royal Decree nos. 920 of 2 December 1997 and 951 of 12 December 1997 specify the composition, competence and tasks of the Competition Council and the Competition Authority. Both the Competition Council and the Competition Authority are, for purposes of administering and enforcing the Competition Act, independent of the Minister of Commerce, the Commentary at pp. 32 and 33.
20 A copy of the application form is attached to Merger Decree, note 8, above.
21 Section 7 of Merger Decree, note 8, above.
22 Also excluded from publication is information on customers in companies which are subject to the supervision of the Danish Supervisory Authority of Financial Affairs.
23 This appears from the responses to questions posed to the Committee of Commerce of the Danish Parliament, especially Question nos. 77, 107, 108 and 112.
24 Obviously, joint venture agreements between large competitors may be a step on the way leading to the abuse of a dominant position, thus triggering the application of Section 11 of the Competition Act.
25 It appears from recital 25 in the EC Merger Regulation, the Commission's Notice on Ancillary Restraints, O.J. (1990) C 203/5 and the Commission's Notice on the assessment of cooperative joint ventures, O.J. (1993) C 43/2, at point 65 concerning ancillary restraints, that additional agreements which qualify as "ancillary" are to assessed together with the joint venture.
26 See the notices referred to in note 25.
27 It should be noted that the notification of anticompetitive agreements in joint venture agreements must be filed on the "K1" form which is used for notifying anticompetitive agreements within the scope of Section 6 of the Competition Act (as opposed to the K2 form used for notifying mergers, acquisitions and amalgamations).
28 However, it may be mentioned that in the annotated edition of the Competition Act, "Konkurrenceloven", note 18, above, at pp. 94 and 95 it has been suggested that anticompetitive agreements in joint venture agreements are to assessed under the Commissions notice on ancillary restraints regarding the EC Merger Regulation. The reasons for this choice are not set out, however.
29 Section 1(3) of Merger Decree, note 8, above.
30 Upon submitting a K2 form for purposes of notifying under the Danish rules it must be indicated whether a filing also has been made at EU level in respect of the same transaction,

see further Section A(3) above. See further, on the issue of double filings as a consequence of overlapping jurisdiction, the article "Konkurrencerådet eller EU-Kommissionen" (i.e. the Competition Council or the Commission) by Miriam Holm-Nielsen, published in "Advokaten" No. 4 of 16 April 1998.

31 A second *de minimis* rule provides that where the market share criteria of 10% is exceeded, parties to an anticompetitive agreement may still escape the prohibition in Section 6 if their combined annual turnover does not exceed DKr 150 million (approx. € 20 million).

32 Section 23(1) No. 3 and Section 9 in Royal Decree 461, note 8, above.

Finland

Christian Wik

Contents

1. Introduction 133
2. Relevant legislation and authorities 133
3. Definition of a concentration 133
   3.1. Acquisition of control of a business, or a merger 134
   3.2. Joint ventures 134
   3.3. Acquisitions by financial institutions 135
4. Which concentrations are caught 136
   4.1. Turnover thresholds 136
   4.2. Transactions between foreign companies 137
5. Timing of the notification 138
6. Preparation of the notification 138
   6.1. Notification form 138
   6.2. Pre-notification meeting 139
7. Time-limits and procedure 140
   7.1. Time-limits 140
   7.2. Procedure 140
   7.3. Insurance companies 141
8. Suspension 142
9. Substantive test for clearance 143
   9.1. Dominance 143
   9.2. Ancillary restraints 144
   9.3. Conditions 144
10. Judicial review 145

1. Introduction

Merger control was introduced in Finland on 1 October 1998. Prior to this date there was no actual merger control system in Finland. The structure of the merger control rules corresponds to a large extent to those of the EC Merger Regulation. Since the rules have entered into force only recently, there exist only a few merger decisions by the competition authorities. Thus, it remains to be seen how the authorities interpret and apply the merger control rules in practice.

2. Relevant legislation and authorities

The merger control rules are contained in Finland's Act on Restrictions on Competition (480/92) (the "Competition Act"). In addition, the Ministry of Trade and Industry has issued two decisions concerning the application of the merger control rules. The first decision concerns the calculation of turnover of the parties involved and the second decision contains the notification form. Moreover, the Finnish Competition Authority has given fairly detailed guidelines concerning the interpretation of the merger control rules. Such guidelines concern the duty to notify, the calculation of turnover, joint ventures, ancillary restraints, and the assessment of the concentrations by the Competition Authority.

The authorities which investigate concentrations are the Finnish Competition Authority (the FCA), and the Competition Council, which exercises judicial power in competition matters. The FCA investigates the concentration in the first stage, and either clears it, with or without conditions, or requests the Competition Council to block it. The Competition Council is entitled to prohibit the concentration.

3. Definition of a concentration

The merger control rules apply to concentrations defined in the Competition Act as:
- an acquisition of control in another company;
- an acquisition of the whole business of another company, or a part thereof;
- a merger; or
- a creation of a joint venture.

3.1. Acquisition of control of a business, or a merger

A concentration may be formed as a result of purchase of shares in a company. The acquisition of control does not necessarily require the acquisition of a majority shareholding to be considered a concentration as defined in the Competition Act. An acquisition of a majority of the votes in another company is, however, always deemed to constitute an acquisition of control. This is the case even if the bye-laws of the target company provide that the amount of votes that can be used by one shareholder is restricted.

An acquisition of a minority shareholding may be deemed to constitute a concentration if the acquiror obtains a *de facto* control in the target company. Such control may arise if the other shares in the company are widely dispersed and the acquirer would in practice have the majority of votes in a shareholders' meeting. Furthermore, such control may be based on the acquiror's right to appoint a majority of the members of the board of directors, or the acquirer's right to decide on the strategic commercial behaviour of the target company. Such rights may for example be given in a shareholders' agreement concerning the target company. Control may be acquired by one party (sole control) or by several parties (joint control).

The acquisition of a business constitutes a concentration for purposes of the Competition Act. The issue to be established is whether the transaction is a transfer of a business or a transfer of some assets only. If staff, know-how and agreements with customers are transferred in addition to assets, the transaction is likely to constitute a concentration. The authorities have, nevertheless, indicated that even a transfer of important intellectual property rights might be caught by the merger control rules, despite no staff being transferred. This could be the case in a high-technology branch where intellectual property rights are of great importance.

A merger may be implemented by merging two companies into a new company established by them or by merging one company into another company.

3.2. Joint ventures

The creation of a joint venture is caught by the merger control rules provided that the joint venture performs on a lasting basis all the functions of an autonomous economic entity. The assessment under the Competition Act of whether the joint venture is considered to constitute a so-called full-function joint venture is likely to correspond to the assessment made under the EC Merger Regulation. Thus, the joint venture must have sufficient financial and other resources, such as staff, including operative management, premises and independent financial situation, and in the long term it must not be dependent on supplies from, or purchases by, its parent companies. Should the joint venture not constitute a full-function joint venture, it may be assessed under the provision of the Competition Act concerning horizontal co-operation between competitors, and it may require an exemption.

The merger control rules of the Competition Act do not address the situation where the parent companies of a full-function joint venture are engaged in co-operation which may restrict competition. Such co-operation may be assessed by the FCA based on the provision of the Competition Act concerning horizontal co-operation between competitors mentioned above. However, unlike the current rules of the EC Merger Regulation, the Competition Act does not require the assessment to be made within the time-limits set for the processing of the merger control notification. Alternatively, the FCA could possibly, depending on the type of the co-operation, consider the co-operation between the parents as a restraint ancillary to the concentration.

3.3. Acquisitions by financial institutions

Under the Competition Act, an acquisition of control by a credit institution or other financial institution or insurance company must be notified to the FCA, although the control would be retained only for a short period of time. Thus, the Competition Act does not contain any exception concerning such temporary acquisitions similar to that of the EC Merger Regulation.

Summary: A concentration is constituted by an acquisition of control in another company, e.g. by an acquisition of shares, an acquisition of a business, a merger, or the creation of a full-function joint venture. If the joint venture does not constitute a full-function joint venture, it may require an exemption under the Competition Act.

4. Which concentrations are caught

4.1. Turnover thresholds

Under the Finnish merger control rules, a concentration as defined above must be notified to the FCA where:
  (i) the combined aggregate world-wide turnover of the parties exceeds FIM 2 billion (approx. € 335 million);
  (ii) where the aggregate world-wide turnover of at least two of the parties exceeds FIM 150 million (approx. € 25 million); and provided that
  (iii) the target company, or a company controlled by it, is engaged in business activities in Finland.

If the above conditions are met, the filing of a notification with the FCA is mandatory. The parties whose turnover is relevant under the Competition Act are the company or companies which acquire control on the one hand, and the target of the acquisition on the other. Thus, the turnover of the seller is not taken into account. As regards the party acquiring control, the turnover of the whole group of companies where it belongs shall be taken into consideration. As regards the target company, only the target company and any companies controlled by it are taken into account. The competition authorities will look at the latest annual accounts. Any acquisitions and divestments that have taken place after the preparation of the accounts are taken into consideration.

The Ministry of Trade and Industry has given a decision containing rules concerning the calculation of the turnover. The decision includes among other things rules concerning situations where there is a shift from sole to join control or changes in joint control. Moreover, the FCA has issued fairly detailed guidelines concerning the calculation of turnover.

If the target company is acquired in stages over a period of two years, under the Competition Act all such acquisition are taken into account in the turnover calculation. Moreover, if the same company acquires several companies operating in the same field, the turnover thresholds are deemed exceeded if the combined world-wide turnover of the target companies acquired during the last two years exceeds the threshold, even though the turnover of each acquired company does not exceed FIM 150 million. The problem with the application of this rule is that it is somewhat unclear which companies are considered to operate in the same field. It seems that the concept of the same field refers to a wider product market than the relevant product market. These rules, however, apply only to acquisitions made after the entry into force of the merger control rules, i.e. after 1 October 1998.

The Competition Act contains rules on the calculation of the turnover of credit institutions, investment companies and other financial institutions. Such companies' total amount of income items, excluding extraordinary items, are deemed to constitute their turnover. The turnover of insurance and pension institutions shall, under the Competition Act, comprise their gross premium.

4.2. Transactions between foreign companies

Transactions between foreign companies are also caught by the Finnish merger rules provided that the turnover thresholds are exceeded and that the target of the acquisition or the joint venture is engaged in business activities in Finland. This requirement is also fulfilled where a company controlled by the target company or the joint venture is engaged in business activities in Finland. In the case of a merger between two companies, the transaction is caught by the merger control rules where one of the merging companies or a company controlled by any such company is engaged in business activities in Finland.

The requirement of being engaged in business activities in Finland is considered fulfilled where any of the above companies offer for sale goods or services in Finland through a subsidiary, a branch, a sales office or other establishment in Finland. Direct imports to Finland by the target company established abroad or by a distributor appointed by it would not, as such, lead to the application of the merger control rules. The same concerns a registered seat in Finland without any actual commercial activity. If the target company has appointed an agent for the sale of its products to Finland, it is somewhat unclear whether the authorities would consider this to constitute business activities by the target company in Finland.

Summary: The turnover thresholds are the following: the combined aggregate world-wide turnover of the parties must exceed FIM 2 billion (approx.€ 335 million), and the aggregate world-wide turnover of at least two of the parties must exceed FIM 150 million (approx.€ 25 million). The target company, or a company controlled by it, must be engaged in business activities in Finland in order that the concentration may be caught by the Competition Act.

5. Timing of the notification

The notification must be filed within one week from one of the following events, whichever occurs first:
- the signing of a binding agreement to implement an acquisition, a merger or a joint venture;
- the acquisition of control or the acquisition of a business;
- the decision to merge by the companies involved;
- the holding of the constitutive meeting of the joint venture; or
- the publication of a public bid.

This means that in an ordinary acquisition of a company the notification must be filed within one week from the signing of a binding acquisition agreement. It seems that the signing of a letter of intent would not trigger the notification requirement. The notification obligation lies with the party or parties which acquire control in the target company, or in the case of a merger, with the merging companies. Failure to comply with the filing obligation may lead to fines between FIM 5,000 and FIM 4 million, or in exceptional cases, up to 10% of the turnover of the relevant undertaking. Nevertheless, fines would not be imposed unless deemed necessary in the interests of competition. Thus, it appears that fines might not be imposed for example in a case where the notification is slightly late, or where it was clearly open to interpretation whether the concentration would be caught by the Competition Act.

Summary: The notification is mandatory, and it must be filed within one week from the signing of the binding acquisition agreement, or another event which triggers the notification obligation, whichever is earlier.

6. Preparation of the notification

6.1. Notification form

The Ministry of Trade and Industry has issued a notification form which to a large extent corresponds to Form CO of the EC Merger Regulation. The notification must be submitted either in Finnish or in Swedish, even though the FCA also accepts enclosures to the notification in English. Detailed information on the

relevant markets is required if the parties to the concentration compete and have a combined market share exceeding 15%, or where the parties have a vertical relationship and at least one of them has a minimum market share of 20%. The main items required in the notification are the following.
- Information on the parties to the concentration (including the whole group of companies) and the seller.
- Description of the transaction.
- Turnover of the parties to the concentration.
- Acquisitions by the parties during the two years preceding the concentration in the same branch.
- Shareholdings and board representation of the parties in other companies in the relevant markets.
- All the relevant product markets where at least two of the parties to the concentration conduct business and where their combined market share is a minimum of 15% in Finland or a relevant part therein.
- All the relevant product markets where a party to the concentration operates and which are upstream or downstream in the manufacturing chain or the distribution channel of a product market where another party operates, provided that the market share of the party in question exceeds 20% in Finland or a relevant part therein.
- Markets closely related to the relevant product markets.
- Various information on the above markets, such as size of the market, sales, market shares, competitors, customers, suppliers, imports and exports, barriers to entry and detailed information on the market conditions.
- Trade associations.
- Ancillary restraints.

6.2. Pre-notification meeting

The FCA encourages the notifying party or parties to arrange a meeting with the FCA prior to filing the notification. Any competition issues that seem to arise in connection with the concentration, or questions relating to the market definition, can be addressed in such meeting, and thus a smooth processing of the notification by the FCA may be facilitated. In addition, the FCA may grant a waiver in respect of the information required in the notification form, if such information is deemed unnecessary for the investigation or if the transaction affects competition only to an insignificant extent. This is particularly important in view of the detailed nature of the questions in the notification form, which may be unnecessarily burdensome to complete. Waivers could be granted for instance in a transaction between two foreign companies which have only minor activities in Finland. The meeting with the FCA may also serve the purpose of ensuring that the notification will be considered complete by the FCA. The time-limit for the decision-making by the FCA will not start to run until the FCA deems the notification complete.

7. Time-limits and procedure

7.1. Time-limits

The Competition Act contains strict time-limits for decision-making by the FCA and the Competition Council. If such authorities fail to make a decision within the set time-limits, the concentration is deemed allowed.

The notification is filed with the FCA, which investigates the concentration at the first stage. The FCA must within one month either clear the concentration, decide that the transaction does not fall under the Competition Act, or decide to initiate an in-depth investigation. It seems likely that most of the concentrations will be cleared within the one month period. In particular, temporary acquisitions by financial institutions and insurance companies will most likely be permitted within this first stage.

If an in-depth investigation is carried out, the FCA must within three months (or five months with the permission of the Competition Council) of the decision to initiate the investigation, permit the concentration, or request the Competition Council to block it. After the receipt of the request by the FCA, the Competition Council must make its decision to clear or prohibit the concentration within three months. If a concentration is investigated during the maximum period allowed by the Competition Act, such investigation may extend up to nine months. Nevertheless, this is expected only in exceptional cases where significant competition issues must be resolved.

7.2. Procedure

In the investigation, the FCA will as a rule hear competitors, customers and suppliers of the parties to the concentration. It will send a questionnaire to them with the aim of establishing the structure of the market and the competition conditions therein, and to hear the views of the competitors, customers and suppliers of the planned concentration. If it is clear that the concentration will not result in any competition issues and that it will be allowed without any material investigation, the above inquiries may not be made. Nevertheless, if the FCA carries out an in-depth investigation, it may send more detailed questions to the competitors, customers and suppliers. The views given and the case will be discussed with the parties and, if necessary, formal hearings will be held.

The Competition Council will, at the preparatory stage, hear the parties and possibly competitors, suppliers and customers. If an oral hearing is held after the preparatory stage, experts and witnesses may also be heard.

If the concentration seems to pose problems under the Competition Act, the FCA and the Competition Council may impose conditions on the parties. The conditions would, as a rule, be negotiated with the FCA during its investigation, and not be left to be negotiated with the Competition Council. In fact, the Competition Act provides that the FCA should always endeavour to negotiate with the parties and impose conditions rather than request the Competition Council to prohibit the concentration.

7.3. Insurance companies

The merger control procedure in the acquisition of an insurance company differs from the procedure described above. Such acquisitions are notified to the Ministry of Social Affairs and Health under the insurance legislation, and the Ministry will, when processing the notification, request a statement from the FCA. If the FCA does not oppose the transaction in its statement, the Competition Act does not require any separate notification to the FCA.

Summary: The competent authorities are the Finnish Competition Authority (the FCA) and the Competition Council. The FCA must within one month from the receipt of the notification either clear the concentration, decide that the transaction does not fall under the Competition Act, or decide to initiate an in-depth investigation. If an in-depth investigation is carried out, the FCA must within three months (or five months with the permission of the Competition Council) of the decision to initiate the investigation, permit the concentration, or request the Competition Council to block it. After the receipt of the request by the FCA, the Competition Council must make its decision to clear or prohibit the concentration within three months.

8. Suspension

According to the Competition Act, the transaction may not be closed prior to clearance from the FCA or the Competition Council, as the case may be. However, when the Competition Council is investigating a concentration at the request of the FCA, the suspension obligation will cease within a month from such request, unless the Council orders the suspension to continue.

Thus, under the main rule no steps are allowed to be taken to implement the transaction prior to the decision of the authorities. Nevertheless, the provisions of the Competition Act leave some room for interpretation as to which measures are considered implementing measures. The FCA and the Competition Council may, upon application, permit implementing measures during the investigation. However, since there are not, as yet, precedents in this matter, it is unclear to what extent the authorities would in practice permit any measures. It seems that in order to obtain such permit, the suspension obligation should cause material harm to the parties.

A party that has launched a public bid can purchase the shares offered before clearance, although it is not entitled to use its voting rights to determine the competitive behaviour of the target company. The same rule applies in certain cases where shares are redeemed.

If the transaction is closed prior to the decision of the FCA or the Competition Council, fines of between FIM 5,000 and FIM 4 million, or in exceptional cases, up to 10% of the turnover of the relevant company, can be imposed. Moreover, consequences for not notifying or closing before clearance may occur at a later stage, since the Competition Council can, at the request of the FCA, order the concentration to be dissolved. Such a request of the FCA must be notified to the parties within one year from the closing of the transaction.

Summary: The transaction may generally not be closed prior to clearance from the FCA or the Competition Council, as the case may be.

9. Substantive test for clearance

9.1. Dominance

Under the Competition Act, a concentration may be prohibited if it creates or strengthens a dominant position as a result of which competition would be significantly impeded in the Finnish market or a substantial part of it. Thus, the assessment by the competition authorities requires that the relevant product market and the relevant geographic market are defined, and that the position of the concentration in the relevant market is established. In addition, if dominance seems to be created or reinforced, the authorities must decide whether the concentration significantly impedes competition in Finland or part of Finland.

An undertaking may be considered dominant under the Competition Act if it can significantly influence the price level, delivery conditions, or other competition conditions at a certain production or distribution level. When the FCA and the Competition Council are assessing dominance, the market share is not the only criterion, nor is there any specific market share threshold which such authorities would consider as establishing dominance. The authorities also consider other factors, such as the economic and financial strength of the concentration, the wideness of the selection of products offered by the concentration, vertical effects, the bargaining power of the customers and the suppliers, potential competition, barriers to entry, and the saturation of the markets. The creation of a dominant position may not, as such, result in a prohibition of the concentration, as the Competition Act requires that the concentration must in addition significantly impede competition. The authorities will take into consideration any increase in efficiency resulting from the concentration, which is passed on to the customers. The FCA has in its guidelines confirmed that they will also investigate whether the notified concentration results in joint dominance.

In their assessment, the FCA and the Competition Council may not take into account any public interest issues, such as employment or environmental considerations. Nor do any other authorities have the right to intervene in the decision-making under the Competition Act. However, the Competition Act contains a specific provision concerning the electricity market. A concentration whereby the parties would obtain in the aggregate a 25% share of the electricity distribution in Finland in a network with a capacity 400V can be prohibited. The purpose of this special provision is to control any negative effects of vertical integration between electricity producers and distributors and it relates to the recent liberalisation of the Finnish electricity markets.

Summary: The substantive test is dominance and a significant impediment for competition in Finland or a substantial part of Finland. A concentration whereby the parties would obtain in the aggregate a 25% share of the electricity distribution in Finland in a network with a capacity 400V can be prohibited. No political intervention is possible.

9.2. Ancillary restraints

Any restraints ancillary to the concentration must be notified to the FCA, and such restraints may be cleared in the decision to permit a concentration. Non-compete clauses, licensing agreements, supply and distribution agreements and, in case of a joint venture, agreements between the parents and the joint venture would, under the main rule, be notified as ancillary restrictions. The FCA has issued guidelines concerning the ancillary restraints, and it seems that it will assess such restraints following the guidelines and the decisions of the European Commission. A non-compete provision may, for example, be permitted up to five years, provided that in addition to the customers and goodwill, know-how is transferred to the purchaser. If no know-how is transferred, the clause may be allowed up to two years. If a certain arrangement is not approved of as an ancillary restraint by the authorities, the parties may, if they wish, apply for an individual exemption from the FCA for such arrangement. If this is not done, the FCA may on its own initiative, or based on a complaint, start to investigate whether the arrangement actually breaches the Competition Act.

9.3. Conditions

Both the FCA and the Competition Council may clear the concentration on conditions imposed by them. As mentioned above, the Competition Act provides that the FCA should always endeavour to negotiate with the parties to the concentration and impose conditions rather than request the Competition Council to prohibit the concentration. Conditions that may be imposed include, among other things, obligation to divest a subsidiary or a business, sell or license intellectual property, or give up exclusive agreements. The FCA and the Competition Council may impose a conditional fine in connection with the condition. If the condition is breached by the parties, the Competition Council may order the conditional fine to be paid.

10. Judicial review

The decision of the FCA may be appealed to the Competition Council, and the decision of the latter may be appealed to the Supreme Administrative Court. Nevertheless, the decision of the FCA on whether it will carry out an in-depth investigation may not be appealed, nor the request of the FCA for the Competition Council to prohibit a concentration. Parties which are directly affected by the decision are entitled to appeal. This means that the parties to the concentration have the right of appeal. It is unclear whether competitors, suppliers and customers could in an individual case be considered to be directly affected by the decision, and thus have the right of appeal.

France

Pierre Kirch

Contents

1. Introduction 149
2. The definition of concentration 153
    2.1. Concentration by way of a transfer of assets, rights and obligations 153
    2.2. Concentration by acquiring a "decisive influence" over one or several undertakings 154
3. Control thresholds 160
    3.1. The definition of "economically-linked" undertakings 161
    3.2. Pre-tax turnover threshold 162
    3.3. Market share threshold 163
4. Procedure 167
    4.1. Benefits and disadvantages of a notification 168
    4.2. Notification procedure 169
    4.3. Opinion of the Competition Council 172
    4.4. Relationship between the French authorities and the European Commission 173
5. Criteria used for determining whether a concentration is admissible .. 174
    5.1. First step of the analysis: Consequences of the concentration on the competitive market situation 175
    5.2. Second step of the analysis: Economic benefits/disadvantages analysis 178
6. Final decision of the Minister of the Economy 181
    Notes 184

FRANCE

1. Introduction

Concentrations between or among previously independent undertakings, however effected, have been regulated in France since the entry into force of the law of 19 July 1977, which introduced threshold criteria and procedures for the control of concentrations under French law. Amendments were made to the original legislation in 1985. Shortly thereafter, the Ordinance of 1 December 1986 (the "1986 Ordinance"), which set out rules applicable to competition in France in general, set forth a somewhat modified version of the rules on concentrations which has remained in force in France to this day. In addition, the 1986 Ordinance replaced the body originally charged with enforcing competition rules and advising the Government on their application, the Competition Commission (*Commission de la Concurrence*), with a new, independent administrative body with reinforced powers, the Competition Council (*Conseil de la Concurrence*). Procedural rules are set forth in a Government Decree of 29 December 1986 (the "1986 Decree").

Although the rules set out in the 1986 Ordinance are broad in scope, some economic sectors are subject to special legal provisions. Concentrations in the French coal and steel sector are subject to the application of Article 66 of the Treaty of Paris of 18 April 1951 forming the European Coal and Steel Community (ECSC)[1]. Special rules apply to concentrations in the press sector. However, this exception has been construed narrowly as applying to concentrations involving daily newspapers covering general and political information, but not other publications, including daily economic newspapers and weekly news magazines[2]. With regard to banks, the law of 24 January 1984, as modified, which provides for general rules in the banking sector, explicitly states that the antitrust rules (anti-competitive agreements, abuse of dominant market position) set forth in Articles 7 and 8 of the 1986 Ordinance are applicable to banks, but does not mention the rules applicable to concentrations. While some scholarly writers interpret this as excluding the banking sector from the scope of the rules of the 1986 Ordinance on the control of concentrations, the Government considers that the 1986 Ordinance is applicable to the sector in its entirety[3]. This said, it should be noted that, as of mid-1998, no decision had been rendered under the provisions of the 1986 Ordinance in connection with concentrations between banks. Finally, with regard to the broadcasting sector, a law of 17 January 1989 explicitly excludes the application of the 1986 Ordinance to that sector. Nevertheless, it would

149

appear that both the Government and the Competition Council consider that the 1986 Ordinance is applicable whenever a concentration in the broadcasting sector has effects on other markets, such as the advertising market[4] (it would appear, moreover, that concentrations in the broadcasting sector would inevitably have effects in other markets).

Where the threshold criteria set forth by the 1986 Ordinance are met, a concentration may be subject to control by the Minister of the Economy and by those other Government Ministers whose portfolios cover the economic sectors affected by the concentration[5].

There is no legal obligation for the undertakings concerned to notify a concentration. In the absence of notification, however, the Minister of the Economy, acting through the B3 Office of the DGCCRF (*Direction générale de la concurrence, de la consommation et de la répression des fraudes*, "General Office of Competition, Consumption, and Repression of Fraud"), the administrative office within the Ministry of the Economy charged with carrying out the application of the rules of the 1986 Ordinance on concentrations to specific transactions, may decide to review such a concentration at any time. Conversely, if a notification is filed, the Government's power to control the concentration will be limited to a specific time-frame.

The voluntary nature of the French notification procedure constitutes its essential distinguishing feature in comparison with European Community rules under Council Regulation (EEC) No. 4064/89 on the control of concentrations between undertakings, as modified from time to time (the "EC Merger Regulation")[6]. Presuming that a contemplated transaction does not fall within the scope of the EC Merger Regulation, the fundamental initial analysis undertaken by the parties to a concentration and their advisers in France consists in a preliminary assessment of *whether* to notify and, in particular, an assessment of the risk that, in the absence of notification, Government authorities take interest in the transaction and either apply pressure on the parties to notify or themselves open the formal review procedure by referring the matter to the Competition Council for an opinion.

In this respect, it should be emphasised that, until recent years, concentrations were rarely notified and reviewed in France and even major transactions often went unnotified. In the last several years, the situation has evolved significantly, in such way that it would seem fair to state that Government officials expect that high profile transactions involving significant French market share and which are not of Community dimension as defined in the EC Merger Regulation *will* be notified. For this reason, it is now often recommended that, for certain types of transactions, voluntary notification be carried out.

Pursuant to figures published by the French Government, between 1977 (when the first law on the control of concentrations entered into force) and 1996, a total of approximately 350 concentrations were the subject of voluntary notification. This would appear to represent a small percentage of the total number of concentrations in France, at least according to official Government statistics [7]. In 1993, 903 concentrations were listed as having taken place in France, of which 21 were the subject of voluntary notification under the 1986 Ordinance. In 1994, according to the same source, there were 691 concentrations in France, and 20 notifications. In 1995, of 536 concentrations, 20 were notified. Finally, in 1996, of 472 concentrations, 27 were notified [8]. These figures, however, should be regarded with some caution. The Government figures do not indicate how many concentrations actually met the conditions to fall within the scope of the rules on concentrations. In addition, it is possible that some concentrations which have met the very broad legal definition of a concentration under French law have remained unknown to Government officials and thus have not appeared in the statistics. Several years ago, an official of the Competition Council nevertheless estimated that 200-300 concentrations per year met the control thresholds and thus qualified for referral to the Competition Council [9].

Where a concentration, whether notified or not, is reviewed by the Minister of the Economy, the formal review process may last up to a total of six months. The Minister of the Economy may take formal action on behalf of the Government prohibiting a concentration or subjecting its approval to conditions or other measures imposed upon the parties only after having received a non-binding opinion from the Competition Council.

Final Government decisions as well as the relevant opinion of the Competition Council are published in the *Bulletin Officiel de la Concurrence, de la Consommation et de la Répression des Fraudes* (BOCCRF). In practice, in some cases, after having referred a concentration to the Competition Council for its opinion, the Government does not make a formal decision and thus may be deemed to have tacitly approved the transaction. Of the 44 referrals made from 1992 to 1997, 36 were the subject of a formal decision [10]. Competition Council opinions are also made known to the public through publication in its Annual Report (*Rapport d'activité*). The Annual Report is available through the Official Journal (*Journal officiel de la République française*), 26 rue Desaix, 75727 Paris Cedex 15, France. In cases where the Minister of the Economy has deemed that a matter did not need to be referred to the Competition Council, the practice has been, in recent years, for the Minister of the Economy to send a letter to a representative of the parties to the transaction to outline briefly the reasons for not referring the matter to the Competition Council (and thus approving the transaction). These letters are also now published in the BOCCRF.

Published Government decisions and letters and Competition Council opinions provide a valuable interpretative aid to the 1986 Ordinance. Published Government statements on its enforcement policy concerning the 1986 Ordinance are also available. In July 1992, the Government issued guidelines entitled *"Méthode d'analyse pour le contrôle des concentrations"* (the "Guidelines"). In 1995, the Government published an "appendix" to the earlier policy document explaining the procedure to be followed for defining the relevant market, entitled *"Le marché pertinent: Annexe à la méthode d'analyse pour le contrôle des concentrations"* (the "Market Definition Guidelines"). Moreover, it is generally agreed that decisions and opinions issued prior to the 1986 reform, as well as official Government interpretations of the rules on concentrations in force before that reform, and in particular the Government instructions (*circulaire*) on concentrations published in 1978[11], may also be used to elucidate the rules now in force.

Below are explained the different steps of the concentration review procedure under French law. First, parties to a transaction should verify whether the transaction is a concentration as this term is understood under French law (section 2), and whether the transaction meets the threshold criteria set forth by the 1986 Ordinance (section 3). If the parties decide to notify the transaction or if the Minister of the Economy decides to review the transaction *sua sponte*, the parties will have to comply with a specific control procedure (section 4). The review process implies an analysis of the concentration's effects, based on specific analytical criteria (section 5). This process generally leads to a final decision by which the Minister of the Economy approves or prohibits the transaction, or approves the transaction subject to conditions or other measures imposed upon the parties (section 6).

2. The definition of concentration

Transactions such as mergers, take-overs, purchases of business assets and joint ventures may all give rise to a concentration. Yet the scope of French law goes beyond these types of concentrations to include other transactions as well. Under Article 39 of the 1986 Ordinance, a concentration results from any act, whatever its form, (i) which transfers ownership or possession of all or part of the assets, rights and obligations of an undertaking, or, alternatively, (ii) the purpose or effect of which is to enable an undertaking or group of undertakings to exercise, directly or indirectly, a "decisive influence" (*influence déterminante*) over one or several other undertakings. In practice, the authorities tend to characterise a transaction as a concentration by using either of the alternative tests set forth under Article 39 of the 1986 Ordinance, in cases where they consider that the transaction should be reviewed, often by general reference to Article 39 without clarification as to which of the alternative criteria effectively applied.

2.1. Concentration by way of a transfer of assets, rights and obligations

The first of the two alternative criteria set forth under Article 39 of the 1986 Ordinance refers to transactions which involve structural change. The structural change criterion is often referred to as defining a concentration in terms of the "means" used to carry out the concentration (whereas the second test, relating to the obtaining of a "decisive influence", is often referred to in terms of the "result" of the concentration).

The structural change test is often used in order to review transactions which involve the acquisition by an undertaking of a business activity previously operated by another undertaking[12]. In practice, the structural change test is sometimes given a very broad application by the French authorities. In the *Gaumont/Pathé* case, the reciprocal acquisition of movie theatres between two leading French operators of chains of movie houses was considered as a concentration because it resulted in a transfer of ownership of assets, rights and obligations[13]. In the *Kimberley-Clark/Peaudouce* case of 1996 and the *Solvay Pharma* case of 1998, the Minister of the Economy considered that the mere acquisition of a brand involved a transfer of ownership of assets, rights and obligations, and could therefore be characterised as a concentration[14].

2.2. Concentration by acquiring a "decisive influence" over one or several undertakings

The 1986 Ordinance does not specify what is meant by "decisive influence". According to the Guidelines, the term "decisive influence" should be construed according to economic criteria based on a review of the factual consequences of a particular transaction[15]. The decisive influence test is generally construed as referring to the "results" of a concentration (as opposed to the "means" under the structural change test). In what follows, the issue of acquisition of decisive influence is analysed according to the type of transaction involved: transaction without acquisition of shares (2.2.1), transaction by way of acquisition of shares (2.2.2), joint control ("joint decisive influence") in the framework of a joint venture (2.2.3).

2.2.1. Acquisition of decisive influence without the acquisition of shares

The "decisive influence" test allows the review of agreements which, without involving genuine structural changes, result in one company gaining the power to influence another company's management decisions and therefore potentially restrict competition in the market concerned. In the absence of a statutory definition, 1978 published Government instructions on concentrations have given a broad interpretation of the term according to which it is generally assumed that an undertaking, without acquiring control, may nevertheless acquire a "decisive influence" over another undertaking through, *inter alia*, subcontracting or distribution agreements[16].

In this respect, in its 1991 opinion concerning the agreements entered into between Gillette Company and Eemland Management Services, which owned the Wilkinson Sword shaving goods business, the Competition Council considered that mere potential control of Eemland by Gillette, through the acquisition by the latter of the convertible bonds issued by Eemland, could entail the acquisition of a decisive influence over Eemland. Three factors, in conjunction with the acquisition of convertible bonds, brought the Competition Council to that conclusion: (i) the existence of first refusal rights over the sale of ordinary shares of Eemland, (ii) the status of Gillette as an important creditor of Eemland as a competitor on the shaving goods market, and (iii) the acquisition by Gillette of the Wilkinson Sword trademark in the territory outside of the EC and the United States, given that this acquisition gave Gillette control of the commercial policy for the Wilkinson Sword products for that territory: according to the Competition Council, such a situation had an impact on the commercial policy in France and therefore indirectly granted Gillette decisive influence over Eemland in France as well. The Competition Council's opinion concerning the transaction was confirmed by the Government's decision of 11 March 1992, which authorised the transaction, subject to certain conditions relating to the upholding of separate marketing networks in France[17].

In the same way, in a 1995 opinion, which was confirmed by the Minister of the Economy, the Competition Council specifically referred to the distinction made by the European Commission in the *Warner Lambert/Gillette* case [18] between "virtual effects" of the agreements under review, such as the acquisition of a minority shareholding interest, and "potential effects", such as a creditor-debtor relationship, convertible bonds or first refusal rights over newly issued shares [19].

2.2.2. Acquisition of decisive influence involving the acquisition of shares

The acquisition of a majority shareholding interest[20] or of the totality[21] of the shares manifestly allows the buyer to exert a decisive influence over the target company. The acquisition of a minority shareholding interest may be also deemed to confer a decisive influence and thus to constitute a concentration. As is the case under the EC Merger Regulation, such minority shareholding interest may give rise to issues of analysis in such a way that other factors must be reviewed to determine whether they confer to the acquirer a decisive influence over the target undertaking[22]. In this respect, according to the Guidelines, it is necessary to determine whether provisions of the by-laws or a shareholders agreement grant to the minority shareholder a role in management or the possibility of determining the general commercial policy of the target undertaking[23]. In practice, the authorities use a "body of evidence" approach to assess whether the relationship between the parties is characterised by the power of one of them to exert a decisive influence over the other.

For example, the Competition Commission analysed, in a 1981 case, a transaction pursuant to which the French company *Grange Frères* was to be controlled by the German company IWKA as majority shareholder with 51% of the shares, with Compagnie Générale des Eaux holding a minority interest with 35% of the shares. In its opinion, despite the majority interest held by IWKA, the Competition Commission considered that Compagnie Générale des Eaux, by holding a 35% minority stake in Grange Frères, also had to be regarded as a party to the concentration, since such stake gave it an "influence on management" through a veto power in shareholders meetings over, *inter alia*, proposed amendments to the by-laws, resolutions on reductions or increases in capital and mergers and spin-offs[24]. Going even further, the Competition Council admitted in a 1988 opinion that the acquisition of a 13.6% minority shareholding could potentially lead to the obtaining of a decisive influence over the target undertaking, given that the minority shareholder was also an operator in the same market as the target[25]. In both cases the Minister of the Economy agreed with the Competition Commission and the Competition Council, respectively, as to the characterisation of the transactions.

The Guidelines also state that, where the minority shareholding has been acquired by a financial institution, there is a refutable presumption that said shareholding constitutes a simple financial investment for the minority shareholder without said shareholder having any decisive role in the undertaking[26]. For example, in the above-mentioned *Gillette/Eemland Management Services* case, the fact that Gillette was an industrial operator in the same market as Eemland and not a financial institution appears to have been an important consideration in the finding of the Competition Council and the Minister of the Economy that the acquisition of convertible bonds could entail the creation of a decisive influence[27].

The use of a body of evidence approach instead of clear-cut rules can result in conflicting decisions and opinions. In a 1997 case, involving the acquisition of 42.39% of the shares of GMB, a retail distribution group, by a competitor, Carrefour, the Minister of the Economy and the Competition Council disagreed about whether the shareholding qualified as a concentration. The Competition Council concluded that Carrefour was prevented from exercising a decisive influence over GMB due to a shareholders' agreement entered into by the other shareholders (representing 54.6% of the capital), as well as the absence of Carrefour representatives on the board of directors. The Minister of the Economy, on the other hand, argued that the transaction qualified as a concentration because there were certain safeguards set out in the shareholders' agreement. The Minister of the Economy informed the concerned companies that he would re-examine the file if there were any change in the ownership or organisation of GMB, since the Competition Council had also stated that if Carrefour were to increase its shareholding or were to become a member of the board, there could be synergy between Carrefour and GMB, which could result in the new group enjoying a dominant position in local markets[28]. It should be noted that the Minister of the Economy's approach in this case is more in accordance with the Competition Council's opinion in previous cases, according to which a virtual or potential decisive influence suffices to characterise the transaction as a concentration.

Finally, it should be noted that the Minister of the Economy sometimes characterises the acquisition of shares as a concentration because such transaction involves the transfer of assets, rights and obligations, without verifying whether this leads to the acquisition of a decisive influence over the target undertaking. For example, in the *Renault Véhicules* case, the Minister of the Economy characterised the acquisition of 50% of a holding company's shares by Renault as a concentration because it resulted in the transfer of the assets, rights and obligations of Heuliez Bus, a subsidiary of the holding company[29]. This suggests that, in practice, the Minister of the Economy is ready to use any one of the two alternative criteria set forth by Article 39 when he considers that a transaction should be subject to control.

2.2.3. Acquisition of joint decisive influence by two or more undertakings: The case of joint ventures

As explained below, there appears to be a divergence of views between the Competition Council and the Government concerning the application of French rules on the control of concentrations to joint ventures.

(a) The Competition Council's position
In its annual report for 1990, the Competition Council stated its position concerning the application of rules on competition to joint ventures in general terms. Nonetheless, as illustrated by three opinions, Competition Council policy appears to be still somewhat undecided as to the circumstances under which a joint venture may be deemed to constitute a concentration.

In 1988, the Minister of the Economy requested that the Competition Council issue an opinion concerning a proposed 50/50 joint venture partnership, Loselle, between Henkel France and Colgate Palmolive which had been notified pursuant to the voluntary notification procedure. While being under tight control and joint decision-making by the parent companies, Loselle was to manufacture household cleaning products for both, and undertake common research and development projects. The parent companies, however, were to continue marketing individually under their own trademarks the products which had been manufactured by the joint venture undertaking.

The Competition Council found that the joint venture did not constitute a concentration between Henkel France and Colgate Palmolive, basing its view solely on the consequences of the transaction with regard to the consumer market for household cleaning products. The Competition Council emphasised that the joint venture partners would have continued to have independent commercial strategies. It noted that the joint venture would be involved only in production and research for the joint venture partners and thus would not be directly involved in various markets for household cleaning products. In such situation, according to the Competition Council, the proposed structure would not in itself tend to allow one of the joint venture partners to have a decisive influence over the marketing policy of the other undertakings[30].

In another case, concerning Médiavision and Circuit A, two French firms specialised in selling advertising time for movie house screenings, the Competition Council stated that the formation of an economic interest grouping did not constitute a concentrative joint venture, since such grouping did not involve the transfer of property or rights thereof and did not have an economic activity independent of that of the undertakings involved in the grouping. In this case, the Médiavision/Circuit A joint venture was to be formed for nine years and was limited solely to a joint effort to find new advertisers, with each party acting independently in the sale of movie screening advertising time. In its opinion, the Competition Council considered that the joint venture grouping did not constitute an autonomous economic entity[31].

A third opinion rendered by the Competition Council in 1990 illustrates the application of the rules of the 1986 Ordinance to a joint venture considered as a concentration. Four companies active in the French sugar market, Générale Sucrière S.A., Commerciale Sucre Union, Sucre Union Distribution and Compagnie Française de Sucrerie, created a joint venture in the form of a partnership (*société en nom collectif*) called Eurosucre which would handle for those companies the marketing of all household and industrial sugar products on the French and European markets. The joint venture partners undertook to refrain from marketing household or industrial sugar products within the European Community or to deal in this regard with any company other than Eurosucre. Eurosucre was to allocate orders among the joint venture manufacturers based on demand predictions, productivity and location. In this context, the Competition Council characterised the joint venture as a concentration since the new entity had a "decisive influence over the production policies of the undertakings concerned by the transaction". On the merits, the Competition Council advised in its opinion that the concentration should be approved[32].

(b) The Government's position
In the 1978 published Government instructions concerning concentrations, it was stated that the creation of a joint venture undertaking could constitute a concentration subject to control[33]. Going further, the Guidelines, published in 1992, while conceding that difficulties may arise in the application of the rules on concentrations to joint ventures, state that the French authorities are not bound to adopt the EC law distinction between concentrative and co-operative joint ventures and that, pursuant to the decisive influence criterion described above, the acquisition or creation of a joint venture falls within the scope of French rules on concentrations, regardless of whether the joint venture would be characterised as concentrative under EC law[34].

The 1988 *Henkel France/Colgate Palmolive* case, described above, illustrates the policy adopted by the Minister of the Economy. Although the Competition Council had concluded that the contemplated transaction did not constitute a concentration between the parties, the Minister of the Economy apparently did not agree with the Competition Council, since, as stated in the Guidelines, he raised informal objections to the contemplated transaction and was able to have the parties agree to changes thereto without the Government having to resort to a formal decision.

(c) Perspectives
The Government's position does not seem likely to change, although, with the entry into force of the modified version of the EC Merger Regulation in March 1998, the distinction, for EC merger control purposes, between concentrative and co-operative joint ventures no longer applies, and the "full function" nature of a joint venture has become the sole criterion governing application of the EC Merger Regulation. This said, it would seem fair to state that, although the "full function" criterion at European level should have for effect to broaden the scope of application of the EC Merger Regulation to joint ventures, the Government's position remains even broader still.

It seems that the Government will continue to apply an analysis which allows for wide-ranging interpretation of the concept of concentration. Indeed, going back to the DGCCRF's Annual Report for 1993, the Government has stated that it did not agree with the Commission's policy, which in its opinion is too theoretical and narrow with regard to the reality of concentrations. As a consequence, Government practice has been to give a strict, albeit broad interpretation to Article 39 of the Ordinance and thus consider as potentially falling within its scope any transaction which involves *any* type of transfer of control over an undertaking, including joint control.

Finally, although no clear-cut solution has yet been given as to the risk of conflicting decisions of the Minister of the Economy, implementing the rules applicable to concentrations, and the Competition Council, implementing Article 7 of the 1986 Ordinance, which sets forth a prohibition of anti-competitive agreements in terms similar to those of Article 85(1) of the Treaty of Rome, the Court of Cassation (*Cour de Cassation*), France's highest Court in civil and commercial law matters, has confirmed a Paris Appeals Court ruling stating that, in a case where the Minister of the Economy had already characterised the crossed purchase of movie theatres as a concentration, by way of an assets swap, the transaction could not be contested afterwards before the Competition Council acting as the enforcement authority with regard to Article 7 of the 1986 Ordinance[35]. It therefore appears that a Government decision to characterise a transaction as a concentration would prevent competition authorities from reviewing the structural aspects of the transaction on grounds of Article 7.

3. Control thresholds

A transaction which may be characterised as a concentration under French law may be subject to review only where the undertakings which are parties to the concentration, which are the subject of the concentration or which are "economically linked" to such undertakings have either (i) realised together more than 25% of the sales, purchases or other transactions in a national market for substitutable goods, products or services or in a substantial part of such market, or have (ii) realised together in France a total annual before-tax turnover of more than FFr 7 billion (approx. € 1.07 billion), provided, in the latter case, that at least two parties to the concentration have each realised an annual turnover of at least FFr 2 billion (approx. € 305 million). Pursuant to Article 27 of the 1986 Decree, all threshold calculations relate only to business activity which takes place in French territory.

With regard to territorial aspects of the French rules, as early as 1984, under the old 1977 law, the Government accepted to review a concentration between two undertakings which had their head offices in the United States of America on grounds that the transaction had effects on the French market[36]. This acknowledgement of the "effects doctrine" was confirmed after the entry into force of the 1986 Ordinance[37]. As a consequence, a concentration involving undertakings which do not have their head offices in France but which has effects on the French market may be subject to review by the Minister of the Economy, as long as it meets the thresholds as set forth by the Ordinance.

As a general rule, the wording of and criteria set forth in Article 38 have as their consequence to facilitate the exercise by the Government of its power to review concentrations, and this for two reasons. First, the notion of "economically linked", cited above, is sufficiently vague to enable the authorities to have considerable leeway in defining the undertakings concerned by the concentration for threshold calculation purposes. Secondly, whereas the EC Merger Control Regulation limits threshold criteria to turnover calculations only, the French rules include an alternative market share criterion which may allow the authorities to act even where a concentration involves small undertakings provided that the undertakings are active on the same specifically defined market or markets and have a significant market share thereof.

3.1. The definition of "economically-linked" undertakings

As stated above, the definition of this notion bears some importance since it may be used by the authorities to determine the perimeter of a concentration for purposes of making threshold calculations. The term itself, however, is not defined in the 1986 Ordinance and there is no opinion of the Competition Council or case law which deals specifically with the meaning of the term. Nevertheless, it is generally agreed that reference should be made to the 1978 published Government instructions mentioned above, which interpreted the original 1977 legislation on concentrations. Pursuant to those instructions, an "economic link" between undertakings may involve those links deriving from company law (shareholdings, "groupings" of companies, common directors), from financial or commercial ties (supply agreements, subcontracting) or, as a general rule, from any other agreements which may create "lasting links" between the undertakings concerned[38]. It should be pointed out, however, that the notion of "economically linked" does not necessarily appear to coincide with that of "concentration", since the Competition Council has excluded the formation of an economic interest grouping – which creates "links" between undertakings – from the French definition of a concentration. In the Guidelines, the Government admits that the assessment of the number of undertakings concerned by a transaction is done, in fact, on a case-by-case basis[39].

In the case of a *partial* acquisition of an undertaking's assets, the selling company's turnover and market shares should logically be excluded from the calculations, since those figures are not pertinent for the evaluation of the new entity's market power. This is the situation under Article 5(2) of the EC Merger Regulation. However, the French authorities do not seem to apply such reasoning in a consistent manner. For example in the *Total/Bolloré* case, in which the Bolloré group sold its shareholding in a third company to Total, the Competition Council decided that the undertakings to be taken into account for the threshold calculations were both Bolloré, as a group, including the target undertaking group, and Total, as purchaser[40]. However in the *Exide/ CEAC* case, in which Fiat and Alcatel-Alsthom sold their shareholdings in a third company to Exide, the Competition Council only took into account the turnover and market shares of Exide and the target undertaking[41]. In both cases, the Minister of the Economy followed the Competition Council's opinion without further analysis. It is not clear whether those conflicting views are based on a specific reasoning, or are due to an absence of any firm policy on the issue.

3.2. Pre-tax turnover threshold

The first alternative threshold, as set forth in Article 38 of the 1986 Ordinance, is expressed in absolute terms of pre-tax turnover of the undertakings concerned, amounting to combined turnover in France of FFr 7 billion (€ 1.07 billion), provided that at least two of the undertakings have each obtained in France a turnover of at least FFr 2 billion (€ 305 million). This threshold is not as simple as it appears, however, as the conflicting positions of the Minister of the Economy and the Competition Council in the 1993 *Prodirest/Discol* case indicate. The Competition Council concluded that because the pre-tax turnover of Prodirest was inferior to FFr 2 billion (€ 305 million), the threshold was not reached and as a result, the operation was not controllable in terms of turnover. The Minister of the Economy, on the other hand, stated that the relevant turnover was that realised by all of the companies belonging to the same *group*. Since Prodirest was a subsidiary of Promodès, which had a 1992 turnover of FFr 84.2 billion (€ 12.84 billion), the Minister of the Economy deemed the threshold to be reached and the concentration controllable[42].

The turnover to be taken into account is thus the *total* turnover of the group, and not only the turnover which arises from sales in the markets concerned. This condition allows French authorities to control concentrations between relatively large undertakings (which obtain turnover amounts greater than the threshold levels indicated above but less than those set under the EC Merger Regulation) doing business in competitive markets in which they do not obtain through the transaction combined market share of more than 25%.

The relevant period for making turnover calculations is that of the last accounting period year preceding the transaction.

3.3. Market share threshold

The other threshold as set forth in Article 38 of the 1986 Ordinance is expressed in relative market share terms set at 25% of "sales, purchases, or transaction" in the French market or in a "substantial part" thereof.

According to the Guidelines, the market share threshold applies even where the concentration involves, on the one hand, an undertaking which already has a market share greater than 25% and, on the other hand, a second undertaking which has no business activity in the same market[43]. Moreover, the Minister of the Economy considers that a concentration affecting several markets must be considered controllable in its entirety as long as the threshold in relative market share is reached in one or several of these markets[44].

It should be noted that the reference to 25% of "sales, purchases or other transactions" in the French market has allowed the authorities to exercise considerable leeway in applying the threshold. For instance, in the 1990 *Eurocom/Carat* case, the Competition Council relied on the relative volume of purchases of advertising space to evaluate market share and not on invoiced purchase amounts since the concerned undertakings were able to obtain higher discounts on their purchases than their competitors[45].

The market share threshold condition leads to some legal insecurity for the undertakings involved in a concentration and to a possible broad exercise of power by the authorities, given that this threshold condition applies regardless of the size of the undertakings concerned and that its applicability depends on market definition, which encompasses the definition of one or several product and geographic market(s).

3.3.1. Product market definition

In 1995, the DGCCRF published the Market Definition Guidelines, which explain the procedure followed by the Minister of the Economy for defining the relevant market. This document, as a methodological tool, enumerates four steps in the reasoning process of defining a relevant product market.

In the first step, the authorities consider all the products and services which may reasonably be thought of as alternative means of satisfying a single demand. This quality of substitutability is the common denominator of products and services belonging to the same market. For instance, in the *Henkel/Loctite* case, involving a concentration in the glue industry, the Competition Council observed that professionals and the general public employ the same glues differently, with professionals using glue according to its chemical qualities and the general public according to the use prescribed by the manufacturer. The Competition Council found that there is a greater variety among glue's chemical composition than among its recommended uses; as a result, the same glues were divided into seven markets for professionals and three for the general public. (The Competition Council's opinion was approved by the Minister of the Economy.)[46]

The remaining steps of the DGCCRF's market definition method involve narrowing down the concerned markets by gradual removal from the market scope of non-substitutable products and services.

Thus, in step two of the DGCCRF method, an "objective" narrowing takes place, involving the identification of products and services rendered non-substitutable on technical, contractual, legal, and regulatory grounds. For instance, as noted in the Market Definition Guidelines, butter and margarine would be considered as non-substitutable from the point of view of professionals because regulations prohibit the use of margarine for the production of certain goods. As another example of this step two analysis, with regard to cinema entertainment, in the *Gaumont/Pathé* case, it was considered that showing a movie in a theatre is a type of service inherently different from, and therefore not substitutable with, showing movies on television or by way of videocassettes[47]. However, it should be noted that even an important difference in the technical characteristics of products does not necessarily exclude the possibility that the products belong to the same relevant market, where there is demand side substitutability. For example, aluminium, steel and plastic cables have been classified by the Minister of the Economy in the same market, because they are perceived by the consumer as having the same function [48].

The third step of the DGCCRF's market definition method involves the same process, but employs a more subjective approach. The authorities examine reports, studies and surveys in order to assess the substitutability of the products with regard to the consumer demand. For example in the 1993 *Gaumont/Pathé* case, it was observed that the attendance index for Paris theatres was 12.68, for theatres in the suburbs it was 1.56, and the national average was 2.07. It was reasoned that individual Parisians and suburbanites had the same propensity to attend movies, but that more suburban duellers go to Parisian movie theatres than Parisians go to suburban movie theatres, with the conclusion that movie theatres in Paris and in its suburbs are not substitutable [49]. Another example can be found in the distribution sector, where the authorities distinguish between distribution networks intended for retailers and those intended for consumers, the latter being segmented into further market segments [50]. Moreover, when analysing the substitutability of a range of similar products (e.g. mattresses of different sizes and shapes), the authorities have considered that products belong to the same market as long as they respond to a common demand of the consumers, except for expensive luxury goods [51]. In this respect, the French authorities acknowledge the existence of specific market segments composed of luxury goods (characterised by their higher prices and quality, and specific consumer demand characteristics) within a defined product range.

The fourth and final step in the DGCCRF's market definition method involves the price elasticity of products. Generally speaking, as noted in the Market Definition Guidelines, if a price increase of product A leads to an increase in consumption of product B, the products are deemed to be substitutable. For example, in the *Continental Pet* decision of 1993, the Competition Council found that metal and glass containers did not belong to the same product market as plastic containers because producers of liquids continued to use metal and glass containers despite their much higher cost [52]. The Competition Council's opinion was approved by the Minister of the Economy. In another case, *Coca-Cola/Pernod Ricard*, both the Competition

Council and the Minister of the Economy rejected Coca-Cola's argument that "cola drinks" do not form a proper product market, although Coca-Cola had submitted several price studies in support of its argument[53]. The authorities did not agree with those studies for the following reasons: (i) the price studies compared prices, and not price variations, (ii) the prices were not weighted to take into account seasonal variations (different results were obtained for the same prices when compared, for example, from January to January and from November to January), (iii) the "hypothetical monopolist test" had been performed with price increases of 20% instead of the 10% usually applied by competition authorities. This case reveals important information to undertakings as to how price studies should be presented to the French authorities. It appears, moreover, to constitute an acknowledgement by the French authorities of the use, where applicable, of the "hypothetical monopolist test", which consists in verifying whether an important price increase would deprive a manufacturer of the monopoly or quasi-monopoly it has concerning a specific product, because consumers would switch to similar products presumably belonging to different markets.

In general, it would appear that the aim of the French authorities in using the "four-step method" described in the Market Definition Guidelines is to constitute a body of evidence in order to assess the substitutability of products on the demand side. Indeed, in practice, the consumer's choice of products seems to be the most important factor for the definition of the relevant product market. Contrary to European Commission practice, the fact that there may be manufacturers which are not present in the relevant product market but which could adapt their production processes to manufacture the concerned products is usually not taken into account by the French authorities[54].

In practice, it would appear that the use of narrow market definition techniques involves sufficient flexibility so as to potentially be used as a means to assert control over a concentration which would not otherwise meet the turnover threshold test. In the 1989 *Nestlé S.A./Rowntree* case, although Nestlé had group turnover of FFr 13 billion (€ 1.98 billion), Rowntree PLC's group turnover was less than FFr 1.5 billion (€ 229 million), and thus below the FFr 2 billion (€ 305 million) turnover threshold. However, by applying the market share threshold, the Competition Council, in its opinion, was able to assert control over the transaction (purchase by Nestlé S.A., a Swiss company, of Rowntree PLC, a British company). Rather than define a broad market in chocolate bars and tablets, the Competition Council distinguished, essentially according to the shape of the packaged product, among five different types of consumer chocolate products, including, *inter alia*, chocolate bars and chocolate tablets, each of which was deemed to constitute a separate consumer market. On three of the five markets, the combined market shares in France of the undertakings concerned exceeded 25% (ranging from 29.3% to 38.5% market share)[55].

3.3.2. Geographic market definition

The product market(s), as defined under the reasoning process explained above, must be confined to a geographic area, where offer and demand for the concerned product meet. Most often, the geographic market in control cases is deemed to be national, but cases arise where, as a result of factors such as the cost or time of transport, demand for a product may be considered to exist only in a limited area. This was the situation in the 1994 *Holdercim/Cedest* case, which involved ready-to-use concrete. Because such concrete had to be used soon after production, the Minister of the Economy, in his decision, stated that the geographic market was limited to the local area of the site of production, which the Competition Council, in its opinion, had set at a radius of 30 kilometers[56].

It should be kept in mind that, even where the relevant geographic market is smaller than the French territory, Article 38 allows for control where the 25% threshold is obtained in a "substantial part" of the national market. The adjective "substantial" does not appear to be interpreted by the authorities as being substantial in a purely geographical sense. For instance, in the *Gaumont/ Pathé* case, the authorities ruled that Parisian movie theatres played an essential role in the commercial success of movies and, therefore, that Paris constituted a substantial part of the national market for the showing of movies in theatres[57]. In the same way, in another case, the geographic market for crude oil storage was confined by the Minister of the Economy to the French oil refineries likely to use crude oil[58].

4. Procedure

The concentration review procedure may be initiated either upon the filing of a notification to the Minister of the Economy (DGCCRF) by the concerned undertakings or upon a decision of the Minister of the Economy to review the concentration, generally following an administrative inquiry. After a transaction has been notified or after the Minister of the Economy has decided to review a transaction *sua sponte*, the Minister of the Economy may decide to refer the matter to the Competition Council for an opinion, before reaching a final decision.

4.1. Benefits and disadvantages of a notification

In deciding whether to notify a transaction, the parties should take into account the risk that, in the absence of notification, the French authorities become interested in the transaction and, thus, the risk that an already completed concentration be reviewed and potentially subject to negative measures such as a partial divestment or total demerger order. Such risk assessment often involves a variety of considerations including, *inter alia*, market share; configuration of the market in its horizontal and vertical aspects; nature of the relevant markets (whether the transaction involves a "sensitive" sector from an economic, Governmental, or socio-cultural point of view); media interest in the transaction; possibility that competitors, suppliers or customers could file complaints concerning the transaction to the DGCCRF or to Government authorities having a particular interest in the sector. In borderline cases, the concerned undertakings may find it advantageous to notify the transaction, since notification procedures allow for a "first shot" by the undertakings at making market definitions and analysis, as well as at preparing an economic analysis of the consequences of the concentration which corresponds to an assessment of the transaction in its most favourable light from their point of view. In addition, the chances that a significant transaction would simply go "unnoticed" by the authorities would appear to be somewhat remote. The DGCCRF claims to "conduct systematic examinations of all operations attaining the thresholds for reviewability set forth under Article 38 of the 1986 Ordinance"[59]. While it used to be somewhat rare that undertakings notify a concentration, an increasing percentage of all statistically recorded concentrations carried out in France over the past several years would now appear to be the subject of voluntary notification.

In addition, notification gives undertakings the advantage of legal security in that, through notification, they may oblige the Minister of the Economy to act within a specified time-frame, limited to two months where clearance is given without referral to the Competition Council and to six months where the Minister of the Economy issues a decision concerning the transaction (which may be negative) only after having obtained an opinion of the Competition Council.

In current practice, it would appear that the Minister of the Economy is somewhat reluctant to prohibit outright a transaction which was completed some time before the carrying out of the control procedure, as evidenced by the *Sensormatic/Knogo* case in 1994. In that case, the Competition Council concluded that Sensormatic's acquisition of Knogo conferred it a dominant position on the French anti-theft device market and therefore should not be approved. The Minister of the Economy, however, making his decision a full year after the merger's completion, elected to approve the concentration on grounds that it could not be undone, but did impose conditions on Sensormatic's operations in France. It should be noted that those measures, though limited to French territory, were by no means insignificant, since the parties were ordered to (i) eliminate their general conditions of sale, rental or maintenance *for France*, to the extent that those conditions excluded the guarantee for use with by-products which were not sold by Sensormatic or Knogo and (ii) renounce the use *in France* of a specific technology which was acquired by way of the transaction. Moreover, the Minister of the Economy justified his refusal to prohibit the transaction by a specific set of facts: (i) the transaction was a merger *stricto sensu*, meaning that one of the companies was absorbed by the other and disappeared totally, (ii) the previous activities of the absorbed company had been continued by the new entity (the absorbing company) after the merger[60]. The reluctance of the Minister of the Economy to order a demerger in that case may have been motivated by the idea that it was truly impossible to come back to the *status quo ante*.

4.2. Notification procedure

The parties to a concentration may proceed with notification of the transaction to the Minister of the Economy on a voluntary basis either before or within three months of the effective date of the transaction. The notification may be coupled with commitments by the notifying parties for the purpose of maintaining competition in the markets affected by the transaction.

The notification information required of the parties is straightforward and does not involve the same quantity of complex data analysis as that involved in the mandatory notification procedures under the EC Merger Regulation.

This said, the quantity of notification information required under the French review procedure was substantially increased by 1995 amendments to the applicable rules.

Although there is no statutory provision to this effect, Government officials request the filing of at least three copies of a notification. The file should be sent to the Minister of the Economy, for the Attention of *Bureau B3 (Concentrations, études financières, aides), Direction Générale de la Concurrence, de la Consommation et de la Répression des Fraudes* (DGCCRF), Carré Diderot, 3-5 boulevard Diderot, 75572 Paris Cedex 12, France. Receipt is recorded in a special registry. In some cases, Government officials may contact the parties after notification in order to obtain further information. If said information is necessary to complete the notification file, the limited period of time allowed for Government action concerning the transaction (2 or 6 months, depending on whether the case is referred to the Competition Council) will begin only once the file has been completed.

Pursuant to Article 28 of the 1986 Decree, as amended in 1995, notifying parties must supply the following information:

- A copy of the relevant contract giving rise to the concentration, a presentation of the transaction's legal and financial aspects, as well as its economic objectives.
- Information concerning the undertakings involved in the transaction, and "economically-linked" undertakings, including, *inter alia*:
  - the by-laws;
  - management and the main shareholders or partners;
  - the extent of shareholdings in companies belonging to the same group;
  - relevant shareholders' agreements;
  - information on employees;
  - financial statements for the previous fiscal year, including turnover, in France;
  - financial agreements between the parties to the transaction and economically-linked undertakings;
  - a list of concentrations completed within the past three years.
- A definition of the markets affected by the transaction, specifying the criteria employed for selecting the products or services that the parties consider to be substitutable.
- A definition of the geographic markets, specifying the criteria employed in their definition.

- The characteristics of the markets affected by the transaction, including, *inter alia*:
    - an estimate of the value and size of these markets;
    - the names of the main competitors and their market share;
    - the flow of imports and exports;
    - the main professional associations;
    - the main factors in determining prices;
    - the evolution of prices over the previous five years;
    - a presentation of the factors likely to affect entry to the concerned markets (applicable regulations, such as prior authorisation requirements to exercise the activity, access to raw materials, expenses for research and development and for advertising, the existence of standards, licenses for patents or other rights, the importance of economies of scale, necessary technology, etc.).
- The position of the undertakings participating in the concentration on the markets affected by the transaction, including, *inter alia*:
    - an estimate of the market shares held by the undertakings, as well as their evolution;
    - prices and sales conditions;
    - the names of the main clients and suppliers;
    - location of the principal business units;
    - the distribution agreements;
    - contracts entered into with public bodies;
    - rights affecting the products or services corresponding to these markets;
    - expenses for research and development and for advertising.
- Where relevant, undertakings made by the participants in order to foster competition.

If the notifying companies consider that some of the requested information is of a confidential nature, they may inform the Minister of the Economy which pieces of information they do not want to be made public.

In 1997, a "single and common notification form" in France and two other European Union countries, the United Kingdom and Germany, was introduced. This form may be used by the parties to a transaction which is likely to be controllable in at least two of the three countries. Although the common notification form is intended to simplify the notification procedure, it must be sent to each of the concerned national authorities. Moreover, for transactions which are controllable in France, this procedure only obliges the French authorities to inform the notifying parties, within one month, whether a formal notification under French law is necessary. Indeed, the filing of the common notification form does not constitute a substitute for the ordinary national notification form, but rather would appear to be comparable to informal pre-notification procedures.

The following information is requested under the common notification form:
- an evaluation of the countries in which the transaction is likely to be reviewed;
- the name, position and address of a sole representative concerning the transaction;
- a description of the transaction and of its time-frame;
- a description of the concerned parties, including their world-wide turnover and their turnover in France, Germany and the United Kingdom, as well as the world-wide assets of the target undertaking;
- an evaluation of the markets affected by the transaction.

4.3. Opinion of the Competition Council

The Minister of the Economy may refer the case to the Competition Council for an opinion only after having informed the parties to the transaction of his intention to do so (Article 29 of the 1986 Decree). As of May 1998, according to official figures, the Minister of the Economy had referred, over the approximately 21 years which have elapsed since the original legislation on concentrations entered into force in 1977, some 57 concentration cases to the Competition Council (and to its predecessor institution, the Competition Commission)[61].

In the Guidelines, the Government has stated that, as a general rule, a transaction, whether notified or not, would be submitted to the Competition Council for an opinion where, in particular, (i) the case at hand is rather complex and controversial and thus the opinion of the Competition Council would be useful, (ii) the transaction clearly has a negative effect on competition in the concerned market but contributes to economic progress, (iii) the market or sector concerned has been the subject of decisions implementing antitrust rules in the past, which shows that this market or sector is "problematic" as to competition requirements, (iv) one of the parties to the transaction clearly has a dominant position in the concerned market, (v) the concerned market is characterised by a significant legislative and regulatory environment, (vi) the Minister of the Economy wishes to render a decision which differs from that of other country's competition authorities, (vii) the case has a Community dimension but was referred back to the French authorities by the European Commission under Article 9 of the EC Merger Regulation[62].

Even where the proposed transaction will not result in a concentration, the Minister of the Economy may still submit the matter to the Competition Council for an opinion pursuant to Article 5 of the 1986 Ordinance, which allows the Government to ask the Competition Council for an opinion concerning any question related to competition. For instance, in a 1997 case involving a partial acquisition of the retail distribution group GMB by Carrefour, the Minister of the Economy requested that the Competition Council examine the effects of the transaction on competition even though the Competition Council had determined that the operation did not qualify as a concentration[63].

The opinion of the Competition Council is not binding upon the Minister of the Economy who, acting in conjunction with other ministers whose portfolios cover the economic sector affected by the transaction, has final discretionary power over concentrations which fall within the scope of the 1986 Ordinance. Indeed, it is the Government authority (rather than an independent administrative body such as the Competition Council) which has final decision-making authority, with the exercise of such discretionary power involving, in the French concept of merger control, a delicate appraisal of the balance between the economic and social benefits of the transaction, on the one hand, and the competition disadvantages in the concerned market, on the other hand.

4.4. Relationship between the French authorities and the European Commission

The entry into force of the EC Merger Regulation in 1990 has not in all cases stripped the French authorities of their power to control concentrations of some economic importance. For instance, the June 1991 concentration between the retail distribution group Carrefour and Euromarché, of considerable importance since it led to a new group having a combined turnover of some FFr 105 billion, was informally reviewed, and acted upon by the French Government with the Minister of the Economy giving conditional approval of the transaction by an unofficial letter of 5 September 1991[64]. Moreover, even where the European thresholds are met, the French Government may request and obtain from the European Commission a transfer of cases which have local effects on the French market, pursuant to Article 9 of the EC Merger Regulation[65]. It should be added that Commission merger control policy and practice have, in many cases, a discernable influence on the approach adopted by the French authorities, and the Competition Council and the Minister of the Economy often refer to the merger control policy of the European Commission in their own analysis, such as, for example, with regard to the definition of the relevant market[66] or even the effects of a transaction on the competitive market situation[67].

5. Criteria used for determining whether a concentration is admissible

Article 38 of the 1986 Ordinance states that the Minister of the Economy may submit a transaction to the Competition Council for an opinion where it is "of such nature to restrict competition by, in particular, creating or strengthening a dominant position". In such case, the Competition Council "evaluates whether the proposed concentration or the concentration entails a contribution to economic progress that is sufficiently important so as to compensate the negative effects on competition". The Competition Council is required to take into account the competitiveness of the undertakings involved with regard to international competition (Article 41 of the 1986 Ordinance). However, it should be noted that those criteria do not bind the Minister of the Economy, who only has an obligation to give the grounds for his decisions (Article 44 of the 1986 Ordinance).

In practice, the Minister of the Economy and the Competition Council use a similar approach in their analysis, which is described in the Guidelines as encompassing two steps: (i) first, the authorities evaluate whether the concentration restricts competition in the relevant market, (ii) secondly, in the event that the concentration has been considered to have negative effects on competition, the authorities then assess whether the transaction contributes to economic progress and whether this contribution suffices to compensate for the restrictions on competition[68]. Whereas the Competition Council is bound to the criteria set forth in Article 41 of the 1986 Ordinance, the Minister of the Economy tends to motivate his decision in detail only when he prohibits a transaction or imposes conditions on the parties to a transaction. Letters in which the Minister of the Economy accepts a concentration without conditions, even after referral to the Competition Council, usually contain only a very brief summary of the reasoning leading to the decision to approve the transaction.

5.1. First step of the analysis: Consequences of the concentration on the competitive market situation

A transaction may have negative effects on the competitive market situation, in the wording of Article 38 of the 1986 Ordinance, "creating or strengthening a dominant position" of an undertaking. It should be noted that French law does not consider the fact that an undertaking gains significant market power in terms of additional market share through a concentration as a condition leading automatically to a prohibition of the transaction. The main concern of the French authorities at this stage of the assessment of a concentration, is whether the transaction restricts competition in the relevant market. Thus, the structure of the market also plays an important part in the analysis.

5.1.1. Market share

The Competition Council specified in its Annual Report for 1996 that a transaction which confers a "pre-eminent" position to an undertaking because of its market share does not automatically imply that such transaction has created or strengthened a dominant position[69]. This reasoning is also accepted by the Government, as stated in the Guidelines[70]. It allows the authorities to assess the consequences of transactions which have only a limited or no effect on market share. For example, in one case, both the Minister of the Economy and the Competition Council considered that a merger between a manufacturer and a distributor (vertical integration) would not change the manufacturer's market share, but strengthen his market power and reduce the possibility for other manufacturers to distribute their products or buy raw materials[71]. Moreover, a concentration between two undertakings which are not active in the same market, may also increase the new entity's economic strength and market power although it does not result in an important increase in market share. For example, in the *Coca-Cola/Pernod Ricard* case, the Minister of the Economy and the Competition Council considered that, although the

175

acquisition by Coca-Cola of the "Orangina" activity of Pernod Ricard would result in the new entity having only between 20% and 30% of market share in the market of non-alcoholic carbonated beverages, such concentration would result in the association of the two most famous brand marks in the French markets of cola beverages and of carbonated non-alcoholic beverages, thus allowing Coca-Cola to increase its market power and offer the most attractive "beverage portfolio" to distributors, in such way that competitors such as Pepsi-Cola would be discouraged from having an aggressive strategy in the French market. (The Minister of the Economy issued a negative decision.)[72]

Finally, in cases where the transaction only results in a negligible increase in market share of the new entity, the Competition Council seems to take into account other factors, such as market structure, in deciding whether there is a restriction of competition in the relevant market. For example, in the *Codes Rousseau/Media Communication* case, the Competition Council (opinion followed by the Minister of the Economy) considered that a transaction involving an increase in market share of 2.7% had negative effects on competition in the market, because (i) there were only two operators left in the market, the new entity included, (ii) the new entity had considerable turnover, (iii) the other operator in the market had limited financial resources, and (iv) the market was characterised by significant barriers to entry[73].

5.1.2. Market structure

As a general rule, the markets to be considered for assessing the admissibility of a transaction are not only those in which the parties (and economically linked undertakings) are active, but also those which may be indirectly affected by the transaction. Thus, in the *Vivendi/Havas* case, the Competition Council decided that the markets concerned by the concentration included the various business sectors of Canal Plus, although this company was not, *stricto sensu*, a party to the concentration[74]. Vivendi owned 34% of shares of Canal Plus and had concluded a shareholders agreement with another shareholder owning 15% of Canal Plus shares. Vivendi had stated that it planned to have an aggressive commercial strategy and to become a global player in all fields of the communications sector, including those in which Canal Plus was active. The Minister of the Economy approved the transaction without going into much detail[75].

Moreover, although threshold calculations take into account only the French market, analysis concerning the market consequences of the transaction sometimes takes into account the European and international market context. Thus, in an opinion of 22 March 1979, concerning a merger in the tubes sector, the Competition Commission noted that, although the concentration resulted in a dominant market position in France, competition would be maintained due to the free access of imports into France[76]. Contrariwise, the situation in European or international markets may be deemed to have a negative effect where one of the parties concerned by the transaction has a significant presence in those markets. In a Competition Commission opinion of 10 May 1984 concerning the acquisition of Ashland Chemical France S.A. by Cabot Corporation, Cabot's strong situation in international markets as an exporter to the French market was deemed to represent a significant negative factor, exacerbating the effects in France of the creation of a dominant market position[77]. The Competition Commission issued a negative opinion concerning the Cabot transaction that was followed by a decision by the Minister of the Economy prohibiting the carrying out of the transaction. Said decision was, however, overturned by the Courts on procedural grounds[78].

The market structure is often used as a factor which allows the Competition Council or the Minister of the Economy to compensate for the potential increase of market power gained by the parties to a concentration by other factors. First, anticipated shifts in market share enter into the authorities' decision-making process. For instance, in the 1997 *Henkel* case, the Competition Council listed as one of its reasons for approving Henkel's purchase of Loctite the fact that although this new group, through its "Superglue" brand, had significant market share, the "Superglue" market share was, in fact, steadily declining. (The Minister of the Economy approved the transaction.)[79] Moreover, the authorities may take into account the fact that the market is undergoing transformation because product technology is in constant evolution. For example, the Minister of the Economy focused on the evolution of the market in approving Thomson's purchase of Matra's "imagery business", a system for the numeric retransmission of television programs. The Minister of the Economy reasoned that a strong market position would not prevent competition in such a young, undeveloped market[80]. The Competition Council used the same type of reasoning to diminish the significance attributed to Vivendi's market position in internet services and broadcasting[81].

Another important factor is the existence or absence of potential competition. For the purpose of measuring whether a concentration results in an undertaking gaining a dominant position, it is necessary to assess whether the relevant market is characterised by significant barriers to entry, or whether, on the contrary, the market structure allows potential competitors to challenge the parties to the concentration. Barriers to entry may result from various factors, such as, *inter alia*, applicable regulations (for example, the need for an administrative authorisation), investment requirements, technology or brand-name recognition factors. In the *Coca-Cola/Pernod Ricard* case, one of the main reasons why the acquisition by Coca-Cola of the "Orangina" brand was prohibited by the Minister of the Economy resided in the fact that the soft drinks market was highly dependent on brand recognition factors, and that Coca-Cola's main competitor, Pepsi-Cola, would probably not elect to mount an aggressive commercial strategy in France in the event that Coca-Cola owned the two most famous brands in the French market[82].

Finally, the authorities also appear to take into account the market situation deriving from previous decisions rendered in concentration cases in the same market. For instance, in 1997, the Minister of the Economy based his approval of the purchase of Nethold by Canal Plus, which would give the latter a dominant position in the pay-per-view market, in part on a 1995 decision prohibiting Canal Plus from having exclusive broadcast rights for certain major sporting events[83].

5.2. Second step of the analysis: Economic benefits/disadvantages analysis

After reviewing anti-competitive effects which derive from the concentration, the Competition Council and the Minister of the Economy review whether the economic benefits thereof outweigh the disadvantages. This method, which is an essential characteristic of the French rules, is explicitly provided for under Article 41 of the 1986 Ordinance, as concerns the Competition Council, which must assess whether the "economic progress" resulting from the concentration compensates its negative effects on competition.

The concept of "economic progress" may generally encompass productivity gains or various commercial or financial synergies that the group or entity deriving from the concentration will be able to obtain. In this respect, the French authorities have introduced what could be called a "proportionality test", which consists in verifying whether the economic progress resulting from the transaction could not be obtained by means which would have a less restrictive effect on competition. For instance, in the *Coca-Cola/Pernod Ricard* case, it was deemed that the economic benefits from a reduction in Coca-Cola's distribution costs and the possibility for Pernod Ricard to concentrate on its primary activities, two factors of economic progress, could have been achieved by other means than the contemplated concentration (application of a "proportionality test")[84]. It should also be noted that the Competition Council and the Minister of the Economy specified in the *Coca-Cola/Pernod Ricard* case that for Pernod Ricard to gain considerable financial resources from the sale of the Orangina business could not be considered as an economic progress "for the collective good". This interpretation of the concept of "economic progress" would appear to correspond to concepts included in Article 10(2) of the 1986 Ordinance, which allows the Competition Council, when acting as an ordinary competition authority, to exempt restrictive agreements and concerted practices subject to the condition that they contribute to economic progress and that consumers benefit directly from at least part of this economic progress.

In addition, the Competition Council appears to have accepted, in a 1996 opinion, the concept of *failing company defence*, in a case concerning the acquisition of a company which had been making losses for several years. In its opinion, the Competition Council noted that the transaction was the only way of avoiding the disappearance of said company (no other buyer had been found). The Competition Council accepted the transaction as contributing to "economic progress" only to the extent that the buyer of the target undertaking committed to (i) continue selling the products manufactured by the undertaking for at least three years or (ii) licence the technology necessary for the manufacture of those products to other undertakings. The Minister of the Economy followed the Competition Council's opinion, as concerns the two conditions for accepting the transaction, but indicated that he did not consider the acquisition of a failing company which otherwise would disappear as a contribution to economic progress[85].

Moreover, Article 41 of the 1986 Ordinance states that the "Competition Council takes into account the competitiveness of the concerned undertakings with regard to competition in international markets". Indeed, a concentration which involves a number of restrictions on competition at the national level may produce various benefits in an international perspective, such as increased export capacity or increased size necessary to compete in Europe, as well as potential consequences on the unit costs of the undertakings or on their ability to innovate, diversify their business activities or increase their productivity[86].

The 1990 *Eurocom/Carat* case (concerning a complex deal in which a British Company in the advertising field, WCRS, was to take control of Eurocom, pursuant to which two French companies, Eurocom and Carat, were to merge their advertising space businesses) illustrates the manner in which concerns relating to international competitiveness may affect the review of a transaction. The Competition Council accepted the analysis of the parties according to which the merger between Eurocom and Carat for the purchase of advertising space would contribute to the competitiveness of the new group in international markets, but concluded that such international benefits could be obtained in the absence of concentration of the undertakings' business activities in the French market. Although the Minister of the Economy approved the transaction in his decision of 3 September 1990, said approval was only granted subject to the condition that the concentration between the business activities of Eurocom and Carat involve the purchase of advertising space for "international clients" who request space not only in France but at the same time in several other countries, and that the businesses remain separate in the domestic market.

Finally, the French authorities consider not only the economic welfare of the concerned undertakings, but also that of their competitors and clients. In 1997, the Competition Council rendered two favourable opinions, which were "globally approved" by the Minister of the Economy, in part because of the benefits which would accrue to the new group's clients in the form of lower prices resulting from savings in production costs derived from economies of scale [87]. In 1998, the Minister of the Economy approved the acquisition of Prisunic by Monoprix in part because the operation "could allow the merged group to stimulate competition with regard to other market participants"[88].

Ministerial control takes into account not only the economic benefits of a concentration, but also the "social" benefits. This results from Article 42 of the 1986 Ordinance, pursuant to which the Minister of the Economy may accept a concentration subject to the condition that the parties comply with specific requirements designed to contribute to "economic and social progress". It is generally agreed that such social benefits include employment and consumer protection. The Minister of the Economy is thus empowered to act not only on the grounds of antitrust considerations but general policy considerations in other areas as well. In the 1994 *Metaleurop/Heubach & Lindgens* case, the Competition Council extended its assessment of what constituted economic progress to environmental concerns: "... the development of economic progress may also be qualified by a contribution to the fight against pollution of the environment".

Nonetheless, in his decision, the Minister of the Economy approved this concentration without referring to environmental protection[89].

6. Final decision of the Minister of the Economy

The Minister of the Economy may prohibit a transaction, by way of a formal decision (*arrêté*). If he decides to approve a transaction, he may (i) approve the transaction without referring the matter to the Competition Council for an opinion, by way of a simple letter, (ii) impose conditions on the parties involved by way of a formal decision, or (iii) approve the transaction, by way of a simple letter, but subject to the condition that the parties comply with specific undertakings they may have submitted, at any time during the procedure, in order to compensate or attenuate restrictions on competition. Before rendering a formal decision, the Minister of the Economy must notify a proposal for such decision to the parties concerned, with a copy of the opinion of the Competition Council, and set a time period during which the parties may make observations (Article 30 of the 1986 Decree).

It should be noted that, unlike the EC Merger Regulation, French law and practice do not acknowledge any particular procedure for approval of restrictions ancillary to the concentration, such as non-competition clauses, confidentiality agreements or distribution and supply agreements in the case of joint ventures.

It is relatively rare that the Government prohibit outright a concentration. Of some 57 cases submitted to the formal control procedure between 1977 and mid-1998, 28 were approved with no conditions, 22 with conditions, and only 3 were prohibited outright[90].

It appears that, where possible, the Government favours partial divestment as a means of reducing the disadvantages of a concentration over outright prohibition. In the *Elf France* decision rendered on 10 May 1991, the Government noted that the acquisition by Elf France of two competing companies would create a dominant position in several regional markets which could limit the access of independent operators to oil supplies. The Government thus ordered that assets covering certain oil supply capacities be sold by the companies involved in the concentration to independent operators so as to safeguard the access of said independent operators to those supply capacities[91]. In another case, *Carrefour/Euromarché* in September 1991, in informal negotiations between the Government and the concerned parties which did not give rise to a formal review procedure, the Government approved Carrefour's purchase of Euromarché only after Carrefour agreed to sell off its stores in areas where the acquisition would lead to a dominant market position.

A more common Government response when faced with a concentration which may restrict competition is to apply conditions – short of partial divestment – which will alleviate the threat to competition. Such conditions include, *inter alia*, limiting the geographical market for a product, upholding independent marketing strategies for certain trademarks and separate distribution networks, and requiring periodic filing with the Minister of the Economy of status updates on compliance with the conditions.

Generally speaking, however, the Government favours the imposition of conditions which involve a one-time structural change, as in the *Elf France* and *Carrefour/Euromarché* cases mentioned above, over the monitoring of a company's behaviour. In the *CLT/Fun/M40* case of 1994, the Competition Council proposed a modification of the pricing scheme of the concerned undertakings, but the Minister of the Economy opposed this condition on the grounds that it was a purely behavioural measure that would require permanent monitoring of the companies' behaviour[92]. Since this decision, as of mid-1998, the Minister of the Economy had imposed conditions on some 7 transactions, 2 of which involved a partial divestment and 3 of which required some degree of monitoring of the participants' behaviour.

The conditions imposed on the parties to a concentration may also result from proposed commitments favourable to competition which the parties have submitted to the Minister of the Economy. If the Minister of the Economy has accepted the transaction subject to compliance by the parties with those commitments, any case of later non-compliance may give rise to penalties, but only after referral of the matter to the Competition Council for an opinion. It should be noted that proposed commitments may be submitted by the parties at any time during the concentration review procedure. For instance, in the 1997 *Callebaut/Barry* case, the Minister of the Economy imposed as a condition upon the concerned companies the obligation to carry out "structural changes" (no further indication given), although those proposed commitments had been submitted to the Minister of the Economy after the Competition Council had rendered a negative opinion concerning the contemplated transaction[93]. Such practice, although it may be criticised for its lack of transparency, has the advantage of providing more leverage to the Minister of the Economy in dealing with difficult cases.

Finally, it appears that the Minister of the Economy may deliberately elect to allow specific circumstances, such as international situations or mergers which have already been completed, to have an impact on his decision.

In international situations, when confronted with concentrations which have negative effects on competition in the French market, the Minister of the Economy generally neutralises those negative effects by imposing measures on the concerned undertakings instead of ordering an outright prohibition of the concentration. In accordance with the principle of territoriality, those measures are confined to the French territory. For example, in the *Sensormatic/Knogo* case, the Minister of the Economy ordered the parties to (i) modify their general conditions of sale, rental and maintenance *for France,* and (ii) commit not to use a specific technology *in France*[94]. It should be noted that the Competition Council had recommended an outright prohibition of the concentration. In the *Eurocom/Carat* case, the Minister of the Economy accepted a concentration by which Eurocom acquired control of Carat, both companies being active in the market of advertising space purchases on an international scale, subject to the condition that Eurocom and Carat would not group together those activities *in France*, except for advertising campaigns which would concern at the same time the French market and the markets of several other countries[95]. This decision was rendered in accordance with the opinion of the Competition Council. Finally, in the *Gillette/Eemland Marketing Services* case, in which Gillette acquired a decisive influence over Eemland, which owned the Wilkinson Sword brand, the Minister of the Economy ordered (i) Gillette to avoid having any influence over the distribution of Wilkinson Sword razors *in France*, and (ii) Eemland to cease distributing Wilkinson Sword razors itself *in France*. This decision was rendered in accordance with the opinion of the Competition Council[96].

The issue remains open whether the full exercise by the Minister of the Economy of the power to control concentrations in France is somewhat hindered by the existence of an optional, rather than mandatory notification procedure. Since there is no principle of prior approval, mergers are often completed before notification or before the Minister of the Economy has taken the initiative to control an unnotified merger. In the *Sensormatic/Knogo* case, the Minister of the Economy elected not to prohibit a concentration which had been completed one year earlier without being notified[97]. This said, it should be noted that (i) the Minister of the Economy's reluctance to prohibit that particular transaction appeared to have been justified by the specific circumstances of the case (following the transaction, the undertakings involved had fully combined their business activities) and (ii) the Minister of the Economy did impose, in his decision, constraining measures on the combined entity, in order to attenuate the concentration's negative effects on competition. Moreover, the Minister of the Economy remains free to adopt a different approach in future decisions, since the 1986 Ordinance does not set forth any obstacles to a prohibition of concentrations.

Notes

1. *Cf.* Direction Générale de la Concurrence, de la Consommation et de la Répression des Fraudes ("DGCCRF"), *Méthode d'analyse pour le contrôle des concentrations*, 1992, pp.9-10.
2. Law of 1 August 1986, *Journal Officiel de la République Française* ("JORF"), 2 August 1986, and Law of 27 November 1986, JORF, 28 November 1986. For an example of application of the 1986 Ordinance to the Press sector, *cf.* Minister of the Economy, letter, 4 August 1993, *Société Générale Occidentale/le Point,* and opinion of the Competition Council, 6 July 1993, *Bulletin Officiel de la Concurrence, de la Consommation et de la Répression des Fraudes* ("BOCCRF"), 10 September 1993, p. 268.
3. DGCCRF, *Méthode d'analyse pour le contrôle des concentrations*, 1992, p. 11.
4. *Cf.* Minister of the Economy, letter, 19 December 1994, *CLT/Fun Radio/M40,* and opinion of the Competition Council, 15 November 1994, BOCCRF, 28 December 1994, p. 585.
5. In what follows, for purposes of simplification, reference will be made only to the Minister of the Economy. However, where appropriate in a decision-making context, this reference should also be understood as encompassing any other Government Ministers who share decision-making powers with the Minister of the Economy in any given case.
6. *Official Journal of the European Communities* (OJEC), 1989, L 395/1, corrigendum published OJEC, 1990, L 257/14, as modified.
7. Annual Report of the DGCCRF for 1996, p. 8.
8. *Ibid.*
9. F. Jenny (at the time, *rapporteur-général* of the Competition Council), *International Antitrust Law & Policy*, Fordham Corporate Law Institute, 1991, p. 120.
10. Figures obtained from Annual Reports of the Competition Council for the years 1992 to 1997.
11. Government instructions, 14 February 1978, BOSP, 17 February 1978, p. 82.
12. For a recent straightforward example of the structural change test, *cf.* Minister of the Economy, letter, 21 August 1998, *Elf Atochem/Air Liquide,* BOCCRF, 30 September 1998, p. 531, in which the acquisition of Elf's "hydrogen peroxide activity" was considered as being a transfer of ownership of assets, rights and obligations.
13. Competition Council, opinion, 12 January 1993, *Gaumont/Pathé,* and letter of the Minister of the Economy, 18 March 1993, BOCCRF, 26 March 1993, p.95.

14 Minister of the Economy, letter, 13 November 1996, *Kimberley Clark/Peaudouce*, BOCCRF, 27 December 1996, p. 627. Minister of the Economy, letter, 22 September 1998, *Solvay Pharma*, BOCCRF, 7 October 1998, p. 578.
15 DGCCRF, *Méthode d'analyse pour le contrôle des concentrations*, 1992, p. 11.
16 Government instructions, 14 February 1978, BOSP, 17 February 1978, p. 82.
17 Competition Council, opinion, 15 October 1991, *Gillette Company/Eemland Management Services*, and decision of the Minister of the Economy, 11 March 1992, BOCCRF, 1992, p. 84.
18 European Commission, decision, 10 November 1992, *Warner-Lambert/Gillette*, OJEC 1992, No. L 116/21.
19 Competition Council, opinion, 11 July 1995, *De Dietrich/GEC Alsthom/Ferromeca*, and letter of the Minister of the Economy, 3 August 1995, BOCCRF, 8 September 1995, p. 369.
20 *Cf.* Competition Council, opinion, 9 July 1996, *Brasserie Fischer/Sogebra*, and decision of the Minister of the Economy, 20 August 1996, BOCCRF, 25 March 1997, p. 171, in which the acquisition of a 54.4% shareholding interest was held to be a concentration because it conferred 74.8% of the voting rights.
21 *Cf.* Competition Council, opinion, 14 October 1997, *Henkel/Loctite Corp*, and letter of the Minister of the Economy, 6 November 1997, BOCCRF, 28 February 1998, p. 87.
22 *Cf.* Competition Council, opinion, 20 June 1995, *Total Raffinage Distribution*, and letter of the Minister of the Economy, 21 July 1995, BOCCRF, 25 August 1995, p. 329: acquisition of a 31.81% shareholding interest.
23 DGCCRF, *Méthode d'analyse pour le contrôle des concentrations*, 1992, p. 15.
24 Competition Commission, opinion, 26 February 1981, *Grange Frères*, and decision of the Minister of the Economy, 10 March 1981, BOSP, 11 March 1981, p. 63.
25 Competition Council, opinion, 22 March 1988, *Saint Louis S. L. B*, and decision of the Minister of the Economy, 13 April 1988, BOCCRF, 16 April 1988, p. 95.
26 DGCCRF, *Méthode d'analyse pour le contrôle des concentrations*, 1992, p. 15.
27 Competition Council, opinion, 15 October 1991, *Gillette Company/Eemland Management Services*, and decision of the Minister of the Economy, 11 March 1992, BOCCRF, 1992, p. 84.
28 Competition Council, opinion, 1 July 1997, *Carrefour*, and letter of the Minister of the Economy, 29 July 1997, BOCCRF, 7 October 1997, p. 685.
29 Minister of the Economy, letter, 25 March 1998, *Renault Véhicules*, BOCCRF, 15 May 1998, p. 215.
30 Competition Council, opinion, 26 April 1988, *Henkel France/Colgate Palmolive*, Annual Report for 1988, p. 154.
31 Competition Council, opinion, 10 July 1990, *Médiavision Cinéma/Circuit A*, Annual Report for 1990, p. 184.
32 Competition Council, opinion, 12 June 1990, *Sociétés Générales Sucrières Commerciale Sucre Union/Sucre Union Distribution*, Annual Report for 1990, p. 176.
33 Government instructions, 14 February 1978, BOSP, 17 February 1978, p. 82.
34 DGCCRF, *Méthode d'analyse pour le contrôle des concentrations*, 1992, pp. 15-16.
35 Court of Cassation (Commercial Chamber), 26 November 1996, *Bull. civ.* IV, No. 291.
36 Minister of the Economy, decision, 19 June 1984, *Cabot/Ashland*, and opinion of the Competition Commission, 10 May 1984, BOSP, 22 June 1984, p. 182.

37 *Cf., inter alia*, Minister of the Economy, decision, 11 March 1992, *Gillette/Eemland Management Services*, and opinion of the Competition Council, 15 October 1991, BOCCRF, 14 March 1992, p. 84.
38 Government instructions, 14 February 1978, BOSP, 17 February 1978, p. 82.
39 DGCCRF, *Méthode d'analyse pour le contrôle des concentrations*, 1992, p. 28.
40 Competition Council, opinion, 20 June 1995, *Total Raffinage Distribution*, and letter of the Minister of the Economy, 21 July 1995, BOCCRF, 25 August 1995, p. 329.
41 Competition Council, opinion, 9 May 1995, *Exide/CEAC*, and letter of the Minister of the Economy, 9 June 1995, BOCCRF, 25 July 1995, p. 295.
42 Competition Council, opinion, 9 November 1993, *Prodirest/Discol*, and letter of the Minister of the Economy, 3 December 1993, BOCCRF, 11 December 1993, p. 339.
43 DGCCRF, *Méthode d'analyse pour le contrôle des concentrations*, 1992, p. 20.
44 For a recent example, *cf.* Minister of the Economy, letter, 29 July 1997, *Ruggieri/Lacroix*, BOCCRF, 30 August 1997, p. 577.
45 Competition Council, opinion, 10 July 1990, *Eurocom/Carat*, BOCCRF, 4 September 1990, p. 349.
46 Competition Council, opinion, 14 October 1997, *Henkel/Loctite*, and letter of the Minister of the Economy, 6 November 1997, BOCCRF, 28 February 1998, p. 87.
47 Competition Council, opinion, 12 January 1993, *Gaumont/Pathé*, and decision of the Minister of the Economy, 18 March 1993, BOCCRF, 26 March 1993, p. 95.
48 Minister of the Economy, letter, 30 January 1996, *Legrand/Tehalit*, BOCCRF, 12 April 1996, p. 115.
49 Competition Council, opinion, 12 January 1993, *Gaumont/Pathé*, and decision of the Minister of the Economy, 18 March 1993, BOCCRF, 26 March 1993, p. 95.
50 For a recent example, *cf.* Competition Council, opinion, 5 May 1998, *Casino/Franxprix-Leader Price*, and letter of the Minister of the Economy, 30 May 1998, BOCCRF, 15 September 1998, p. 479.
51 Competition Council, opinion, 25 January 1994, *Epeda/Merinos*, and letter of the Minister of the Economy, 22 February 1994, BOCCRF, 8 March 1994, p. 81.
52 Competition Council, opinion, 16 November 1993, *Continental Pet*, and letter of the Minister of the Economy of 16 December 1993, BOCCRF, 1993, p. 351.
53 Competition Council, opinion, 29 July 1998, *Coca-Cola/Pernod Ricard*, and decision of the Minister of the Economy, 17 September 1998, BOCCRF, 7 October 1998, p. 555.
54 However, for a case *contra:* Minister of the Economy, letter, 5 May 1995, *Bayer/Florasynth*, BOCCRF, 16 June 1995, p. 197.
55 Competition Council, opinion, 31 January 1989, *Nestlé SA/Rowntree*, BOCCRF, 22 February 1989, p. 43.
56 Competition Council, opinion, 20 September 1994, *Holdercim/Cedest*, and decision of the Minister of the Economy, 4 October 1994, BOCCRF, 1994, p. 458.
57 Competition Council, opinion, 12 January 1993, *Gaumont/Pathé*, and decision of the Minister of the Economy, 18 March 1993, BOCCRF, 26 March 1993, p. 95.
58 Minister of the Economy, letter, 5 January 1998, *SOGELFA*, BOCCRF, 30 June 1998, p. 367.
59 DGCCRF, *Méthode d'analyse pour le contrôle des concentrations*, 1992, p. 57.
60 Competition Council, opinion, 29 August 1995, *Sensormatic/Knogo*, and decision of the

Minister of the Economy, 12 December 1995, BOCCRF, 12 February 1996, p. 21.
61 *Cf.* annual reports of the Competition Council and of the Competition Commission for the years 1977 to 1997.
62 DGCCRF, *Méthode d'analyse pour le contrôle des concentrations*, 1992, p. 63.
63 Competition Council, opinion, 1 July 1997, *Carrefour*, and letter of the Minister of the Economy, 29 July 1997, BOCCRF, 7 October 1997, p. 685.
64 The letter was not officially published in the BOCCRF. Presumably the case fell within the "two-thirds" exception set forth in Article 1 and thus outside the scope of the EC Merger Regulation.
65 For a recent example: Minister of the Economy, letter, 5 January 1998, *SOGELFA*, BOCCRF, 30 June 1998, p. 367, in which the Minister of the Economy reviewed an acquisition of shares between undertakings active in the storage of petrol products (to the extent that this activity took place in local markets in France).
66 *Cf.* Minister of the Economy, decision, 17 September 1998, *Coca-Cola/Pernod Ricard*, BOCCRF, 7 October 1998, p. 555, in which three decisions of the European Commission are mentioned.
67 *Cf.* Competition Council, opinion, 31 August 1998, *CGE/Havas*, BOCCRF, 7 October 1998, p. 565.
68 DGCCRF, *Méthode d'analyse pour le contrôle des concentrations*, 1992, pp. 35-51.
69 Competition Council, Annual Report for 1996, p. 93.
70 DGCCRF, *Méthode d'analyse pour le contrôle des concentrations*, 1992, p. 32.
71 Competition Council, opinion, 19 March 1991, *Les Fils de Jules Bianco/Elf France*, and decision of the Minister of the Economy, 10 May 1991, BOCCRF, 11 May 1991, p. 129.
72 Minister of the Economy, decision, 17 September 1998, *Coca-Cola/Pernod Ricard*, and opinion of the Competition Council, 29 July 1998, BOCCRF, 7 October 1998.
73 Competition Council, opinion, 13 September 1994, *Codes Rousseau/Media Communication*, and decision of the Minister of the Economy, 7 October 1994, BOCCRF, 20 October 1994, p. 455.
74 Competition Council, opinion, 31 August 1998, *CGE/Havas*, BOCCRF, 7 October 1998, p. 565.
75 Minister of the Economy, letter, 9 September 1998, *CGE/Havas*, BOCCRF, 7 October 1998, p. 565.
76 Competition Commission, opinion, 22 March 1979, *Vallourec/Les Tubes de la Providence*, BOSP, 19 May 1979, p. 139.
77 Competition Commission, opinion, 10 May 1984, *Cabot/Ashland*, and decision of the Minister of the Economy, 19 June 1984, BOSP, 22 June 1984, p. 182.
78 Conseil d'Etat, *Société Cabot Corporation*, 22 May 1985, *Rec.*, 1985, p. 158.
79 Competition Council, opinion, 14 November 1997, *Henkel/Loctite*, and letter of the Minister of the Economy, 6 November 1997, BOCCRF, 28 February 1988, p. 87.
80 Minister of the Economy, letter, 6 February 1998 *Thomson/CSF*, BOCCRF, 13 March 1998, p. 115.
81 Competition Council, opinion, 31 August 1998, *CGE/Havas*, BOCCRF, 7 October 1998, p. 565.
82 Competition Council, opinion, 29 July 1998, *Coca-Cola/Pernod Ricard*, and decision of the Minister of the Economy, 17 September 1998, BOCCRF, 7 October 1998, p. 555.

83 Minister of the Economy, letter, 20 February 1997, *Canal Plus*, BOCCRF, 29 April 1997, p. 305.
84 Competition Council, opinion, 29 July 1998, *Coca-Cola/Pernod Ricard*, and decision of the Minister of the Economy, 17 September 1998, BOCCRF, 7 October 1998, p. 555.
85 Competition Council, opinion, 31 January 1996, *Seiko-Seiki*, and decision of the Minister of the Economy, 22 May 1996, BOCCRF, 20 August 1996, p. 415.
86 Competition Commission, opinion, 22 March 1979, *Vallourec/Les Tubes de la Providence*, and decision of the Minister of the Economy, 16 May 1979, BOSP, 19 May 1979, p. 139.
87 Competition Council, opinion, 15 November 1997, *MAAF/DEKRA*, and letter of the Minister of the Economy, 6 November 1997, BOCCRF, 29 January 1998 p. 3; Competition Council, opinion, 14 January 1997, *EBS/CFS*, and letter of the Minister of the Economy, 5 February 1997, BOCCRF, 29 April 1997, p. 295.
88 Minister of the Economy, letter, 17 February 1998, *Monoprix*, BOCCRF, 15 May 1998, p. 215.
89 Competition Council, opinion, 17 May 1994, *Metaleurop/Heubach & Lindgens*, and letter of the Minister of the Economy, 14 June 1994, BOCCRF, 14 July 1994, p. 264.
90 The remaining four cases were deemed to fall outside the scope of review. *Cf.* annual reports of the Competition Council (and, until 1986, of its predecessor, the Competition Commission) for the years 1977 to 1997.
91 Minister of the Economy, decision, 10 May 1991, *Les Fils de Jules Bianco/Elf France*, BOCCRF, 11 May 1991, p. 129.
92 Minister of the Economy, letter, 19 December 1994, *CLT/Fun/M40*, BOCCRF, 28 December 1994, p. 585.
93 Minister of the Economy, decision, 5 February 1997, *Callebaut/Barry*, and opinion of the Competition Council, 7 February 1997, BOCCRF, 7 May 1997, p. 307.
94 Minister of the Economy, decision, 12 December 1995, *Sensormatic/Knogo*, and opinion of the Competition Council, 25 August 1995, BOCCRF, 12 February 1996, p. 21.
95 Minister of the Economy, decision, 3 September 1990, *Eurocom/WCRS/Carat Espace*, and opinion of the Competition Council, 10 July 1990, BOCCRF, 4 September 1990, p. 349.
96 Minister of the Economy, decision, 11 March 1992, *Gillette/Eemland Management Services*, and opinion of the Competition Council, 15 October 1991, BOCCRF, 14 March 1992.
97 Minister of the Economy, decision, 12 December 1995, *Sensormatic/Knogo*, and opinion of the Competition Council, 25 August 1995, BOCCRF, 12 February 1996, p. 21.

Federal Republic of Germany

Dr. Thomas Jestaedt

Dr. Martin Sura

Contents

Introduction	192
1. Definition of concentration	193
1.1. Overview	193
1.2. General: merger control applies to "enterprises" only	194
1.3. Merger by acquisition of assets	194
1.4. Merger by acquisition of shares	195
1.5. Merger by acquisition of control	197
1.6. Merger by exercise of influence which is substantial as regards competition	198
1.7. Exceptions	200
2. Joint Ventures	201
3. Notification thresholds/jurisdiction issues	202
3.1. Basic turnover thresholds for German merger control to apply	202
3.2. Effect of mergers in Germany, in particular: Foreign-to-foreign mergers	202
3.3. De minimis thresholds for exceptions from German merger control	203
3.4. Specific thresholds for newspaper/magazine publishing and broadcasting	203
3.5. Reasons for changes of relevant turnover thresholds	204
3.6. Method of calculating turnover	205
4. Notification/sanctions	206
4.1. Mandatory pre-merger notification without official form	206
4.2. Content of notification	206
4.3. Exception from notification requirement: Referral by European Commission	207
4.4. Sanctions	208
5. No time-limits for notifications	209
6. Procedure	210
6.1. Time-frame and standstill obligation	210
6.2. Imposition of conditions/undertakings by clearance decision	211
6.3. Fees charged by the BKartA	211

    6.4. Written statement of reasons: increased transparency 212
    6.5. Third party rights 212
7. Substantive test: dominance 213
    7.1. General rule: Prohibition of dominant positions/possibility
         to override anti-competitive effects of merger 213
    7.2. Creation of market dominance or strengthening of an
         already existing position of market dominance 214
    7.3. Presumption of market dominance 217
    7.4. Possibility to override: Balancing clause 218
8. Competent authorities 219
    8.1. Federal Cartel Office (Bundeskartellamt, BKartA) 219
    8.2. Approval by Federal Minister of Economics 219
    8.3. Judicial review 220
Summary 221
Annex 1 224
Annex 2 232
    Notes 235

Introduction

The main source of merger control legislation in Germany is the Act Against Restraints of Competition of 1958 (*Gesetz gegen Wettbewerbsbeschränkungen,* GWB [1]), which was amended for the sixth time on 26 August 1998[2]. The amendment took effect on 1 January 1999. One of the main areas of change were the rules on merger control in sections 35 to 43[3].

Merger control has existed in the Federal Republic of Germany since 5 August 1973 when the merger control provisions of the GWB entered into force[4]. Until 31 December 1998, merger control in Germany was characterised by a two-tier system providing for both substantive post-merger and pre-merger control depending on the size of the transaction. The principal aims[5] of the Sixth Amendment to the GWB in the area of merger control were:
- to abolish substantive post-merger control and to set forth new (lower) turnover thresholds for pre-merger notifications (thus extending the scope of substantive pre-merger control as the only form of control along the lines of the merger control system under the European Merger Control Regulation, EMCR);
- to "streamline" the German rules that described six different forms of merger events (as opposed to the broad concept of "acquisition of control" under Article 3 EMCR) by reducing them to four merger events only (one of them now being modelled on the "acquisition of control" principle of the EMCR); and
- to provide for a more transparent procedure by creating an obligation for the Federal Cartel Office (*Bundeskartellamt*, BKartA) to give a reasoning not only when a merger is prohibited, but also when a merger is cleared (in second phase proceedings), and to simultaneously provide for *locus standi* to third parties in this case.

The following features of the "old" German merger control system were not, however, affected by the Sixth Amendment:
- the substantive test criterion for prohibition of a merger, i.e. the question of whether a merger will result in creating or strengthening a market dominant position of either a single company or an oligopoly; and
- the possibility for the Federal Minister of Economics to approve a prohibited merger (if anti-competitive effects of a merger are balanced by overall economic advantages or if the merger is justified by an overriding public interest).

1. Definition of concentration

1.1. Overview

Section 37 now combines the former concept of an exhaustive list of merger events and the broad concept of "acquisition of control" of the EMCR (Article 3(3)). The following specific situations continue to be considered a "merger":
- the acquisition of the assets of another enterprise as a whole or to a significant extent, section 37(1)(1)[6];
- the acquisition of shares in another enterprise if such shares alone or together with other shares already belonging to the transferee represent 50% or 25% of the capital or of the voting rights of the target, section 37(1)(3) (a) and (b)[7];
- any relationship between or among enterprises whereby one or several enterprises are enabled to exercise directly or indirectly an influence on another enterprise which is substantial as regards competition, section 37(1)(4)[8].

Moreover, a "merger" will also be present in the case of:
- the acquisition of direct or indirect control by one or more enterprises over the entirety or parts of one or more other enterprises.

Such control can be based on rights, agreements, or other means that allow for the possibility (based on all factual and legal circumstances) of exercising a controlling influence on the activities of the enterprise, in particular ownership in the entirety or parts of the assets of an enterprise, or rights or agreements that allow for a controlling influence on the composition, deliberations, and decisions of governing bodies of an enterprise. This rule corresponds to the concept of Article 3(3) EMCR and is new in the system of German merger control as it lays down a broad principle of control. The "old" GWB already provided for some rules[9] that described situations where an acquisition of control occurs. The Sixth Amendment has eliminated these rules as these situations will now automatically be included in the broad concept of section 37(1)(2)[10] (according to the view expressed by the German Government in the Statement of Reasons at p. 44 and p. 58).

1.2. General: merger control applies to "enterprises" only

Only enterprises (as opposed to private individuals or to the state which exercises public functions) come within the scope of German merger control rules. However, the GWB interprets the notion of enterprise (*Unternehmen*) in a broad sense to include corporations and other business entities such as sole proprietorships or partnerships not having legal personality, associations and groups of companies, state-owned enterprises, regions or municipalities that participate in the economic process (e.g. through subsidiaries of municipalities), public law broadcasting stations or broadcasting corporations, and individuals that hold a majority participation in an enterprise[11].

1.3. Merger by acquisition of assets

The acquisition of assets may occur by way of agreement on the sale and transfer of assets, but also by way of transfer of assets as a result of a liquidation of a company or the dissolution of a joint venture, as well as by merger (*Verschmelzung*) or transformation (*Umwandlung*). The assets of the transferring (or of the entirely acquired) enterprise are all material or immaterial goods such as rights or legal positions. Even the possibility of acquiring certain rights may constitute "assets" on condition that they have a monetary value, i.e. are traded or tradable in economic life, such as a trademark, copyright or publishing rights in a publishing house. Typical examples of assets would be production facilities or plants of a company.

If all the assets of another company are acquired, it is clear that a merger has occurred. However, if this is not the case, it needs to be determined whether the assets acquired are a substantial part of the assets of the transferring company. In the absence of a broad concept of acquisition of control such as in Article 3(3) EMCR, before 1 January 1999, it was emphasised by German case-law and scholars that under German merger control the mere acquisition of a large amount of assets did not necessarily constitute a merger within the meaning of the German rules, if the assets acquired were not "substantial". As the broad concept of acquisition of control has now been introduced into German law, it remains to be seen if the question of whether the acquired assets form a substantial part will continue to be important in Germany. This issue is one of the reasons why German scholars and practitioners have criticised the Sixth Amendment because it might lead to an unclear coexistence of the broad concept of acquisition of control and certain specified (narrower) merger events.

When determining whether assets form a substantial part of an enterprise, German courts apply a test based on both quantitative and qualitative criteria. The quantitative criterion is met if the assets acquired correspond to a large proportion of the total assets of the transferor. For the qualitative criterion German courts look to whether the assets acquired form a separate or distinct entity with its own specific business purpose (e.g. production or marketing purpose). This requirement will be met if the acquisition of assets allows the purchaser to change its position in the market, e.g. by assuming the transferor's market position. Therefore, the acquisition of an independently functioning business operation or business establishment (*Betriebsstätte*) will be considered as an acquisition of a substantial part of the assets and hence be a merger. The same would apply to portions of businesses that are restructured following the transaction so as to become an independently functioning business operation. The following assets have been considered to be a substantial part of the business of the target:

- three retail stores in a major German city[12],
- the lease contracts as well as orders in hand, subscribers and copyright and publishing rights of an advertising publication[13],
- the organic pigments business of the transferor[14],
- the cement plant of a large steel producer[15],
- three small production plants on condition that the transferor ceases to compete on the relevant market thereby influencing market conditions[16], and
- a trademark together with the corresponding business documentation such as customer lists and advertising material[17].

1.4. Merger by acquisition of shares

The acquisition of shares in a company (which is by far the form of merger most frequently notified in Germany) will be considered a merger under German merger control rules if, together with those shares that the transferee already holds in the company, the acquisition results in a shareholding of 50% or of 25% of the shares or of the voting rights. In the event of successive acquisitions of shares, a merger will, therefore, occur each time the thresholds of 25% and 50% of the share capital or voting rights are reached. The acquisition of shareholdings of more than 50% come within the scope of the merger event of acquisition of (sole or joint) control pursuant to section 37(1)(2)[18] (see below 1.5).

The "old" GWB contained a provision[19] under which merger control was also extended to transactions not resulting in the acquisition of 25% of the share capital but involving voting rights that correspond to those of a minority shareholder that holds more than 25% of the voting capital. This rule was meant to catch attempts to circumvent the merger control provisions. It was not included in the Sixth Amendment to the GWB because these situations were deemed caught as of 1 January 1999 by either the broad concept of acquisition of control in section 37(1)(2) or by the "catch-all clause" in section 37(1)(4) (see Statement of Reasons at p. 58).

The acquisition of shares may relate to both corporations (*Kapitalgesellschaften*) and partnerships not having legal personality (*Personengesellschaften*) to the extent that the latter have partnership interests. The acquisition of shares may result from an agreement on the sale and assignment of shares or from legal provisions or provisions laid down in the articles of association of a corporation regarding accrual of shares in the case of partnerships (e.g. under section 738 German Civil Code, *Bürgerliches Gesetzbuch*, BGB) or regarding the redemption of shares in a private limited company (*Gesellschaft mit beschränkter Haftung*, GmbH).

The acquisition of minority shareholdings of 25% or more is subject to merger control because such shareholdings typically trigger a specific influence on the company by the minority shareholder. It depends, however, on the substantive test (see below 7.2) to decide whether a mere minority shareholding leads to the creation or strengthening of a market dominant position (e.g. through an increase of entrepreneurial resources).

When calculating the share percentage that may trigger merger control, it is not only those shares that are held by the transferee that will be taken into consideration. Those shares in the target company that are held by affiliated undertakings of the transferee[20] as well as those shares that third parties hold in trust for the transferee or, if the owner of the transferee is a sole proprietor, other shares which are held by the sole proprietor (section 37(1)(3)(2)) must be taken into account as well. Shares held by third parties, in particular trustees, will be imputed to the transferee if e.g. pursuant to the contractual relationship between transferee and trustee it is the former that carries the economic risk of the trustee's shareholding, or if the trustee is subject to instructions by the transferee regarding the exercise of rights linked to the shareholding. The same applies if the transferee can exercise an option to acquire the shares from the trustee[21].

1.5. Merger by acquisition of control

One of the reasons for introducing the broad concept of acquisition of control laid down in Article 3(3) EMCR into the German GWB was that the flexibility of this concept allows all situations to be dealt with where an entrepreneurial influence is acquired over a target company. In order to balance the negative aspects of the broad concept, i.e. the uncertainty as to its exact scope (which depends very much on the individual circumstances of a case as well as on the decision practice of the European Commission) it was, however, deemed necessary to maintain other more precise descriptions of merger events in the German rules on merger control.

The Federal Government admitted, however, in the Statement of Reasons for the Sixth Amendment that in many cases in the future these two concepts could overlap in the future. For instance, the acquisition of a majority of shares almost always constitutes acquisition of control. Also, the Statement of Reasons expressly specified that it was anticipated that the BKartA would apply the broad concept of acquisition of control along the lines of the well-established case-law of both the European Commission and the Luxembourg courts.

The concept encompasses both sole and joint control. Therefore, a merger will be deemed to be present where one or several companies obtain a significant degree of influence over another. Normally, such influence is obtained by acquisition of shares. Minority shareholdings as such are, however, not sufficient (unlike under the German concept outlined above) but have often been construed as joint control by the Commission. Moreover, control can be obtained also through the acquisition of assets or through financing, technical assistance, franchise, supply or similar arrangements. It has already been pointed out above (under 1.3) that it remains to be seen to what extent the "coexistence" of two different concepts of a merger event will lead to changes to the BKartA's and the courts' practice developed under the "old" GWB (in particular regarding asset deals where the acquired assets needed to be "substantial" up to 31 December 1998 for a merger to be present).

1.6. Merger by exercise of influence which is substantial as regards competition

This rule is meant to apply to situations that fall short of the above thresholds or that do not constitute acquisition of control but nonetheless meet concern from a merger control standpoint. It was not introduced into the GWB until the Fifth Amendment in 1989[22]. It relates, for example, to situations where a minority shareholding (below 25%) is linked to particular rights to information or participation of the shareholder that put him into a position to influence the behaviour of the enterprise in the market. In the past, the corresponding "old" provision was applied to cases where the acquisition of shares was effected by several companies that co-operated with each other, or, for example, by members of the same family, if the result was a majority shareholding of the various companies or family members in the aggregate.

The first case where the BKartA prohibited a merger based on the "old" provision was *Gillette/Wilkinson*[23]. *Gillette* wished to acquire the *Wilkinson* business of *Stora*. Because of merger control concerns, the European *Wilkinson* activities of *Stora* were contributed into a holding company in which *Wilkinson* held 22.9% of the shares. The other shares were held by banks and other investors. The financing of *Wilkinson's* acquisition by the holding company was secured by *Gillette*, which could influence both the financial resources and the structure of liabilities of the holding. Moreover, *Gillette* had rights of first refusal regarding the shares in the holding and had concluded various exclusivity and delimitation agreements with *Wilkinson*. This network of shareholdings and other ancillary agreements was found to give *Gillette* a substantial influence on *Wilkinson*.

Another example was the prohibition of the acquisition of *Kolbenschmidt* by *T & N*[24]. The acquisition was split into various transactions. First, a shareholding slightly lower than 25% of the share capital in *Kolbenschmidt* was acquired by a bank with the approval of *T & N*, which was granted an option to acquire this shareholding. Under the option agreement with the bank, *T & N* was under an obligation to reimburse any difference between the purchase price paid by the bank and the price to be obtained by a third party transferee in the event that *T & N* did not exercise its option. As *T & N* bore the economic risk linked to the bank's shareholding, the BKartA imputed this shareholding directly to *T & N*. As the participation in *Kolbenschmidt's* annual shareholders' meetings moreover, was clearly lower than 100%, the shareholding of almost 25% was held to give *T & N* the factual position of a minority shareholder with a blocking minority.

A third example was the prohibition of the acquisition of almost 25% in *Stadtwerke Bremen AG* by a company of the *VEBA* Group[25]. This prohibition was *inter alia* based on the fact that both parties concerned were utilities with neighbouring territories which might have affected competition between *Stadtwerke Bremen AG* and the *VEBA* Group. Another consideration was that through its shareholding, the *VEBA* company acquired access to a co-ordination committee within *Stadtwerke Bremen AG* where the considerable know-how of the *VEBA* Group in energy and economic matters could be used to influence the co-shareholders.

Finally, the BKartA prohibited the acquisition of 24% of the shares in the press retailer S*tilke* by the publishing house *Axel Springer*[26]. Under the articles of association of *Stilke*, *Axel Springer* was given extensive information rights, but no blocking minority. The only other shareholder holding 76% in *Stilke* had a right to withdraw from the company if *Axel Springer* was prohibited from becoming shareholder in *Stilke*. The BKartA argued that this showed that the other shareholder expected a specific entrepreneurial behaviour from *Axel Springer* thus granting *Axel Springer* considerable freedom to influence the business activities of *Stilke*, in particular the distribution of its own products by *Stilke*.

The above examples show that it may be quite difficult to assess whether a merger within the meaning of section 37(1)(4) GWB is present. For this reason, this type of merger event was exempted from pre-merger control under the old law[27]. This exemption was abolished by the Sixth Amendment. Therefore, the obligation to file a pre-merger notification (see below 4.1), and the prohibition from consummating a merger before it is cleared by the BKartA as well as the corresponding sanction of voidness of any infringing transaction (see below 4.4.3) place a considerable burden on companies and on their counsel in situations where it is unclear whether the requirements of this merger event are met by a transaction. In cases of doubt a notification should be made as a precaution.

1.7. Exceptions

1.7.1. Transactions between affiliated companies, restructuring of groups

Transactions in situations where the participating companies were already affiliated due to a prior merger or where a group of companies is restructured only internally normally fall outside the scope of merger control. Section 37(2) clarifies that such a situation will be a merger only if the transaction (e.g. the transfer of a shareholding from one group company to another) leads to a substantial strengthening of the already existing combination of companies[28]. A substantial strengthening will, of course, be present if in the course of the transaction a mere minority shareholding is increased to 50% or even beyond that (the second threshold in section 37(1)(3) would then be met). If the shareholding, however, remains unchanged and is simply transferred from one group company to another, a substantial strengthening may still result from an increase in the rights granted to a shareholder, e.g. due to the conclusion of a domination or of a transfer of profits and losses agreement. The (group) companies which participate in the transaction bear the burden of proof that section 37(2) applies in their favour, i.e. leads to the result that there is no merger present. In cases where it is doubtful whether a substantial strengthening may be the result of a transaction, it is advisable to file a notification as a precaution.

1.7.2. Acquisition of shares by banks etc.

Acquisitions of shares made by banks, other financial institutions or insurance companies for the purpose of subsequent assignment of the shares will not be considered as mergers, as long as no voting rights linked to the shares are exercised (section 37(3)). In addition, these transferees must assign the shares to third parties within one year for the exception to apply. This one-year deadline may be extended by the BKartA upon application if it is substantiated that no assignment could reasonably be made within the original deadline. This rule already existed for banks in the "old" GWB[29] and has now been extended to insurance companies and financial institutions other than banks along the lines of Article 3(5) EMCR.

2. Joint Ventures

Joint ventures may come within the scope of German merger control (section 37(1)(3)(3)). The creation of a joint venture company by either a simultaneous or successive acquisition of shares (meeting the 25%/50% thresholds) by more than one company is considered a merger of the shareholding companies in the markets of the joint venture company[30]. However, this rule, whose purpose is to deal with the so-called "group-effect" resulting from the creation of a joint venture, does not extend merger control to other business activities of the parent shareholders in the joint venture. Section 37(1)(3)(3), therefore, is a rule that provides for a so-called "partial" (horizontal) merger (in addition to the vertical mergers taking place between each parent shareholder and the joint venture company). In addition, the newly introduced concept of acquisition of control (section 37(1)(2)) expressly refers to acquisition of "joint" control and, consequently, also covers joint ventures.

It is worth noting that, according to the case-law of German courts and the BKartA, joint venture companies of a co-operative nature may simultaneously and independently from each other come within the scope of both the rules on merger control and of the general rules prohibiting restrictions of competition between companies (section 1 *et seq.*)[31]. A joint venture is regarded, as a general rule, as not infringing the restrictive practices provisions of the GWB if it is a so-called full-function joint venture acting as an independent market participant, if it is not exclusively or predominantly active in upstream or downstream markets of its parent companies, and if the parent companies are not active in the relevant product markets of the joint venture[32].

Unlike Article 2(4) EMCR (where the European Commission appraises co-ordination effects of notified joint ventures under Article 85(1) and (3) EC Treaty within the time-frame set by the EMCR) the BKartA will not investigate such potential anti-competitive effects of joint ventures within the deadlines for investigation under the German merger control rules[33]. Clearance of a joint venture by the BKartA under the merger control rules, therefore, does not prevent third parties from challenging joint ventures under the restrictive practices rules of the GWB.

3. Notification thresholds/jurisdiction issues

3.1. Basic turnover thresholds for German merger control to apply

Section 35 sets the thresholds that must be met for German merger control to be triggered[34], i.e. for an obligation to notify to exist. A merger will come within the scope of German merger control if:
- the participating companies have combined world-wide sales of more than DM 1 billion (section 35(1)(1)), i.e. of approx. € 510 million[35]; and
- at least one participating company has sales of more than DM 50 million in Germany, i.e. approx. € 25.5 million (section 35(1)(2)).

These turnover/sales thresholds must be met during the business year preceding the merger. The purpose of section 35(1)(2) is to exempt those mergers from German merger control that will only have marginal effects in Germany[36].

3.2. Effect of mergers in Germany, in particular: Foreign-to-foreign mergers

Section 35(1)(2) will be of particular relevance in cases where German companies are taken over by foreign companies or where foreign companies that have only minor business activities in Germany merge (foreign-to-foreign mergers[37]). The rule brings a helpful clarification compared to the situation before the Sixth Amendment. Under the "old" law, foreign mergers were subject to German merger control if they had an "effect" within Germany. However, the concept of "effect" was not precisely defined and, therefore, was interpreted by the BKartA on a case-by-case basis. The BKartA looked to whether a foreign-to-foreign merger could produce immediate and noticeable effects in Germany[38]. This criterion was, for example, held to be met where a foreign-to-foreign merger would lead to decreasing sales or production activities in Germany[39], or, in any event where (one of) the merging companies had subsidiaries in Germany.

Under section 35(1)(2) no German business establishment of the participating companies is required for German merger control to apply. Mere sales in

Germany (i.e. to customers located in Germany) made from abroad will suffice if they meet the threshold. If none of the participating (group of) companies achieves sales of more than DM 50 million/€ 25.5 million in Germany, the merger will be exempt from German merger control.

3.3. *De minimis* thresholds for exceptions from German merger control

Section 35 (2) provides for two exceptions from the scope of German merger control:
- A merger where one party is an independent company (i.e. a company not affiliated with other companies) that had world-wide sales of less than DM 20 million, i.e. approx. € 10.2 million, in the business year preceding the merger will be exempted[40]. This *de minimis* rule, however, does not apply to mergers in the newspaper/magazine publishing sector (including distribution) which is characterised by comparatively low turnover figures of many market participants.
- Also, no merger control will take place if a merger affects a *de minimis* market which has existed for at least five years and in which aggregate sales of less than DM 30 million, i.e. approx.€ 15.3 million, were generated in the last calendar year[41]. This exemption, however, applies only if no other markets exceeding the DM 30 million/ € 15.3 million threshold are affected by the same merger[42].

3.4. Specific thresholds for newspaper/magazine publishing and broadcasting

Specific thresholds apply to the newspaper and magazine publishing sector (including distribution) and the broadcasting sector (television and radio). Mergers between companies active in these areas come within the scope of merger control if the aggregate world-wide sales of the participating companies are at least DM 50 million, i.e. approx. € 25.5 million, and if at least one participating company achieved sales in Germany of more than DM 2.5 million, i.e. approx. € 1.28 million in the business year preceding the merger. This follows from section 38(3) which provides that with respect to newspaper and magazine publishing (including distribution) and broadcasting activities[43] the relevant turnover must be calculated by multiplying the effective turnover figure by 20 [44]. Therefore, mergers between companies in these areas with turnover figures that are considerably lower than the thresholds set forth in section 35(1) are caught by German merger control[45].

3.5. Reasons for changes of relevant turnover thresholds

Until 31 December 1998, German law distinguished between pre-merger notifications which had to be submitted before a transaction was closed, and post-merger notifications. Under these rules, a pre-merger notification was required where either one of the participating companies achieved a (world-wide) turnover of DM 2 billion, i.e. approx. € 1.02 billion or more or where at least two parties achieved a (world-wide) turnover of DM 1 billion, i.e. approx. €510 million, each. Post-merger notification was required where the participating companies achieved an aggregate (world-wide) turnover of at least DM 500 million, i.e. approx. € 255 million.

This former two-tier system was fundamentally changed by lifting the minimum turnover threshold which triggers merger control (from DM 500 million/approx. € 255 million to DM 1 billion/ € 510 million), and by simultaneously reducing the former applicable minimum thresholds for pre-merger notification by applying a uniform threshold of an aggregate turnover of more than DM 1 billion/ € 510 million.

According to the German Federal Government (Statement of Reasons at p. 43 *et seq.*) the purpose of lifting the threshold was to reduce the BKartA's workload. It has been estimated that about two-thirds of the mergers that were subject to post-merger notification up to 31 December 1998 (i.e. all mergers meeting the DM 500 million/ € 255 million threshold) would be outside the scope of merger control as of 1 January 1999. Moreover (and perhaps more importantly), efficient post-merger control had proved to be almost impracticable. Until 31 December 1998 it was possible for the BKartA to issue an order to dissolve a completed merger within one year after post-merger notification[46]. The legal and practical difficulties which resulted from such an order by the BKartA and the resulting risks for the parties involved were widely considered unsatisfactory.

In the past, it was widespread practice to voluntarily file a pre-merger notification (where the parties involved wished to avoid any uncertainty as to the validity of the transaction). Approximately 80% of all pre-merger cases were cleared by the BKartA within the initial one-month stage of the summary investigation.

3.6. Method of calculating turnover

Section 38 lays down the rules on how turnover must be calculated (and hence the market shares on which the investigation of the merger will to a large extent rely; see below under 7.).

Section 38(1)[47] provides that the turnover calculation is based on section 277(1) of the German Commercial Code (*Handelsgesetzbuch*, HGB) which states that "turnover" means all profits resulting from sales, rental, lease of products and goods or services reflecting the typical business of a company (exclusive of any reduction of proceeds and VAT). Any intra-group turnover (i.e. turnover generated between affiliated companies) will not be taken into consideration. Unlike the old rule, this new rule does not specify that turnover generated in foreign currencies must be converted into DM on the basis of the official exchange rate. This conversion will, however, undoubtedly have to be made in the future also[48]. The Statement of Reasons specified (at p. 58) that the basis for the conversion is the annual average exchange rate of the Frankfurt Stock Exchange.

For distribution (as opposed to production) companies only 75% of the turnover calculated on the above basis will be taken into account because mere distribution activities are less likely to be used to restrict competition (Statement of Reasons at p. 59). As far as publishing, production and distribution of newspapers, magazines and parts thereof and the production, broadcast and organisation of radio and TV programmes as well as the sale of radio and TV advertising time are concerned, the annual turnover has to be multiplied by 20 to obtain the relevant turnover; thus, these companies come within the scope of merger control even if they achieve only modest turnovers. This rule extends the "old" corresponding rule[49] beyond the scope of press publishing in order to adequately deal with the regionalisation of broadcasting markets (Statement of Reasons at p. 59)[50].

Section 38(4) provides for a specific method of calculating turnover for credit institutions and other financial institutions as well as for insurance undertakings which is based on certain types of revenue (e.g. from interest payments and commissions for credit institutions) as well as on gross premiums written for insurance undertakings. This calculation method is modelled on Article 5(3) EMCR.

In the case of an asset deal, only the portion of assets that are transferred has to be taken into consideration for the purpose of calculating turnover of the seller (section 38(5)).

4. Notification/sanctions

4.1. Mandatory pre-merger notification without official form

The BKartA must be notified of all mergers (that meet the turnover thresholds outlined above) prior to consummation (section 39(1)). Pre-merger notification is thus mandatory.

The obligation to notify is incumbent on all the companies participating in the merger as well as on the party that sells assets and/or shares to an acquiring party (section 39(2)). This obligation to notify must be discharged by the legal representatives of the companies. In practice, only one notification is made on behalf of all the participating companies or on behalf of one of these companies with the other participating companies consenting to the notification.

Unlike under the EMCR there is no official form for notifications[51]. The GWB limits itself to briefly describe the indispensable information to be provided in a notification. In simple and straightforward cases a notification may well only consist of a three- to five-page letter to the BKartA.

Business secrets contained in a notification will be kept confidential by the BKartA if they are specifically identified (unless it cannot be reasonably held that the information is confidential).

As with the "old" merger control system up to 31 December 1998, the participating companies are still under an obligation to notify the consummation of a merger immediately[52] (*Anzeige*). This *Anzeige*, which under the former system served substantive purposes in post-merger notification cases, now has exclusively statistical significance.

4.2. Content of notification

The notification must indicate the form of the merger (section 39(3)). In addition, the following information is mandatory with respect to each participating company:

- corporate name and other designation as well as place of business or corporate seat;
- the type of business;
- the turnover in Germany, in the European Union and world-wide[53]; with respect to credit and other financing institutions as well as insurance undertakings the particular calculation method laid down in section 38(4) must be applied;
- market shares together with the basis for their calculation or estimation; however, this indication is compulsory only where combined market shares of the participating companies have reached at least 20% in either the entire German market or in a substantial part thereof;
- in the case of an acquisition of shares in another company, the amount of shares acquired as well as of the aggregate shareholding;
- the designation of a person in Germany who is authorised to accept service on behalf of a participating company which does not have its seat in Germany[54].

If one participating company belongs to a group, the corporate name or other designation, the place of business or the corporate seat, as well as of the type of business must be indicated for all affiliated companies. Indications as to turnover and market shares must be made for a participating company and its whole group in the aggregate. In addition, precise information on the nature of the intra-group relations (e.g. means of exercise of control within the group, shareholdings in the group, etc.) must be provided[55].

The BKartA has the power to request information from the participating companies about market shares including the methods of their calculation and estimation as well as about the turnover regarding specific goods or services produced/rendered by the company in the business year preceding the merger.

4.3. Exception from notification requirement: Referral by European Commission

A notification will not be required if the European Commission refers a case to the BKartA under Article 9(2) EMCR. The purpose of this new rule is to reduce the burden on the companies linked to establishing a notification. However, the exception applies only if the information outlined above is available to the BKartA in the German language. The BKartA will immediately inform the participating companies on the date of receipt of the referral decision by the European Commission.

4.4. Sanctions

4.4.1. Incomplete notification

In the event that a notification does not contain the above elements, it will be considered incomplete by the BKartA. An incomplete notification does not trigger the deadlines of the merger control procedure. The BKartA will ask the notifying party instead to comprehensively provide the required information. Making an incomplete notification will, therefore, lead to longer proceedings and delay consummation of the transaction.

4.4.2. Failure to notify

Under section 81(1)(7), section 81(2) a fine of up to DM 50,000, i.e. approx. € 25,000, can be imposed if a merger is not notified at all, notified incompletely or if facts are misrepresented.

4.4.3. Prohibition to consummate

The most important sanction available in cases where no notification has been made can be found in section 41(1). This provision prohibits the consummation of mergers that are not cleared by the BKartA. Any legal transaction that infringes upon this prohibition is void. If the prohibition is infringed a fine of up to DM 1 million, i.e. approx. € 510,000, and beyond that of up to three times the economic benefit resulting from the infringement can be imposed under section 81(1)(1) and section 81(2).

Upon application, the BKartA may grant exemptions from the prohibition to consummate a merger if the participating companies put forward substantial reasons, in particular if an exemption avoids serious detriment to a participating company or a third party (section 41(2)). Such exemption may be granted at any point in time, even before the notification is made. The exemption may be made subject to conditions/undertakings. In case of non-compliance with these conditions/undertakings the exemption may be withdrawn. The Statement of Reasons specified (at p. 61) that situations where this provision may become

GERMANY

relevant are likely to be reorganisation mergers (*Sanierungsfusionen*) and foreign mergers, where the notification is incomplete and the notifying party substantiates that it is prevented by foreign law or other circumstances from providing the required information.

4.4.4. Dissolution of consummated mergers

By virtue of section 41(3), a consummated merger must be dissolved if it has been prohibited by the BKartA or if a clearance decision has subsequently been withdrawn by the BKartA (unless the Federal Minister of Economics has given its approval; see below under 8.2). The BKartA may order the measures which are necessary in respect of the dissolution of a merger. However, in this respect it will not necessarily be required to restore the *status quo ante*. Therefore, dissolution may be made, for example, through the sale of the relevant assets to a third party.

The BKartA may impose single or multiple fines (coercive payments) ranging between DM 10,000 and DM 1 million each in order to implement its orders that aim at dissolving a merger. The BKartA may also prohibit or restrict the exercise of voting rights, or appoint a trustee that is in charge of carrying out the dissolution (section 41(4)).

5. No time-limits for notifications

The GWB does not stipulate a time-limit for the filing of a notification[56] (except for the rule in section 39(1) that notification must be made prior to consummation). However, a merger must not be consummated before the BKartA has carried out its investigation (which may take up to four months as a general rule; straightforward cases will be cleared within one month from notification). Parties must, therefore, take this time-frame into account when planning a transaction.

Unlike Article 4(1) EMCR, no guidance is given in the GWB as to the point in time when notification must be filed[57]. Nor is there any indication as to the earliest point in time when a notification may be filed (if notification can be made while the transaction is still being negotiated the impact of waiting periods pending the BKartA's decision may be substantially reduced). Although the new law appears to deviate from the former situation where the "intention" to merge had to be notified (in scenarios falling within the scope of pre-merger

209

control[58]) by stating that "mergers" must be notified[59], the practice developed under the "old" law will continue[60]. In accordance with established practice, it was not acceptable to notify the BKartA of intended mergers that had not yet been put into concrete form by the negotiating parties (e.g. mergers envisioned by one party only). However, a signed agreement was not required for notification. As soon as the parties are in the position to provide the information required under section 39(3) (see above under 4.2) – most importantly the form of the merger and turnover and market share data – they can file a notification with the BKartA.

6. Procedure

6.1. Time-frame and standstill obligation

The BKartA may prohibit a merger only if it informs the notifying parties within one month of receipt of the notification that it has entered into an in-depth investigation of the matter (*Hauptprüfverfahren*, section 40(1)). The BKartA then has a period of four months (from receipt of the notification) to investigate the case. The in-depth or "second phase" investigation needs to be terminated by either a formal prohibition or a formal clearance decision by the BKartA (section 40(2)). If within this four-month deadline no decision is handed down (and duly served upon the parties participating in the proceedings) by the BKartA, the merger is deemed to be cleared (section 40(2)(2)), unless the notifying companies have consented to an extension of the deadline (or misrepresentations were made, requests for information were not duly answered, or there is no person authorised to accept service for a foreign company).

The in-depth investigation will, as a rule, commence only if the case so requires due to the complex nature and competition concerns. Cases that do not present problems are cleared at the initial stage by an informal clearance letter that is not subject to appeal[61].

Unless an exemption from the general prohibition to consummate a merger before clearance is granted (upon application)[62], the parties will have to suspend consummation until the investigation ends with a positive decision by the BKartA.

6.2. Imposition of conditions/undertakings by clearance decision

Pursuant to section 40(3) the BKartA can now impose conditions or undertakings in connection with clearance decisions under section 40(2). However, mere behavioural remedies must not be used in this context (section 40(3)(2)). No such rule was contained in the "old" GWB. It was, however, normal practice under the "old" law that remedies such as, for example, the restructuring of a transaction by divesting overlapping businesses (such remedies aimed to have a structural effect in the market) were used both prior to a clearance decision and in the form of undertakings to be implemented after the deadline for a prohibition of a merger by the BKartA had lapsed. Such undertakings were usually contained in a contract between the companies concerned and the BKartA which as a rule provided that in the event of non-performance the BKartA was free to re-enter the prohibition procedure or to immediately order the dissolution of the merger. However, it has proved to be difficult to enforce such an undertaking, once a merger has been fully consummated[63]. The new rule, therefore, serves to clarify the legal situation because in the event of non-fulfilment of a condition or non-compliance with an undertaking connected to a clearance decision such a decision would lose its effectiveness thus opening the way for the BKartA to prohibit the merger.

6.3. Fees charged by the BKartA

Any notification of a merger and any decision of the BKartA pursuant to a notification triggers administrative fees (section 80(1)) that must be borne jointly by the notifying parties. Section 80(2) limits the aggregate fees for a notification and the BKartA's corresponding decision to a maximum of DM 100,000 (i.e. approx. € 51,000) as a rule. The fees are assessed by the BKartA either in its decision on the merits (clearance or prohibition) or in a separate decision. The amount of the fee depends on both the amount of work triggered by the handling of a notification and the economic importance of the notified transaction (section 80(2)). If the amount of work triggered and the economic importance of the matter are extraordinarily high, the amount of the fee may be increased up to twice the above "normal" maximum fee (section 80(3)).

MERGER CONTROL IN THE EU

Hence, a maximum fee of DM 200,000 (i.e. approx. € 102,000) may be assessed in these cases.

The BKartA's decision assessing the fees contain a statement of reasons explaining which factors were taken into consideration when calculating the fees[64]. Straightforward cases where no second phase investigation is entered into will rarely trigger fees that exceed DM 10,000 to 20,000 (i.e. approx. € 5,100 to 10,200).

Measures taken by the BKartA under section 41 with respect to dissolving consummated mergers or to granting exemptions from the prohibition to consummate[65] may trigger separate fees to which the above limits also apply.

It is finally worth noting that in proceedings before the BKartA each party involved bears its own costs and expenses. These expenses (e.g. lawyer's fees) cannot be recovered from other parties involved (unlike in judicial review proceedings subsequent to a complaint against a decision by the BKartA[66]).

6.4. Written statement of reasons: increased transparency

Unlike under the "old" law not only prohibitions, but also "second phase" clearances will be made through formal decisions (section 40(2)(1)) which must contain a detailed statement of reasons[67] and must be published[68]. It is therefore expected that this will make merger decisions of the BKartA more transparent[69]. Until 31 December 1998, transparency and critical public discussion of cleared mergers were safeguarded to some extent only by the Main Expert Opinions (*Hauptgutachten*) published every two years by the Monopolies Commission (*Monopolkommission*)[70] as well as by the biannual reports on the activities of the BKartA (*Tätigkeitsbericht*)[71].

6.5. Third party rights

6.5.1. Challenge of clearance in court

Another result of the BKartA's duty to render a decision if it clears a merger is that third parties[72] may challenge clearances in court so as to obtain their annulment[73] (however, no action could be brought that aims to obtain a prohibition of a merger). Such a claim must be brought before the Higher Regional Court (*Oberlandesgericht,* OLG or *Kammergericht,* KG) of the seat of the BKartA (section 63(4)). As the BKartA is due to move from Berlin to

Bonn in 1999, venue for these actions will shift from the KG Berlin to the OLG Düsseldorf.

If a clearance decision is annulled by a court decision, a new four-month deadline for investigation starts to run when the court decision becomes final (section 40(6)).

6.5.2. Prerequisite for court action: participation in proceedings before BKartA

As the right to challenge the BKartA's decisions is limited to the parties involved in the procedure before the BKartA (section 63(2)), it is imperative for third party competitors to file an application with the BKartA to be admitted to the proceedings as interveners. Third parties will, upon application, qualify as interveners if their interests are materially affected by a pending merger (section 54(2)(3)). Usually, competitors, customers and suppliers which can show a specific economic interest in the outcome of the proceedings will fulfil this requirement. Although merger notifications are not officially published in Germany, the BKartA will confirm upon a specific inquiry (which can be made by telephone) that a merger notification has been filed in a particular case.

7. Substantive test: dominance

7.1. General rule: Prohibition of dominant positions/ possibility to override anti-competitive effects of merger

The BKartA must prohibit any merger which is certain to lead to either the creation of a market dominant position, or to the strengthening of an already existing market dominant position (section 36(1)). Therefore, the BKartA has no discretion regarding the prohibition of a merger.

However, the participating companies may prove that the merger will also lead to improvements in competitive conditions and that those improvements outweigh the detrimental effects of market dominance so as to avoid a prohibition by the BKartA (section 36(1)). Also, the Federal Minister of Economics has the power to approve a merger that was prohibited by the BKartA upon a corresponding application by the participating companies, if the restraints of competition that result from the merger are balanced by the overall economic benefits of the merger or are justified by an overriding public interest (section 42; see below under 8.2).

7.2. Creation of market dominance or strengthening of an already existing position of market dominance

7.2.1. Definition of market dominance

Market dominance is defined by the GWB in the context of the rules on abuse of market dominant positions[74]. This definition also applies to merger control. In this definition, a company is in a market dominant position as either a supplier of goods or services or as a customer:
- if it has no competitors or is not subject to any substantial competition; or
- if it has a superior market position in relation to its competitors; this assessment will be based on the following aspects:
    - market shares;
    - financial strength;
    - access to supply and sales markets;
    - corporate ties to other companies;
    - legal or factual barriers to market entry by other companies;
    - actual or potential competition by companies located either in Germany or abroad[75];
    - a capability to shift offer or demand to other goods or services;
    - the possibility of the other market side to switch to other companies.

Two or more companies are considered market dominant if together they fulfil the above criteria and if there is no substantial competition between them.

7.2.2. Assessment of market dominance

Section 36 (1) requires a prognosis about the likely results of a merger in the future. It is not necessary that such results are produced immediately. In practice this prognosis is based on empirical knowledge.

The structural elements of the market concerned will play a decisive role in this prognosis. Elements to be taken into consideration are the potential market entry of new companies or the likely departure of competitors from the market, technological innovation, changes in customer behaviour, the development of new markets, political changes etc. For the purposes of assessing conditions in the market, market shares and turnover of the participating companies will be added and resources of a parent company will be imputed to an affiliate.

However, structural changes of a market concerned will only be taken into consideration if they are actually caused by the merger. If the same result had occurred without the merger, the change in market conditions could not be seen as a consequence of the merger. One example is a so-called reorganisation merger (*Sanierungsfusion*), i.e. a situation where the target company would have gone bankrupt but for the merger so that the market shares of the bankrupt company would have accrued to the acquiring company anyway (because it is the only competitor in the market). In this example, the structural change in the market will not be seen as a result of the merger.

7.2.3. Creation of a market dominant position

A market dominant position will be created if as a result of a merger the conditions for substantial competition will in all likelihood disappear or if the merged entity acquires an independent scope of conduct, which will be present if its business decisions are no longer affected by the market behaviour of competitors. This analysis will be based on criteria such as market shares (which is the most important criterion), leading position *vis-à-vis* competitors, excess capacity of competitors or existence of potential competitors that are ready to enter the market. Also, the deterring effect of a merger on competitors may play a role. Conditions that affect all competitors in a market, as for example a strong position of the demand side or strong competition by substitution products, will not be taken into consideration.

Examples where the creation of a market dominant position were held to result from a merger are:
- a merger between the two leading companies in the market[76];
- the creation of a duopoly[77];
- the creation of an oligopoly as a result of a merger between the two leading companies[78].

As a rule, if combined market shares are below 20%, no creation of a market dominant position will result from a merger.

7.2.4. Strengthening of a market dominant position

This criterion for the assessment of whether a merger must be prohibited or not was far more relevant in German practice up to now than the above criterion of the creation of a market dominant position. The purpose of this criterion is to protect the residual competition in a market where a dominant position already exists. Therefore, even very slight changes in the elements that determine market power will lead to a prohibition if they result in increased restrictions for residual competition. An example is the elimination of potential competition from neighbouring markets. A strengthening does not necessarily require an increase of market shares. A merger of a German company having a quasi-monopoly in Germany with the world market leader which had, however, no sales at all in Germany was indeed held to lead to the strengthening of the German company's market dominant position (*inter alia* because the foreign acquiror ceased to be a potential competitor). The merger was, consequently, prohibited [79]. Each increase of a company's scope for independent conduct resulting from a structural change in the market will indeed be sufficient. The increase in resources for the merged entity is of particular relevance in this context as this criterion reflects an increase in the deterring potential resulting from a merger.

Other examples of the strengthening of a market dominant position are:
- the elimination of substitute competition coming from neighbouring markets mainly if the merged entity is – unlike its competitors – put into a position to offer all product ranges that are necessary to satisfy customer demand [80];
- the sale of the market dominant company from one parent to another if the acquiring parent is "closer" to the affected market thereby increasing the likelihood that its resources will be used for the purposes of the acquired entity [81];
- the acquisition of a remaining competitor by one member of a narrow oligopoly [82];
- the acquisition of a well-known trademark by the leading company in the market [83];
- every increase in the shareholding in another company as this shows an increased interest of the shareholder in its shareholding which also increases the likelihood that the shareholder's resources will be used for the purposes of the other company [84].

Even the acquisition of a very small competitor by the market leader may be relevant as this impedes other competitors from strengthening their position through the acquisition of this small competitor[85].

Potential deterring effects are of greater relevance for the strengthening than for creation of a market dominant position. The accumulation of resources on which the deterring effects theory is based will be taken into account in particular if the acquiring company has activities which are "close" to the affected market or if it pursues a business strategy of diversification as these elements show that the shareholding reflects business purposes which go beyond pure investment goals.

Finally, the strengthening of an existing market dominant position must be appreciable (although not substantial). The higher the degree of market concentration, the lower the requirements are for noticing a strengthening of an existing market dominant position. In highly concentrated markets, minor increases of market shares by 1%, for example, may suffice.

7.3. Presumption of market dominance

Under the following conditions set out by section 19(3), in the context of abuse of a dominant position, the existence of market dominance will be presumed by a way of a refutable presumption:
- if a company has a market share of at least one-third;
- if three or fewer companies together have an aggregate market share of at least 50%; or
- if five or fewer companies together have an aggregate market share of at least two-thirds.

These presumptions of either single or oligopolistic market dominance will, however, not apply if the company or companies concerned prove that based upon competitive conditions, substantial competition (in the case of an oligopoly between its members) may be expected or that it or the members of an oligopoly considered together do not possess a superior market position compared to other competitors. Proof of the latter situation may be successfully established if competitors are bigger or at least have more resources. Proof that substantial competition will exist may successfully be established if functioning competition on price or quality continues to exist, e.g. due to low market entry barriers, potential competition, substitute competition from neighbouring markets, terms of distribution, particular technologies or a high degree of technological innovation. In fact, in the vast majority of cases in the past, the notifying parties were able to successfully refute the presumption of market dominance.

7.4. Possibility to override: Balancing clause

The BKartA cannot prohibit a merger if the parties to a merger prove that it will (also) result in improvements of competitive conditions which outweigh detrimental effects of market dominance[86] (section 36(1)).

7.4.1. Improvement of competitive conditions

The improvements to be taken into account must have been caused by the merger, must be of a structural nature and must relate to competitive aspects (as opposed to the elements that have to be taken into account for ministerial approval under section 42 GWB, which may well have a "general interest" nature). As the GWB does not specify in which market the improvements must be realised, the BKartA as a rule first compares negative consequences as well as improvements resulting from the merger in the same market and secondly looks at whether other improvements have occurred in third markets.

7.4.2. Balancing

The improvements must outweigh the detrimental effects of a merger. The application of this test is usually very difficult. An easy solution may be found where for example negative effects in comparatively small markets concur with substantial improvements in important markets.

7.4.3. Examples

An improvement of competitive conditions will be held to exist if, for example, the foundation of a joint venture in a neighbouring market to a market which is highly concentrated will lead to the creation of substitute competition as may be the case in energy markets if a new joint venture will compete with oil suppliers through the supply of gas[87]. Likewise, a relevant improvement may occur if a merger leads to the entry of a powerful competitor in a highly concentrated market. Another example may be a case where market entry cannot be made by one company alone[88]. In the case of a reorganisation merger (*Sanierungsfusion*), the balancing clause may be complied with if all participating companies would have to leave the market but for the merger[89]. Another example in this context may be the creation of an entity second only to the market leader through a merger, if the position of the market leader would have been further strengthened without the merger[90].

8. Competent authorities

8.1. Federal Cartel Office (*Bundeskartellamt*, BKartA)

The BKartA has exclusive competence in the area of merger control (section 48). The BKartA is a federal agency supervised by the Federal Ministry of Economics. However, it is generally accepted by German legal writers that the Federal Ministry of Economics is not allowed to give instructions to the BKartA in pending proceedings[91]. Instructions by the Federal Ministry of Economics may, therefore, be given only as general instructions (which are published in the Federal Gazette, section 52).

Mergers are handled by all ten executive divisions (*Beschlußabteilungen*) of the BKartA depending on which sector of economy is concerned. The BKartA will move its seat from Berlin to Bonn in 1999.

8.2. Approval by Federal Minister of Economics

As under the "old" law mergers that are prohibited by the BKartA may nonetheless be approved by the Federal Minister of Economics by means of an application under section 42[92] (so-called "*Ministererlaubnis*"). This application has to be filed within one month after receipt of a prohibition decision (or, if the prohibition is challenged in court upon the decision becoming final). The Federal Minister of Economics may, if appropriate, subject to conditions and/or undertakings, clear the merger. The prerequisites are that the restraints of competition resulting from the merger are balanced by overall economic advantages of the merger or that the merger is justified by an overriding public interest. When making this assessment the ability of the participating companies to compete in markets outside Germany must also be taken into account. No approval may be granted if the restraints of competition resulting from the merger would jeopardise the system of the market economy. The Federal Minister decides on an application for approval within four months[93]. Before doing so, he asks for an expert opinion of the Monopolies Commission.

As in the case of a clearance decision subject to conditions and/or undertakings pursuant to section 40(3), approval by the Federal Minister under conditions and/or undertakings must not amount to a mere behavioural control of the companies. If conditions are not fulfilled and/or undertakings not complied with, the approval – just like a clearance decision – may be withdrawn.

Up until now, sixteen applications for approval by the Federal Minister have been made, five of which were subsequently withdrawn by the applicants because of lack of likelihood of success. In six cases, approval was granted by the Minister (in four cases subject to conditions). Grounds of public interest that outweighed restraints of competition resulting from a merger[94] were:
- to safeguard the long-term supply of crude oil in Germany in order to secure a certain energy supply[95];
- to safeguard jobs in economically weak regions[96];
- to safeguard jobs together with the need to safeguard a specific technological potential, embodied in the human resources, of the target company, which would have gone bankrupt but for the merger[97];
- to increase supply of crude oil and gas in Germany[98];
- to safeguard or create jobs unless this would harm competing companies[99];
- to reduce state subsidies through privatisation as well as to increase international competitivity as well as benefiting from synergies[100].

8.3. Judicial review

The decision of the BKartA either to prohibit or to clear the merger (after a second phase investigation) is subject to a complaint (*Beschwerde*) to the Higher Regional Court competent for the BKartA (section 63)[101]. If an application for approval by the Federal Minister of Economics is made subsequently to a prohibition by the BKartA a complaint to the Higher Regional Court is possible after the decision of the Federal Minister. The filing of a complaint must be made within one month of the service of the BKartA's decision or within one month of service of the Federal Minister's decision (section 66(1)[102]). The complaint must be justified within one further month after filing has taken place. Companies (and individuals) must be represented by a lawyer in complaint proceedings.

An appeal (*Rechtsbeschwerde*) against decisions of the Higher Regional Court may be lodged at the Federal Supreme Court (*Bundesgerichtshof,* BGH). Such an appeal must, however, be admitted by the Higher Regional Court (section 74). Leave to appeal must be granted by the Higher Regional Court if the appeal concerns a legal question of fundamental importance, or if the development of the law or the maintenance of a uniform jurisprudence requires a decision by the BGH. Thereafter, no further appeal is possible.

Court fees are assessed in accordance with the normal German statutory rules. Court and lawyer's fees and other expenses may, as a general rule be recovered from the party that is defeated in court proceedings.

Summary

Under the German merger control rules set forth in the GWB (which were substantially modified as of 1 January 1999 by the Sixth Amendment), a concentration or merger will be present if one of four specific merger events occurs. A merger will be present in the event of acquisition of control over another company (this newly introduced broad concept of acquisition of control is modelled on Article 3(3) EMCR), if either all the assets or at least a significant portion of the assets of another company are acquired, if a shareholding of 25% or of 50% in another company is acquired, and failing that if a company is in a position to directly or indirectly exercise influence on another company which is substantial as regards competition. Various exceptions in the GWB provide that there is no merger present if for example a group of companies is restructured internally only and if shares are acquired by banks, other financial institutions or insurance companies for the purpose of subsequent assignment as long as no voting rights linked to the shares are exercised.

The establishment of a joint venture company will, as a rule, come within the scope of German merger control. Moreover, co-ordination effects of such a joint venture company may come within the scope of the restrictive practices rules of the GWB. Therefore, clearance of a joint venture by the German Federal Cartel Office does not prevent the joint venture from being challenged by third parties under the restrictive practices rules.

German merger control is triggered if the companies participating in a merger have combined world-wide sales of more than DM 1 billion (approx. € 510 million) and if at least one participating company has sales of more than DM 50 million (approx. € 25.5 million) in Germany. Any foreign-to-foreign merger satisfying these turnover thresholds falls within the jurisdiction of the BKartA. De *minimis* rules provide that no merger control will take place if one party to a merger is an independent company that had world-wide sales of less than DM 20 million (approx. € 10.2 million) in the business year preceding the merger. Also, if a merger exclusively affects a market that has existed for at least five years on which aggregate sales of less than DM 30 million (approx. € 15.3 million) were generated in the last calendar year, no merger control will take place.

Pre-merger notification is mandatory in Germany. The GWB merely describes the necessary contents of a notification but does not provide for an official form to be used for notifications. If a notification is incomplete, the deadlines for the investigation by the Federal Cartel Office will not be triggered. If no notification is made, fines of up to DM 50.000 (approx. € 25,000) may be imposed by the BKartA. Before clearance is given by the BKartA, a merger must not have been consummated. Mergers that are consummated nonetheless will be dissolved by the Federal Cartel Office. In addition, fines of up to DM 1 million (approx. € 510,000) or of up to three times the economic benefits resulting from pre-mature consummation may be imposed.

The GWB does not set forth time limits for a notification. A pre-merger notification can be filed as soon as the parties are in a position to indicate the form of the merger as well as the required turnover and market (share) data.

Following a notification the BKartA undertakes its investigation within a four-month deadline if, within one month of receipt of the notification, it informs the notifying parties that it has entered an in-depth investigation of the matter. Straightforward cases are cleared within the initial one-month period by an informal decision not subject to appeal. Any decision (prohibition or clearance) taken in "second phase" proceedings must be made by way of a formal decision, which may also be appealed by third parties.

The substantive test applied by the Federal Cartel Office is whether a merger will lead to either the creation of a market dominant position or to the strengthening of an already existing market dominant position. However, even if a merger leads to the creation of market dominance or to the strengthening of pre-existing market dominance, the Federal Cartel Office must not prohibit it if the parties to the merger prove that the merger will also result in improvements of competitive conditions which outweigh the detrimental effects of market dominance. In addition, the German Federal Minister of Economics may approve a merger that has been prohibited by the Federal Cartel Office upon application by the parties if restraints of competition resulting from the merger are balanced by overall economic advantages or by an overriding public interest.

The Federal Cartel Office has exclusive competence to deal with merger notifications. In addition, parties may apply for approval by the Federal Minister of Economics as outlined above. A judicial review is possible by way of a complaint to the competent Higher Regional Court, as well as by a way of an appeal against the decision of the Higher Regional Court to the Federal Supreme Court.

Annex 1

GWB[103]

First Part. Restraints of Competition

Section Seven. Control of Concentrations

Section 35 Scope of Provisions on Control of Concentrations.

(1) The provisions on control of concentrations shall apply if during the business year preceding the concentration
  1. the participating companies achieved an aggregate world-wide turnover of more than DM one billion and
  2. at least one participating company achieved a turnover in Germany of more than DM fifty million.

(2) Paragraph 1 does not apply,
  1. if a company which is not dependent within the meaning of section 36 paragraph 2 and which achieved a world-wide turnover of less than DM twenty million in the last business year merges with another company, or
  2. if a market is affected in which goods or commercial services have been offered for at least five years and in which a turnover of less than DM thirty million has been generated during the last calendar year.

To the extent the concentration affects competition in the newspaper or magazine publishing sector including production and distribution of newspapers or magazines or of parts thereof, only sentence 1 no. 2 shall apply.

(3) The provisions of this Act do not apply to the extent the Commission of the European Communities has exclusive jurisdiction pursuant to Regulation (EEC) no. 4064/89 of the Council of 21 December 1989 on the Control of Concentrations between Undertakings as amended from time to time.

Section 36 General Principles for the Investigation of Concentrations.

(1) Any concentration which must be expected to either create or strengthen a

market dominant position must be prohibited by the Federal Cartel Office, unless the participating companies prove that the concentration will also lead to improvements of conditions of competition and that such improvements outweigh the detrimental effects of market dominance.

(2) If a participating company is a dependent or dominating company within the meaning of section 17 of the Stock Corporation Act, or a group company within the meaning of section 18 Stock Corporation Act, the companies that are affiliated in such a way must be considered as a single company. If several such companies jointly exercise a dominating influence over another company they will each be considered as dominating company.

(3) A person or an association of persons which is not a company but holds a majority share-holding in another company will be considered a company.

Section 37 Concentration.

(1) A concentration shall be present in the event of:
1. the acquisition of all or of a substantial part of the assets of another company;
2. the acquisition of direct or indirect control by one or more companies over all or parts of one or several other companies. Control is constituted by rights, contracts, or other means which, either separately or in combination and having regard to the considerations of fact or law involved, confer the possibility of exercising decisive influence on the activities of another company, in particular by:
   a) ownership or the right to use all or part of the assets of a company,
   b) rights or contracts which confer decisive influence on the composition, voting, or decisions of the organs of a company;
3. the acquisition of shares in another company, if these shares alone or in combination with other shares already held by the company constitute
   a) 50% or
   b) 25%
   of the capital or the voting rights of the other company. The shares held by a company shall include those shares that are held by a third party on account of this company and, if the owner of the company is a sole proprietor, also those shares that are included in the owner's other assets.

If several companies simultaneously or successively acquire shares in the above mentioned amounts in another company, this shall be considered a concentration also between the shareholder companies in the markets in which the other company is active;
4. any other combination of companies pursuant to which one or more companies may directly or indirectly exercise an influence over another company which is substantial as regards competition.

(2) A concentration shall be present also if the participating companies were already combined, unless the concentration does not lead to a substantial strengthening of the already existing combination of companies.

(3) No concentration is present, if credit institutions, financial institutions or insurance companies acquire shares in another company with a view to re-selling the shares, as long as they do not exercise voting rights linked to these shares and provided that disposal of these shares occurs within one year. This period may be extended by the Federal Cartel Office if it is substantiated that disposal of the shares was not reasonably feasible within the period.

Section 38 Calculation of Turnover and Market Shares.

(1) Section 277 paragraph 1 of the Commercial Code shall apply to the calculation of turnover. Turnover resulting from supplies and performances between affiliated companies (intra-group turnover) as well as excise duties shall not be taken into account.

(2) With respect to the trade in goods three quarter of the turnover shall be taken into account only.

(3) With respect to the publishing, the production and the distribution of newspapers, magazines and parts thereof, the production, the distribution, and the organisation of broadcast programmes and the sale of broadcast advertising time, twenty times the turnover is to be taken into account.

(4) In place of turnover, the following shall be used for credit institutions, financial institutions and building loan savings banks: the aggregate amount

of the proceeds set forth in section 34 paragraph 2 sentence 1 no. 1(a) to (e) of the Regulation on the Accounting of Credit Institutions of 10 February 1992 (BGBl. I p. 203) after deduction of value added tax and other taxes directly levied on those proceeds. For insurance companies the value of gross premiums written during the last full business year shall be relevant. Gross premiums written shall be the revenues from direct and reinsurance activities including parts expended for reinsurance.

(5) With respect to the acquisition of the assets of another company the transferred assets will be taken into account only for the purpose of calculating market shares and turnover of the transferor.

Section 39 Obligation to Notify.

(1) Concentrations must be notified to the Federal Cartel Office prior to consummation in accordance with paragraphs 2 and 3.

(2) The following have an obligation to notify:
1. the companies participating in the concentration,
2. in the case of section 37 paragraph 1 no. 1 and 3 the transferor also.

(3) The form of the concentration must be indicated in the notification. In addition, the notification must contain the following information for each participating company:
1. the corporate name or other designation and the place of incorporation or the business seat;
2. the nature of business activities;
3. the turnover in Germany, in the European Union and world-wide; in place of turnover, with respect to credit institutions, financial institutions and building loan savings banks the aggregate amount of proceeds pursuant to section 38 paragraph 4 shall be indicated; for insurance companies the value of gross premiums;
4. market shares including the bases for their calculation or estimation, if combined for all participating companies they reach at least 20% in the territory to which this Act applies or in a substantial part thereof;
5. in the event of an acquisition of shares in another company the amount of the shareholdings acquired and held in the aggregate;

6. a person in Germany authorised to accept service if the seat of the company is outside the territory to which this Act applies.

If a participating company is an affiliated company, the information pursuant to sentence 2 no. 1 and 2 must be provided for its affiliated companies also, and the information pursuant to sentence 2 no. 3 and 4 must be provided jointly for each company participating in the concentration and the companies affiliated with it, and intra-group relationships, as well as relationships of dependence and shareholdings between the affiliated companies must be communicated. The notification must not contain or make use of false or incomplete information to induce the cartel authority to refrain from a prohibition under section 36 paragraph 1 or from a communication under section 40 paragraph 1.

(4) No notification is required if the Commission of the European Communities has referred a concentration to the Federal Cartel Office and if the information required under paragraph 3 is available to the Federal Cartel Office in the German language. The Federal Cartel Office informs the participating companies without undue delay on the date of receipt of the referral decision.

(5) The Federal Cartel Office may request information from each participating company on market shares including the bases for their calculation or estimation as well as on the turnover of a specific kind of goods or commercial services that the undertaking has generated during the last business year before the concentration.

(6) The participating companies must notify the Federal Cartel Office without undue delay of consummation of the concentration.

Section 40 Procedure of Control of Concentrations.

(1) The Federal Cartel Office may prohibit a concentration of which it has been notified only if it informs the notifying companies within a period of one month from receipt of the complete notification that it has entered into the investigation of the concentration (main investigation procedure). The main investigation procedure shall be commenced if a further investigation of the concentration is necessary.

(2) In the main investigation procedure the Federal Cartel Office decides by formal decision whether the concentration is prohibited or cleared. If the formal decision is not handed down within a period of four months from receipt of the complete notification, the concentration is deemed cleared. This shall not apply if
1. the notifying companies have consented to an extension of the period,
2. the Federal Cartel Office has omitted the communication under paragraph 1 or the prohibition of the concentration due to false information or information not supplied in time under section 39 paragraph 5 or section 50,
3. a person in Germany authorised to accept service is no longer designated in violation of section 39 paragraph 3 sentence 2 no. 6.

(3) Clearance can be linked to conditions and undertakings. These must not aim to put the participating companies under a continuous control of behaviour. Section 12 paragraph 2 sentence 1 no. 2 and 3 shall apply *mutatis mutandis*.

(4) Prior to a prohibition the supreme State authorities of the area where the participating companies have their seat must be given the opportunity to make observations.

(5) In cases pursuant to section 39 paragraph 4 sentence 1, the periods pursuant to paragraphs 1 and 2 sentence 2 shall start upon receipt of the referral decision by the Federal Cartel Office.

(6) If a clearance by the Federal Cartel Office is either partly or wholly annulled by a court order that has become final, the period under paragraph 2 sentence 2 shall start anew at the point in time at which the court order becomes final.

Section 41 Prohibition to Consummate, Dissolution.

(1) Before expiration of the periods under section 40 paragraph 1 sentence 1 and paragraph 2 sentence 2, the companies must not consummate a concentration which has not been cleared by the Federal Cartel Office or take part in the consummation of this concentration. Legal transactions that infringe this prohibition are void. This shall not apply to agreements on the transformation, incorporation or establishment of a company and to company

agreements within the meaning of sections 291 and 292 of the Stock Corporation Act as soon as they have become valid through registration with the competent register.

(2) The Federal Cartel Office may, upon application, grant exemptions from the prohibition to consummate if the participating companies put forward substantial grounds therefor, in particular in order to protect a participating company or third parties from serious detriment. The exemption may be granted at any time, also prior to the notification and may be linked to conditions and undertakings. Section 12 paragraph 2 sentence 1 no. 2 and 3 apply *mutatis mutandis*.

(3) A consummated merger which has been prohibited by the Federal Cartel Office or with respect to which it has withdrawn the clearance, must be dissolved unless the Federal Minister of Economics grants the approval of the concentration under section 42. The Federal Cartel Office orders the measures necessary for the dissolution of the concentration. The restriction of competition may be removed by other means than by restitution of the previous situation also.

(4) In order to enforce its order the Federal Cartel Office may in particular
1. assess a coercive payment of DM 10,000 to DM 1 million once or several times,
2. prohibit or restrict the exercise of voting rights linked to shares in a participating company that are held by another participating company or that must be attributed to it,
3. appoint a trustee that carries out the dissolution of the concentration.

Section 42 Approval by Federal Minister of Economics.

(1) The Federal Minister of Economics may upon application grant approval of a concentration which has been prohibited by the Federal Cartel Office, if in the individual case the restriction of competition is outweighed by overall economic advantages of the concentration, or if the concentration is justified by an overriding common interest. In this respect, the ability of the participating companies to compete in markets outside the territory to which this Act applies

is to be taken into account. Approval must be granted only, if the dimension of the restriction of competition does not jeopardise the system of market economy.

(2) The approval may be linked to conditions and undertakings. Section 40 paragraph 3 applies *mutatis mutandis.*

(3) The application must be made in writing to the Federal Ministry of Economics within one month of receipt of the prohibition. If the prohibition is challenged, the period starts from the date when the prohibition becomes final.

(4) The Federal Minister of Economics shall decide on the application within four months. Prior to a decision, an expert opinion shall be obtained from the Monopolies Commission, and the supreme State authorities of the area where the participating companies have their seat shall be given the opportunity to make observations.

Section 43 Publications.

The following shall be published in the Federal Gazette:
1. the notification of consummation of a concentration,
2. the formal decision by the Federal Cartel Office under section 40 paragraph 2,
3. the application for grant of approval by the Federal Minister of Economics,
4. the approval by the Federal Minister of Economics, its refusal and amendment,
5. the withdrawal and the revocation of the clearance by the Federal Cartel Office or of the approval by the Federal Minister of Economics,
6. the dissolution of a concentration and the corresponding measures ordered by the Federal Cartel Office under section 41 paragraphs 3 and 4.

Section 39 paragraph 3 sentence 1 as well as sentence 2 no. 1 and 2 shall apply *mutatis mutandis* to the contents of the publication.

Annex 2

Common Form
For Mergers in the United Kingdom, in France and in Germany

Introduction

The purpose of this document is to provide a voluntary system for simplifying the examination of mergers which may be subject to control in more than one of the following countries: France, United Kingdom, Germany.

The completed form provides a formal notification of a merger in Germany and it provides an informal notification in the United Kingdom and France; it does not replace any formal notification in France or the formal pre-notification of mergers in the United Kingdom. In any case it does not exclude the possibility that more information may be needed by the competition authorities in order to reach a decision under their respective laws (see Annex).

Companies using this form will be told, within one month of the receipt by the competition authorities in Germany, whether further examination is required; in France, whether a formal notification is advisable; and in the United Kingdom, whether a merger qualifies for investigation by the Monopolies and Mergers Commission. The three competition authorities will also seek, where possible, to co-ordinate their timetables for final decisions.

Please answer the following questions in typescript on separate sheets of paper

I. General Information

   1. In which countries does the proposed merger fall under merger provisions? Which other competition authorities (including France, United Kingdom, Germany) have been contacted?

   2. Please indicate which of the data given are business secrets. Can any

GERMANY

business secrets given *not* be disclosed to the authorities in France, the United Kingdom and Germany also examining this merger? In which case, please specify.

3. Please give names, position, company (or firm) and contact numbers (telephone, fax) of any authorised representative acting on your behalf and/or persons to which any correspondence should be sent.

II. The Merger Situation

Give a full description of the proposed merger and the form it will take by replying to the following questions in typescript on separate sheets of paper. For definitions of relevant terms, see Annex.

1. Describe briefly the merger proposal (including the reasons for the transaction), the merging enterprises and the proposed arrangements by which they will merge. Give details of any factors upon which completion of the merger is conditional. Supply copies of any agreements or contracts on which the merger is based.

2. If not completed, what is the expected timescale for the completion of the merger?

3. In the United Kingdom, if the offer is subject to the City Code on Takeovers and Mergers, please supply two copies of the Offer Documents and Listing Particulars. If these are not yet available, provide copies of the latest drafts and supply the final versions as soon as they are issued. Please also indicate what is likely to be the effective closing date and whether the offer has been recommended by the Board of the target company?

4. Give the following details about the merging enterprises and of any associated enterprises, both domestic and foreign and before and after the merger:
   - name and official addresses of the enterprises;
   - ownership and control;
   - types of businesses;

- group relationships, degrees of dependency and percentages of holdings;
- when shares in another enterprise are acquired, the amount of the shareholding acquired and the total shareholding owned in it;
- turnover for the last business year:
- total worldwide for each group,
- total for each group in each France, United Kingdom, Germany, and
- for each individual enterprise concerned in each France, United Kingdom and Germany.

5. Give the gross worldwide assets of the enterprise being acquired.

6. Enclose a list of the notified mergers involving any of the merging enterprises in the UK, France, Germany and any other country during the last three years.

7. Supply, for each of the merging enterprises, three copies of the latest annual report, if any, and accounts.

8. Describe in your view, each product or service market affected and whether the geographic markets are international, national, regional or local. Give reasons for your statements. (For definition of "affected" markets see Annex)

9. For the different relevant markets, give the following information. Refer to industry data where available. Use the most recent figures available, specify the period they cover and explain the basis for your estimates:
    1) an estimate of the value, preferably, or volume of each market and of its evolution; if the affected market is not a national one, also give an estimate for the national market;
    2) turnover and market shares of the merging enterprises in each relevant market [and the evolution of that share];
    3) the names and market shares of your competitors (including overseas companies/importers) with over five% of a market.

10. Give details of the nature and extent of any vertical links between the merging enterprises.

GERMANY

Notes

1 See the translation of the GWB's rules on merger control in Annex 1. The GWB refers to "concentrations" instead of "mergers".
2 The Sixth Amendment to the GWB was published on 2 September 1998 in the Federal Gazette (*Bundesgesetzblatt*, BGBl.) at BGBl. I 2521. The Act Amending the Public Procurement Rules (*Vergaberechtsänderungsgesetz*, VgRÄG) of the same date (published on 2 September 1998 at BGBl. I 2512) incorporated the German rules on public procurement into the GWB. Both the Sixth Amendment and the VgRÄG led to material changes and also to a complete re-numbering of the sections in the GWB. The GWB was, therefore, entirely re-published on 2 September 1998 in the BGBl. I 2547.
3 References are to sections of the "new" GWB in force as of 1 January 1999 unless otherwise specified.
4 Merger control rules were set forth by the Second Amendment to the GWB, published in the BGBl. I 1973, 917; the subsequent Third to Fifth Amendments to the GWB (of 28 June 1976, published in the BGBl. I 1976, 1697; of 26 April 1980, published in the BGBl. I 1980, 458; and of 22 December 1989, published in the BGBl. I 1989, 2486) introduced various changes to the rules on merger control.
5 The aims of the Sixth Amendment are set out in detail in the official Statement of Reasons for the draft Sixth Amendment by the German Federal Government in: Acts of the German Federal Council (*Bundesrat*) no. 852/97 of 7 November 1997 at p. 43.
6 This rule corresponds to the former rule in s. 23(2)(1) GWB (old).
7 This rule corresponds to the former rule in s. 23(2)(2)(1)(a) and (b) GWB (old).
8 This rule largely corresponds to the former "catch-all" in s. 23(2)(6) GWB (old). Its purpose was to deal with situations where acquisitions of shares did not exceed the threshold of 25% or where no majority of members could be appointed to an enterprise's governing bodies.
9 In s. 23(2)(3), (4) and (5) as well as in s. 23(2)(2)(1)(c) GWB (old).
10 These rules mainly dealt with agreements between enterprises on the creation of a group of enterprises (*Konzern*) within the meaning of s. 18 of the German Stock Corporation Act (*Aktiengesetz*, AktG), with agreements on the transfer of profits and losses, and with agreements on the lease of an enterprise to another enterprise, on the nomination of at least half of the members of a governing body of an enterprise which are identical with the members of another enterprise, as well as combinations of enterprises whereby one or more enterprises can exercise directly or indirectly a dominating influence on another enterprise.
11 The latter rule for individuals is expressly provided in s. 36(3), which corresponds to s. 23(1)(10) GWB (old), the so-called "*Flick* clause" introduced into the GWB by the Fourth Amendment in 1980 in order to deal with the various shareholdings of the German industrialist *Flick*.
12 KG decision of 22 May 1985, WuW/E OLG 3591, 3594, *Coop Schleswig-Holstein/Deutscher Supermarkt*.
13 KG decision of 13 January 1988, WuW/E OLG 4095, 4102, *W + 1-Verlag/Weiss-Druck*
14 BGH decision of 29 May 1979, BGHZ 74, 322, *Organische Pigmente*.

235

15   BGH decision of 23 October 1979, WuW/E BGH 1655, *Zementmahlanlage II.*
16   BGH decision of 12 February 1980, WuW/E BGH 1763, 1771, *Bituminöses Mischgut.*
17   BGHZ 119, 117, *Melitta/Kraft (Frapan).*
18   The old law contained a third threshold for mergers by acquisition of shares in s. 23(2)(2)(c) GWB (old). Under this rule the acquisition of majority shareholdings within the meaning of s. 16 German Stock Corporation Act (*Aktiengesetz*, AktG) constituted a separate merger event.
19   S. 23(2)(2)(4) GWB (old).
20   S. 36(2) states that affiliated undertakings within the meaning of s. 17 and s. 18 AktG are treated as one company for the purpose of merger control in general, i.e. also for the purpose of calculating thresholds.
21   KG, AG 1985, 167; BKartA WuW/E BKartA 2178, *Klöckner/SEN II.*
22   See the corresponding rule in s. 23(2)(6) GWB (old).
23   BKartA, decision of 23 July 1992 – B 5-42/90.
24   BKartA, decision of 6 July 1995, WuW/E BKartA 2829, 2835.
25   BKartA, decision of 29 May 1996 – B 8-148/95.
26   Decision of 6 November 1997, WuW/DE-V 1.
27   See s. 24a(1)(2) *in fine* GWB (old). Even if the relevant "pre-merger control" thresholds were met, only a post-merger notification was, therefore, required after consummation. The BKartA then disposed of a one-year deadline to prohibit the merger (and ask for its dissolution). As such transactions could not infringe a prohibition to consummate, they were legally valid pending a potential prohibition by the BKartA.
28   A corresponding rule was already set forth in the GWB (old) in s. 23(3)(1).
29   S. 23(3)(2) GWB (old) which was, however, limited to acquisitions by banks of new shares in the course of the creation of a stock corporation or during a capital increase.
30   This rule corresponds to the former rule of s. 23(2)(2)(3) GWB (old) with the sole difference that the "old" rule set forth a legal definition of a joint venture company. The new rule no longer gives a definition of a joint venture company because the creation of a joint venture may not only occur through acquisition of shares but also through acquisition of control as of 1 January 1999 under s. 37 (1)(2).
31   BGH decision of 1 October 1985, WuW/E BGH 2169, *Mischwerke*; BGH decision of 13 January 1998, WuW/E DE-R 115, *Carpartner.*
32   OLG Düsseldorf decision of 9 November 1993, WuW/E OLG 5213, *Gemischtwirtschaftliche Abfallverwertung.*
33   The Federal Government had announced in the Statement of Reasons (at p. 58) its intention to decide during the legislative proceedings leading to the enactment of the Sixth Amendment whether such "double control" by the BKartA of joint venture mergers should be provided for. This has, however, not been realised.
34   S. 35(3) specifically states that the GWB, i.e. its rules on merger control as well as its rules on restrictions of competition set forth in s. 1 *et seq.*, do not apply to mergers that come within the exclusive competence of the European Commission under the EMCR.
35   All conversions from DM into € are made on the basis of the official exchange rate of 1.95583.
36   The general rule set forth by the GWB in this respect is, that it applies to all restraints of competition that have an effect in Germany even if the cause takes place outside German

territory, s. 130(2).
37 Foreign-to-foreign mergers represent approx. one eighth of the mergers dealt with by the BKartA.
38 See e.g. decision of the KG of 1 July 1983, WuW/E OLG 3051, *Morris/Rothmans*.
39 See decision of the BKartA of 23 July 1992 in *Gillette/Wilkinson*, – B 5-42/90.
40 The old *de minimis* rule provided that mergers were exempted that involved one independent company with a turnover not exceeding DM 50 million, i.e. approx. € 25.5 million, unless such a company was taken over by a company with a turnover of at least DM 1 billion, i.e. approx. € 510 million, and had itself a turnover of at least DM 4 million, i.e. approx. € 2.04 million. This rule was considered to be too narrow because too many cases which did not present competition problems were subject to German merger control. The BKartA will apply the new *de minimis* rule also to situations where the target company is not independent but where aggregate world-wide sales of the group of the seller are lower than DM 20 million/€ 10.2 million.
41 The old *de minimis* rule provided that a merger could not be prohibited if it affected a market that had existed for at least five years in which aggregate sales of less than DM 10 million were generated in the calendar year preceding the merger. However, this rule did not exempt the parties from the obligation to notify the BKartA about the merger.
42 Also, the BKartA will not apply this exception if a merger affects several neighbouring (regional or local) markets which, considered independently from each other, would benefit from the *de minimis* rule.
43 For details see 3.6.
44 This specific method of calculating turnover, however, exclusively applies to publishing/broadcasting activities of the participating companies as opposed to activities that they may carry out in other business fields.
45 The underlying reason is that due to the trend for markets in these business fields to become regional, even merely local efficient merger control cannot rely on the "normal" turnover thresholds; see Statement of Reasons at p. 59.
46 Pursuant to s. 24(2)(2) of the GWB (old).
47 This rule largely corresponds to the former rule in s. 23(1)(3) GWB (old).
48 The BKartA so far accepted both conversions based on the average annual exchange rate of as well as conversions based on the exchange rate applicable on 31 December of the relevant business year.
49 In s. 23(1)(7) GWB (old).
50 See also above under 3.4.
51 It is worth noting that, together with the competition authorities of France and the UK, the BKartA has established a "Common Form" for mergers that are subject to control by at least two of these authorities. Compliance with this form (see Annex 2) is voluntary.
52 Such notification will be published in the Federal Gazette (*Bundesanzeiger*) pursuant to s. 43(1).
53 This deviates from the former rule in s. 23(5)(1)(3) GWB (old) that required indication of turnover without further specifying it. By virtue of the much more specific new requirement, the BKartA is enabled to control whether the new threshold of *de minimis* turnover is exceeded in Germany as contained in s. 35(1)(2); moreover, the BKartA will be able to verify, on the basis of the detailed turnover information, whether a notification comes

within the scope of the EMCR and consequently will be exempt from German merger control by virtue of s. 35(3).
54 This new rule is meant to avoid any uncertainties when the BKartA serves decisions on foreign companies.
55 It is widespread practice to attach annual reports of the group of a participating company to the notification and to refer to its contents regarding specific information about the members of the group. Nonetheless full information as outlined above should be provided with respect to any member of the group that has business activities in Germany and/or business establishments or subsidiaries in Germany.
56 The "old" law contained an obligation to file a post-merger notification (*Anzeige*) forthwith, i.e. without undue delay, upon consummation (s. 23(1)(1) GWB (old)).
57 Under Article 4(1) EMCR notification must be made, *inter alia*, within one week of signature of the relevant agreement.
58 S. 24a(1)(1) and (2) GWB (old).
59 S. 39(1).
60 The Statement of Reasons specifies (at p. 59) that no material deviation from the "old" law is intended in this respect.
61 Like the European Commission, the BKartA is ready to discuss intended mergers informally with the parties on the basis of a draft notification. Such informal discussions based on a detailed draft notification are highly advisable indeed in complex cases as they may help the parties to elaborate issues deemed problematic by the BKartA more precisely and thus accelerate the handling of the case by the BKartA, once the notification is officially lodged (or even avoid a "second phase" investigation and the corresponding risk that third parties challenge a clearance decision; see below under 6.5).
62 See above under 4.4.3.
63 In the *Krupp-Hoesch* case, *Krupp* undertook to divest a certain business but later did not comply with this undertaking. *Krupp* rather invoked substantial subsequent changes in the affected market. Therefore, *Krupp-Hoesch* terminated the contract containing the undertaking. The BKartA disputed the validity of this termination and issued a decision enjoining the divestiture of the relevant business on 25 February 1994, WuW/E BKartA 2625. This decision was challenged in court by *Krupp-Hoesch* which, however, divested subsequently some of the relevant activities for other reasons whereupon the litigation was brought to an end by mutual consent of the parties.
64 For judicial review of this assessment of fees see below under 8.3.
65 See above under 4.4.4 and 4.4.3.
66 See below under 8.3.
67 As a rule, s. 61(1) requires a statement of reasons for any decision by the BKartA.
68 Under s. 43(3), all decisions by the BKartA pursuant to s. 40(2) GWB must be published in the Federal Gazette (*Bundesanzeiger*).
69 The Statement of Reasons emphasised at p. 45 that experience drawn from the European Commission's case-law under the EMCR shows that clearance decisions are far more likely to trigger a specific need for critical public discussion than prohibitions.
70 It is governed by s. 44 to 47.
71 They are published pursuant to s. 53.
72 In addition, companies that are the target of a hostile takeover bid can now also challenge

clearance decisions.
73 Under s. 63(1) all decisions by the BKartA are subject to challenge by way of a complaint (*Beschwerde*).
74 In s. 19(2).
75 This criterion for determining market strength has been newly incorporated into the GWB by the Sixth Amendment. A recent decision by the German Federal Supreme Court (*Bundesgerichtshof*, BGH) of 24 October 1995, WuW 1996, 3026 – *Backofenmarkt* gave rise to some misunderstandings in this respect. In this decision, the BGH held that the geographical market which is relevant for purposes of German merger control may not exceed the territory of Germany. Hence, clarification was needed to stress that actual or potential competition from outside Germany may nonetheless influence the assessment of market dominance.
76 BKartA, WuW/E BKartA 2405, *MAN/Sulzer*; WuW/E BKartA 2421, *Unilever/Braun*.
77 BKartA, AG 1987, 253, *Hüls/Condea*; WuW/E BKartA 2405, *MAN/Sulzer*; BKartA, decision of 23 July 1992 – B 5-42/90, *Gillette/Wilkinson*.
78 BGH AG 1988, 47, *Gruner + Jahr/Zeit II*.
79 BKartA, decision of 27 February 1997, WuW/E BKartA 2885, *Kali + Salz/PCS*. The parties in this case applied for an approval by the Federal Minister of Economics (see below under 8.2), which was, however, also refused: decision of the Federal Minister of Economics of 22 July 1997, WuW/E BMW 225.
80 BKartA AG 1988, 387, *Messer Griesheim/Buse*.
81 BKartA AG 1988, 391, *Wieland/Langenberg*.
82 BKartA TB 1989/90, 77.
83 BGHZ 119, 117, *Melitta/Kraft (Frapan)*.
84 BGHZ 119, 346, *Springer/Beig (Pinneberger Tageblatt)*; BGHZ 121, 137, *WAZ/IKZ*.
85 BGH AG 1992, 120 (122), *Linde/Lansing (Auslandstochter)*.
86 In the first draft of the Sixth Amendment, the balancing clause had been eliminated. The Statement of Reasons explained (at p. 57) that the criteria for the balancing clause were difficult to determine and, moreover, clearance decisions by the BKartA could be made subject to conditions and undertakings pursuant to s. 40(3). At a later stage of the legislative process, however, the balancing clause was re-inserted into the Sixth Amendment.
87 BGHZ 73, 65, *Erdgas Schwaben*.
88 BKartA WuW 1978, 554, *DWK*.
89 BKartA, WuW/E BKartA 1571, *Kaiser-VAW*.
90 BKartA WuW 1977, 692, *Benteler/Niederrheinstahl*.
91 No case has become known where the Federal Ministry of Economics tried to directly influence pending proceedings.
92 This provision largely corresponds to the rules in s. 24(3) to (5) GWB ("old").
93 The application for approval and the subsequent decision by the Federal Minister will trigger a fee to which the method of assessment and limits set forth above under 6.3 apply.
94 If it is determined that grounds of public interest outweigh restraints of competition the Federal Minister has no discretion as to whether to grant an approval or not.
95 Decision of 1 February 1974 WuW/E BWM 147, *VEBA-Gelsenberg II*.
96 Decision of 17 October 1976 WuW/E BWM 155, *Babcock-Artos*.
97 Decision of 1 August 1977 WuW/E BWM 159, *Thyssen-Hüller*.

98 Decision of 5 March 1979 WuW/E BWM 165, *Veba-BP*.
99 Decision of 9 December 1981 WuW/E BWM 177, *IBH-Wibau*.
100 Decision of 6 September 1989 WuW/E BWM 191, *Daimler-MBB*.
101 A complaint can also be lodged against the assessment of fees by the BKartA.
102 Likewise, a complaint must be lodged within one month of service of a decision that (separately) assesses the BKartA's fees.
103 Unofficial translation by the authors.

Greece

Nikolaos Korogiannakis

Contents

1. Introduction 243
   1.1. Development of the law 243
   1.2. First and second amendment of Act 703/1977 by Acts
        1934/1991, 2000/1991 244
2. Legislation of the merger control rules: Current position 245
   2.1. Definition of concentration 246
   2.2. Obligation to notify 251
   2.3. Obligation to pre-notify 253
   2.4. Preventive control of concentrations: Main procedure 256
   2.5. Suspension of concentrations 259
3. Competent authorities 259
   Notes 261

1. Introduction

No legislation existed in Greece for the control of mergers until the Act No 703 of 26 September 1977 "on the control of monopolies and oligopolies and the protection of free competition". This Act, as amended by Acts No 1934 of 8 March 1991, No 2000 of 24 December 1991 and No 2296 of 2 February 1995, still constitutes the main framework of the Greek competition legislation. Compliance with the provisions of Act 703/1977 is regulated by the Competition Committee which is administratively independent and is supervised by the Minister of Commerce. However, a concentration that has been prohibited by the Competition Committee may be approved by a specifically justified decision of the Ministers of National Economy and Commerce provided that certain conditions are met.

1.1. Development of the law

Competition law in Greece developed in the mid-70s due to the then imminent accession of Greece to the European Community and the need to compete with foreign companies which experienced economies of scale. Also, given the growth rate of Greece at the time, increase of the size of businesses and therefore mergers and concentrations were regarded as a necessary consequence. This position was illustrated in Article 4, paragraph 2 of Act 703/1977 which provided that "a concentration, according to the present act, shall be deemed to arise: a) by the creation of a new undertaking, b) by the absorption of one or more undertakings by another undertaking, c) by the acquisition of one or more undertakings by another undertaking".

The newly created legal instrument did not introduce the systematic control of mergers between companies but instead followed the example of the EC Treaty. Mergers and acquisitions were considered to be permissible and only the abuse of a dominant position was regarded to substantially fetter competition and therefore was prohibited. In the preamble of Act 703/1977 it was stressed that: "It is commonplace that the protection of free competition, in other words the prevention of the creation of monopolistic or oligopolistic situations which could impede the normal functioning of the market and thus harm the interests of consumers and that of the national economy in general, constitutes one of the most significant duties of the State in conditions of liberal economy. This area is to be covered by the Bill introduced for voting. This has been drafted in accordance with that in force in the EEC so as also to constitute the harmonization of the national economy with the principles of the Common Market under this heading".

As regards the obligation to notify, it was provided that an omission of the obligation to notify a merger resulted in the imposition of a fine of Drs 3 million[1].

1.2. First and second amendment of Act 703/1977 by Acts 1934/1991, 2000/1991

The first amendment to the Act 703/1977 introduced a general obligation to notify every concentration between undertakings that would either hold a market share over 10% in the Greek market or in a substantial part of it, or the combined aggregate turnover of all the undertakings concerned in the Greek market would be in excess of € 10 million. The preventive control of concentrations is preserved for those operations where the market share of the products or services to which the concentration is concerned represents within the national market or in a substantial part of it, at least 35% of the combined aggregate turnover of identical products or where the combined aggregate turnover of all the undertakings concerned is equivalent to or exceeds the amount of € 75 million[2]. The relevant provisions in effect introduced a peculiar form of control of concentrations. On the one hand it required as obligatory the prior notification of all concentrations that satisfied the above criteria but on the other hand it prohibited the formation only of certain concentrations before a final decision had been issued by the competent authority.

It is also worth mentioning that according to the new Article 4b it was provided that, following a common decision adopted by the Ministers of National Economy and Commerce, it was possible to submit to preventive control concentrations of homogeneous companies which operate in sectors where the degree of concentration could lead to the prevention, restriction or distortion of competition. This provision was never actually implemented. It however received heavy criticism since it attempted to introduce a type of control which would be exercised in portions from sector to sector. It also provided for the preventive control of homogeneous companies leaving in this way horizontal and vertical concentrations without control.

It is accepted that the second amendment did not effect any significant alteration to the applicable control of concentrations. It only reduced the criteria for the application of the preventive control of concentrations from 35% to 30% and the combined aggregate turnover from € 75 million to € 65 million. Additionally, it provided that concentrations could no longer fall under Article 2 regarding the prohibition of the abuse of dominant position.

2. Legislation of the merger control rules: Current position

The present position in relation to merger control has been significantly modified following the third and final amendment of Act 703/1977 by Act 2296/1995. Contrary to previous amendments that made the activation of preventive control dependent on the issue of a common ministerial decision by the Ministers of National Economy and Commerce, a new general system of control of concentrations is introduced which covers all sectors of economy.

The basic principles which govern the applicable system on the control of concentrations, each of which is discussed in the text that follows, are:

    a. Concentrations: the Act applies to concentrations which are defined in conformity with the relevant provisions of Regulation (EEC) 4064/1989. A distinction is made between concentrative and co-operative joint ventures.

    b. Obligation to notify: the obligation to notify or to pre-notify a concentration depends on the market share of the products or services to which the concentration is concerned and on the combined aggregate turnover of all the undertakings concerned.

    c. Preventive control of concentrations – main procedure: the Competition Committee will investigate mergers that fall under the notification thresholds of the Act in order to test their compatibility with the protection of free and unimpeded competition in the national market or in a substantial part of it. Mergers that are incompatible within this sense may be blocked. In special circumstances a concentration that has been prohibited by the Competition Committee may be approved by a specifically justified decision of the Ministers of National Economy and Commerce.

d. *Suspension of concentrations:* concentrations will be suspended for a limited period following notification. Special reference is made to cases of derogation from the provisions on the suspension of concentrations.

2.1. Definition of concentration

Article 4(2) of Act 701/1977 includes two types of operations that correspond to the notion of concentration. In particular it is provided that a concentration shall be deemed to arise where:
"(a) two or more previously independent undertakings merge in any manner,
(b) one or more persons already controlling at least one undertaking or one or more undertakings, acquire direct or indirect control of the whole or parts of one or more undertakings".[3]

It is apparent that the addition of the phrase "in any manner" differentiates the merger of two or more independent undertakings under the Greek law from the equivalent provision of Article 3(1)(a) of Regulation (EEC) 4064/89. Whereas Regulation 4064/89 includes the formation of a merger that is effected by formation of a new company and by absorption (buying out), paragraph 2(a) of Act 703/1977 refers also to mergers which are created following the take-over of one company by another[4].

The provision of paragraph 2(a) covers not only mergers between companies limited by shares (*anonymi etairia* "A.E.") and between companies with limited liability ("E.P.E.") which are already regulated under Greek law[5], but also mergers between personal companies or between those companies and limited liability companies or companies limited by shares or personal companies. However, it should be mentioned that mergers which are created on the basis of Article 68 of Act 2190/1920 and 54 of Act 3190/1955 benefit from the advantages which are provided by the relevant provisions (Article 69, par. 2 of Act 2190), in other words the transfer of the assets of the merged undertakings is effected by a "quasi universal succession" without dissolution and liquidation of the undertakings concerned. In all other cases the transfer of assets takes place by special succession following the dissolution and liquidation of the undertakings concerned.

As far as the provision of paragraph 2(b) is concerned it should be mentioned that the word "person" could mean either a legal or a natural person. In this way, they could qualify as undertakings legal persons of private law (institutions, societies), legal persons of public law (e.g. municipalities, communities) and public companies. The application of paragraph 2(b) is made dependant on the prior exercise of control of at least one undertaking by those undertakings that acquire control of one or more undertaking. The definition of control is given in Article 4(3) which provides that:

"control shall be constituted by rights, contracts or any other means which, either separately or in combination and having regard to the considerations of fact or law involved, confer the possibility of exercising decisive influence on an undertaking, particularly by:
   (a) ownership of the right to use all or part of the assets of an undertaking
   (b) rights or contracts which confer decisive influence on the composition, voting or decisions of the organs of an undertaking".

According to Article 4(4) control is also acquired by person(s) or undertakings which:

"(a) are holders of the rights or entitled to the rights under the contracts concerned; or
(b) while not being holders of such rights or entitled to rights under such contracts concerned, have the power to exercise the rights deriving therefrom".

The acquisition of control by one person or undertaking may give sole control for the purpose of Article 4(3). On the other hand, where the control of an existing company or a company which has just been established is acquired by two or more persons or undertakings, this may lead to the acquisition of joint control. In the latter case the relationship between the persons or undertakings which have acquired joint control is governed by contracts that are concluded between them and which normally incorporate terms for the exercise of joint control, the rights of each person or undertaking which has acquired control, etc. As opposed to cases of acquisition of sole control, in cases of joint control it is important to examine the contract that governs the relationship between the persons or undertakings that acquire jointly the control of another undertaking or form a joint undertaking. It is this very agreement whose subject-matter according to Article 4(2) constitutes the concentration.

For the purpose of interpretation of Article 4(3), a trader who carries out business activities and participates in a concentration within the meaning of Article 4 could also qualify as an undertaking. The same applies to the general partners of a general partnership and to the general partners of a limited partnership who also have commercial capacity.

Article 4(2)(b) makes a distinction between the acquisition of direct and indirect control. Direct control is acquired when a company has the ownership or the usufruct of the whole or part of an undertaking. Within this meaning it is not necessary to acquire a property right but it is sufficient to rely on contractual rights, as for example in the cases of assignment of a company or of the leasing of another company. What is always crucial is to acquire the right of disposal of the whole or parts of an undertaking. For the determination of the parts of the undertaking that should form the object of control, it is necessary to take into account not only the quantitative but also the qualitative importance of those parts in relation to the position of the buyer in the relevant market.

An example is *Nutricia/Milupa*[6] where Nutricia acquired from Milupa the tangible and intangible goods relating to the production and distribution of child nutrition, diet and similar products in Germany, some real estate property and its subsidiary companies in Germany. The Competition Committee accepted implicitly the creation of a merger without examining whether the acquired property constituted a significant part of Milupa's assets. Similarly, in *Kraft/Chipita*[7] the issue to be considered was the acquisition of the bakery production of Kraft by a subsidiary of Chipita.

2.1.a. Creation of joint ventures which qualify as concentrations for the purposes of merger control

In full conformity with Article 3(2) of Regulation 4064/1989, Greek law makes a distinction between concentrative and co-operative joint ventures. Specifically, Article 4(5) provides that:

"Operations, including the creation of a joint venture, which have as their object or effect the co-ordination of the competitive behaviour of undertakings which remain independent, shall not constitute a concentration within the meaning of paragraph 2(b). The creation of a joint venture performing on a lasting basis all the functions of an autonomous economic entity which does not give rise to co-ordination of the competitive behaviour of the parties among themselves or between them and the joint venture, shall constitute a concentration within the meaning of paragraph 2(b)."

The creation of a joint venture requires the exercise of joint control by the parties. This implies the existence of "common will" and "joint exercise" of decisive influence. The mere fact that a party holds a majority shareholding in another party does not exclude the existence of joint control. On the contrary, the particular circumstances in every case and the agreements between the parties are of crucial importance. Therefore we have a case of joint control between two parties where each party holds 75% and 25% of the share capital respectively, provided that the partner with minority shareholding participates with equal votes in a committee of shareholders which approves the most significant administrative decisions of the joint venture.

In *Petrolina/EKO*[8], Petrolina and EKO established a joint venture, OPTIMUM. Each parent owned equal shares. Petrolina appointed 3 directors and the managing director whereas EKO appointed 2 directors. Resolutions in crucial matters had to be passed with a majority of 4/5 of the Board of Directors. The Competition Committee found that joint control existed on the basis not only of the equal approportionment of shares but also on the additional contract signed by the parties which provided that the election and revocation of the Board of Directors' members required the prior agreement of the parent companies (each party voted for the appointment and revocation of the directors of the other party).

Article 4(5) provides that for a joint venture to be concentrative, two conditions must be satisfied, one positive and one negative. The positive condition is that the joint venture should perform on a lasting or long-term basis all the functions of an autonomous economic entity. In *Petrolina/EKO* the Competition Committee found that a joint venture which was established for a period of 15 years could not qualify as a concentration. Nevertheless, it was accepted that significant capital investment for the establishment of a joint venture company, a transfer to the new entity of an existing company and/or of significant know-how could render the joint venture autonomous after an initial period. Additionally, it is crucial to examine the ability of the joint venture company to determine independently its own commercial policy on the basis of its own economic interests[9]. The mere fact that the parent companies exercise the right to take important decisions for the development of the joint venture does not affect the financial independence of the latter as long as the joint venture is not used by the parent companies as a vehicle to satisfy their interests.

The negative condition is that the creation of the joint venture must not have as its object or effect the co-ordination of the competitive behaviour of undertakings that remain independent of one another. The application by the Greek Competition Committee of both the positive and the negative condition for the distinction between concentrative and co-operative joint ventures stands in full conformity with the Commission's Notice on Co-operative and Concentrative Joint Ventures [10].

2.1.b. Acts which do not constitute a concentration.

Article 4(6) provides that a concentration shall not be deemed to arise when:
"a) credit institutions or other financial institutions or insurance companies, the normal activities of which include transactions and dealing in securities for their own account or for the account of others, hold on a temporary basis, securities which they have acquired in an undertaking with a view to reselling them, provided that they do not exercise voting rights in respect of those securities with a view to determining the competitive behaviour of that undertaking or provided that they exercise such voting rights only with a view to preparing the disposal of all or part of that undertaking or of its assets or the disposal of those securities and that any such disposal takes place within one year from the date of acquisition. That period may be extended for a reasonable period of time by the Competition Committee, where such institutions or companies can show that the disposal was not reasonably possible within the period set;

b) the operations referred to in paragraph 2(b) are carried out by financial holding companies, provided however that these rights are exercised, in particular in relation to the appointment of members of the management and supervisory bodies of the undertakings in which they have holdings, only to maintain the full value of those investments and not to determine directly or indirectly the competitive conduct of those undertakings."

The provision of this Article applies only in relation to credit institutions or other institutions whose normal activities include transactions and dealings in securities. The way in which the securities are acquired as well as the person in whose favour the acquisition takes place are immaterial. This provision concerns only participation rights in anonymous companies since according to Article 1a, par. 1 of Act 2190/20[11] only those rights could be incorporated in securities. The acquisition of securities must be performed with the intention of reselling them. It is not sufficient if the securities are resold to affiliated companies or to credit institutions, insurance companies or other financial institutions that belong to the same group of companies.

On the basis of the above provisions it is implied that a concentration is performed when one of the following conditions is fulfilled:
   a) credit institutions or other institutions acquire securities with the intention to influence the competitive behaviour of the company;
   b) they refrain from reselling the securities within a year from the date of acquisition;
   c) their intention of reselling is no longer present.

2.2. Obligation to notify

Act 703/1997 makes a distinction between the obligation to notify and the obligation to pre-notify concentrations which fall within the scope of this Act. In particular, Article 4a provides that every concentration shall be notified to the Competition Committee within one month of its realisation where:

"a) the market share of the products or services to which the concentration is concerned, as defined in Article 4f, represents within the national market or in a substantial part of it, with respect to the particular characteristics of the products or services, at least 10% of the combined aggregate turnover of the products or services which are regarded as identical because of their properties, their price and their intended use, or

b) the combined aggregate turnover of all the undertakings concerned, as defined in Article 4f, is at least equal to the equivalent to the drachma amount of € 10 million."

The law focuses on the size of the undertakings involved and not on their market power. The jurisdictional test for the delimitation of the undertakings which are obliged to notify relies on two quantitative criteria: the market share and/or the combined aggregate turnover. The intention of the legal draftsman was clearly to bring all types of concentrations within the scope of this provision.

For the purpose of the above provision a concentration is realised with the accomplishment of all formal requirements. However, if the completion of the concentration depends on the fulfilment of a conditional option, the concentration is realised when this option is fulfilled. In case of unconditional options or conditional time options, the realisation is effected immediately following the conclusion of the relevant contract[12].

With regard to those concentrations whose realisation depends respectively on their registration in public records (e.g. in the Register of Companies Limited by Shares, in the records of the Court of First Instance as regards personal companies or in the Land Registry for transferring ownership of interests in land) or on completion of the publication formalities of Article 8, Act 3190/55 in relation to limited liability companies, the obligation to notify starts as from their registration in the relevant public records. In the case of transfer of shares or securities the time-limit for notification runs as from the time of their acquisition. If the operation concerns the acquisition of existing shares, the realisation of the concentration and therefore the obligation to notify applies following the agreement for the transfer of ownership and delivery of the securities. In case of nominal shares, the concentration is realised with their registration in the partners' records (Article 8b Codified Law 2190/90).

In case of a culpable omission of the obligation to notify, the Competition Committee shall impose a fine not exceeding 5% of the aggregate turnover, as defined in Article 4f (Article 4a(4)). In effect this provision grants to the Competition Committee the discretion to determine the amount of the fine depending on the type and gravity of the infringement[13].

According to Article 4a, paragraph 2, the following are obliged to notify:
"a) each of the undertakings in the case where the concentration is the subject of an agreement between undertakings being parties to the merger;
b) the persons, the undertakings or the groups of persons or undertakings acquiring control of the whole or parts of one or more undertakings, in all other cases."

The Competition Committee has produced a standard form for the purpose of notification. In order to complete this form the notifying firms must provide the Competition Committee with substantial information in order to enable it to reach a decision within the prescribed time-limits[14].

Section 1 of the form requires details of the undertakings concerned; section 2 requires information on the nature and the method of the notified merger;

section 3 refers to the undertakings concerned and to those companies controlled by them; section 4 concerns general information regarding the distribution system of products or services which is applied by each of the undertakings concerned in the relevant market; in addition, this section incorporates a declaration that in case the Competition Committee concludes that the notified operation does not constitute a concentration within the meaning of Article 4, the parties wish the present application to be regarded as a notification for clearance on the basis of Article 1 para. 3 or negative clearance on the basis of Article 11 of Act 703/1977.

Apart from the administrative sanction which provides for the imposition of fines in cases of culpable omission to notify, Article 29 makes provision for penal sanctions imposed against any person acting in breach of Articles 4 to 4f. This fine should not be less than 1 million drachmas nor more than 5 million drachmas and in case of relapse, the aforementioned limits shall be doubled. In addition, Article 30(1) provides that natural persons who act contrary to the relevant provisions for the control of concentrations as defined in Articles 4 to 4f, shall be liable to the extent of their personal property and by personal detention, jointly with one another and along with the legal entity concerned for the payment of the fines imposed on the latter. According to the same provision, the aforementioned persons against which criminal prosecution is exercised and a penalty is imposed pursuant to Article 29(1), are, in case of personal undertakings, the entrepreneurs, in case of partnerships, the general partners, in case of limited liability companies and co-operatives, the administrators, and in case of joint-stock companies, the members of the Board of Directors.

The decisions of the Competition Committee may be challenged on appeal to the Athens Administrative Court of Appeal within 20 days from their notification (Article 14). Against the decisions of the Athens Administrative Court of Appeal the parties shall be allowed to appeal by a writ of error to the supreme administrative court of Greece, the Council of State (Article 15).

2.3. Obligation to pre-notify

The obligation to pre-notify a concentration to the Competition Committee within ten working days from the conclusion of the agreement, or the announcement of the public bid to buy or exchange, or the acquisition of a controlling interest applies according to Article 4b where:

"a) the market share of the products or services to which the concentration is concerned, as defined in Article 4f, represents within the national market or in a substantial part of it with respect to the particular characteristics of the products or services, at least 25% of the combined aggregate turnover of the products or services which are regarded as identical because of their properties, their price and their intended use, or

b) the combined aggregate turnover of all the undertakings concerned, as defined in Article 4f, is at least equal to the equivalent to the drachma amount of € 50 million, and the aggregate national turnover of each of at least two of the undertakings concerned is more than the equivalent to the drachma amount of € 5 million."

It should be noted that the limit of 25% of the combined aggregate turnover which is set by the law does not constitute an irrefuttable legal presumption but simply a criterion for the delimitation of large concentrations. This implies that even concentrations with an aggregate turnover of 25% could be prohibited if one of the undertakings concerned and mainly the acquiring company has significant market power and the remaining market shares are widespread among competitors.

The Competition Committee has produced a standard form for the purpose of pre-notification, the use of which is compulsory. Section 1 requires information and data in relation to the undertakings concerned and the appointment of an attorney or representative; section 2 requires detailed information regarding the notified concentration; section 3 concerns the ownership and control which is acquired over one or more undertakings; section 4 refers to personal and financial relations and to previous takeovers by the undertakings concerned; section 5 concerns any attached documents; section 6 refers to the definition of the relevant product and geographical market; section 7 requires information in relation to neighbouring markets which are affected by the concentration; section 8 requires information as to the general conditions of the affected markets as for example the nature of supply and demand, entry barriers, research and development, co-operation agreements, commercial unions; section 9 refers to general elements in relation to the market as well as to secondary restrictions regarding the concentration; finally, section 10 incorporates a declaration that in case the Competition Committee concludes that the notified operation does not constitute a concentration within the meaning of Article 4, the parties wish the present application to be regarded as a notification for clearance on the basis of Article 1 para. 3 or negative clearance on the basis of Article 11 of Act 703/1977.

Culpable omission of the obligation to pre-notify the concentration leads to the imposition of a fine not exceeding 7% of the aggregate turnover of the undertakings concerned, as defined in Article 4f (Article 4b(4))[15]. As far as those obliged to notify are concerned, Article 4b(3) provides that the provisions of paragraph 2 of Article 4a shall apply. Within this context it should be mentioned that Article 4b(4) differs from the notification requirement of Article 4a in terms of the amount of the applicable fine, which in the present case is calculated on the basis of the aggregate turnover of the "undertakings concerned". The use of the phrase "undertakings concerned" instead of the phrase "undertakings obliged to notify" implies that in principle those obliged to notify are the parties to the notified operation since most concentrations constitute the subject matter of an agreement. However, in the exceptional case that the operation is not the subject matter of an agreement, the fine is imposed on the basis of the aggregate turnover of the persons or undertakings acquiring control of the whole or parts of one or more undertakings.

In case the undertakings concerned proceed to the realisation of the concentration without prior notification then Article 4b(4) and Article 4e(1)(3) apply in conjunction. Article 4e prohibits a concentration that has not been notified in accordance with Article 4b to be put into effect. In case of breaching this obligation, a fine not exceeding 15% of the aggregate turnover of the undertakings concerned, as defined in Article 4f, is imposed by the Competition Committee. Similarly, the provision of incorrect and inadequate information results not only in the imposition of a fine but also in the suspension of the time-limits for the examination of the planned concentration by the Competition Committee. Nevertheless, in *SKW/Sandoz*[16] the Competition Committee held that delay in the notification of a concentration may be justified and therefore escape sanctions in exceptional circumstances as for example in cases of *force majeur*.

As was mentioned above, apart from the administrative sanctions of Articles 4b and 4e, Article 29 makes provision for penal sanctions which may be imposed against any person acting in breach of Articles 4 to 4f.

2.4. Preventive control of concentrations: Main procedure

The substantive test for the control of concentrations is provided by Article 4c of Act 703/1977. This Article incorporates in effect the basic criterion for the prohibition of concentrations which have been notified in accordance with Article 4b (Article 4c, para. 1) as well as the criterion for the approval of a concentration which has been prohibited where the concentration in question presents advantages of general economic nature (Article 4c, para. 3).

Specifically, Article 4c, para. 1 provides that:
> "Every concentration between undertakings that is subject to prior notification and may significantly impede competition in the national market or in a substantial, with respect to the characteristics of the products or services, part of it and particularly by creating or strengthening a dominant position, shall be prohibited by decision of the Competition Committee."

As opposed to Regulation 4067/89, the concept of a dominant position is not central to the working of this Act. The control of concentrations focuses on the potential of significantly impeding competition and the creation or strengthening of a dominant position is indicated as a particular case where competition in the market is significantly restricted. The definition of the relevant product and geographical markets is an essential part of the process of appraising the potential effect of the notified operation on competition.

Also Article 4c, para. 2 states that:
> "Within the scope of appraising the possibility of a concentration to constitute significant impediment of competition within the meaning of paragraph 1 of the present Article, the following shall be taken into account, especially the structure of all the relevant markets concerned, the actual or potential competition from undertakings located either within or outside Greece, the existence of any legal or other barriers to entry, the market position of the undertakings concerned and their financial and economic power, the alternatives available to suppliers and users by the undertakings concerned as well as by the actually or potentially competitive undertakings, their access to suppliers or markets, the supply and demand trends for the relevant goods or services, the interests of the intermediate and ultimate consumers and their contribution in the development of technical and economic progress provided that it is to consumers' advantage and does not form an obstacle to competition".

Therefore, even if the combined market share of the undertakings concerned in a concentration is less than 25% in the relevant market, the concentration could still be prohibited if the financial and economic power of the undertakings could significantly impede competition. Similarly, high market shares indicate that a concentration may impede competition only if other factors, such as the allocation of market shares between competitors, the position of the other companies in the market and the existence of passive competition, are taken into account. So in *Fresenius A.G./Pharmacia&Upjohn A./B.* the combined market share of the parties to the notified operation was 65.4%. The Competition Committee took into account: a) the small size of the market for full intestinal nutrition, b) the fact that multinational pharmaceutical companies (Baxter and Brawn) and other import companies (Diapit) operated in the relevant market, c) the prices of the relevant products were determined by the State, and d) demand depended directly on the attendant doctor. On this basis it concluded that the high market share which was to be acquired by the buyer would not significantly alter the conditions of competition which existed in the relevant market.

In *Ellinika Petrelea A.E./Mamidakis & Sia A.E.E.P.* the Competition Committee found that the combined market share of the parties to the notified concentration would represent 29.8% in the market of simple petroleum, 25.7% in the market of operating petroleum, 47% in the market of crude oil 3500, 30.4% in the asphalt market, 61.6% in the paraffin fuel market, 38.2% in the shipping diesel market, 43.2% in the ocean-going diesel market, 32.8% in the shipping crude oil market, and 39.4% in the ocean-going crude oil market. Given the position held by the undertakings concerned in each of the above product and services markets and the presence of existing competition, the Competition Committee allowed the notified concentration.

Similarly, in case 108/1998, the Competition Committee found that the notified concentration between the French companies Goodyear SA, Goodyear Tyre & Rubber Co. and the Slovenian company Sava Gumarska in Keminca Industrija D.D. did not significantly impede competition within the meaning of Article 4c of Act 703/1977. In reaching this conclusion the Competition Committee took into account the fact that the relevant market was developing, supply exceeded demand, there were no legal or actual barriers to entry, 15 companies already operated in the relevant market, the most significant competitors were members of powerful international groups and the customers of most of these companies were wholesalers and retailers who preferred to have alternative sources of supply.

If the market is oligopolistic, the creation of a concentration may contribute in the development of the conditions of competition provided that the market shares of the undertakings concerned are relatively small (cases of toehold acquisition). In the case *Sara Lee/Bravo*[17] the Competition Committee held that the acquisition of Bravo by Sara Lee would increase competition since a company with significant financial and economic power would enter the Greek market in order to support its subsidiary company Bravo in competing with the other companies which are nevertheless stronger in the market and would therefore help it remain in the market. On the contrary, a concentration may not improve the conditions of competition when oligopoly is symmetrical, in other words, when all the undertakings which operate in the relevant market hold equal shares.

Article 4c(3) states that:

> "A concentration that has been prohibited by the Competition Committee, pursuant to paragraph 1, may be approved by a specifically justified decision of the Ministers of National Economy and Commerce as particularly provided in Article 4d(7), where the concentration in question presents advantages of a general economic nature that counterbalance the resulting restriction of competition, or it is regarded as being indispensable for the public interest, especially where it contributes to modernisation and rationalisation of production and economy, attraction of investments, strengthening of competitiveness in the European and international market and creation of new employment positions."

The above provision incorporates in effect the failing company defence argument. In *Kraft/Chipita*[18] the Competition Committee found that the creation or strengthening of a dominant position which would result from the notified operation could be weakened or altered if in the absence of the concentration the acquired company would have otherwise been forced to liquidation. In *Kamari/Bosinakis*[19] it was held that in a tight oligopoly the acquisition of Bosinakis by Kamari could not restrict competition since the sale of the acquired company was performed in order to confront its financial difficulties.

2.5. Suspension of concentrations

Article 4e(1) requires automatic suspension of concentrations until one of the decisions provided for in Article 4d, paras. 2-7 on the procedure for the preventive control of concentrations is issued. In case of breaching this prohibition, a fine not exceeding 15% of the aggregate turnover of the undertakings concerned shall be imposed by the Competition Committee. Although in this case the legal draftsman does not require the existence of a culpable omission to notify, it is regarded that the proof of culpability is necessary for the imposition of the fine.

Article 4e provides that the Competition Committee may, on request, grant a derogation from the obligation mentioned herewith, in order to prevent serious damage to one or more undertakings concerned by the concentration or to a third party. This decision may be made subject to certain conditions and obligations in order to ensure conditions of effective competition and to prevent situations that could hinder the execution of a possible prohibiting final decision.

Also, according to Article 4e(4), where the concentration has already been realised in breach of the decisions or provisions prohibiting its realisation, the Competition Committee may require that the undertakings or assets brought together to be separated or the cessation of joint control. Again, in case of non-compliance with this decision, a fine not exceeding 15% of the aggregate turnover of the undertakings concerned and a penalty payment of up to Drs 3 million for each day of delay to comply with, shall be imposed by the Competition Committee. The issuance of such a decision does not preclude the possibility of the concentration being approved by the Ministers of National Economy and Commerce provided that the requirements of Article 4c(3) are met.

3. Competent authorities

The applicable provisions on the control of monopolies and oligopolies and the protection of free competition require the participation of two bodies which are entrusted with the performance of certain tasks. In particular, the Competition Committee is the responsible body that supervises the application of Article 4a and issues decisions regarding the observance or not of the notification provisions of Article 4b(1) as well as the effect of a concentration on the conditions of competition. On the other hand, according to Article 4c(3), the Ministers of National Economy and Commerce are responsible for the approval of a concentration which has been prohibited by the Competition Committee pursuant to paragraph 1 of Article 4c.

When a concentration is notified, the Competition Committee examines the concentration as soon as the relevant notification is submitted (Article 4d, para.1). Where it is found that the concentration notified does not fall within the scope of Article 4b(1), the President of the Competition Committee records that finding by means of a relevant decision issued within one month from its notification (Article 4d, para. 2). On the contrary, if within the period of one month from notification, the Competition Committee finds that the concentration notified falls within the scope of Article 4b(1), the case in question is introduced to the Competition Committee for further examination on the basis of Article 4c(1) and the persons or undertakings that submitted the notification are accordingly informed (Article 4d, para. 3).

In case the Competition Committee finds that the notified concentration following modifications made by the undertakings concerned if necessary, can not lead to a significant restriction of competition, it issues a relevant decision within two months from the introduction of the case to it. The Competition Committee may attach to its decision conditions and obligations intended to ensure that the undertakings concerned comply with the commitments they have entered into *vis-à-vis* the Competition Committee with a view to modifying the original concentration plan. This decision shall also cover restrictions directly related and necessary to the implementation of the concentration (Articles 4d, paras. 4, 5).

Where the Competition Committee finds that the concentration can lead to a significant restriction of competition, it issues within two months from the introduction of the case a decision prohibiting its realisation. This decision is served to the undertakings concerned within ten days from its issuance. Within one month following the notification of the decision prohibiting the concentration the interested persons or undertakings concerned may request the Ministers of National Economy and Commerce to approve the concentration on the basis of the conditions mentioned in Article 4c(3). This decision shall be issued within a time limit of two months from its request and may be subject to conditions and obligations. The lapse of the two-month

GREECE

period is considered equivalent to the request being rejected (Article 4d, paras. 6, 7).

All the above time-limits may be extended if the participating undertakings reach an agreement, if the information contained in the notification is incomplete or if the notification is incorrect or misleading. Also, the decisions issued according to paragraphs 2, 4 and 7 of Article 4d can be revoked by the competent authority in case its issuance was based on incomplete, incorrect or misleading information; and if the undertakings concerned commit a breach of the conditions and obligations attached to the decision.

Notes

1. Article 21, paragraph 3 of Act 703/1977.
2. Articles 4a – 4e of Act 703/1977 (amendment by Act 1934/1991).
3. It should be noted that an operation which does not qualify as a concentration falls under the scope of Article 1 of Act 703/1977.

    Article 1(1) provides that: "The following shall be prohibited: all agreements between undertakings, all decisions by associations of undertakings and concerted practices of whatsoever kind which have as their object or effect the prevention, restriction or distortion of competition, and in particular those which:
    a) directly or indirectly fix purchase or selling prices or any other trading conditions;
    b) limit or control production, markets, technical development or investment;
    c) share markets or sources of supply;
    d) apply dissimilar conditions to equivalent transactions with other trading parties, thereby impeding competition, in particular by refusing without valid justification to sell, purchase or conclude any other transaction;
    e) make the conclusion of contracts subject to acceptance by the other parties of supplementary obligations, which by their nature or according to commercial usage, have no connection with the subject of such contracts".
4. Note that according to Act 2190/1990 a concentration between companies limited by shares (*anonymi etairia* "A.E.") is effected either with absorption or with the establishment of a new company.
5. Articles 68 and 69 of Act 2190/1920 and Article 54 of Act 3190/1955.
6. Case 21/1996.
7. Case 23/1996.
8. CC 31/1996.
9. See decision DSM/BASF, CC 54/1997.
10. OJ 94/C 385/1.
11. Act 2190/1920 on Anonymous Companies.
12. See case 17/1995 *Niki/Kokkinidis*.

13 See cases 165/94 *Atlantic/Kipseli*, 167/94 Dr. Michalis, 223/95 *The Lion/A.B. Vassilopoulos*, 226/95 ABC-KEM-Anistal.
14 See Article 4d of Act 703/1977.
15 See cases 120/1998 *Sarantis ABEE/Sanitas-Sanitas AE*, 116/1998 *Stakor ABEEA/Krikos ABETE*, 110/1998.
16 CC 50/1997
17 Case 12/1995.
18 Case 23/1996.
19 Case 40/1996.

Ireland

Damian Collins

Gerald FitzGerald

Contents

1. Introduction 266
   1.1. The Mergers and Take-overs (Control) Act, 1978 (as amended) . 266
   1.2. The Competition Act, 1991 (as amended) 266
   1.3. Other relevant legislation 267
2. Transactions to which the Mergers Act's notification
   obligation applies 267
   2.1. The notification obligation 267
   2.2. Asset acquisitions 270
   2.3. Thresholds 271
   2.4. Newspaper transactions 272
   2.5. Non-application of the Mergers Act 272
3. Joint ventures 273
   3.1. The Mergers Act 273
   3.2. The 1991 Competition Act 273
4. Notification of mergers and take-overs under the Mergers Act 274
   4.1. Notification by the parties 274
5. Procedure under the Mergers Act 274
   5.1. The two-stage procedure 274
   5.2. First stage: Clearance without reference to the
        Competition Authority 275
   5.3. Second stage: Reference to the Competition Authority 276
   5.4. The Minister's decision 276
   5.5. Appeals 277
6. The substantive criteria applied in the review of mergers
   and take-overs 277
   6.1. Legislative framework for the substantive criteria 277
   6.2. The Section 8 criteria 278
   6.3. Practical application of the substantive criteria 278
7. Mandatory nature of filing 279
   7.1. Obligation to notify 279
   7.2. Criminal consequence 279
   7.3. Title to shares or assets 280
8. The application of the Mergers Act to transactions involving
   non-Irish parties 280
   8.1. Lack of precision in thresholds 280

IRELAND

 8.2. Practice in relation to non-Irish transactions 281
9. Other procedural issues under the Mergers Act 281
 9.1. Protection of business secrets and confidentiality 281
 9.2. Publicity, complaints and interveners 281
10. The Competition Act 282
 10.1. Application of the Competition Act to mergers
  and take-overs 282
 10.2. The Competition Act's prohibitions 282
 10.3. Procedure under the Competition Act 283
 10.4. The Competition Authority's view on the application
  of the Competition Act to mergers and take-overs. 284
 10.5. The substantive analysis of mergers and take-overs
  in the Authority's notice 285
11. Proposals for reform 289
 11.1. Expert group 289
 11.2. Recommendations 289
12. Regulation of acquisitions in the banking and financial
 services sectors 290
 12.1. The Central Bank Act, 1989 290
 12.2. Notification under the Central Bank Act, 1989 290
 12.3. Notification under the Investment Intermediaries
  Act, 1995 and the Stock Exchange Act, 1995 291
 12.4. Notification under the Non-Life Insurance Framework
  Regulations, 1994 and the Life Assurance Framework
  Regulations, 1994 292
13. Other clearances 293
 13.1. IFSC companies 293
 13.2. Companies in receipt of incentives 294
Annex 1 295
Annex 2 297
 Notes 298

1. Introduction

1.1. The Mergers and Take-overs (Control) Act, 1978 (as amended)

The principal legislation regulating mergers and take-overs in Ireland is the Mergers and Take-overs (Control) Act, 1978 (as amended)[1] ("the Mergers Act"). The Mergers Act provides for the compulsory notification of mergers and take-overs, prior to their implementation, to the Minister for Enterprise, Trade and Employment (the "Minister").[2] The Minister reviews the proposed transaction by reference to "the exigencies of the common good" which include competition-based criteria as well as broader policy criteria (for example, employment, regional development, research and development). Following her review, the Minister may clear the proposed transaction, prohibit it absolutely or permit it to proceed subject to conditions. Before reaching her decision, the Minister may refer the proposed transaction to the Competition Authority, an independent statutory body established under the 1991 Competition Act, for investigation and report. (If she wishes to be in a position to prohibit a proposed transaction, or to impose conditions in relation to it, the Minister *must* first refer it to the Authority.)

1.2. The Competition Act, 1991 (as amended)

The Competition Act 1991 (in this chapter referred to, including its subsequent amendment,[3] as "the Competition Act") introduced, at Section 4, a prohibition on anti-competitive agreements and arrangements and, at Section 5, a prohibition on the abuse of dominant position. These prohibitions are substantively based on Articles 85 and 86 of the EC Treaty. The Competition Authority, which is responsible for the enforcement of the Competition Act, maintains that the provisions of that Act may apply to mergers and take-overs (notwithstanding the prior existence of a merger control system in the Mergers Act). This interpretation of the Act by the Authority is controversial and has not yet been confirmed by the Irish Courts (which, in the Irish constitutional system, are ultimately responsible for the interpretation of Irish legislation). The Authority has issued a notice outlining its approach to the application of the Section 4 prohibition to mergers and take-overs.

1.3. Other relevant legislation

Clearances for mergers and take-overs may also be required under other legislation relating to specific economic sectors (in particular, banking, insurance, investment services). Clearances may also be required in respect of transactions involving companies operating in the Dublin International Financial Services Centre and involving companies in receipt of incentives for investment in Ireland.

2. Transactions to which the Mergers Act's notification obligation applies

2.1. The notification obligation

The Mergers Act's prior notification obligation applies to a proposed transaction which:
(a) is a "merger or take-over" within the meaning given to that phrase in the Mergers Act; and
(b) involves two or more enterprises each having either turnover or gross assets with a value in excess of thresholds fixed in the Mergers Act.

2.1.1. "Merger or take-over"

The Mergers Act includes a number of provisions intended to clarify the meaning of the phrase "merger or take-over". Within the scheme of the Mergers Act, these provisions play a rôle roughly equivalent to Article 3 of the EC Merger Control Regulation which defines the meaning of "concentration".

As its basic principle, the Mergers Act provides that a "merger or take-over" shall be taken to exist where two or more enterprises, at least one of which carries on business in the State[4], "come under common control"[5]. As an appreciation of the scope of this basic definition of the phrase "merger or take-over" depends on an understanding of a number of key terms and concepts used in the Mergers Act, these key terms will be examined individually in the following paragraphs.

2.1.2. "Enterprise"

"Enterprise" is defined as being a person (a term sufficiently broad, in Irish legal terminology, to include legal persons such as companies) or partnership engaged for profit in the supply or distribution of goods or the provision of services.[6] Expressly included in this definition are:
  (i) societies, including credit unions, registered under the Industrial and Provident Societies Acts;
  (ii) societies registered under the Friendly Societies Acts;
  (iii) societies registered under the Building Societies Act.

To fall within the definition, an enterprise must be engaged for profit in the supply of goods or the provision of services; the term "goods" is not defined but "services" is.[7] The definition of "services" is important because it excludes a number of fields of economic activity from the scope of the Mergers Act. "Service" includes any professional service but does not include:
  (a) banking services provided by the holder of a licence granted under the Central Bank Act, or the Trustee Savings Banks Acts;[8]
  (b) any service provided under a contract of employment;[9]
  (c) any service provided by a local authority as defined by the Local Government Act;[10]
  (d) the owning or transfer of land where this activity is the sole activity of the enterprise concerned.[11]

Holding companies are also expressly included in the definition of "enterprise" in the Mergers Act.[12]

2.1.3. "Carry on business in the State"

A proposed transaction will only be a merger or take-over if one of the enterprises which will be brought under common control as a result of the proposed transaction carries on business in the State. The obvious intention behind the inclusion of this requirement was to restrict the potentially universal application of the Mergers Act and to limit its ambit to transactions involving enterprises with an economic link to Ireland. To a limited extent this objective is achieved, although, as discussed further below, the imprecise drafting of the Mergers Act's threshold provision causes confusion in the appraisal of its application to proposed transactions involving non-Irish parties with limited economic activity in Ireland. However, the inclusion of the requirement that one of the enterprises coming under common control should carry on business in Ireland does at least confirm that mergers or take-overs involving parties with no business activity in Ireland are outside the scope of the Mergers Act.

It is also suggested that the "carry on business" requirement excludes from the application of the Mergers Act situations in which a purchaser who does not carry on business in Ireland acquires from a vendor a business which is not engaged in any business activities in Ireland, even if that vendor carries on, through a part of its business which it will retain, business activities in Ireland. This suggestion is made on the grounds that, in applying the "merger or take-over" test, the correct analysis must focus on the enterprises which will come under common control as a result of the proposed transaction. Where the part of its business which is active in Ireland is retained by the vendor and the purchaser does not carry on business in Ireland, it will usually not be possible to identify any enterprise carrying on business in Ireland which comes under common control as a result of the proposed transaction.

The Mergers Act does not include any definition of the phrase "carry on business". The relatively general nature of the phrase can give rise to difficulties in the appraisal of the Act's application. It seems clear that an enterprise will be regarded as carrying on business in Ireland if it maintains a factory, has established a subsidiary, has registered a branch or operates through a wholly integrated agent in Ireland. More difficult questions arise when an enterprise's products are distributed in Ireland by an independent distributor. The decision as to whether or not an enterprise in this situation carries on business in Ireland may need to be reviewed by reference to the place of transfer of title to the products in question.

2.1.4. "Common control"

In the EC Merger Control Regulation, a concentration is deemed to arise either where enterprises "merge" or where direct or indirect "control" is acquired[13]. The Irish Mergers Act combines both concepts within the notion of enterprises being brought under "common control". In an attempt to clarify the meaning of "common control", the Mergers Act deems enterprises to come under "common control" if:

(a) the decision as to how or by whom each shall be managed can be made either by the same person or by the same group of persons acting in concert;[14] or
(b) an enterprise, whether by means of acquisition or otherwise, obtains the right to appoint or remove a majority of the board or committee of management of a second enterprise;[15] or
(c) an enterprise, whether by means of acquisition or otherwise, obtains the right to shares which carry more than 25% of the total voting rights in a second enterprise (unless before the acquisition the first enterprise already controlled more than 50% of the voting rights in the second enterprise).[16]

The drafting of these "common control" deeming provisions leaves something to be desired in terms of clarity; this lack of clarity is compounded by the absence of any published decisions or guidelines by the Minister's Department on the scope of the deeming provisions' application. Considerable difficulties of appraisal can arise in the context of the granting of options or conversion rights in respect of shares. Similarly, while it seems that the deeming provisions apply to incremental increases in a holding of voting shares between 25% and 50%, this is not stated expressly in the legislation.

2.2. Asset acquisitions

The Mergers Act also includes a provision which brings certain asset acquisitions within the definition of "merger or take-over".[17] The Act deems a proposed transaction to be a "merger or take-over" where the assets (including goodwill) or a substantial part of the assets of an enterprise are acquired by another enterprise if the result would be to place the acquiring enterprise in a position to replace (or substantially to replace) the selling enterprise in the business in which that enterprise was engaged immediately before the acquisition. An asset acquisition is a "merger or take-over" only if the value of the assets acquired is more than IR£ 10 million (€ 12.69 million) or the value of the turnover generated by the assets acquired exceeds IR£ 20 million (€ 25.39 million).

2.3. Thresholds

The prior notification obligation in the Mergers Act applies to a proposed transaction which is a "merger or take-over" only if, in their most recent financial year, the value of the gross assets of each of two or more of the enterprises involved in the proposal is not less than IR£ 10 million (€ 12.69 million) or the turnover of each of two or more enterprises involved is not less than IR£ 20 million (€ 25.39 million).[18] The Mergers Act specifically provides that turnover does not include any payment in respect of VAT on sales or in respect of duty of excise.[19]

It should be noted that the Mergers Act's thresholds are not specifically limited to the value of the parties' Irish assets or their Irish turnover (see section 8 below).

It should also be noted that the Act does not specify which enterprises should be regarded as "involved" in a proposed transaction. In particular, the Mergers Act includes no provision equivalent to Article 5(2) of the EC Merger Control Regulation relating to the calculation of turnover in the case of the acquisition of part of an undertaking. This lack of precision in the Mergers Act occasionally gives rise to suggestions that the assets and turnover of the vendor should be taken into account in the application of the Mergers Act's thresholds to take-overs. While the better view seems to be that the Mergers Act's thresholds should be applied only to the enterprises which will come under common control as a result of the proposed transaction, given the vagueness of the wording it may be prudent to consider the vendor's assets and turnover as well.

Furthermore, the Mergers Act does not include any rules, equivalent to Article 5(4) of the EC Merger Control Regulation, to assist in identifying the turnover (or assets) which should be attributed to the enterprises involved. It is generally assumed, however, that, subject to the approach explained in the preceding paragraph, an enterprise involved in a proposed transaction should have attributed to it the turnover and assets of the group to which it belongs, roughly in accordance with the rules outlined in Article 5(4) of the EC Merger Control Regulation. It is occasionally suggested that an enterprise should have attributed to it the turnover and assets of any other enterprise in which it holds, or which holds in it, more than a 25% voting rights interest. This suggestion is made on the basis that such enterprises are deemed to be under "common control" by the Mergers Act.[20]

The Mergers Act does not contain any special rules for calculating the turnover of credit institutions or other financial institutions, or of insurance enterprises equivalent to those contained in Article 5(3) of the EC Merger Control Regulation.

The Minister has wide powers as regards the thresholds in the Mergers Act. First, she may by order increase the thresholds.[21] Secondly, where the Minister is of the opinion that the exigencies of the common good require it she may order that the Act shall apply to proposed transactions of a particular class even though the thresholds are not met.[22]

2.4. Newspaper transactions

The power to apply the Mergers Act's notification obligation to all transactions of a particular class was exercised by the Minister in an order which effectively brought all acquisitions in the newspaper sector within her control. The relevant provisions require the notification of any proposed merger or take-over which involves at least one enterprise engaged in newspaper printing or publication regardless of the turnover or gross assets of the enterprises concerned.[23] The definition of "newspaper" in the order is not confined to newspapers printed or published in Ireland, although trade and professional newspapers are excluded.

2.5. Non-application of the Mergers Act

The Mergers Act specifies a number of situations in which, although enterprises come under common control, its provisions do not apply:
    (a) where two or more bodies corporate are involved each of which is a wholly owned subsidiary of the same body corporate;[24]
    (b) where the person acquiring control through shares or voting rights is an underwriter or jobber acting as such;[25]
    (c) where the person who can make the management decisions about the enterprises concerned is a receiver or a liquidator acting as such;[26]
    (d) where an acquisition of assets by which one enterprise can replace another is made by a receiver or liquidator acting as such;[27]
    (e) where the enterprises come under common control solely as a result of testamentary disposition or intestacy.[28]

3. Joint ventures

3.1. The Mergers Act

Unlike the EC Merger Control Regulation, the Mergers Act does not include any provision relating specifically to joint ventures. It is, however, generally agreed that the Mergers Act may apply to certain types of joint venture. In particular, where an enterprise obtains shares with more than 25% of the voting rights in an existing second enterprise in order to operate that second enterprise as a joint venture with a third enterprise, that share acquisition for the purposes of forming the joint venture may be a "merger or take-over" within the meaning of the Act. Application of the turnover and asset thresholds will determine whether or not the arrangement is notifiable under the Mergers Act.

It is less easy to identify how the Mergers Act would apply to the formation of a *"de novo"* joint venture, where the parties do not take any interest in an existing enterprise. It will be recalled that, for a "merger or take-over" to exist under the Mergers Act, two or more "enterprises" must come under "common control". Although the acquisition of more than 25% of the voting rights in an enterprise may be sufficient for a transaction to be deemed to be a "merger or take- over", there must be a significant question as to whether the *de novo* non-trading joint venture company in which the partners take their shares is an "enterprise". It will be recalled that a company or partnership is an "enterprise" within the meaning of the Mergers Act only where it is "engaged for profit in the supply or distribution of goods or provision of services". Newly established non-trading entities would not normally fall within this definition.

3.2. The 1991 Competition Act

As will be seen below, the Competition Act introduced into Irish domestic law a competition law system analogous to the EC system based on Articles 85 and 86 of the EC Treaty.

Although the experience of the Competition Authority (which enforces the Competition Act) in respect of the joint ventures is limited, it is generally assumed that the Competition Act may apply to joint ventures where their object or effect is the prevention, restriction or distortion of competition. As a result, it might be necessary to consider notification of certain joint ventures to the Competition Authority.

The Authority has not distinguished between co-operative and concentrative joint ventures; in any event, the distinction may be of little consequence in Irish law and practice since the Authority appears to take the view that the Competition Act applies to concentrative transactions which would be regarded as "mergers or take-overs" under the Mergers Act.

4. Notification of mergers and take-overs under the Mergers Act

4.1. Notification by the parties

Where the Mergers Act applies to a proposed merger or take-over, each of the enterprises involved is required to notify the Minister in writing with full details within one month of the making of an offer capable of acceptance, the effect of which would be to bring the enterprises under common control.[29]

Although the Mergers Act provides for separate notification by each party to the proposed transaction, the practice of joint notification has developed for agreed or friendly transactions (which constitute the vast majority of notified transactions). The requirement that both parties notify can allow the target of a hostile bid some control over the timing of the Act's review procedure.

There is no particular form to be completed for the purposes of notification. However, guidelines indicating the information to be supplied in the notification to the Minister have been issued (Annex 1).

A IR£ 4000 (€ 5079) fee is payable on notification.[30]

5. Procedure under the Mergers Act

5.1. The two-stage procedure

The Mergers Act essentially provides for the possibility of a two-stage review procedure. Transactions which do not raise concerns (in practice, the large majority of cases) are usually cleared during the first stage by the Minister acting alone. The second stage of the review procedure, which involves the reference of the proposed transaction to the Competition Authority, is initiated by the Minister only in cases which give rise to serious competition or other policy concerns.

5.2. First stage: Clearance without reference to the Competition Authority

For a period of one month following the receipt of the notification (or the last notification if there are separate notifications) the Minister may request further information in writing from any of the parties involved in the transaction.[31] The Minister does not have an express power under the relevant part of the Mergers Act to seek information from individuals or enterprises who are not parties to the proposed transaction. The information requested must be provided within a specified period and there are criminal sanctions for failure to reply.[32]

In this chapter, for ease of comprehension, the phrase "Notification Date" means whichever is the latest of the dates on which the Minister receives:
  (i) the notification; or
  (ii) the last notification, if there were separate notifications; or
  (iii) any additional information which she may have requested.

Within 30 days of the Notification Date, the Minister must decide whether or not to refer the transaction to the Competition Authority under the Mergers Act; the Minister can prohibit a proposed transaction or impose conditions in respect of a transaction only where she has referred that transaction to the Competition Authority and considered the Authority's report.

If the Minister decides not to refer a proposed transaction to the Authority, she is obliged "as soon as practicable" to inform the parties that she does not intend to prohibit the transaction or impose conditions.[33] The Minister's letter informing the parties of first stage clearance is usually very short and does not explain in detail the basis for her decision. If the Minister fails to take any action, the transaction will be deemed to be approved three months after the Notification Date. In practice, this first stage clearance is usually communicated to the parties within three or four weeks of the submission of a joint notification (although the time scale for a first stage clearance may be longer in cases involving separate notifications or where additional information is requested).

5.3. Second stage: Reference to the Competition Authority

The large majority of transactions notified under the Mergers Act are cleared without the initiation of the second stage procedure.

Where the Minister decides to open the second stage by referring a transaction to the Competition Authority for investigation, she must specify a time period within which the Authority should report back to her.[34] The Minister, in setting the date, must allow at least 30 days from the date of the reference for the Competition Authority's investigation.[35] Given the time-limits imposed on the Minister, the maximum period within which the Authority could be allowed to report cannot exceed three months from the Notification Date. In practice, Ministers have tended not to allow the Authority much more than the minimum 30 days for submission of its report.

In its report to the Minister, the Authority is required to state its opinion concerning the proposed transaction by reference to the competition and other substantive criteria mentioned in the Mergers Act.[36]

5.4. The Minister's decision

Where the second stage of the procedure has been opened and a proposed transaction referred to the Competition Authority, the Minister may, following receipt of the Competition Authority's report:
  (a) prohibit the proposed transaction absolutely;[37] or
  (b) permit the proposed transaction subject to conditions;[38] or
  (c) take no action, thus clearing the transaction by default.[39]

The default clearance referred to at (c) comes into effect if the Minister has taken no action in respect of the proposed transaction within three months of the Notification Date. In practice, clearance by default is exceptional; it appears to have occurred only in one case since the Act's adoption.

Prohibition or conditional approval orders made by the Minster must state the reasons for their adoption and, in the case of a conditional order, may have retrospective effect.[40] Where she makes a conditional order, the Minister must include a condition requiring the merger or take-over to be effected within 12 months of the making of the order.[41] Every order must be laid before both Houses of the Oireachtas (the Irish Parliament) either of which may, by resolution, annul the order.[42] Parliamentary annulment of an order does not prejudice the validity of anything previously done under the order.[43]

It is a criminal offence to contravene an order by the Minister which either prohibits a proposed transaction or approves a proposed transaction subject to conditions.

The Minister may revoke an order which she has made or, with the agreement of the enterprises concerned, may amend an order.[44] In practice, the Minister can use this power of revocation or amendment to accept a modified version of a proposed transaction which she has previously prohibited or approved subject to conditions.

A written statement by the Minister that she has decided not to prohibit a proposed transaction ceases to have effect after 12 months if the enterprises have not come under common control during that period. [45]

Annex 2 contains an overview of the number of notifications, references and orders made under the Mergers Act since its entry into force.

5.5. Appeals

Any enterprise referred to in a prohibition order or conditional approval order may appeal the order to the High Court on a point of law.[46] Where the Court allows the appeal, the Minister must amend or revoke the order.[47]

6. The substantive criteria applied in the review of mergers and take-overs

6.1. Legislative framework for the substantive criteria

The Mergers Act provides that the Minister may prohibit a proposed transaction absolutely or make it subject to conditions where she thinks that the "exigencies of the common good so warrant".[48] The Mergers Act states that those "exigencies of the common good" shall include, but are not confined to, the criteria in Section 8 of the Act,[49] which outlines the issues on which the Competition Authority is required to express opinions and views in the report to the Minister on a proposed transaction which has been referred to it for review.

6.2. The Section 8 criteria

In its review, the Competition Authority is, first, required to express its opinion "as to whether the proposed merger or take-over concerned would be likely to prevent or restrict competition or restrain trade in any goods or services".[50] It is, secondly, required to express its opinion as to whether the proposed transaction "would be likely to operate against the common good".[51] The Authority in dealing with this second "common good" criterion is required to give its view on the likely effect of the proposed transaction in respect of:
- (i) continuity of supplies or services,
- (ii) level of employment,
- (iii) regional development,
- (iv) rationalisation of operations in the interests of greater efficiency,
- (v) research and development,
- (vi) increased production,
- (vii) access to markets,
- (viii) shareholders and partners,
- (ix) employees,
- (x) consumers.[52]

6.3. Practical application of the substantive criteria

In practice, the Competition Authority's reviews of proposed transactions referred to it are focussed almost exclusively on the competition criterion. The other "common good" criteria are usually canvassed in a fairly perfunctory manner. In relation to the competition criterion, the substantive similarity in its formulation ("prevent or restrict competition or restrain trade") with Section 4 of the Competition Act (which prohibits arrangements which "have as their object or effect the prevention, restriction or distortion of competition in trade") will be noted. For this reason, it is not surprising that the Competition Authority, when reviewing proposed transactions referred to it by the Minister, tends to use as the basis for its substantive analysis the approach it outlined in its notice on the application of Section 4 of the Competition Act to mergers and take-overs.[53] This notice is discussed in section 10 below.

In practice, the Competition Authority recommends prohibition only in the case of a proposed transaction which give rise to serious concerns in respect of competition. No recommendation for prohibition has ever been made by the Authority and no prohibition order has ever been made by the Minister on the basis of the other "common good" criteria.

7. Mandatory nature of filing

7.1. Obligation to notify

The requirement to notify a "merger or take-over" which satisfies the Mergers Act's thresholds may be regarded as mandatory since it is a criminal offence to fail to notify and the Mergers Act also provides that title to any assets and shares shall not pass to a purchaser where a notifiable transaction has not been notified.

7.2. Criminal consequence

Failure to notify (or to provide additional information requested following notification) may result in criminal liabilities for the "person in control" of the enterprise concerned. The "person in control" is:
   (a) in the case of a body corporate, any officer of the body corporate who knowingly and wilfully authorises or permits the contravention;
   (b) in the case of a partnership, each partner who knowingly and wilfully authorises or permits the contravention;
   (c) in the case of any other form of enterprise, any individual in control of that enterprise who knowingly and wilfully authorises or permits the contravention.[54]

Where a person in control is found guilty of a failure to notify (or to supply information), he may be liable:
   (i) on summary conviction, to a fine not exceeding IR£ 1,000 (€ 1270) and, for continued contravention, to a daily default fine not exceeding IR£ 100 (€ 127), or
   (ii) on conviction or indictment, to a fine not exceeding IR£ 200,000 (€ 254,000) and, for continued contravention, to a daily default fine not exceeding IR£ 20,000 (€ 25,400).[55]

The daily default fines continue for as long as the contravention continues.[56]

7.3. Title to shares or assets

Section 3 of the Mergers Act provides that, in relation to a proposed merger or take-over, title to any shares or assets concerned will not pass until one of the following events has occurred:
  (a) the Minister has issued a first stage clearance; or
  (b) the Minister has made a conditional approval order; or
  (c) the transaction has been cleared by default.

The Mergers Act also permits the vendor to sue the purchaser in respect of a loss suffered as a result of the application of this invalidity sanction.

The invalidity provision operates as a *de facto* suspension provision. The Mergers Act does not include any express provision requiring parties to a proposed transaction to suspend its implementation pending clearance and does not impose criminal sanctions in respect of pre-clearance implementation. The effect of the invalidity provision is, however, to render invalid, under Irish law, any transfer of shares or assets implemented in disregard of the Mergers Act's notification requirement or prior to clearance. It should be noted, however, that some commentators have queried the effectiveness of the invalidity provision in respect of transactions which do not involve any asset or share transfers directly subject to Irish law.

8. The application of the Mergers Act to transactions involving non-Irish parties

8.1. Lack of precision in thresholds

It has already been noted that the Mergers Act thresholds are not expressly limited to the value of the parties' Irish gross assets or their Irish turnover. As a result, there is some doubt about the application of the Act's notification obligation to transactions involving non-Irish parties where their world-wide assets or turnover exceed the thresholds but their Irish assets and turnover fall below the thresholds. In practice, the officials in the Minister's Department responsible for the administration of the Mergers Act routinely take the view that where the value of the world-wide gross assets or the world-wide turnover of the parties exceeds the thresholds, the notification obligation in the Act only applies if the business over which control will change as a result of the proposed transaction has either the value of either the gross assets or turnover in Ireland in excess of the Act's thresholds.

8.2. Practice in relation to non-Irish transactions

The Minister's officials recognise the difficulties which arise as a result of the ambiguous drafting of the Mergers Act's threshold provision and have developed a procedure often referred to as "short-form notification". In response to a submission by the parties (the principal purpose of which is to show that the value of the Irish gross assets and the Irish turnover of the business over which control will change do not exceed the Act's thresholds), the Minister will issue a so-called "no-jurisdiction" letter, which confirms that, in her view, the transaction is not notifiable and that, as a result, she does not intend to make a prohibition order or an order imposing conditions. This "no-jurisdiction" letter is usually regarded as sufficient to allay any concerns in relation to criminal enforcement or the validity of the transfer of title to shares and assets under Irish law.

9. Other procedural issues under the Mergers Act

9.1. Protection of business secrets and confidentiality

The Mergers Act includes provisions designed to protect the business secrets of notifying parties in the event of the publication of information concerning the review procedure under the Act. In addition, the officials of the Minister's Department and the officers of the Competition Authority are bound by general obligations to maintain the confidentiality of the cases in which they are engaged. It is usual practice, when notifying, to request confidential treatment for material submitted in connection with the notification.

9.2. Publicity, complaints and interveners

Transactions dealt with by the Minister alone during the Act's first stage procedure involve very little, if any, publicity. Although the Act does not include any provisions on the participation of complainants or other third parties in the review procedure, it is always possible for them to make submissions to the Minister if they are aware of a proposed transaction. Where the second stage procedure is initiated and a transaction is referred to the Competition Authority, it is the Authority's usual practice to publish a notice inviting third party observations on the transaction. In such cases, it has become the practice of the Minister's Department to give the parties to the proposed transaction an opportunity to comment on the Competition Authority's report before the Minister takes her final decision. The reports of the Authority to the Minister are published.[57]

10. The Competition Act

10.1. Application of the Competition Act to mergers and take-overs

The Competition Act introduced into Irish law prohibitions on anti-competitive arrangements and the abuse of dominant position based substantively on Articles 85 and 86 of the EC Treaty. The Competition Authority has taken the view that the provisions of the Competition Act may apply to mergers and take-overs, notwithstanding the prior existence of a merger control system in the Mergers Act. This is a controversial view and it has not yet been confirmed by the Irish Courts (which, in the Irish constitutional system are ultimately responsible for the interpretation of Irish legislation). The Competition Authority has issued a notice outlining its approach to the application to mergers and take-overs of the Competition Act's prohibition on anti-competitive arrangements. In practice, relatively few mergers and take-overs are notified to the Competition Authority under the Competition Act.

10.2. The Competition Act's prohibitions

Section 4(1) of the Competition Act prohibits and renders void
> " ... all agreements between undertakings, decisions by associations of undertakings and concerted practices which have as their object or effect the prevention, restriction or distortion of competition in trade in any goods or services in the State or in any part of the State including in particular, without prejudice to the generality of this subsection, those which:

(a) directly or indirectly fix purchase or selling prices or any other trading conditions;
(b) limit or control production, markets, technical development or investment;
(c) share markets or sources of supply;
(d) apply dissimilar conditions to equivalent transactions with other trading parties thereby placing them at a competitive disadvantage;
(e) make the conclusion of contracts subject to acceptance by the other parties of supplementary obligations which by their nature or according to commercial usage have no connection with the subject of such contracts."

The similarity of Article 81(1) of the EC Treaty is apparent.

Section 5(1) of the Competition Act prohibits:
"Any abuse by one or more undertakings of a dominant position in trade for any goods or services in the State or in a substantial part of the State."

Section 5(2) provides examples of behaviour which may constitute the abuse of a dominant position in the following terms:
"(a) directly or indirectly imposing unfair purchase or selling prices or other unfair trading conditions;
(b) limiting production, markets or technical development to the prejudice of consumers;
(c) applying dissimilar conditions to equivalent transactions with other trading parties, thereby placing them at a competitive disadvantage;
(d) making the conclusion of contracts subject to the acceptance by other parties of supplementary obligations which by their nature or according to commercial usage have no connection with the subject of such contracts."

Again, the similarity to Article 82 of the EC Treaty is apparent.

10.3. Procedure under the Competition Act

The Competition Act provided for the establishment of the Competition Authority, which was given the task of reviewing applications for licences and certificates under the Act. Licences are the equivalent of exemptions under Article 85(3) of the EC Treaty and certificates are the equivalent of negative clearances in the EC system. Licences and certificates are available only in respect of the Section 4(1) prohibition; there is no provision for clearance under Section 5.

Licences and certificates under the Competition Act may be issued only by the Competition Authority. Applications are made on the Form CA which is drafted in terms very similar to the Form A/B used by the European Commission.

Since the entry into force of the Competition (Amendment) Act, 1996, infringement of Section 4(1) or Section 5 is a criminal offence. The Competition Authority or the Minister may initiate criminal prosecution in respect of violations of the Competition Act's prohibitions.

In addition, the Minister, the Authority or any party who is aggrieved "in consequence of any agreement, decision, concerted practice or abuse which is prohibited under Section 4 or 5"[58] may bring an action in the Hight Court for relief against any party to the agreement, decision or concerted practice or any party which has abused a dominant position. The Minister or the Authority may seek a declaration that the activity complained of is unlawful and/or an injunction requiring the parties to take or to refrain from taking action specified in the Court's order. Where an aggrieved party initiates Court proceedings in respect of a breach of the Competition Act, he is entitled to ask the High Court for relief by way of injunction, declaration and damages (including exemplary damages).[59]

10.4. The Competition Authority's view on the application of the Competition Act to mergers and take-overs.

Unlike other systems,[60] there is no provision in the Mergers Act, or the Competition Act, which expressly excludes the application of the generally applicable rules on competition (i.e. Sections 4 and 5 of the Competition Act) to mergers and take-overs. The Competition Authority has repeatedly expressed the view that, notwithstanding the prior enactment of the Mergers Act, the prohibitions contained in Sections 4 and 5 of the Competition Act may apply, in certain circumstances, to mergers and take-overs (whether or not notifiable under the Mergers Act).

In a 1997 Notice,[61] the Authority adopted a Category Certificate (a form of group negative clearance) under the Competition Act in respect of mergers and take-overs. The Authority's objective in publishing this notice was, of course, to alleviate concern caused by its affirmation of the dual application of the Mergers Act and the Competition Act to mergers and take-overs. The Authority sought in its Notice to offer guidelines to identify the situations in which it believed, according to its own interpretation, that the Competition Act did not apply to mergers and take-overs. The Notice is, generally speaking, drafted in clear terms and fulfills the useful subsidiary function of providing an insight in the Authority's approach to the application of the Mergers Act's competition criterion to proposed transactions referred to it by the Minister. However, given that the Notice repeats the Authority's view that the Competition Act may apply to mergers and take-overs, it now seems that the imbroglio of the dual application of that Act and the Mergers Act to mergers and take-overs will be resolved only through judicial clarification or the enactment of primary legislation.

10.5. The substantive analysis of mergers and take-overs in the Authority's notice

10.5.1. Basic concepts

In considering the application to mergers and take-overs of the Competition Act's Section 4(1) prohibition of anti-competitive agreements, the Authority distinguishes between horizontal transactions (i.e. transactions between undertakings which are competitors in one or more markets) and vertical transactions (i.e. transactions between undertakings which operate at different stages in the production or distribution process). Horizontal transactions require closer analysis under competition law, the Authority says, because they are more likely to result in a reduction or diminution of competition.

10.5.2. Vertical transactions

In its Notice, the Authority explains its views on the application of Section 4(1) of the Competition Act to vertical transactions, that is mergers between firms which operate at different stages in the production or distribution process (including mergers between a firm and its suppliers or between a firm and its distributors or retailers). In the Authority's view, these vertical transactions generally pose less risks to competition than mergers or take-overs involving actual or potential competitors. The Authority states that, in general, vertical transactions will not contravene Section 4(1) of the Competition Act. However, the Authority expresses the concern that in certain circumstances, vertical integration resulting from vertical mergers or take-overs could have anti-competitive effects where, for example, the transaction has the effect of blocking access either to sources of raw materials or to distribution outlets. The Authority explains that it will regard any merger between firms which had the effect of foreclosing entry to one or more markets as contravening Section 4(1). The Authority explains that its analysis of vertical transactions will focus on the share of the market foreclosed to competitors, entry barriers and any elimination of potential competition.

10.5.3. Horizontal transactions

Among the factors which the Authority believes need to be considered in order to decide whether a proposed horizontal transaction would have the effect of preventing, restricting or distorting competition are the actual level of competition in the market, the degree of market concentration and how it is affected by the merger, the ease with which new competitors may enter the market and the extent to which imports may provide competition to domestic suppliers.

The Authority believes that where post-merger market concentration levels are relatively low, a proposed horizontal transaction will not have any adverse effect on competition in a market. For the assessment of the degree of concentration, the Authority uses two relevant measures of market concentration: the four firm concentration ratio and the Herfindahl-Hirschman Index (HHI).[62]

10.5.4. Application of the HHI

In the Authority's view, the HHI is a better measure of market concentration than the four firm concentration ratio since it takes into account the relative size of all of the firms in the relevant market. The Authority acknowledges that because information on market shares of all the firms in a market is required, in certain cases it may be difficult to calculate the HHI. However, as the HHI provides more accurate information on market structure and concentration, the Authority believes that it should be used wherever possible. Where there is inadequate information on market shares to estimate the HHI to a reasonably high degree of accuracy, the Authority uses the four firm concentration ratio.

In its Notice, the Authority explicitly refers to the 1984 US Department of Justice Merger Guidelines,[63] which use the HHI to classify markets into three categories. Under those US Guidelines, where the post-merger HHI is below 1000 the market is regarded as unconcentrated and mergers and take-overs in such markets are considered unlikely to have adverse effects on competition. Where the post-merger HHI lies between 1000 and 1800, the market is regarded as moderately concentrated. Mergers and take-overs which increase the HHI by more than 100 points in such markets are viewed, in the US Guidelines, as giving rise to potentially significant competitive concerns depending on other factors. When the HHI exceeds 1800, the market is regarded as highly concentrated, although even in this case, the US Guidelines indicate that a merger raising the HHI by less than 50 points is considered to be unlikely to have adverse competitive consequences.

The Authority recognises that in a small economy such as Ireland market concentration ratios in many sectors may be high relative to those which exist in much larger economies. The Authority also recognises that, where market concentration following a merger is found to be relatively high, the merger or take-over need not necessarily restrict competition. While recognising that the thresholds applied in the US Guidelines were developed for larger economies, the Authority nevertheless considers that they provide a useful guide. The Authority adopts the conclusion that a proposed transaction is unlikely to have any adverse effect on competition where:

  (i) the post-transaction HHI is below 1000; or
 (ii) the post-transaction HHI is between 1000 and 1800 but has increased by less than 100 points as a result of the merger or take-over; or
(iii) the post-transaction HHI is above 1800 but has increased by less than 50 points as a result of the merger or take-over.

The Authority states that where a merger or take-over satisfies the above criteria, it does not contravene Section 4(1).

10.5.5. Application of the four firm concentration ratio

The Authority also provides for the use of the four firm concentration ratio as an alternative to the HHI. Where the four firm concentration ratio is used to calculate market concentration levels, the Authority considers that if the post-transaction four firm concentration ratio is 40% or less, a proposed transaction would be unlikely to have any adverse effect on competition. Therefore, the Authority states that it will not regard a proposed transaction as contravening Section 4(1) of the Competition Act if the four firm concentration ratio in the relevant market following the transaction is below 40%.

10.5.6. "Irrespective of the level of concentration"

It is important to note, however, that the Authority considers that, even in relatively highly concentrated markets, a proposed horizontal transaction will not have an adverse effect on competition in the absence of barriers to entry or where there is a significant level of competition from imports. The Authority's Notice provides that, irrespective of the level of market concentration following the proposed transaction, Section 4(1) of the Competition Act will not apply unless it can be shown that there are barriers which would prevent other firms entering the market or that there is little prospect for purchasers of the products concerned to obtain supplies from outside the State.

10.5.7. Creation or strengthening of a dominant position

The Authority also refers in its Notice to proposed transactions which could potentially create or strengthen a dominant position. The Authority states that the form of negative clearance provided for in its Notice is not available to a horizontal transaction between two undertakings where either firm already has a 35% share of a relevant market. Such transactions, in its view, require individual scrutiny.

10.5.8. Ancillary restrictions

The Authority Notice also contains guidance on the application of the Competition Act to ancillary restraints on post-sale competition. The Authority's approach is based on the main EU competition precedents.

11. Proposals for reform

11.1. Expert group

The application of the Mergers Act and the Competition Act to mergers and take-overs is currently subject to review by a high level expert group appointed by the Minister. The group has recently published a report which includes recommendations for the reform of the current legislative and administrative framework.

11.2. Recommendations

The group's principal recommendations were:
- the retention of the current mandatory prior notification system for mergers and take-overs;
- the abolition of the asset threshold;
- an increase in the turnover threshold to IR£ 30 million (€ 38 million) in respect of each party to a proposed transaction;
- the introduction of threshold in respect of Irish activity which would be determined by reference to the parties' combined Irish turnover and would be fixed at IR£ 30 million (€ 38 million);
- the notification of proposed transactions to the Competition Authority (rather than to the Minister, as is the case currently);
- the retention by the Minister of the final decision power in respect of notified transactions;
- a greater focus on competition-based criteria in the review of proposed transactions;
- the non-application of Section 4 and 5 of the Competition Act to all mergers and take-overs and to ancillary restrictions.

At the time of writing (January 1999), it is not possible to say whether the Expert Group's recommendations will be adopted by the Minister as the basis for reform of the current system.

12. Regulation of acquisitions in the banking and financial services sectors

12.1. The Central Bank Act, 1989

Special rules apply to the acquisition of interests in banks in Ireland. The Central Bank Act provides that the acquisition of an interest in a bank entitling the holder to more than 10% of the voting rights or to appoint or remove some or all of the board requires prior approval from the Central Bank.[64]

12.2. Notification under the Central Bank Act, 1989

Under the Central Bank Act, 1989, the approval of the Central Bank is required where a person (or more than one person acting in concert) acquires shares or other interests in a bank which:
  (a) exceed a specified proportion (at present 10%) of the total shares, or of the total voting rights attached to shares
  (b) do not exceed that 10% threshold but confer (along with any other interest held) a right to appoint or remove some or all of the board of directors.[65]

Where such an acquisition is proposed, each of the undertakings involved and having knowledge of the existence of the proposal is required to notify the Central Bank in writing of the proposal "as soon as may be".[66] Within one month of receipt by it of a notification, the Central Bank may request further information in writing.[67]

Failure to notify is an offence punishable on summary conviction by a fine of up to IR£ 1,000 (€ 1270) or by imprisonment for up to 12 months, or by both, or on conviction on indictment by a fine of up to IR£ 50,000 (€ 63,500) or by imprisonment for up to five years.[68]

Title to any shares or other interest concerned will not pass in the case of an invalid acquisition.[69] Under the Act, the Central Bank may not refuse its approval unless it is satisfied that the transaction would not be in the interests of the orderly and proper regulation of banking.[70]

Where an acquisition involves a bank which controls at least 20% of the total assets of all banks in Ireland, the Central Bank Act 1989 also requires the consent of the Minister of Finance to the proposed transaction.[71]

12.3. Notification under the Investment Intermediaries Act, 1995 and the Stock Exchange Act, 1995

A similar notification and approval regime applies to the acquisition of interests in authorised investment business firms in Ireland under the Investment Intermediaries Act, 1995. Investment business firms are defined in the Act as persons which provide one or more investment business services or investment advice to third parties on a professional basis.[72] Investment business services are widely defined and include receipt and transmission of orders in relation to investment instruments, execution of such orders, dealing with investment instruments on own account, portfolio management on a client-by-client basis and underwriting or placing issues of investment instruments.[73] Member firms of the Irish Stock Exchange, however, are subject to a separate regime.[74]

An acquiring transaction or a disposal in an authorised investment business firm must be notified to the Central Bank[75] and acquiring transactions must also be approved by the Central Bank.[76] An "acquiring transaction" means any direct or indirect acquisition where a person (or more than one person acting in concert) acquires shares or other interests in an authorised investment business firm after which:
  (a) the proportion of voting rights or capital held by the person or persons exceeds a qualifying holding. A qualifying holding is a direct or indirect holding of 10% of capital or voting rights but may cover holdings of less than 10% where, in the opinion of the Central Bank, the holding makes it possible for the persons concerned to control or exercise a significant influence over the management of the authorised investment business firm; or
  (b) the proportion of voting rights or capital held by the person or persons would reach or exceed 20%, 33% or 50%; or
  (c) the authorised investment business firm would become a subsidiary of the acquirer.[77]

A disposal means any direct or indirect disposal by a person (or more than one person acting in concert) of a qualifying holding or a disposal which would reduce such a qualifying holding so that the proportion of the voting rights or of the capital held by the person or persons would fall below 20%, 33% or 50% or so that the investment business firm would cease to be its subsidiary.[78]

Any persons proposing to make an acquiring transaction or a disposal must notify the Central Bank in writing.[79] Where an authorised investment business firm becomes aware of a proposal to make an acquiring transaction or disposal, it must inform the Central Bank of any such transactions that cause holdings to exceed or fall below a qualifying holding, or 20%, 33%, or 50% of the capital or voting rights or that cause an authorised investment business firm to cease being a subsidiary.[80] The Central Bank may request further information from any of the persons concerned with the transaction within one month of receipt by it of a notification.[81]

For an acquiring transaction to go ahead, the Central Bank must either give its approval in writing or fail to refuse to approve within a three-month period from the later of the date of its receipt of the notification (or its receipt of the additional information it has requested).[82] The Central Bank may refuse approval where it is not satisfied as to the suitability of the persons proposing to make the acquiring transaction or where it is of the opinion that the transaction is likely to be prejudicial to either or both of the sound and prudent management or the proper and orderly regulation and supervision of an authorised investment business firm.[83] As is the case with banks, title to any shares or other interests shall not pass in the case of an invalid acquisition.[84]

The Stock Exchange Act, 1995 regulates the acquisition of interests in approved stock exchanges, including the Irish Stock Exchange, and member firms of approved stock exchanges. It follows the same structure as the Investment Intermediaries Act, 1995, requiring the notification of acquiring transactions and disposals in approved stock exchanges or member firms of such exchanges to the Central Bank and the approval by the Central Bank of acquiring transactions[85].

12.4. Notification under the Non-Life Insurance Framework Regulations, 1994 and the Life Assurance Framework Regulations, 1994

Where a person proposes to acquire, directly or indirectly, a qualifying holding in an authorised non-life insurance or life assurance undertaking or to increase a qualifying holding such that the level of voting rights or capital of the holding reaches or exceeds 20%, 33% or 50% resulting in the undertaking becoming a subsidiary of that person, the relevant Minister (currently the Minister of State at the Department of Enterprise, Trade and Employment) must be notified and given an indication as to the size of the proposed acquisition.[86] A qualifying holding is a direct or indirect holding which represents 10% or more of the capital or voting rights or a holding which makes it possible to exercise a significant influence over the management of the undertaking.[87] The Minister has three months from the date of notification to oppose the acquisition.[88] If the Minister has reason to believe that the control exercised by the person acquiring the holding in question is likely to operate against the prudent and sound management of the insurance undertaking, the Minister may, for the purposes of putting an end to that situation, apply to Court for such order by way of injunction, suspension of exercise of voting rights or otherwise as the Court sees fit.[89] Similar action may be taken on breach of the notification requirements.[90]

If a holding is acquired in breach of the statutory provisions, the Court may, on application of the Minister, order the suspension of the corresponding voting rights or the nullity of votes cast in addition to any other order which may be made.[91]

A person is also required to notify the Minister where he disposes of a qualifying holding or decreases a qualifying holding such that the percentage level of the voting rights or capital which he holds falls below the levels previously mentioned.[92] An undertaking must likewise inform the Minister when it becomes aware of an acquisition or disposal of holdings in its capital which exceed or fall below any of the percentage levels mentioned.[93]

13. Other clearances

13.1. IFSC companies

Tax certificates for companies operating in the International Financial Services Centre ("IFSC") are conditional on the company agreeing to notify the Department of Finance of material changes in control and obtain pre-clearance of the change in control. Companies providing services to investment funds are subject to a separate Central Bank regime which requires approval by the Central Bank of any proposed change in ownership or in significant shareholdings, defined as shareholdings of 10% or more in the firm.[94]

13.2. Companies in receipt of incentives

Agreements with companies relating to incentives granted for investment in Ireland may include a requirement for the prior approval by the State entity granting those incentives in the event a change in control of the companies concerned.

The main State entities which grant these investment incentives include: the Industrial Development Authority ("IDA"); the Shannon Free Airport Development Company Limited ("SFADCO"); Udaras na Gaeltachta (which is responsible for the industrial development of the parts of Ireland in which the Irish language is spoken); and An Foras Aiseanna Saothair ("FAS"). The IDA is by far the most important of these. Standard IDA grant agreements include a prohibition on change of ownership without its prior consent. Failure to obtain consent may entitle the IDA to claim repayment of all or part of the grant paid.

The authors acknowledge the assistance of Niamh Moloney of McCann FitzGerald in the preparation of this chapter.

Annex 1

Notice published by the Department of Enterprise, Trade and Employment concerning notifications under the Mergers Act

The following note sets out, in general terms, the information needed in order to examine a proposed merger or take-over requiring to be notified under Section 5(1) of the above Act.

(1) Details of each of the enterprises to be involved in the proposal including ownership, current activities/numbers employed and financial performance in recent years.
   Note: In the case of public companies such information may be contained in annual reports and accounts.

(2) Details of the proposed transaction including means of control (share, asset acquisition, etc.), consideration involved and period within which transaction is to take place.
   Note: Copy of the draft legal contract (or offer document in the case of publicly-quoted companies) will generally suffice for this purpose.

(3) Estimated national market share of each of the enterprises involved in the sector(s) in which they are engaged and details of any further acquisitions which may be planned by them in these or any other sector(s) in the foreseeable future.

(4) Reasons for the proposal insofar as each of the enterprises involved is concerned.

(5) Details of any changes planned in the operation of any of the enterprises as a result of the proposal (e.g. change of product or production methods, management practices, purchase/distribution patterns, level of employment, terms and conditions of employees or geographical location).

(6) Details of any other agreement, (e.g. option purchase, exclusive dealing) which is being entered into in conjunction with, or at the same time as, the proposal.

Where non-Irish enterprises are involved:
- details or any legal sanctions or clearances which may be necessary in other jurisdictions in relation to the proposal
- details of any investigations or prosecutions instituted in respect of the enterprise(s) concerned by other national authorities in relation to antitrust or other competition law matters. Full disclosure, on the basis set out above, will normally be sufficient to allow a notified proposal to be examined without a formal request for information as provided for under Section 5(2) of the Act. However, emphasis on various points obviously varies from case to case and different issues may well arise in individual instances.

Notifying parties should, of course, feel free to submit any other information which is felt to have a bearing on the case or which is considered relevant, particularly in relation to the criteria scheduled in the Act.[95]

Annex 2

	No. notifications	No. mergers/ take-overs cleared by Minister	No. referred[96] to Examiner/ Competition Authority	No. orders made
1978/79	45	18	1	None
1980	40	20	2	None
1981	55	34	4	Conditional order, newspaper sector
1982	47	33	None	None
1983	59	29	None	None
1984	78	42	2	Conditional order, bank / building society sector
1985	65	37	2	None
1986	75	37		
1987	85	39	1	None
1988	107	56	5	Prohibition Order, Conditional Order (both alcohol sector)
1989	125	47	2	Conditional Orders for both made in 1990 (meat sector)
1990	126	62	4	None
1991	137	55	1	None
1992	142	79	1	Prohibition Order (newspaper sector)
1993	115	58	1	None
1994	124	48	None	None
1995	123	63	1	Conditional Order made in 1996 (oil distribution sector)
1996	171	54	2	None
1997	201	62	1	None

Notes

1. The following acts of primary legislation amended or repealed provisions of the Mergers and Take-overs (Control) Act 1978: the Restrictive Practices (Amendment) Act, 1987; the Competition Act, 1991; the Competition (Amendment) Act, 1996. The Mergers and Take-overs (Control) Act, 1978 has also been amended by a number of secondary legislative measures. No official consolidated version of the Mergers and Take-overs (Control) Act, 1978 (as amended) is available. However, a number of consolidated versions have been commercially published (e.g. Irish Competition Legislation, Competition Acts 1991 and 1996, Mergers and Take-overs (Control) Acts, 1978-1996, published by Baikonur, Wicklow, 1996).
2. At the time of writing (January 1999), the Office of Minister for Enterprise, Trade and Employment is held by the Tánaiste (Deputy Prime Minister), Mary Harney T.D.
3. The Competition Act, 1991 was amended by the Competition (Amendment) Act 1996.
4. The phrase "the State", frequently used in Irish legislation refers to Ireland, to the exclusion of Northern Ireland which is part of the United Kingdom. In this chapter, reference to "Ireland" or "the State" should also be understood to exclude Northern Ireland.
5. The Mergers Act, Section 1(3)(a).
6. The Mergers Act, Section 1(1).
7. The Mergers Act, Section 1(1).
8. The Mergers Act 1(1) (as amended by the Central Bank Act, 1989, Section 32); in practice, the exemption of licensed banks from the control of the Mergers Act rarely operates as most licensed banks are brought back within the scope of the Mergers Act as holding companies.
9. The Mergers Act, Section 1(1).
10. The Mergers Act, Section 1(1).
11. The Mergers Act, Section 1(1) (as amended by the Competition Act, 1991, Section 15(1)).
12. The Mergers Act, Section 1(1); This section of the Mergers Act makes specific reference to Section 155 of the Companies Act, 1963 which defines the term "holding company".
13. EC Merger Control Regulation, Article 3(1).
14. The Mergers Act, Section 1(3)(b).
15. The Mergers Act, Section 1(3)(c)(i).
16. The Mergers Act, Section 1(3)(c)(ii).
17. The Mergers Act, Section 1(3)(e).
18. The Mergers Act, Section 2(1)(a).
19. The Mergers Act, Section 2(1)(b).
20. The Mergers Act, Section 1(3)(c).
21. The Mergers Act, Section 2(4). The thresholds were increased to the present levels by the Minister by order in 1993 (S. I No. 135 of 1993).
22. The Mergers Act, Section 2(5).
23. S. I No. 17 of 1979.
24. The Mergers Act, Section 1(3)(g).
25. The Mergers Act, Section 1(3)(f).
26. The Mergers Act, Section 1(3)(f).

27 The Mergers Act, Section 1(3)(f).
28 The Mergers Act, Section 2(3).
29 The Mergers Act, Section 5(1).
30 The Mergers Act, Section 5(1A).
31 The Mergers Act, Section 5(2), 1978 Act.
32 The Mergers Act, Section 5(3), 1978 Act.
33 The Mergers Act, Section 7(a).
34 The Mergers Act, Section 8(1).
35 The Mergers Act, Section 8(1).
36 The Mergers Act, Section 8(2).
37 The Mergers Act, Section 9(1).
38 The Mergers Act, Section 9(1).
39 The Mergers Act, Section 3(1)(c).
40 The Mergers Act, Section 9(2).
41 The Mergers Act, Section 9(1)(b).
42 The Mergers Act, Section 9(5).
43 The Mergers Act, Section 9(5).
44 The Mergers Act, Section 9(4).
45 The Mergers Act, Section 3(2).
46 The Mergers Act, Section 12(1).
47 The Mergers Act, Section 12(2).
48 The Mergers Act, Section 9(1).
49 The Mergers Act, Section 9(1).
50 The Mergers Act, Section 8(2)(a).
51 The Mergers Act, Section 8(2)(b).
52 The Mergers Act, Section 8(2)(b).
53 Competition Authority, Decision No. 489, Category Certificate in Respect of Agreements involving a Merger and/or Sale of a Business (2 December 1997, Amended version, 21 January 1998).
54 The Mergers Act, Section 5(3)(c).
55 The Mergers Act, Section 5(3)(a).
56 The Mergers Act, Section 5(3)(b).
57 The Mergers Act, Section 8(2).
58 The Competition Act, Section 6(1).
59 The Competition Act, Section 6(3).
60 For example, EC Merger Control Regulation, Article 22.
61 Competition Authority, Decision No. 489, Category Certificate in respect of Agreements involving a Merger and/or Sale of Business (2 December 1997, amended version, 21 January 1998).
62 The four firm concentration ratio measures the combined market share of the four largest firms in the relevant market. The HHI is the sum of the squares of the shares of all firms in a market.
63 The provisions of these 1984 Department of Justice Guidelines in relation to horizontal transactions have been replaced by 1992 Guidelines on Horizontal Mergers which were in turn revised in 1997.

64 The Central Bank Act, Section 76.
65 The Central Bank Act, Section 76.
66 The Central Bank Act, Section 82(1).
67 The Central Bank Act, Section 82(2).
68 The Central Bank Act, Section 82(3)(a).
69 The Central Bank Act, Section 76(i).
70 The Central Bank Act, Section 78(1).
71 The Central Bank Act, Section 77.
72 The Investment Intermediaries Act, Section 2(1).
73 The Investment Intermediaries Act, Section 2(1).
74 Member firms are regulated by the Stock Exchange Act, 1995, discussed *infra*.
75 The Investment Intermediaries Act, Section 39(1) and (2)
76 The Investment Intermediaries Act, Section 40.
77 The Investment Intermediaries Act, Section 38(2).
78 The Investment Intermediaries Act, Section 38 (3).
79 The Investment Intermediaries Act, Section 39(1) and (2).
80 The Investment Intermediaries Act, Section 39(3).
81 The Investment Intermediaries Act, Section 39(4).
82 The Investment Intermediaries Act, Section 40.
83 The Investment Intermediaries Act, Section 44(1).
84 The Investment Intermediaries Act, Section 43(i).
85 The Stock Exchange Act, Sections 39-49.
86 European Communities (Life Assurance) Framework Regulations, Article 40(1).
87 European Communities (Life Assurance) Framework Regulations, Article 40(9); European Communities (Non-Life Insurance) Framework Regulations, Article 20(9).
88 European Communities (Life Assurance) Framework Regulations, Article 40(2); European Communities (Non-Life Insurance) Framework Regulations, Article 20(2).
89 European Communities (Life Assurance) Framework Regulations, Article 40(6); European Communities (Non-Life Insurance) Framework Regulations, Article 20(6).
90 European Communities (Life Assurance) Framework Regulations Article 40(8); European Communities (Non-Life Insurance) Framework Regulations Article 20(8).
91 European Communities (Life Assurance) Framework Regulations Article 40(8); European Communities (Non-Life Insurance) Framework Regulations, Article 20(8).
92 European Communities (Life Assurance) Framework Regulations, Article 40(3); European Communities (Non-Life Insurance) Framework Regulations, Article 20(3).
93 European Communities (Life Assurance) Framework Regulations, Article 40(5); European Communities (Non-Life Insurance) Framework Regulations, Article 20(5).
94 Central Bank UCITS Series of Notices, Notice 2.0, para 14; Central Bank NU Series of Notices, Notice 5.3, para 12.
95 Authors' note: Now contained in the Mergers Act, Section 8
96 From October 1, 1991 the Competition Authority replaced the Examiner of Restrictive Practices

Italy

Giovanni De Berti

Federico Regaldo

Contents

1. The Italian merger control system 303
2. The Italian Antitrust Authority 304
3. Relationship between the Authority and the European Commission and other authorities 305
4. Definition of concentration 306
5. Operations which do not constitute a concentration 307
6. Filing a notification: Thresholds, deadlines 309
7. The clearance procedure 311
8. Implementation prior to clearance 313
9. Powers of the Authority 314
10. The rights of parties involved in the investigation 316
11. Publicity and confidentiality 316
12. Substantive tests for clearance 317
13. Oligopolistic dominance 319
14. Remedies 320
15. Behavioural remedies 321
16. Structural remedies 322
17. Operations forbidden by the Authority 322
18. Clearance or prohibition due to national economic interest 324
19. Judicial review and redress 324
20. Special sectors 326
21. Conclusion 327
    Notes 328

1. The Italian merger control system

A comprehensive and thorough merger control system was introduced in Italy only recently, by comparison with other European countries, through the enactment of Law No. 287 of 10 October 1990[1] ("the Antitrust Act"), which went through Parliament without considerable debate, as if Italy were eventually adopting antitrust legislation more to cope with European responsibilities than to satisfy internal economic needs.

Actually, several attempts to introduce antitrust legislation had been made during the '50s and '60s, but they were unsuccessful and, above all, none of them had been aimed at introducing a comprehensive merger control system.

The lack of regulation in this field may also have been due to other factors. The Italian market had for many years been characterised by the massive presence of state-owned enterprises, which were originally regarded as a weapon against anti-competitive behaviour adopted by private undertakings. The Italian Constitution of 1948, whose provisions were often the result of a compromise between the leading, but opposite, Catholic and Marxist forces, contains provisions on both free enterprise and private property, namely Articles 41 and 42. These provisions mitigate rather than proclaim both principles, which are not even stated to be fundamental rights. Indeed some of its authors believed that "dangerous" private initiatives could have been easily neutralised by invoking the Constitution: the idea being that capitalistic private property had to be recognised only insofar as it had a "social function". Nowadays, witness the launch of a massive process of privatisation, these arguments seem to have lost a large part of their weight.

Rules checking unfair competition had already been inserted in the Civil Code of 1942. Thus, Italian law had long considered the problems of competition from the point of view of constitutional, civil and commercial law rather than from an administrative, or regulatory, law perspective. Articles 2598 to 2601 of the Civil Code forbid, as unfair behaviour, the use of someone else's name or trademark, the abusive imitation of a competitor's products, the confusion of one's own products or activities with those of competitors, the abusive divulging of news or opinions concerning a competitor's products or activities and, generally, the direct or indirect use of means which contrast with the principles of fair dealing in trade and which are likely to undermine others' business activities.

The scope and aim of these rules were far from those of the comprehensive antitrust rules and regulations adopted in 1990, which instituted a State authority charged with antitrust control.

Nowadays, the legal framework of Italian antitrust provisions include, besides the Antitrust Act, the regulation contained in the Presidential Decree No. 217 of 1998 ("the Antitrust Regulation")[2] and the "Guidelines for the notification of a concentration under Law No. 287 of 10 October 1990" ("the Antitrust Guidelines")[3].

2. The Italian Antitrust Authority

The *Autorità garante della concorrenza e del mercato*, the Italian competition authority ("the Authority"), is a collective body composed of a President and four Members, each appointed jointly by the Presidents of both Chambers of the Italian Parliament for a seven-year, non-renewable term. The Authority is located in Rome and is fully independent. It adopts its decisions on a simple majority basis and is not subject to governmental or parliamentary interference. The Secretary General of the Authority supervises services and offices and is appointed by the Ministry of Industry, upon the proposal of the President of the Authority[4].

The Authority exercises control over agreements restricting competition, abuses of dominant position and concentrations that may either create or strengthen a dominant position so as to substantially and lastingly eliminate or reduce competition. The Authority also has jurisdiction in the field of misleading advertising, according to Law Decree No. 74 of 1992; furthermore, it has the right to petition both Parliament and the Government and exercises advisory powers. In this latter role the Authority has often spoken out in favour of liberalisation and has criticised the abuses of the old system of State monopolies.

The Authority is divided into seven Directorates and two Offices. Three of the Directorates investigate and analyse restrictive practices and mergers, organised according to the sector of economic activity which they oversee, and are subdivided as follows:
- Directorate A: food and agriculture, mechanics, electro-mechanics, electricity and electronics, information technology and telecommunications, credit, financial services, insurance and commercial distribution;

- Directorate B: general manufacturing, mining, chemical, petrochemical and assimilated industries; construction, energy, environmental services and other public services;
- Directorate C: press and broadcasting industries and the like; transport, tourism and the like; business services.

3. Relationship between the Authority and the European Commission and other authorities

Since its origin, the scope of the Italian Authority has been confined, according to Section 1 of the Antitrust Act, to "agreements, abuses of dominant position and concentrations outside the scope of Article 65 and/or 66 of the Treaty establishing the European Coal and Steel Community, Articles 81 and/or 82 of the Treaty establishing the European Economic Community (EEC), EEC Regulations or Community acts having an equivalent statutory effect". However, due to the heavy workload of the European Commission and the inconvenience of a centralised system, it appears as thought the role of national authorities is going to be seen more and more within the broader framework of the European competition policy. This trend has become evident following the publication of the Commission Notice on the co-operation between the Commission and the competition authorities of Member States in examining the cases governed by Articles 81 and 82 of the Treaty[5] and the revision of the Merger Regulation[6] which has increased the frequency with which cases may be referred to national authorities.

The Italian Authority seems well prepared to cope with the new trend of European competition policy, given that the Antitrust Act expressly states that the provisions on agreements, abuses of dominant position and concentrations "shall be interpreted in accordance with the principles of the European community competition law". Some recent and important cases referred by the European Commission to the Italian Authority under Art. 9(3)(b) of the Merger Regulation are *Schemaventuno-Promodes/Gruppo GS*[7] and *Alliance Unichem/Unifarma*[8].

Mention must also be made of the increasing level of co-operation between the Italian Authority and other European antitrust authorities, namely in case of concentrations, not having a Community dimension, involving undertakings in various European countries.

4. Definition of concentration

According to Section 5(1) of the Antitrust Act:
"a concentration takes place when:
a) two or more undertakings *merge*;"

This can occur either when the two undertakings unite to form a new undertaking or when one undertaking takes over one or more other undertakings. The Civil Code lays down specific rules which are applicable when one or more of the merging undertakings are companies (Section 2501 *ff.* Civil Code).

> "b) one or more persons controlling at least one undertaking or more undertakings, acquire the direct or indirect *control* of the whole or of parts of one or more undertakings, whether through the acquisition of shares or assets, or by contract or by any other means;"

According to the Authority, the acquisition of control of an undertaking occurs when the operation creates a situation in which one or more individuals or corporations are able to exercise a determining influence on the whole or part of one or more undertakings. Acts of various nature, such as leases, shareholders' voting agreements or other kinds of shareholders' agreements, have been deemed by the Authority to establish such a determining influence. The Authority places both direct and indirect control on the same level; control can be sole or joint control, and consist in a power of veto; any substantive changes in a position of control, such as the passage from joint to exclusive control, would be considered as a concentration.

> "c) two or more undertakings create a *joint venture* by setting up a new company."

Although this provision of the Antitrust Act uses a different wording, not covering expressly "contractual" joint ventures which do not involve the incorporation of a new company, the notion of joint venture as elaborated by the European Commission has been adopted in its entirety by the Authority. As indicated *infra*, the Antitrust Act has also kept the distinction between co-operative and concentrative joint ventures and the Authority has established that, for the purpose of determining if there is co-ordination between the concerned undertakings the only relevant relationship is that between the joint venturers [9].

With reference to *concentrative joint ventures*, the Authority, in cases of acquisition of joint control, has scrutinised the relationship between the acquiring undertakings, considering as self-evident the functional autonomy of the joint venture [10]. As under European rules, operations transforming sole control into joint control have been considered concentrations [11].

5. Operations which do not constitute a concentration

According to Section 5 of the Antitrust Act, certain transactions are exempt from the application of the concentration rules.

With regard to *banks* and *financial institutions*, Section 5(2) establishes that:
> "Acquisition of control of an undertaking does not take place in the case of a bank or financial institution acquiring shares in an undertaking when it is formed, or when its share capital is raised, with a view to re-selling them on the market, provided that it does not exercise any voting rights vested in those securities while holding them, and that such holding period shall not exceed 24 months."

Section 5(3) of the Antitrust Act refers to *co-operative joint ventures*, stating that:
> "Operations having as their main object or effect the co-ordination of the activity of independent undertakings shall not constitute concentrations."

This provision excludes the application of the rules on concentrations in case of joint ventures whose prevalent function would be to co-ordinate the competitive behaviour of the founding undertakings. In such case, the relevant operations are subject to the rules concerning agreements which limit free competition.

If the joint undertaking would not constitute an independent economic entity the operation is not considered a concentration.

The Authority has clarified, through Section A(2) of the Antitrust Guidelines, that in order to determine whether a joint venture is co-operative or concentrative, the criteria laid down by the Commission Notice 94/C 385/01, relating to the distinction between concentrative and co-operative joint ventures, shall apply [12].

In border-line cases, the parties are allowed to notify the joint venture as a concentration, but to ask expressly for it to be treated as notification of an agreement, as the case may be.

The approach followed by the Authority in dealing with joint ventures could lead to the conclusion that it would adopt the rules contained in Article 2(4) and 3(2) of the revised version of the European Merger Regulation.

Another exemption relates to *intra-group operations*. The Authority pointed out in its Notice of 28 March 1995 [13] (later incorporated in the Antitrust Guidelines) that operations carried out within a group of non-independent undertakings are considered to be intra-group, and not to constitute mergers, if:

1. they are carried out between a party and one or more undertakings in which the former holds, directly or indirectly, more than 50% either of the capital or of the votes to be cast at the general shareholders' meeting; or
2. they are carried out between companies in all of which the same party holds, directly or indirectly, more than 50% either of the capital or of the votes to be cast at the respective general shareholders' meetings.

Nonetheless, such operations give rise to a concentration and must be notified when, due to statutory or bye-laws provisions, shareholders' resolutions or the purely financial nature of the holding, there is no relationship of dependence between the parties involved.

Concentrations are not deemed to arise either in mergers with, or in acquisitions by or of, companies which neither conduct economic activity nor directly or indirectly hold other undertakings. Such would be the case of a real property company whose only activity is the management of its own property, as long as the acquiror is not an undertaking which operates on the real property market. However such operations may amount to concentrations if the acquired parties hold licences, permits or similar rights entitling them to carry on economic activities, or if such parties control undertakings which, in turn, possess such licenses, etc.

Concentrations which produce *no turnover on Italian markets* are not subject to Italian antitrust rules. Thus, according to Section A(3) of the Antitrust

Guidelines, mergers and acquisitions of foreign undertakings need not be notified if the latter have not produced turnover in Italy over the three years prior to the transaction, either directly or through subsidiaries. However, notification is required if turnover is to be produced in Italy as a consequence of the operation.

Similarly, joint ventures or mergers in which at least one of the parties is a foreign undertaking need not be notified if the foreign party has not produced turnover in Italy over the three years prior to the operation. However, notification is required if the undertaking resulting from the operation is going to carry on economic activities on the Italian market.

6. Filing a notification: Thresholds, deadlines

If an operation meets the criteria of Section 5 of the Antitrust Act and exceeds the thresholds provided, filing is mandatory and must precede implementation.

Thresholds beyond which notification is mandatory are, as from May 1999, either:
- L 710 billion (€ 366.684 million) for the total domestic turnover of all the undertakings concerned; or
- L 71 billion (€ 36.668 million) for the total domestic turnover of the target undertaking.

Such thresholds are reviewed yearly by an amount equivalent to the variation in the so called gross domestic product price deflator index.

"Total domestic turnover" means the aggregate invoiced amounts for products sold and services rendered on the Italian market during the last financial year, net of goods returned, discounts and sale and service taxes (such as VAT). Successive acquisitions of parts of undertakings between the same parties over a period of two years is treated as a single concentration, dated as of the date of the last transaction.

In the case of banks and financial institutions, the turnover shall be deemed to be equal to the value of one-tenth of their total assets, with the exclusion of memorandum accounts and, in the case of insurance companies, to be equal to the value of premiums collected. These criteria, contained in Section 16(2) of the Antitrust Act, reproduce the original text of Council Regulation (EC) No. 4064/89, and are not in line with the amendments introduced therein in 1997.

Concentrations must be notified prior to their implementation. According to Section D(2) of the Antitrust Guidelines, a concentration is deemed to be implemented when "the capability of substantially influencing the economic behaviour of the target company" has been acquired. Hence, the notification must be filed before this moment and after the parties have reached an agreement upon "the essential elements of the operation". In particular:
- mergers must be notified before the execution of the formal deed of merger, drawn up by a notary;
- acquisition of control through a share purchase is deemed to be validly notified in advance, if the closing of the acquisition agreement is conditional upon the approval of the Authority;
- joint ventures established through the incorporation of a new company must be notified prior to the filing of its deed of incorporation with the company registry.

According to Section 19 of the Antitrust Act, "the Authority may impose on undertakings which fail to comply with the prior notification requirements provided by section 16(1) administrative fines of up to one per cent of the turnover of the year prior to the year in which the undertaking is challenged", over and above any other penalties for which they may be liable as a consequence of violation of the order of the Authority finally prohibiting the concentration.

While in the early years of its activity the Authority was more sympathetic towards parties in breach of this provision, it is now rather strict, though fines might not always be as heavy as they could be[14].

A notification of a concentration must contain very detailed information and attach all documents, as indicated in special forms provided by the Authority and published in its Bulletin, as well as any further elements that would enable the Authority to fully evaluate the contents of the relevant transactions.

The notification may contain the indication of a jointly chosen attorney, charged with receiving and/or submitting documents on behalf of each of the notifying parties. According to Section D(1) of the Antitrust Guidelines, the notification has to be filed by the acquiring party. In case of acquisition of joint control, establishment of a joint venture, or merger, the obligation falls upon all undertakings involved, which may file jointly. In case of a take-over bid, the notification has to be filed by the bidder. The above notifications may be made, alternatively, by the ultimate owner of the party that is going to acquire control.

If two or more undertakings involved in the transaction are active on the same relevant market and will hold, following the operation, no less than a 25% market share, a so-called "full form" must be used for notification purposes. The full form must also be used in vertical concentrations, when one of the parties will eventually hold no less than a 40% market share.

In all other cases and whenever the market share of the target undertaking will be less than 1%, a so-called "short form" may be submitted for notification purposes. Nevertheless, the Authority has the right to demand and obtain the filing of a full form, if this will enable it to better assess the operation. The distinguishing feature of the full form is the request of more detailed information on brands and on the general structure of the relevant markets.

The filing is carried out by delivering, by hand or by registered mail, return receipt requested, the notification to the Authority in Rome.

7. The clearance procedure

The procedure to be followed after filing is laid down both in the Antitrust Act and in the Antitrust Regulation.

The investigation conducted by the Authority consists of a two-phase procedure, the second of which is only potential. During the first phase, the Authority carries out a preliminary assessment of the operation, considering whether the concentration notified deserves a fully-fledged investigation, which would constitute the second phase of the procedure.

Upon receipt of a notification, the Authority has 30 days to issue a decision to the undertakings involved regarding the first phase. This term is reduced to 15 days when the transaction consists of a take-over bid.

If the notification is grossly inaccurate, incomplete or untrue, the Authority must inform the parties concerned, and the 30-day term begins to run afresh once the notification has been made accurate, complete and truthful by the interested party [15]. The Antitrust Act does not foresee any sanctions against incomplete filings, other than the delay to the clearance procedure. According to Section D(4)(a) of the Antitrust Guidelines, a notification is deemed to be incomplete e.g. when the undertakings, without due reason, fail to supply the required information, or supply inaccurate or misleading data. To avoid such predicaments, the Authority invites parties who have doubts or questions regarding what to include in the notification to contact its officers prior to filing. In practical terms, this might substantially delay the date of filing, while the filing party negotiates with the officer in charge the completeness of the notification. On the other hand, a claim of incompleteness can become an easy way to delay the proceedings on the part of the Authority, though the Italian Courts have held that the incompleteness must be such as to prevent the Authority to evaluate the very scope and effects of the concentration [16].

Filing parties are also required to inform the Authority without delay of any substantive changes regarding facts and circumstances referred to in the notification. Should such changes substantially undermine the completeness of the notification, the filing is treated as if it were incomplete and the term for its preliminary assessment will start running from the moment in which the Authority is informed of them.

Before the expiration of the 30-day term from the filing (or of its adjournment, as the case may be), the Authority must either:

a) declare the transaction to be compatible with the Italian market; or

b) begin a fully-fledged investigation.

The second phase of the procedure starts only when the Authority deems that the concentration may be subject to prohibition, under Section 6 of the Antitrust Act, as it may create or strengthen a dominant position on the domestic market, thereby eliminating or restricting competition appreciably and on a lasting basis.

The decision which leads to the opening of the fully-fledged investigation is made by the full board of the Authority. The decision must "indicate the essential details concerning the supposed violations, the term by which the procedure must end, the case manager, the office by which the documents pertaining to the procedure may be examined, the term within which the undertakings and entities involved may exercise their right to submit representations"[17].

Statistically, most cases do not reach the second phase, as the Authority deems the relevant transaction to be compatible with the Italian market. When a transaction is cleared, the Authority's decision is notified to the undertakings involved and to the Ministry of Trade and Industry: silence on the part of the Authority would be tantamount to clearance, but this rarely happens, if at all. On the contrary, when the Authority deems that there is reason to suspect that the transaction may be prohibited pursuant to the Antitrust Act, it must serve notice of the opening of the (fully-fledged) investigation to the undertakings concerned, or to their jointly appointed attorney, to the other parties concerned, such as the complainants, as the case may be, and, if insurance companies are involved, to the Regulatory Authority on insurance companies (ISVAP).

Service of this notice may be made by an officer or other employee of the Authority, either by hand or by mail. However, if there is a large number of addressees other forms of service may be adopted, such as advertisements in major newspapers. Notice of the opening of the investigation is also published in the Bulletin of the Authority.

Within 45 days of the opening of the investigation, the Authority must notify the concerned undertakings and the Ministry for Trade and Industry of its conclusions. This period may be extended in the course of the investigation for a period of no more than 30 days, if the undertakings fail to supply the information and data in their possession and requested of them.

The Authority, within the 45-day term set by Section 16 (8) of the Antitrust Act, must close the investigation by either:
a) prohibiting the merger transaction, if it deems the transaction falls under Section 6 of the Antitrust Act; or
b) simply discontinuing the investigation, if it appears that the transaction does not fall under Section 6 of the Antitrust Act or if the concerned undertakings show to have eliminated from the original concentration plan any elements that might have made it fall under Section 6.

If the concentration has already been carried out, the Authority may order such measures as may be needed to re-establish a competitive market and to eliminate the distorting effects of the transaction.

According to Section 16(2) of the Antitrust Regulation, the Authority must give the concerned parties at least seven days' notice of the date of closing of the investigation, and the parties are entitled to a hearing before the Authority.

8. Implementation prior to clearance

When a fully-fledged investigation is set in motion, Section 17 of the Antitrust Act entitles the Authority to order the parties concerned not to carry out the concentration until such investigation is concluded. Thus, implementation of the merger while the clearance procedure is still pending, entails the risk that the Authority might suspend or prohibit the merger following its closing. Although no monetary sanctions are directly linked to the suspension or prohibition of a merger, they will certainly be levied if the merger is carried out despite its prohibition. Monetary fines may also be levied if a concerned party fails to comply with the directions issued by the Authority in order to restore conditions of effective competition and to remove any distortion brought about by the implementation of the merger.

At any rate, the cost of suspending the effects of the concentration or of divesting and complying with the directions of the Authority to restore competition has to be taken into account in the event of a closing of the operation before clearance [18].

9. Powers of the Authority

As indicated above, when the Authority opens the second phase, or fully-fledged investigation, it may order the parties concerned to suspend the carrying out of the relevant transaction until the conclusion of the investigation [19]. The Italian suspension system is thus different from the European one in which, according to the revised Article 7 of the Merger Regulation, suspension is the rule and implementation is the exception.

However, the Authority may not order the suspension of a notified take-over bid provided that the acquiror does not exercise any voting rights vested in the securities in question [20].

The violation of the order of suspension is not sanctioned directly by the Antitrust Act, but it may fall under the provisions of Section 650 of Italian Criminal Code, which considers the refusal to comply with a lawful order of a public authority to be a misdemeanor.

According to Section 6 of the Antitrust Act, the Authority has the power to prohibit concentrations or to authorise them subject to compliance with the necessary measures which it may lay down. It also has powers of investigation which include, according to Section 12, the right to require undertakings, entities and individuals to supply any information in their possession and exhibit any documents of relevance, to conduct inspections of the undertaking's books and records and make copies of them. To carry out such activities, the Authority may obtain the co-operation of the *"Guardia di Finanza"* (a special police body that investigates *inter alia* financial and white-collar crimes) and of other governmental agencies. The Authority has powers to fine up to L 50 million (€ 25,942) anyone who refuses or fails to provide said information or documents without justification. This fine may be increased up to L 100 million (€ 51,884) if untruthful information or documents are submitted.

Finally, according to Section 19(1), the Authority shall impose administrative fines on undertakings which carry out a concentration in violation of an order of prohibition or fail to comply with the directions issued so as to restore conditions of effective competition and remove any effects that distort it. Such fines can range from a minimum of 1% to a maximum of 10% of the turnover of the business that is the object of the concentration.

Hence, direct enforcement powers are vested in the Authority, which does not need to request any judicial authorisation before imposing fines and taking other measures (however, its decisions are subject to judicial review).

The Authority may:
a) request that the undertakings or other interested parties provide information and exhibit documents that are useful to the investigation;
b) order inspections aimed at the verification of business documentation and make copies of such documentation;
c) order economic analyses and expert consultations with reference to any matter relevant to the investigation.

Requests for exhibition documents or information must be in writing and must indicate: the facts or circumstances on which clarifications are requested; the purpose of the request; the term by which the answer must be furnished or the exhibition carried out; the means by which the information is to be provided, or the officers to whom the documents are to be exhibited or the information given; the sanctions to be applied should the concerned party unjustifiably refuse, omit, or delay in providing information or exhibiting documents as requested; the sanctions to be applied should the concerned party furnish untrue information or exhibit untrue documents.

Inspections are ordered by the Authority itself upon request of the case manager. These inspections may be carried out "with regard to anybody who is deemed to possess business documentation useful for the purposes of the investigation"[21].

10. The rights of parties involved in the investigation

The parties involved in the investigation, pursuant to Section 14 (1) of the Antitrust Act and Section 7 of the Antitrust Regulation, have the right to:
a) submit statements in person, with the assistance of their own consultants, or through a special attorney;
b) submit written briefs, documents or opinions in every phase of the investigation until five days prior to the term set for the closing of the investigation;
c) make further statements to the Authority before the closing of the investigation;
d) gain access to documents held by the Authority in the proceedings.

Other parties, or consumer associations, have the right to submit briefs and documents if they are liable to be affected either by the alleged infringement of competition or by the decisions taken by the Authority. Anybody intending to exercise this right must lodge a duly motivated request within 10 days of the publication in the Bulletin of the notice of the investigation's opening. These parties also have a right to access to the relevant file pursuant to Section 13 of the Antitrust Regulation. If a third party has lodged a complaint or filed a petition which caused the opening of the investigation, it is also entitled to a hearing, in accordance with Section 7(3) and 6(4) of the Antitrust Regulation.

11. Publicity and confidentiality

The Authority does not disclose the receipt of a notification. However, it does publish in its *Bulletin* the decisions whether or not to open a fully-fledged investigation, as well as the decisions adopted following such investigations. Some other decisions are published, such as those extending the investigation for 30 days under Section 16(8) of the Antitrust Act, or those extending the term for compliance in case of remedies. The Bulletin also contains opinions given by the Authority and decisions made by the Bank of Italy on concentrations falling under its jurisdiction, as well as relevant opinions given by other authorities in the field of concentrations.

Notwithstanding the extensive publication of the relevant information, the parties are protected against the disclosure of business secrets and confidential information submitted both by Italian law generally and, more specifically, by the Antitrust Act and the Antitrust Regulation. The Antitrust Act provides, in Section 14(3) and 14(4) respectively, that "any information or data regarding the undertakings under investigation by the Authority is wholly confidential and may not be divulged even to other government departments" and that "in the exercise of their functions officers of the Authority shall be considered 'public officials'. They are sworn to secrecy."

The Antitrust Regulation contains two sections which are respectively dedicated to secrecy (Section 12), and to access of files and confidentiality of information (Section 13). The latter section specifically regulates conflicts between access to information and confidentiality, indicates the documents whose examination is excluded or limited and defines the way in which the respective rights may be exercised. Specifically, any party wishing to oppose the confidentiality or secrecy of information submitted in order to avoid its disclosure has to lodge a request, containing the indication of the information to be classified as confidential or secret and the reasons therefor. Should the Authority consider that there are no grounds for protecting the above information, it shall inform the parties concerned by way of a motivated decision.

12. Substantive tests for clearance

Section 6(1) of the Antitrust Act, obliges the Authority to ascertain whether the concentration under scrutiny creates or strengthens a dominant position on the relevant market, with the effect of eliminating or restricting competition appreciably and on a lasting basis.

With reference to the notion of "relevant market", the Authority follows the traditional approach which entails defining both the relevant geographic market and the relevant product market. Furthermore, the product market is normally defined from a consumer or user perspective.

Namely, the "relevant markets" on which the parties to the operation must inform the Authority are those where:
- two or more such parties are active at the same time and will hold, after the concentration, a market share of at least 15%;
- one party will hold, after the concentration, a market share or at least 25%, and another party is active on either an upstream or a downstream market;
- a target undertaking holds a market share of at least 25%, and the other parties are active on unrelated markets.

In turn, a "relevant product market" includes all products and services which the consumers or users may consider as interchangeable or replaceable, in view of their features, price and use; a "relevant geographical market" means the area where the relevant products and services are supplied, which is geographically separated from adjoining areas in view of the features of said goods and services, transportation costs, entry barriers, consumers' preferences, price differences and the like.

With regard to the notion of "dominance", the Authority has explicitly adopted the definition given by the European Court of Justice in *United Brands*[22], i.e. "a position of economic strength enjoyed by an undertaking which enables it to prevent effective competition being maintained on the relevant market by giving it the power to behave to an appreciable extent independently of its competitors, customers and ultimately of its consumers". The Authority indeed is bound to interpret Italian legal provisions "in accordance with the principles of European Community competition law" (Section 1(4) of the Antitrust Act).

The tests for reaching the final assessment are:
- possibility of substitution available to suppliers and users;
- market position of the undertakings;
- access conditions to supplies or markets;
- structure of the relevant markets;
- competitive position of the domestic industry;
- barriers to entry of competing undertakings;
- evolution of supply and demand for the relevant goods and services.

The decisions issued by the Authority contain fairly elaborate opinions, with regard to the definition of the relevant market. Lack of a proper opinion might cause the quashing of the decision by the Administrative Court of the Latium Region, the Italian court having exclusive jurisdiction on appeals against the rulings of the Authority.

From 1991 (the year in which the Authority became fully operational) to 1997, the Authority scrutinised 1596 concentrations, namely 21 mergers, 1556 acquisitions, and 19 joint ventures[23]. An overwhelming percentage of the operations scrutinised were cleared during the "first phase" as they did not raise any competition problems whatsoever.

Some of the operations, on the contrary, raised sensitive issues, such as that of oligopolistic dominance; others were cleared subject to the undertaking of commitments; finally, a few were forbidden.

13. Oligopolistic dominance

The issue of oligopolistic dominance[24] was at stake for the first time in the 1995 case *Ignazio Messina & C/Lloyd Triestino*[25]. In this case, within a highly concentrated market (basically only three undertakings, two with nearly 30% market share each, the other with 39%), the Authority did not find a situation of oligopolistic dominance, given the fully independent behaviour of the market players and the lively competition between them.

The Authority came to a different conclusion in *Heineken/Moretti*[26]. The notified operation was an acquisition in the sector of beer production, trade and distribution. Relevant product markets were that of beer sold on licensed premises and that of beer sold off-licence. The acquiror was Heineken, the second largest brand on the Italian market, with a market share of around 27%; the target company was Moretti, the third competitor, with a market share of 10%; the market leader was Peroni, with a 29% market share; while the fourth and fifth competitor had respectively 10% and 5% market share, the presence of the latter being limited to a small part of the Italian territory. The remaining 19% was covered by imports. The Authority considered that, due to the characteristics of the off-licence market (high concentration, maturity, stability of market shares of the main operators, relevant barriers to entry and absence of potential competition) and to the structural effect of the operation (increase of the overall market share of the two main competitors, increase of the gap between the other competitors, increase of the total concentration rate and elimination of the most dynamic competitor), the operation might have led to oligopolistic dominance by Heineken and Peroni.

Leaving aside the analysis of further factual elements brought before the Authority by the parties, the approach of the Authority can be compared with the one followed by the European Commission in *Nestlé/Perrier*[27]. In this case the Commission pointed out that the disappearance of Perrier from the relevant market would have considerably increased the likelihood of collusive co-ordination between BSN and Nestlé, amongst others, because of the symmetric duopoly pattern, the low demand elasticity and brand loyalty on the part of consumers and the high transparency of prices and terms of transaction. Furthermore, the external competition was very poor due to the marginal influence of imports (1-2%), the relatively stagnant internal demand and the naturally limited access to sources of supply. This did not prove to be the case in *Heineken/Moretti*, in which the leading players were largely asymmetric, the demand was highly elastic, whilst brand loyalty was low or non-existent, and the market was not transparent. Moreover, external competition remained significant, given the substantial market share of imports, the growth, albeit moderate, of internal demand, the absence of natural barriers to entry and the unlimited availability of raw materials.

In its opinion, the Authority suggested that, on this issue, it would follow a case-by-case approach rather than rigid criteria. Whatever the theoretical approach, from a practical point of view the operation was cleared subject to a modest divestiture (sale of a production plant accounting for 5% of the national capacity, with an option for the acquiror of the plant to produce for Heineken during the initial years).

The Authority came across the issue of oligopolistic dominance again in *Unilever/Star*[28]. In this case a "duopoly" in the market of margarine for consumers would have resulted from the planned concentration. This time, the threat of oligopolistic dominance was neatly dismissed, without any need to recur to divestitures, on the basis that there was sufficient spare production capacity in the sector of industrial margarine and relevant countervailing buying power on the part of the main wholesaler, which was already on the market with consumer brands.

Nonetheless, recent developments at the European level, which require a more detailed analysis prior to diagnosing oligopolistic dominance[29], will probably have important repercussions on the Authority's approach to this issue.

14. Remedies

The issue of remedies is one of the most debated in competition policy[30], due to the serious consequences they might have on the market or on the parties to the operation.

A distinction may be drawn between structural and behavioural remedies. Remedies are considered to be "structural" whenever the entity arising out of the operation is requested to divest completely and permanently certain specified assets, capable of producing turnover, such as subsidiaries, production plants, trademark, licences, know how, etc. Remedies are considered to be "behavioural" when they consist of commitments either to undertake, or to refrain from, a certain action, such as obligation to supply or to sell at agreed prices and conditions.

The European Commission policy on remedies shows a preference for the adoption of structural remedies rather than behavioural ones. This attitude is shared by the Authority, which has recently explained that it favours structural remedies, as behavioural ones can often be both easy to overcome and difficult to monitor. Therefore, the Authority seeks to limit the use of the behavioural remedies to cases in which the structural remedies cannot be adopted[31].

This trend has emerged during recent years, while, in the early '90s, behavioural remedies adopted by undertakings concerned were prevalently admitted by the Authority.

Remedies may be adopted either during the preliminary assessment or during the fully-fledged investigation; their adoption may also be connected with the withdrawal of the previous notification and the filing of a new one[32].

15. Behavioural remedies

Behavioural remedies were considered for the first time in 1992[33] when – following several adjournments, amendments and discussions – the Authority made the authorisation of an operation conditional upon the observance of a series of commitments within the context of the acquisition of a company active in the cement business. These commitments included the obligation for the target company not to terminate an import contract of cement from a foreign source, to assign said contract to third parties at the same conditions and to share its harbour and storage facilities with competing importers of cement for at least five years.

A look at a recently adopted behavioural remedy, shows *prima facie* the evolution of the Authority on the matter of remedies. The remedy adopted in a 1998 case[34], actually coupled to the divestiture of a controlling shareholding, is rather straightforward: the remaining minority shareholding must be treated as a purely financial one, without appointing any member to the board of directors of the divested undertaking.

Despite the complexity of some behavioural remedies, a large part of the commitments relate to the classic obligation to supply[35]. In other cases somewhat peculiar commitments were agreed upon[36]. In a few cases the exact nature of the remedy cannot be fully understood due to omissions in the rulings, necessary for the protection of business secrets[37]. Despite such omissions, it appears that behavioural remedies were only ancillary to structural divestitures and mainly aimed at regulating the transitional period before the full completion of the divestiture.

16. Structural remedies

Structural remedies normally entail divestiture of shares, going concerns, production plants or brands[38]. Generally, the Authority lays down the criteria that the prospective buyer has to meet so as to ensure both that the commitments are duly performed by the parties concerned and that they achieve their pro-competition effects.

The Authority reserves the right to evaluate the compliance by the parties of their commitments and may grant extensions of the implementation period, provided they are justified by objective reasons, namely if linked to behavioural remedies aimed at regulating the transitional period[39].

Generally speaking, both behavioural and structural remedies admitted by the Authority, while aimed at protecting or restoring competition, would not be such as to nullify the economic benefits pursued by parties to the concentration.

17. Operations forbidden by the Authority

Up to the end of 1998, out of nearly 2000 concentrations scrutinised, only six have been held to be in breach of Italian antitrust law, and prohibited. Of these prohibitions, two have then been annulled by the competent Court.

The legal monopoly of telephony was at stake in assessing the 1992 joint cases of *Italtel/Mistel* and *Italtel/General 4 Elettronica Sud* [40], the very first operations to be prohibited by the Authority. By means of these two operations, Italtel (a manufacturer of telecommunication equipment, controlled by state-owned STET, the financial holding company of the telecommunication sector) intended to acquire sole control over two undertakings active in the production of small systems and devices for public telecommunications. Since STET already held a dominant position within the sectors concerned and controlled SIP (the public telephone operator at that time which was practically the sole buyer of the system and devices at stake), the operation had the nature of both a vertical and horizontal concentration. According to the Authority, such an operation would have "strengthen(ed) the segmentation and isolation of the national market compared to foreign ones, clearly against the tide of an evolutionary economic and legal trend in the telecommunications sector characterised by clear choices of liberalisation"[41]. However, on appeal by

STET, the Regional Administrative Court of Latium quashed the ruling issued by the Authority [42].

Other operations forbidden by the Authority date back to the early years of its activity. The case *SIO/Pergine* [43], decided in 1993, involved an operation, which had already taken place before the final order of the Authority, creating a dominant position in the carbon dioxide market (75% market share). However, the acquiring party, SIO, appealed against the prohibition and the order was annulled on procedural grounds (the ruling had been issued after expiration of the statutory deadline) [44].

Again in 1993, a forbidden operation was envisaged in the case *Emilcarta/Agrifood Machinery* [45], whereby a company belonging to the Tetra Pak Group intended to acquire sole control over a holding active in paperboard packaging. The relevant product markets were those relating to aseptic and non-aseptic paperboard packaging. Even though the geographical market was Europe-wide and the position of the target company was relatively small (around 1% market share), the Authority stated that "a market in which there is one quasi-monopolistic player, even a small increase in market power of the latter (which in such a case would lead to the elimination by Tetra Pak of a potential competitor, Italpack) may have strong restricting effects on competition"[46]. The operation was therefore forbidden and no appeal was lodged.

A recent case is *Telecom Italia/Intesa* [47], decided at the end of 1997, again a case in which State-owned monopolistic enterprises were closely scrutinised by the Authority, with the declared aim of avoiding operations that would "produce a general effect of strengthening the dominant position of the public operator nation-wide"[48]. The proposed operation foresaw the acquisition by Telecom Italia (owner of a legal monopoly in providing cable telephony) of Intesa, a company jointly owned by FIAT and IBM that operated in the data transmission field. Had the operation been allowed, Telecom Italia (that was at the same time the monopolist in a limited but essential activity of data transmission and market leader in custom-made data transmission services) would have acquired its first competitor in the sector of data transmission services for business customers. The operation would have also led to a vertical integration of Telecom. The Authority issued a negative ruling, which was not appealed and became final.

18. Clearance or prohibition due to national economic interest

Section 25 of the Antitrust Act provides for special issues which the Authority may have to take into account in assessing an operation.

According to Section 25(1), the Council of Ministers shall, upon proposal of the Minister for Trade and Industry, lay down the general criteria to be used by the Authority when an operation should be prohibited under normal circumstances, but "major general interests of the national economy are involved in the process of European integration". In any case, competition shall neither be eliminated from the market nor restricted to an extent that is not strictly justified by the aforementioned general interests. Moreover, in all of these cases the Authority shall prescribe the measures to be adopted in order to restore full competition by a specified date.

According to Section 25(2), if a concentration involves institutions or undertakings, belonging to countries that do not protect the independence of institutions or undertakings through rules having effects equivalent to those laid down in the Antitrust Act or which apply direct or indirect discriminations *vis-à-vis* Italian institutions or undertakings, the Prime Minister may prohibit the concentration on the grounds that it is against essential national economic interests. However, he may do so only on the basis of a resolution of the Council of Ministers, proposed by the Minister of Trade and Industry, within 30 days of receiving notice from the Authority that the operation has been notified. The Authority shall inform the Prime Minister and the Minister of Trade and Industry within five days of receiving notification of a concentration (Section 16(3) of the Antitrust Act).

The Government thus far has not used the above powers and the entire Section 25 may be regarded as a mere safety net, to be used only in exceptional circumstances.

19. Judicial review and redress

According to Section 33(1) of the Antitrust Act, appeals against a decision issued by the Authority may be filed within 60 days of service of the decision on the party.

Among the rulings issued by the Authority which are subject to appeal are those which:
- decide upon concentrations;
- order interlocutory measures during the investigation by the Authority;
- decide whether or not to open an investigation;
- grant or deny access to acts pertaining to the investigation proceedings;
- levy sanctions.

These appeals can be brought exclusively before the Regional Administrative Court of the Latium Region. This exclusive jurisdiction should facilitate the building up of fairly uniform case-law in an area that involves substantial economic interests, while allowing the judges involved to develop a highly specialised expertise in a fairly new area of law. The Court has jurisdiction regardless of the kinds of interests whose protection is sought, be they full rights or the so-called "legitimate interests", that can be succinctly described as the legal action granted to plaintiffs to ensure that their rights would not be *unjustly* sacrificed by public authorities for supposed (but contested) reasons of public interest.

Appeals can be brought both by the parties to the operation under scrutiny (or already forbidden) and by third parties (e.g. competitors) having an interest in the issue of the ruling. Until the beginning of 1998, some 15 appeals had been lodged before the Court, both against interlocutory measures, and against final rulings by the Authority. A number of appeals were apparently abandoned during the proceedings. In only two cases, both decided in 1994, appeals against the decision prohibiting the concentration were allowed by the Court. In the first instance, relating to the *SIO/Pergine* Case, the Authority had notified the prohibition 45 days after communicating the beginning of the investigation, but more than 45 days from its actual beginning. The Court held that, if allowed to do so, the Authority would be able to extend *ad libitum* the statutory deadline, and that business certainty should prevail over unlimited power of control[49].

In the second instance, relating to the joint cases of *Italtel/Mistel* and *Italtel/General 4 Elettronica Sud*, the Court examined the merits of the case and held that the Authority had not conducted a proper investigation with regard to the relevant market, and had actually reached the wrong conclusions in holding that there had been violations of competition rules[50].

Under Section 33 (2) of the Antitrust Act other actions in law fall under the jurisdiction of the ordinary civil courts. Namely, the Court of Appeal of the appropriate venue has jurisdiction over civil actions relating to breaches of provisions contained in the Antitrust Act, brought by a party against another (not being the Antitrust Authority) to obtain interlocutory measures, damages or a declaration of nullity.

However, these actions are not concerned with redress against the rulings issued by the Authority, but with claims against third parties arising out of the provisions of the Antitrust Act.

20. Special sectors

Special application of the rules concerning the control of concentrations is made by the Antitrust Act with regard to the banking, insurance, communications and film industry sectors, due to their special features, that require that competition and concentration issues be examined, either exclusively or jointly, by their overseeing authorities.

As far as the *banking sector* is concerned, control is vested in the Bank of Italy. The role of the Antitrust Authority is limited to the delivery, within 30 days of receiving the notification, of a non-binding opinion. However, the Bank of Italy, in turn, must comply with the same procedural rules that would apply to the Antitrust Authority. The banking sector will surely be one of the most active areas of the Italian market in the years to come as it is going through a remarkable process of concentration. This is proved by the considerable number of opinions given by the Antitrust Authority to the Bank of Italy over the past few years (46 opinions in 1995, 47 in 1996 and 48 in 1997).

The assessments carried out by the Bank of Italy are generally in line with the methods adopted by the Antitrust Authority for operations under its jurisdiction, although sometimes there may be some divergences in assessing the market shares or defining the relevant market.

While the Bank of Italy has exclusive jurisdiction over the banking sector, the Antitrust Authority retains its jurisdiction in assessing a banking operation as to its influence on sectors other than banking, such as financial services. Therefore, a single operation may be examined by more than one authority and this may sometimes create problems, despite the adoption, in 1996, of a co-operation and co-ordination agreement between the two institutions[51].

With reference to the *insurance sector*, the Antitrust Authority cannot dispose any enforcement measure without first hearing the opinion of the Regulatory

Authority on private and of collective interest insurance (ISVAP). Said opinion should be issued within 30 days of receiving the documentation relating to the measure; if within that time the opinion is not given by ISVAP, the Authority may go ahead and adopt the measures which it is empowered to take.

With regard to the *communications sector*, Law No. 249 of 1997, which established the Communications Authority[52], considerably changed the previous regime, which was similar to that applicable to the banking sector, and conferred full powers of assessment upon the Antitrust Authority.

Finally, Section 13 of Law No. 153 of 1994, which calls for urgent interventions in favour of the *film industry*, requires that the Authority be notified of any concentration that consolidates more than 25% of both the market share of the turnover and of the cinemas in the main cities, i.e. Rome, Milan, Turin, Genoa, Padua, Bologna, Florence, Naples, Bari, Catania, Cagliari and Ancona.

21. Conclusion

The present and future role that the Antitrust Authority is willing to play is best described in the words of its President:[53]

> "I understand that in countries like Italy, where the public service sector is characterised by legal barriers to entry and by a widespread presence of special and exclusive rights, the intervention of national competition authorities might seem rather limited or marginal. However, one has to bear in mind that the Authority has carried out and still plays an important role in the liberalisation process and in the reform of legal structures through the powers granted by Sections 21 and 22 of the Antitrust Act.
>
> During 1997 the Authority issued rulings on 292 operations, 64 agreements and 46 abuses of dominant position. Most operations for which the preliminary proceedings were completed were considered not to create or strengthen a dominant position, following the introduction of modifications to the original plan by the parties during the proceedings. On the contrary, to cite an example, the acquisition of a company active in the data transmission services market was prohibited[54], as the operation would have led to the strengthening of the dominant position of the national telecom operator in that market, thus hindering its competitive evolution.

The final goal, shared by all, is to achieve an environment favourable to the development of new opportunities, which will allow new enterprises and especially young people to participate with renewed dignity in the economic and social growth of the Country."

We wish to thank our colleagues Antonella Terranova (with regard to Clearance Procedure and Judicial Review) and Roberto A. Jacchia, for many useful comments and suggestions.

Notes

1. Published in the *Gazzetta Ufficiale* (Official Journal of the Italian Republic) of 13 October 1990, No. 240.
2. Decree of the President of the Republic No. 217, dated 30 April 1998, "Regolamento recante norme in materia di procedure istruttorie di competenza dell'Autorità garante della concorrenza e del mercato", in *Gazzetta Ufficiale* of 9 July 1998, No. 158: it repealed the previous Regulation, contained in Presidential Decree No. 461 of 1991.
3. "Formulario per la comunicazione di un'operazione di concentrazione", Version as amended on 1 July 1996, in *Bollettino*, 1 July 1996.
4. In May 1999, the Authority was composed of the president, Giuseppe Tesauro, a former Advocate General at the European Court of Justice, appointed on 1 January 1998, Giorgio Bernini, Marco D'Alberti, Michele Grillo and Giovanni Palmerio appointed as members on 11 November 1997. The secretary was Marcello Pera.
5. Commission Notice No. 1015/97 of 15 October 1997, in *OJ* C 313 of 15.10.1997, p. 3. As from 1 May 1999, according to the Amsterdam Treaty, reference to Articles 85 and 86 should be read as reference to Articles 81 and 82.
6. Council Regulation (EC) No. 1310/97 of 30 June 1997, in *OJ* L 180 of 09.07.1997, namely Section 22.
7. Case IV/M 1086 *Promodes/S21/Gruppo GS*, decided on 10 March 1998, referred in part to the Italian Authority and dealt with under the reference C3037 *Schemaventuno-Promodes/Gruppo GS*, in *Bollettino*, 6 July 1998. This case involved an acquisition by Promodes of 36% of GS, the balance remaining almost entirely in the hands of Schemaventuno, and constituted an acquisition of joint control of a joint venture. The Commission, upon the Authority's request, referred the case to the Authority with reference to certain distinct markets in the retail sector situated in the Turin, Vercelli and Aosta areas. The Authority cleared the case after a fully-fledged investigation, following commitments by the parties, on 18 June 1998.
8. Case IV/M.1220 *Alliance Unichem/Unifarma*, decided on 23 July 1998, referred in whole to the Authority and dealt with under the reference C3198 *Alleanza Salute Italia/Unifarma*

Distribuzione, decided on 15 September 1998, in *Bollettino* No. 37-38 of 1998. This operation envisaged the acquisition of joint control of Unifarma Distribuzione by Alliance Unichem, through its Italian subsidiary, Alleanza Salute. The impact of the operation was limited to Northwest Italy and the Commission therefore accepted to refer the case. The case was cleared shortly thereafter by the Authority, which did not deem to open a fully-fledged investigation.

9   Autorità garante della concorrenza e del mercato, *"Relazione sull'attività svolta"* (Rome, Istituto Poligrafico e Zecca dello Stato, 1995), p. 145.
10   Case C2411 *Banca Commerciale Italiana-Investitori Associati/Novamont*, in *Bollettino*, 10 June 1996; Case C2318 *Holdco/O.F.R. Officine Fratelli Riello in Bollettino*, 11 March 1996; Case C2539 *Advent Logistic Investment Company-Pechel Industries/Tecnologistica*, in *Bollettino*, 23 September 1996.
11   Case C2242B *Casse di Risparmio/Caralt/Riscossione Novara Tortona*, in *Bollettino* of 18 March 1996.
12   Commission Notice 94/C 385/01 in *OJ* C 385, 31.12.1994, p. 1.
13   "Notice on the previous notification of concentrations of 28 March 1995", in *Bollettino*, 10 April 1995. This notice, excluding the obligation to notify a large part of intra-group operations, had an important impact on Italian undertakings, since 50.8% belong to groups or are family-owned, while this percentage is much lower in other European countries, e.g. 27% in France, 16.9% in Germany and 13.3% in the UK (Cannari, Marchese, Pagnini, "Forma giuridica, quotazione e struttura proprietaria delle imprese italiane: prime evidenze comparate", in: Banca di Italia, *Il mercato della proprietà e del controllo delle imprese: aspetti teorici e istituzionali* (Rome, Banca di Italia, 1994), p. 257.
14   Fines levied by the Authority for the infringement of Section 19(2) amounted to L 72 million (€ 37,185) to one party and L 48 million (€ 24,790) to the other in the recent Case C3156B *Costruzioni Elettromeccaniche Ascensori Montacarichi-OTIS/Varie Società*, in *Bollettino*, 15 February 1999.
15   See Article 5 (3) of the Antitrust Regulation. It is estimated that between 5% and 10% of filings in 1998 have been held to be incomplete.
16   Regional Administrative Court of Latium, 24 March 1993, No. 497 (a case relating to a ruling issued by the Broadcasting and Publishing Authority, then having jurisdiction over that sector, see *infra*)
17   Section 6 (3) of the Antitrust Regulation.
18   For a case of closing before the final order of the Authority which subsequently prohibited the operation see Case C1115B *Sio/Pergine*, in *Bollettino*, 20 December 1993. The order of prohibition also contained certain "measures to restore competition" which were not disclosed to the public.
19   Section 17 (1) of the Antitrust Act.
20   Section 17 (2) of the Antitrust Act.
21   Sections 9 and 10 of the Antitrust Regulation.
22   Case 27/76 *United Brands Co. v Commission*, (1978) *ECR*, 207, at § 65.
23   Source: Autorità garante della concorrenza e del mercato.
24   "The issue of oligopolies is known to be a particularly difficult one from the perspective of a structural approach to competition. There is not a definitely established approach to the analysis of oligopolies in economic literature, and competition authorities in the EU

and elsewhere have not been prolific in publishing general guidelines on this point. The result is that there is no generally agreed paradigm to identify dominant oligopolies and separate them from situations of oligopolistic supply resulting in a competitive market", J. Briones-Alonso, "Oligopolistic Dominance: is there a Common Approach in Different Jurisdictions? A review of decisions adopted by the Commission under the Merger Regulation", (1995) 6 *ECLR*, p. 334.

25 Case A72 *Ignazio Messina & C/Lloyd Triestino*, in *Bollettino*, 29 May 1995.
26 Case C2347 *Heineken Italia/Birra Moretti*, in *Bollettino*, 22 July 1996.
27 Case IV/M.190 *Nestlé/Perrier*, in *OJ* L 356 of 5.12.1992, p. 1.
28 Case C2980 *Unilever Italia/Star-Stabilimento Alimentare*, in *Bollettino*, 16 March 1998.
29 See Joint Cases C-68/94 and C-30/95 *French Republic v Commission and SCPA and EMC v Commission (re Kali und Salz)*, judgement of 31 March 1998, §§ 220 ff.
30 The issue of remedies in competition law has been the subject of a recent report commissioned by DG IV.
31 Autorità Garante della Concorrenza e del Mercato, *"Relazione sull'attività svolta"*, (Rome, Istituto Poligrafico e Zecca dello Stato, 1998), p. 171.
32 See Case C1179 *Henkel Chimica/Boston*, in *Bollettino* of 6 December 1993.
33 Cases where the Authority adopted behavioural remedies are C337 *Cemensud/Calcementi* in *Bollettino* No. 10 of 1992; C714 *Unichips Finanziaria* in *Bollettino* No. 4 of 1993; C804 *Alitalia/Malev* in *Bollettino* No. 7 of 1993; C2227 *Fiatimpresit-Mannesmann-Techint/Italimpianti*, in *Bollettino* of 4 March 1996; C2309 *Snai Servizi/San Siro-Trenno*, in *Bollettino* of 17 June 1996; C2347 *Heineken Italia/Birra Moretti*, cit.; C2641 *Henkel/Loctite*, in *Bollettino* of 28 April 1997; C2741 *Italcalcestruzzi/Calcestruzzi*, in *Bollettino* of 23 June 1997, C2863 *Cirio/Centrale del Latte di Roma*, in *Bollettino*, 10 November 1997, C2626B *Solvay/Sodi*, in *Bollettino* of 28 April 1997, C2910 *Agip/Tmf energon*, in *Bollettino*, 12 January 1998; C2927 *Euler/SIAC*, in *Bollettino*, 30 March 1998.
34 C2927 *Euler/SIAC*, in *Bollettino*, 30 March 1998.
35 Cases C2910 *Agip/Tmf energon*, cit.; C2227 *Fiatimpresit-Mannesmann-Techint/Italimpianti*, cit.; C714 *Unichips Finanziaria*, cit.
36 Case C2626B *Solvay/Sodi*, cit. The remedy consisted in the obligation not to lobby the Commission in certain anti-dumping matters (and this in order to open the Italian market to American imports) and to lobby the European association of sodium carbonate producers to adopt a similar position *vis-à-vis* the Commission.
37 Cases C2741 *Italcalcestruzzi/Calcestruzzi*, cit., C2863 *Cirio/Centrale del Latte di Roma*, cit.
38 Cases in which the Authority has adopted structural remedies are: C1159 *Ferrovie dello Stato/Sogin*, in *Bollettino* of 10 January 1994; C2347 *Heineken Italia/Birra Moretti*, cit.; C2863 *Cirio/Centrale del Latte di Roma*, cit.; C2741 *Italcalcestruzzi/Calcestruzzi*, cit.; C2641 *Henkel/Loctite*, cit.; C2927 *Euler/SIAC*; cit.; C3037 *Schemaventuno-Promodes/Gruppo GS*, in *Bollettino*, 6 July 1998.
39 See e.g. Decision No. 6347, in *Bollettino* of 7 September 1998 in Case C2741 *Italcalcestruzzi/Calcestruzzi*, cit.
40 Joint Cases C573 & C574 *Italtel/Mistel & Italtel/General 4 Elettronica Sud*, in Bollettino No. 23 of 1992.
41 *Ibid.*, § 20.

42 Regional Administrative Court of Latium, 5 May 1994, No. 652.
43 Case C1115B *Sio/Pergine*, in *Bollettino* of 20 December 1993.
44 Regional Administrative Court of Latium, 24 October 1994, No. 1598
45 Case C812 *Emilcarta/Agrifood Machinery*, in *Bollettino*, 23 August 1993.
46 *Ibid.*, § 29.
47 Case C2833 *Telecom Italia/Intesa*, in *Bollettino*, 1 December 1997.
48 *Ibid.*, § 115.
49 Regional Administrative Court of Latium, 24 October 1994, No. 1598
50 Regional Administrative Court of Latium, 5 May 1994, No. 652.
51 "Accordo" 4 March 1996, in *Bollettino*, 25 March 1996
52 The Authority for the Guarantees in Communications ("Autorità per le garanzie nelle comunicazioni") was instituted by Law No. 249 of 3 July 1997. Before its creation, the relevant powers belonged to the Broadcasting and Publishing Authority.
53 Annual Report of 20 May 1998.
54 Case C2833 *Telecom Italia/Intesa*, in *Bollettino*, 1 December 1997.

The Netherlands

Winfred Knibbeler

Willemijn Jurgens

Contents

I. Introduction 335
II. The Netherlands Competition Authority 335
    Undertaking 336
III. Consequences of an infringement of the NCA 337
IV. Legal Protection 337
V. Merger Control 337
    Compulsory notification of concentrations 337
    Concentration 338
    Creeping mergers 339
    Exception for credit institutions and insurance companies 339
    Jurisdictional thresholds 340
    The notification procedure and the notification form 342
    Exceptions 343
    The licence procedure 344
    Confidential information 345
    Ancillary restrictions 345
    Conditions attached to a licence 346
    Request to the Minister 347
    Practical issues 348
    Practice of the Competition Authority 348
    Notes 350

I. Introduction

The Netherlands Competition Act, hereinafter "the NCA" ("de Mededingingswet"), entered into force on 1 January 1998. The NCA is based on a prohibition system: restrictions of competition, unless eligible for exemption, are prohibited. In this respect, the NCA differs from the previous competition act ("Wet Economische Mededinging"), which was based on an abuse system: restrictions of competition were allowed, until determined otherwise.

The Netherlands has often been stigmatised as a "cartel paradise" because the former act was considered insufficient to ensure workable competition. For example, from 1958, when the Economic Competition Act became effective, to 1986, only one individual declaration of invalidity was issued in respect of an agreement restricting competition. It involved a restriction of competition in an insignificant agreement regarding a Rotterdam shopping centre. In 1993 and 1994 – in anticipation of the NCA – general declarations of invalidity in respect of horizontal price-fixing arrangements, market-sharing arrangements and restrictions of competition in the field of procurement were issued. Prior to the enactment of the NCA there was no merger control in the Netherlands.

One of the basic principles of the NCA is that the Dutch competition rules should be neither more restrictive nor more liberal than the EU competition rules. Most of the substantive provisions of the NCA closely reflect Articles 81 and 82 of the EC Treaty and the European Commission Merger Regulation, hereinafter "the ECMR". The application of the NCA is, and will continue to be, significantly influenced by the interpretation of EU competition law by the Commission, the Court of First Instance and the Court of Justice.

The core of the NCA consists of provisions:
  a. prohibiting arrangements restricting competition and concerted practices in the Netherlands market or part thereof (Article 6 NCA);
  b. prohibiting the abuse of a dominant position (Article 24 NCA);
  c. regarding merger control (Article 34 etc. NCA).

II. The Netherlands Competition Authority

The body that is charged with the enforcement of the NCA is the Competition Authority, headed by a Director-General who is formally the competent authority to take decisions under the NCA. For the time being, the Competition Authority formally operates under the responsibility of the Minister of Economic Affairs. In that respect the Minister may issue general instructions to the Director-General regarding the performance of his duties. These "policy rules" must be published in the State Gazette. The Minister may also issue written instructions in individual cases.

The Competition Authority is empowered to initiate investigations, to order that infringements be terminated and to take administrative measures. The enforcement of the NCA is governed by the general rules on administrative proceedings laid down in the General Administrative Law Act (the "Awb"), in addition to the articles on this subject in the NCA itself.

Certain officials of the Competition Authority, as appointed by order of the Director-General, have extensive investigative powers, comparable to those of the European Commission. These powers are divided into those in respect of supervision and those in respect of investigations in cases where a suspicion exists. Every person who is asked by the above officials to co-operate is obliged to do so, on penalty of a fine. The officials concerned are entitled, *inter alia*, to order examinations of business information and other documents. In the event of a refusal to co-operate, the Director-General may issue an order sanctioned by periodic penalty payments, demanding that the information requested be made available for inspection. The Awb provides that the investigative powers must be exercised in accordance with the principles of proportionality and subsidiarity.

Undertaking

An undertaking is defined in Article 1 of the Competition Act as an undertaking within the meaning of Article 81 of the EC Treaty. As under EU law, public undertakings and undertakings granted special or exclusive rights by the authorities are considered to be undertakings. The Competition Authority has taken several decisions on the concept of undertaking with respect to public undertakings[1]. The Competition Authority considers each unit that performs an economic activity, regardless of its legal form and its funding, to be an undertaking. There is no requirement that the unit aim to make profits.

III. Consequences of an infringement of the NCA

The NCA contains a number of sanctions. Under Article 6 of the NCA, agreements containing restrictions of competition between undertakings are, with certain exceptions, null and void, unless an exemption has been granted. Article 24 of the NCA prohibits the abuse of a dominant position. In the event of an infringement of these provisions, the Director-General of the Competition Authority may impose fines, which may be as high as, but may not exceed, 10% of the turnover of the company/companies involved. Infringement of the relevant provisions may also lead to orders being issued by the Competition Authority, sanctioned by periodic penalty payments. These orders aim at enjoining further infringements or preventing a recurrence of the infringement.

Breach of the obligation to notify a concentration or obtain a licence renders the transaction void, which means that the concentration and all effects thereof must be reversed. In addition, the Competition Authority can impose administrative sanctions, such as fines up to a maximum amount of NLG 50,000 and orders sanctioned by periodic penalty agreements to nullify the infringement.

IV. Legal Protection

An application for administrative review can be filed with the Competition Authority, challenging the decisions of that Authority. If a decision is upheld, an appeal may be lodged with the District Court in Rotterdam and subsequently with the Tribunal for Trade and Industry in The Hague. With respect to decisions related to merger control, it is not necessary to apply for administrative review; a direct appeal can be lodged.

V. Merger Control

Compulsory notification of concentrations

Article 34 of the NCA prohibits the implementation of a concentration that falls within the scope of the NCA before the Director-General has been notified of the envisaged concentration and a subsequent period of four weeks has elapsed. The Competition Act does not require that an agreement be signed or a controlling interest be acquired to trigger the notification requirement. A concrete intention is sufficient to require notification.

The system of merger control does not apply to transactions in which only certain credit institutions and insurance companies are involved. This exception will be revoked two years after the NCA entered into force, i.e. on 1 January 2000.

Concentration

The term concentration refers to:
 a. the merger of two or more previously mutually independent undertakings;
 b. the acquisition of direct or indirect control by:
    1. one or more natural persons who, or legal entities which, already control at least one undertaking, or
    2. one or more undertakings of the whole or parts of one or more other undertakings, by the acquisition of a participating interest in the capital or assets, pursuant to an agreement or by any other means;
 c. the creation of a joint undertaking which performs all the functions of an autonomous economic entity on a lasting basis, and which does not give rise to co-ordination of the competitive behaviour of the parent undertakings.

Control is defined as the possibility of exercising decisive influence on the activities of an undertaking on the basis of actual or legal circumstances. The term activities refers to long-term activities and not those comprising the daily management of the undertaking. In most cases control will be acquired by means of a share purchase or an assets transaction.

In the event a joint venture gives rise to co-ordination of the competitive behaviour of the parent companies, the transaction is considered to be a co-operative joint venture, which falls within the scope of Article 6 of the NCA. Article 6 prohibits arrangements restricting competition. In practice, the Competition Authority follows the European Commission's notice on the distinction between concentrative and co-operative joint ventures[2] in delineating these operations.

Thus, on the subject of merger control, the Netherlands system of merger control does not correspond with the ECMR. Since 1 March 1998, co-operative joint ventures have been characterised under the ECMR as concentrations. The Minister of Economic Affairs has stated that in line with the Commission's policy on structural co-operative joint ventures, the Competition Authority will assess them within the same time-limit as provided for in the case of concentrative joint ventures.

Creeping mergers

A concentration can be realised little by little, in which case it can be difficult to recognise the transition from independence to dependence. The Competition Authority has ruled upon a situation like that in the case "Kalkzandsteen-producenten"[3]. Eleven sand-lime brick factories were united in a co-operative society. In February 1998, the co-operative society and its members (the eleven factories) notified a "pooling agreement", pursuant to which the economic activities, investment policies and personnel policies of the factories would be determined on a central level and the financial results would be pooled. The notifying parties stated that this was not a concentration because the integration had progressed gradually after the founding of the co-operative society in 1989. The Competition Authority held that, prior to the pooling agreement, the co-operative society did not constitute an economic unit since it lacked a lasting character, there was no permanent and common management and each member bore its own risk. The pooling agreement changed this situation, giving rise to a concentration. The Competition Authority subsequently granted a licence for the concentration, as the pooling agreement did not create or strengthen the (already existing) dominant position of the eleven factories.

Exception for credit institutions and insurance companies

A concentration is not deemed to arise where certain credit institutions or other financial or insurance companies hold, on a temporary basis, securities which they have acquired in an undertaking with a view to reselling them, provided that they do not exercise the voting rights in respect of those securities with a view to determining the competitive behaviour of that undertaking, or provided that they exercise such voting rights only with a view to preparing the sale of those securities and that any such sale takes place within one year of the date of acquisition.

In the *Begemann-Tulip* case[4] the Competition Authority did not accept the reliance of Begemann on this exception, as Begemann did not act as a pure investor which did not intend to get involved in the management of the target undertaking (Tulip).

Jurisdictional thresholds

In order to assess whether a concentration falls within the scope of the ECMR or the NCA, the world-wide turnover needs to be determined. Concentrations which are subject to the supervision of the European Commission pursuant to the ECMR do not fall within the scope of the NCA. The European Commission can refer a concentration to a national competition authority under Article 9 of the ECMR. The Commission is obliged to do so if, in its view, the concentration will have a negative impact on the competitive structure of an individual market in a Member State, and this market is not considered a substantial part of the European market. Insofar as this market does concern a substantial part of the European market, the Commission may send the case to a national competition authority. To date, the Commission has once referred a notification to the Netherlands Competition Authority[5].

A concentration falls within the scope of the NCA if, in the preceding calendar year:
   a. the aggregate world-wide turnover of the undertakings concerned exceeded NLG 250 million,
   b. the turnover in the Netherlands of at least two of the undertakings concerned amounted to at least NLG 30 million each.

The NCA is also applicable to foreign mergers, provided that the thresholds are met.

The meaning of the concept "undertaking concerned" is similar to that under the ECMR. Where the concentration is realised through the acquisition of control over parts, whether or not constituted as legal entities, of one or more undertakings, only the turnover relating to the parts which are subject to the transaction will be taken into account in the determination of turnover.

Turnover refers to the net turnover as defined in the Dutch Civil Code (Article 2:377 (6)). This is the income from the supply of goods and services from the business of the legal entity after deduction of rebates and the like and of taxes levied on turnover.

Article 30 (3) NCA provides for the calculation of the turnover of undertakings which are part of a group. These provisions are identical to Article 5 of the ECMR. Article 30 (3) reads as follows:

"the aggregate turnover of an undertaking concerned, within the meaning of Article 29, Clause 1, shall be determined by adding together the respective turnovers of the following undertakings:
 a. the undertaking concerned;
 b. those undertakings in which the undertaking concerned, directly or indirectly:
    1. owns more than half of the capital or business assets, or
    2. has the power to exercise more than half the voting rights, or
    3. has the power to appoint more than half the members of the supervisory board, the administrative board, or bodies legally representing the undertakings, or
    4. has the right to manage the undertaking's affairs;
 c. those undertakings which, in the undertaking concerned, hold the rights or powers listed in b;
 d. those undertakings in which an undertaking as referred to in item c holds the rights or powers listed in item b;
 e. those undertakings in which two or more undertakings, as referred to in items a to d, hold the rights or powers listed in b."

According to Article 30 (5) NCA, transactions between undertakings as referred to in clause 3 shall not be taken into account for the determination of the combined turnover of the undertakings concerned.

Article 31 of the NCA replaces turnover as the criteria for determining whether the Act applies to concentrations involving credit institutions, financial institutions and insurance companies. The turnover of credit institutions and financial institutions is replaced by one tenth of the value of the fixed and current assets as at the end of the preceding financial year, with at least NLG 50 million of tangible fixed assets to be held in the Netherlands. The turnover of insurance companies is replaced by the value of the gross premiums written in the preceding financial year, at least NLG 10 million of which must have been received from Dutch residents.

The notification procedure and the notification form

All concentrations to which the NCA applies must be notified to the Competition Authority. The Competition Authority has produced a standard form for notifications. The notification form requests information on the undertakings concerned, such as a description of the business activities of the undertakings and the sectors in which they are active, information on the group if an undertaking concerned belongs to a group, and a financial outline of the preceding financial year showing the total turnover and the turnover in the Netherlands. Furthermore, the notification form requests a description of the transaction and supporting documentation, such as the most recent annual accounts and reports of the undertakings concerned, the most recent documents purporting to bring about the concentration and powers of attorney from the undertakings concerned to the designated contact person or persons.

The most crucial question covers the description of the affected markets. The demarcation of the relevant markets is based on the product scope and geographical scope of the markets. The Commission's Notice on the definition of the relevant market for the purposes of community competition law[6] is, according to the decision practice of the Competition Authority, relevant in this respect. In defining the relevant product markets, the Competition Authority normally considers demand side substitutability and, if appropriate, supply side substitutability and the potential competition. General factors which are considered in identifying the geographical market include the geographical distribution of market shares, price differences, conditions of competition and transport costs. An affected market is a market on which at least two undertakings concerned are active. The undertakings concerned may have a horizontal or a vertical relationship on these markets.

The affected markets having been defined, the form requests information on the markets to be investigated. These are the affected markets on which a horizontal relationship exists and on which the undertakings concerned hold a market share of at least 15% and the affected markets on which a vertical relationship exists and on which the undertakings concerned hold a market share of at least 20%. The form requests information on the market shares on the markets to be investigated of the undertakings concerned. It further requests the five most important competitors and clients of the undertakings concerned on these markets. The last question on the form is whether the concentration is also subject to control by other (foreign) competition authorities.

THE NETHERLANDS

In comparison with the notification form CO of the European Commission, the notification form of the Competition Authority requires a limited amount of information. If the Director-General decides that a licence is required, a new application form has to be filed, which requires more extensive information. The idea behind this system is to relieve the administrative burden on the notifying parties. In uncomplicated cases, where no overlapping markets are involved, it is not necessary to define the markets since the form only requests information on affected markets. In certain respects, the information requested in the form even seems to be too restricted. The notifying parties are not requested to identify their main competitors and clients if they consider their market share on the affected markets negligible. The Competition Authority, however, can hardly verify this assessment of the notifying parties as long as it does not know the market players. Therefore, it is advisable to take the initiative and include the five main competitors and clients nevertheless. The same advice applies to ancillary restrictions, regarding which the form requests no information either.

After notification, the Competition Authority has a period of four weeks within which it must decide whether a licence is required in order to effect the concentration. This will be the case if, in the opinion of the Competition Authority, it is likely that the concentration will give rise to a dominant position which could significantly impede competition in the Netherlands or any part thereof. The running of this four-week period is suspended if the Competition Authority requests further information relating to the notification, until the day on which such information is provided. Such information may be requested in the event the information supplied is incomplete or insufficient for the purpose of the assessment of the notification. Additional questions not contained in the notification form may be asked.

Exceptions

There are two exceptions to the prohibition against implementing an intended concentration before the notification and before a subsequent period of four weeks has elapsed. The implementation of a public bid for shares is not forbidden provided that the Director-General of the Competition Authority is notified immediately and the acquiring party does not exercise its voting rights on the shares. Furthermore, the Director-General may, for serious reasons (irreparable harm), grant dispensation from the prohibition at the request of one of the notifying parties. In 1998 nine requests for exemptions were filed. In three cases[7] the Director-General granted dispensation from the stand-still obligation to avoid serious financial difficulty on the part of the target company.

The licence procedure

If the Competition Authority decides that a licence is required, an application for such licence can be submitted, initiating a further investigation period of 13 weeks. As mentioned above, the Competition Authority has produced a standard form for this notification. Information is requested on participations and prior acquisitions, market size and market shares, imports, organisation of production, differences in price level in different EC Member States, vertical integration, distribution channels and service networks on the markets requiring investigation, market development, co-operative agreements and market position outside the Netherlands. Within the 13-week period, the Competition Authority must decide whether a licence will be granted. It will not grant a licence if the concentration will give rise to a dominant position which will significantly impede competition in the Netherlands or any part thereof. Although the NCA does not specifically stipulate that further information may be requested during this period, in practice the Competition Authority sometimes requests further information during this period. The Competition Authority takes the view that such requests, similar to those following notification, suspend the running of the 13-week period until the day on which the information is provided.

Although the Competition Authority is not bound by a regulation similar to Regulation (EEC) No. 447/98[8], it does issue its findings in writing to the undertakings concerned and to involved third parties, eight weeks after the application for a licence is filed. The undertakings concerned may respond in writing to this "draft decision". Approximately two weeks after the findings referred to above are issued, there will be a hearing, presided over by an independent advisor of the Competition Authority. On request, the Competition Authority may allow access to the file. It takes the position that neither the undertakings concerned nor third parties are entitled to access to the file on the basis of the Public Information Act.

Confidential information

Both the decision of the Director-General as to whether a licence is required and his decision on the application for a licence are announced in the State Gazette. Business secrets and information which have been provided to the Competition Authority on a confidential basis will not be published. If an undertaking claims that certain other information is also confidential, the Competition Authority will weigh the interests of all parties concerned. If the Director-General decides to publish information in spite of a claim of confidentiality by the undertaking concerned, this undertaking will be given an opportunity to request a provisional ruling of the District Court prior to the disclosure of the information.

Ancillary restrictions

The prohibition set forth in Article 6 of the NCA does not apply to restrictions of competition which are directly related to and necessary for the concentration, the so-called ancillary restrictions. Since the notification form does not request information on ancillary restrictions, the question arises whether the Competition Authority is obliged to investigate officially the existence of ancillary restrictions. The answer seems to be that it does not. Furthermore, it is not clear whether ancillary restrictions which are not mentioned in the notification can benefit from the exemption from Article 6 of the NCA. In practice, the Competition Authority asks for additional information on ancillary restrictions in most cases where the notifying parties have failed to take the initiative and provide such information themselves. It is advantageous to the notifying parties that the Competition Authority consider certain restrictions as ancillary restrictions which are therefore exempted from the prohibition in Article 6 of the NCA, as civil judges and other divisions of the Competition Authority will have to respect this decision once it has become irrevocable.

In its decision on ancillary restrictions, the Competition Authority follows the practice of the European Commission on this subject as laid down in its notice on ancillary restrictions[9]. In a decision with respect to a concentration in the IT sector[10], the Competition Authority considered a no-compete clause to be ancillary for only three years because of the fast-paced technical changes in this sector. The Competition Authority deemed the loyalty of consumers to an IT company not long-lasting. With respect to joint ventures, the Competition Authority allows permanent restrictions on competition between the parent companies and the joint venture. It allowed two telecommunication companies, UPC and NUON[11], to restrict competition between themselves and their joint venture for as long as they owned the joint venture. In the *Sturko Meat-Janssen Group* case [12], the Competition Authority allowed a supply obligation as an ancillary restriction.

Conditions attached to a licence

Contrary to the ECMR, the NCA does not contain a provision granting the notifying parties the right to adjust the notification during the notification procedure in order to avoid a licence procedure or to adjust the notification during the licence procedure. The Competition Authority is not entitled to attach conditions to its decision that a particular concentration does not require a licence.

The Competition Authority may attach certain conditions to a licence, such as that changes be made in the intended transaction, or certain aspects thereof. Experience has shown that where the Competition Authority is not prepared to grant a licence for the transaction as originally envisaged, it is up to the parties themselves to suggest remedies to overcome the Authority's objections so that the licence can be granted. The NCA does not prescribe in which stage of the procedure this should be done. The nature of these remedies may differ from case to case. An example of a remedy is the spin-off of certain group companies or activities which may be acquired under the concentration. Thus, a dominant position on a particular market may be avoided.

Since merger control concerns the structural aspects of the markets, the conditions attached to a licence are more likely to be structural than to refer to certain behaviour. Complainants could argue that the notification is substantially modified by structural conditions attached to a licence and that the modified transaction should have to be notified as such, given that the NCA seems not explicitly to allow the notifying parties to adjust the notification during the notification and licence procedure.

In this respect reference is made to the decision of the Competition Authority in the *Vendex/De Boer Unigro* case [13], a concentration between two supermarkets. During the notification procedure the Competition Authority informed the parties of its viewpoint that if De Boer Unigro, which was to acquire the shares in Vendex Food Group, continued, after the concentration, to be part of the purchase group it had joined before the concentration, this purchase group would acquire a dominant position. The notifying parties subsequently declared that De Boer Unigro would break off relations with the purchase group after the notification. The Competition Authority considered this declaration as an adjustment of the former notification. Taking note of this adjustment, the Competition Authority decided that the concentration did not require a licence. The Competition Authority attached great weight to the commitment of De Boer Unigro that it would not rejoin the purchase group within a certain period after the notification and that it would discuss this matter which the Competition Authority if it considered joining the purchase group after that period.

The reliance of the Competition Authority on the promises of the notifying parties referred to above raises certain questions. The enforceability of these commitments was not certain. This suggests that the Competition Authority would have been wiser to decide that a licence was required. It could have granted a licence conditioned on the promises of the notifying parties. Further case-law on this subject has not yet been developed.

Request to the Minister

If the Director-General of the Competition Authority refuses to issue a licence for an envisaged concentration, the Minister of Economic Affairs may, in response to a request to that effect, decide that a licence will be granted if this is necessary for reasons in the general interest – either economic or not – which outweigh the expected restrictions on competition. The Minister must decide on a request, in accordance with the views of the Cabinet, within eight weeks of the receipt of the request, which must be made within four weeks after the decision to refuse the licence has become irrevocable. An administrative appeal as provided for in the Awb and a request to the Minister can be combined. Article 47 (3) NCA provides that the proceedings before the district court shall be suspended until a final decision is made on the request by the Minister. The decision of the Minister is subject to administrative review and appeal.

Practical issues

It may be presumed that notification of a concentration will in general take place when the parties have reached agreement in principle and when (if required) notification has been effected under the SER Merger Code and advice has been requested from the relevant works councils. Having regard to the periods mentioned above, it is recommended that sufficient time be reserved for the procedure before the Competition Authority. Against this background, it is important to involve competition law at an early stage when contemplating a significant merger, takeover or joint venture in the Netherlands.

Credit institutions will be confronted with the regime on merger control in a number of ways. First, if credit institutions act as matchmakers between companies, an early assessment must be made of the inherent risk, under the system of merger control, that the transaction will be prohibited. The obligation to notify the transaction to the Competition Authority will further have to be taken into account in adopting the agenda for the different stages of any transaction. Such an agenda is frequently kept by the investment banking institution which advises the parties concerned.

Secondly, subsidiaries of credit institutions which provide capital to undertakings, in particular by acquiring holdings in such undertakings, will as a rule have to verify whether a transaction to which they are a party is notifiable.

Although the NCA contains specific provisions replacing turnover as the criteria for determining the applicability of the NCA to concentrations involving a financial holding company, it may – in view of the interpretation of a similar provision in the Merger Regulation by the European Commission – often be necessary to notify a transaction in which a financial holding company participates.

Practice of the Competition Authority

The general assessment of the functioning of the Competition Authority is positive. It has so far dealt with far more concentrations than expected and it has developed a balanced line in its case-law. The investigations are far-reaching where necessary.

In 1998 154 concentrations were notified to the Competition Authority. In six [14] cases, the Director-General decided that a licence was required. In two of these cases, the notifying parties withdrew their application for a licence (Case Nos. 4 and 126). In two cases the Competition Authority granted a licence (Case Nos. 166 and 124). So far it has only once refused a licence for a concentration (Case No. 47). In another case (Case No. 1132) the notifying parties have not yet applied for a licence.

Like the European Commission, the Competition Authority defines product markets rather narrowly. The *Vendex-KBB* case (Case No. 166), for which concentration the Competition Authority has granted a licence, is illustrative. It concerns the concentration of the non-food activities of two sizeable department store groups, Vendex and KBB. The Competition Authority divided the products sold by both department store groups into 22 different categories. It further made a distinction between the various distribution channels: specialised stores, department stores, mail-order companies and the market. It held that department stores and specialised stores do not each form a separate market.

In the *Rotosmeets De Boer/Senefelder* case [15], a concentration between two printing businesses, the Competition Authority decided that in spite of the fact that the combined market share of the undertakings concerned amounted to between 40% and 60% and the market shares of the competitors amounted to between 8% and 9% each, the concentration did not create a dominant position. It considered that the relevant market, the heat-set/offset market, was very competitive, that the customers as well as the suppliers had strong countervailing power, that the two most important competitors were vertically integrated and that the relevant market also suffered competition pressure from product and geographic markets other than the relevant market.

In the *RAI/Jaarbeurs* case (Case No. 47) the Competition Authority refused to grant a licence for a concentration between two undertakings active on the markets for the organisation of trade fairs and the rental of trade fair accommodation. After the concentration, the market share of the notifying parties on both relevant markets would amount to 50%. The Competition Authority expressed the fear that the holding of a 50% market share by a party which both organises trade fairs itself and supplies accommodation for such fairs would aggravate the position of its competitors, other organisers of trade fairs. The notifying parties proposed certain commitments which did not satisfy the Competition Authority as it considered these commitments not sufficiently structural in character.

Notes

1   Case No. 101, *Bloemenmarkt Amsterdam*, 26 November 1998.
    Case No. 119, *Loke-CBR*, 28 August 1998.
    Case No. 52, *Hotel Zuiderduin-Brandweer*, 25 February 1998.
    Case No. 5, *Kunstzinnige vorming en onderwijs*, 31 July 1998.
2   Commission notice on the distinction between concentrative and co-operative joint ventures under Council Regulation (EEC) No. 4064/89 of 21 December 1989 on the control of concentrations between undertakings OJ 1994 C 385/1.
3   Case No. 124, *Coöperatieve Verkoop en Productievereniging van Kalkzandsteenproducenten U.A.*, 23 April 1998.
4   Case No. 770, *Begemann-Tulip*, 8 June 1998.
5   *Vendex/KBB*, OJ C93/28, 28 March 1998 and OJ C111/7, 9 April 1998.
6   OJ C372/5, 9 December 1997.
7   Case No. 69, *Koninklijke BAM Groep N.V. – N.V. Habo*, 2 February 1998; Case No. 849, *Koninklijk Olland Groep B.V. – Olland Vending Finance B.V.*, 26 June 1998; Case No. 676, *Wadco B.V. – VéVéWe Holding B.V.*, 29 April 1998.
8   Commission Regulation (EC) No. 447/98 of 1 March 1998 on the notifications, time-limits and hearings provided for in Council Regulations (EEC) No. 4064/85 on the control of concentrations between undertakings, OJ L 61/1, 2 March 1998.
9   Commission Notice regarding restrictions ancillary to concentrations, OJ C 203/5, 14 August 1990.
10 Case No. 93, *Wang Labaratories, Inc.-Olivetti Solutions S.p.A.*, 11 March 1998.
11 Case No. 439 *United Pan-Europe Communications N.V. en N.V. NUON*, 13 May 1998.
12 Case No. 349, *Sturko Meat B.V., D.J. Janssen's Vee- en Vleeshandel B.V., Robu Holding B.V. en B.V. Gebroeders Jansen Exportslachterij*, 18 May 1998.
13 Case No. 811, *Vendex Food Group B.V./De Boer Unigro N.V.*, 25 July 1998.
14 Case No. 4, *SEP/EPON/EPZ/EZH/UAU*, 29 January 1998.
    Case No. 126, *Internatio-Müller/Brocacef/Drogisten B.V.*, 9 April 1998.
    Case No. 166, *Vendex International N.V./N.V. Koninklijke Bijenkorf Beheer KBB*, 22 June 1998.
    Case No. 124, *Coöperatieve Verkoop- en Productievereniging van Kalkzandsteenproducenten*, 23 April 1998.
    Case No. 47, *Amsterdam RAI B.V./Koninklijke Nederlandse Jaarbeurs*, 25 February 1998.
    Case No. 1132, *FCDF-De Kievit*, 23 December 1998.
15 Case No. 791, *Rotosmeets De Boer/Senefelder*, 15 July 1998.

Portugal

Carlos Pinto Correia

Contents

I. Introduction 353
II. General outline and procedure 354
III. Scope of the law 359
    1. Territorial 359
    2. Material 360
IV. Definition of concentration 361
    1. Control 362
    2. Turnover 363
V. The substantive test 363
VI. Sanctions 364
    Notes 365

I. Introduction

The enforcement of competition rules is a recent phenomenon in Portugal. It was only in 1983, by Decree Law No. 422/83, that the first competition law was adopted, but this should be no surprise to anyone familiar with the country's recent history.

For much of this century, between 1933 and 1974, Portugal was ruled by a corporatist-inspired regime whose official position was one of suspicion of a free market economy. The main culprit of this suspicion lay in access to the more important industrial and financial activities. The Constitution did not recognise the right of free enterprise in these areas and market access was subject to a system of discretionary authorisation. As a result, the Portuguese economy was controlled by a limited number of vast conglomerates and the level of concentration of economic power was high. Free competition was certainly not an objective of such an economic system, and it was not protected by specific legislation[1].

Things started to change gradually after the accession to EFTA, in 1962. Slowly but surely, the system opened up, and by 1972, the first Competition Act was approved. However, it was never enforced because the necessary rules and regulations were never implemented.

In 1974, changing political conditions brought the nationalisation of a number of industrial and financial groups. In a situation where a significant part of the economy was under public control, competition law was not a priority. It was only after negotiations for accession to European Community began that a dynamic private sector again emerged.

The Portuguese legal system lacked the instruments allowing for efficient regulation of a modern market economy. Competition law was one of the most obvious lacunae, particularly since, from the date of accession to the EEC, European antitrust law could be applied to the national market.

In 1983, the first competition law was enacted but it dealt only with restrictive practices, lacking any rules pertaining to the control of mergers. It was only in 1988 that merger control was introduced, through Decree Law No. 422/88, whose preamble indicates that the national legislator had tried to follow the general principles of the proposed Community Merger Regulation.

In 1993, with the experience accumulated over ten years, the whole system was changed. The new competition law, Decree Law No. 371/93 (hereinafter referred to as the "Competition Law"), whose scope is much broader than the previous law, also includes rules on mergers, and thus Portuguese antitrust law is now unified in a single text. This allows for several unified solutions applying to the control of cartels, dominant positions and mergers. The most interesting of these common solutions is the notion of a positive "economic balance" that may allow an otherwise illegal act to be declared lawful.

That notwithstanding, the system of rules applying to mergers differs on a certain number of issues from those of antitrust proper.

The main difference concerns the substantive nature of the actions of the competent authority: in antitrust, the final decisions are taken by the Competition Council, under a proposal by the General Directorate for Trade and Competition of the Ministry of Economy. These decisions can be appealed directly to a judicial court. In merger control, the General Directorate addresses the proposed decision to the Minister and, if it is a negative decision, i.e. against the merger, the Minister is required to hear the Council. The final decision, however, belongs to the Minister. This implies that such decision is an administrative act and thus an appeal has to be brought before the administrative courts.

II. General outline and procedure

The control of mergers can be described as a prior authorisation, two-step procedure.

The parties to a merger are obliged to notify before completion of any legal transactions[2] and specifically before any announcements are made. If the merger is not notified, legal transactions between the parties do not have any effect. The law does not say that these transactions are void or voidable, the two typical consequences for a transaction that violates the law, but just states the absence of legal effect.

That the transactions are not void is clear: if the merger is eventually caught by the authorities, the parties are subject to a heavy fine but this alone does not preclude the possibility of allowing the operation[3]. On the other hand, the fact that they are not voidable means that no one is obliged to bring an action against the legal transactions to have them declared void. Thus those legal transactions are in limbo until the notification is made and clearance is obtained.

Control is carried out by the agency that is empowered to apply antitrust law. This agency, the General Directorate for Trade and Competition[4] (hereinafter referred to as DGCC), has the competence to initiate the procedure and impose sanctions in all matters concerning the violation of the rules on mergers.

According to Article 7, paragraph 1 of Competition Law, mergers subject to prior notification are all those:
- that create or reinforce a market share above 30% in the national market or in a substantial part thereof; or
- whose participating undertakings had a combined turnover exceeding Esc 30 billion (about € 150 million) in the last fiscal year, after deduction of taxes directly related with the turnover.

There are three types of triggering event[5]. The first is the plain merger, which occurs when two previously independent undertakings merge.

The second occurs when (i) one or more persons already controlling at least one undertaking, or (ii) one or more undertakings directly or indirectly acquire control of the whole or part of one or more other undertakings. This covers both the possibility of an individual acquiring control and situations where the entity acquiring control is not an individual but an undertaking. This is the sole reference to individuals, the law otherwise always mentioning undertakings.

Although, in what concerns restrictive practices, the law considers that a group of legally independent companies is an undertaking if these companies maintain ties of interdependence, this does not apply to mergers, where specific rules concerning the definition of control and the non-consideration of corporate entity are used (see below).

The third possibility is the creation of joint ventures. These are described as lasting autonomous legal entities that do not have as their purpose or effect the co-ordination of competitive behaviour, either between the undertakings party to the joint venture or between them and the joint venture. It follows that only concentrative joint ventures are covered by the law and can be approved as such. Co-operative joint ventures are subject to the general regime of competition law.

The notification has to be made by the acquiring undertaking or, in the event of a merger or joint venture, by the group of participating undertakings.

The notification is served to the DGCC. The agency opens a file and analyses it. It has 40 days, from the date of receipt of notification, to conclude the investigation and submit the file to the Minister. Hearing the parties is compulsory and has to take place 10 days before the end of the period. During this hearing, the parties can request further specific investigations by the DGCC. The deadline is suspended until the end of said investigations.

The 40-day deadline is also suspended if the DGCC needs further information. In this case, it will request the new information and suspend the deadline until such information is provided by the parties. In view of its workload, as a matter of practice the agency tends to use this possibility to gain some time to analyse the file.

The file is sent by the DGCC to the Minister for Trade. If, within 50 days of notification, the parties do not receive a decision from the Minister, the merger will benefit from a tacit decision of non-opposition. In general, this happens when the findings of the DGCC are in favour of the merger. As a matter of practice, the DGCC usually informs the parties when its findings are in favour of the merger and before sending the file to the Minister.

If the Minister considers the merger likely to have a negative effect on competition, he must submit the file to the Competition Council for opinion and notify the parties of the request for such opinion. The Minister has 10 days to send the file to the Council.

A second phase of the procedure is then opened. The Council has 30 days to return the file with its opinion, appraising whether the concentration is likely to have a negative effect on competition, according with the criteria provided in paragraph 1 of Article 10; and whether, even if such is the case, the conditions of Article 10, paragraph 2, which allow for a positive decision, are met. The Council's opinion does not bind the Minister.

Within 15 days after receiving the opinion of the Competition Council, the Minister must decide either (i) not to oppose the concentration, (ii) not to oppose the concentration subject to the imposition of conditions and obligations appropriate to the maintenance of workable competition, or (iii) to oppose the concentration. Thus, a notification can take between 50 and 95 days.

In practical terms, the file is submitted to the Competition Council when the findings of the DGCC are against the merger. However, there is at least one case where the Minister decided to send the file to the Council even though the findings of DGCC did not require so. This was an exceptional situation and can be explained because the notifications were filed in a privatisation proceeding. The companies bidding for the privatised undertaking were active in the same market and thus had to notify. However, according to the opinion of the DGCC, not all of these planned concentrations raised doubts as to their compatibility with competition law. Although only where such problems existed was the intervention of the Competition Council necessary, the Minister apparently decided, despite the findings of the DGCC, that all files had to be submitted to the Council[6].

To date, there has never been a decision of opposition to a merger. However, some of the approval decisions have been subject to conditions.

There are several procedural questions that merit development.

Thresholds. Although the DGCC encourages the parties to contact it before a notification is served, it is not empowered to provide the parties with any formal decision before a procedure is concluded. The law does not provide for a preliminary decision by the DGCC formally recognising that the thresholds are not met and thus closing the file without further investigation. This means that whenever the parties have doubts about whether the transaction they are undertaking reaches these thresholds, they have no real alternative other than going through the whole procedure. Only in exceptional circumstances will the DGCC declare, after the filing and before the end of the 40 day period, that a notification was not necessary. This happens, for instance, when the parties have doubts concerning the relevant market and decide to file, but in the market identified by the DGCC the thresholds are not attained.

It follows that the practice of the DGCC is to accept notifications and issue clearing decisions even when the thresholds are not *prima facie* attained. In those cases, however, the DGCC will limit itself to making a somewhat less strict enquiry, inform the parties that the conditions for notification are not met and not send the file to the Minister.

Third parties. The amount of information the parties must provide is significant and the review of this data by the DGCC is quite meticulous. It includes, according to Article 30, the identification of all undertakings that control or are controlled by the notifying undertakings. The definition of control is extremely broad (see below).

The parties have also to provide a list of their main competitors and clients, evaluate their market shares after the concentration, calculate their turnover, including the controlled undertakings, for the last year and provide annual reports for the last three years.

Although the parties must explain the nature of the concentration and its legal form, they are not obliged to provide copies of the contracts they have signed with the notification. Since the amount of information to be provided is so great, from a strictly practical point of view it is useful to be able to contact any local branches or agents of the participating undertakings. The main competitors and clients, whose identification is necessary, are usually contacted by DGCC. However, the rules of procedure do not require a formal hearing of third parties and there is no public notice that a merger procedure is underway. The Competition Law does not grant third parties the right to participate in the procedure.

The fact, however, is that such a hearing is not ruled out either. According to Article 29, when not provided otherwise, the Competition Law is subject to the general rules of administrative procedure[7]. Under these rules, a third party has the right to be heard in an administrative procedure that concerns him. A competitor of merging undertakings can be in this situation and, as such, has the right to be heard. Besides, although there is no public notice of the notification, the main competitors are usually contacted by the DGCC and can present their views on the issue.

However, it should be stressed that Article 35 provides that an appeal can be brought against decisions to prohibit the concentration or to condition its approval. If this is construed as excluding the right to appeal decisions *approving* concentrations, this would limit the right of appeal solely to persons who are party to the transaction, since it would be extremely difficult for a third party to have *locus standi* to appeal an approval under conditions, and an appeal of a prohibition by a third party would be absurd. If the law is construed along these lines, it seems to follow that the decision not to oppose the concentration cannot be appealed [8].

This construction would be an absurd result that violates the right to judicial review recognised by the Constitution. A decision that authorises a merger can obviously violate the rights of competitors. In that case, and if the law is interpreted to mean that those decisions cannot be appealed, the rights of competitors would not be protected. Thus, not only do third parties have the right to be heard but, in any case, they have the right to obtain judicial review of the final decision. Article 35 should be interpreted to mean that a decision authorising the merger cannot be appealed by those same companies that are parties to the merger, a situation which, on the face of it, appears absurd but can be foreseen in the case of a hostile takeover.

Openness of decisions. Only the decisions of the Competition Council are public. This is regrettable since when the procedure ends in the first phase (which includes most of the non-opposition decisions), the file is never submitted to the Council. It follows that the only a very limited number of decisions is made public.

Strictness of procedure. The procedure is quite informal. An example is the practice of the DGCC when it considers that the triggering event was not correctly identified. This happens, for instance, when the purchase of an undertaking is construed as implying, in substance, the creation of a joint venture. Although theoretically the new qualification suggests that the parties to the joint venture thus identified are obliged to come forward and file a notification, in practice the DGCC accepts the information brought by the undertakings that had originally notified.

III. Scope of the law

1. Territorial

As a general rule, Portuguese competition law is applicable to restrictive practices occurring within the national territory or producing, or being able to produce, such effects therein.

In what concerns mergers, the same substantive approach is followed, although the phrasing of the relevant rule, Article 7, is slightly different. It will be remembered that a merger exists whenever a domestic market share of 30% is attained as a result of the operation or the combined turnover in Portugal exceeds Esc 30 billion (approx. € 150 million). It follows that the simple risk of producing effects in the national market is not relevant: the market share, or the level of combined turnover, is either attained or not. In this regard, there is no uncertainty in the scope of the law.

This recognition of the effects doctrine is quite clear, following the established practice in what concerns restrictive practices of both the DGCC and the Council. To these authorities, the fact that a company sells directly to a retailer and does not have any representative or agent in Portugal does not preclude the application of national law[9]. It follows from the text of the law and the interpretation made by national authorities that a concentration where none of the companies is located, or have branches, in Portugal may be subject to Portuguese law.

Since Portugal has a small open economy, a large number of notified concentrations take place outside the country and can even involve undertakings that have no subsidiary or representative in Portugal. In view of the amount of information the parties have to provide (see above), it can be difficult to prepare and file a notification when the undertakings are not represented by a local agent.

National law is "applicable subject to the international commitments of the Republic" [10]. In addition to the more general precepts of the Constitution concerning the reception of Community law, it is through this rule that the articulation between domestic and external (namely Community) legal sources is made. There is no other mention of the effects of Community law on national competition law. It should be stressed that the practice of the national authorities is full co-operation with the Commission, whose decisions are duly recognised. For example, in a recent decision concerning the control of the sole national steel producer, the DGCC declared itself bound by a previous ESCC Commission Decision that cleared the operation [11].

2. Material

Decree Law No. 371/93 is applicable to all economic activities, with two exceptions.

The first concerns undertakings which have been awarded concessions by the State. This exception covers only the scope and execution of the relevant concession agreement. These undertakings benefit from public powers and in general have an exclusive right. In principle, they are not subject to the market. Furthermore, the Government normally has the power to authorise price modifications by the concessionaire, so their behaviour depends on some sort of public control.

This exception has a general nature and covers the whole of competition law, including merger control. This does not mean that such undertakings are free to merge, since the concession agreements generally subject any legal modification of the concessionaire to government authorisation, including the sale of its stock and the infrastructure that pertains to the concession. This follows from the fact that the selection of a concessionaire by the state is highly dependent on the experience and guarantees it offers, so that any fundamental modification of its ownership has to be controlled by the state.

The second exception is limited to the application of merger control rules to the banking sector. Article 7 of the Competition Law exempts credit institutions, financial institutions and insurance companies from its application. Concentrations in the financial sector are directly subject to the Ministry of Finance and the supervision of the Bank of Portugal. The Bank of Portugal must grant prior authorisation to the concentration of credit institutions[12]. If such approval is not obtained, the parties can be fined[13]. Although the relevant texts do not establish a system specifically devoted to merger control, the fact is that such an operation is only subject to those laws and regulations.

In addition to these exceptions, there are two forms of capital acquisitions that are excluded by the law. These are the acquisition of shares as a guarantee of credits and the acquisition of capital under certain special procedures to rescue bankrupt undertakings.

IV. Definition of concentration

As explained above, there are two facts which make notification mandatory: the creation or reinforcement of a market share above 30% or the simple fact that the combined turnover of the parties is above Esc 30 billion.

The first alternative is clearly linked to the legal definition of dominant position. According to Article 3 of the Competition Law, an undertaking with a market share of at least 30% is presumed to have a dominant position. What the law seeks to avoid, thus, is the creation of dominant positions outside the control of antitrust authorities.

The second alternative is independent of any share in the relevant market of the concentration. It obliges all major undertakings to go through the long and potentially cumbersome process of notification just because of their sheer economic importance.

The legal definition is based on the idea of acquisition of undertakings. It does not mention other less obvious ways of acquiring the activity of undertakings such as, for instance, when certain contracts are transferred from the initial provider to the undertaking that somehow acquires them. There is, however, no doubt that such situations are covered by the legal notion of concentration. It should be noted that there are no exceptions for concentrations which are inherently time limited.

The clearest example of the concept of concentration on which the law seems to be based is the purchase of a competitor by an undertaking. This is shown by the fact that notification is mandatory when there is the creation or reinforcement of a market share above 30%. If, however, a company that is not active in a market decides to acquire an undertaking in that same market, there is arguably no creation of a market share but rather the simple transfer of a pre-existent market share.

In one of its opinions, the Council addressed this question, stating in an *obiter dictum* that the mere fact of acquiring a company which has a market share of 30% is not a concentration and, as such, is not required to be notified[14]. For the Council, it is only the fact that an undertaking already holding a market position acquires another market position that is relevant for concentration purposes.

This line of argument can have many practical consequences, since only those concentrations whose notification is mandatory can be prohibited. However, it is extremely difficult to deduce a clear conclusion without considering a particular case. Besides, this position has not had any consequences concerning the practice of the DGCC, which, as far as is known, follows a more traditional interpretation and considers such cases to require notification.

1. Control

In practical terms, the most important triggering event is the acquisition of control by a person or an undertaking of other undertakings. Thus it is essential to define control, a notion that is also important in what concerns the calculation of turnover.

According to Article 9 (2), "control" is defined as the result of any act, whatever its form, that allows the possibility of exerting, jointly or separately, a decisive influence on the activities of an undertaking. The legal and factual circumstances of the case have to be considered when assessing the existence of "control". Article 9 (2) gives the following examples of control:
- acquisition of the whole or part of the capital;
- acquisition of property rights over all or part of the assets of an undertaking, including the right to use or enjoy those assets;
- acquisition of rights or celebration of contracts that confer the possibility of exerting a decisive influence on the composition of the decision-making bodies of the undertaking, or on its decisions.

This includes not only control of the majority of shares but also the possibility of nominating the majority of the members of the company's main boards or

PORTUGAL

the power to conduct the business of the company. In practice, it may be useful to provide copies of the bye-laws of the participating undertakings to clear doubts concerning control and shareholder structure. The parties may have to demonstrate that these rights do not exist, but this could require them to disclose the contracts and agreements made.

2. Turnover

The calculation of turnover must include all undertakings controlled by the parties, as defined above, and all undertakings that control the parties, with the deduction of intra-group sales. The sole exception is the acquisition of a part of an undertaking, where the volume of turnover is limited to the acquired parts.

Although it is clear that turnover of all controlled undertakings have to be considered, there is no rule for jointly controlled undertakings. The law seems to assume that there is always a single controlling company and does not consider the possibility of real joint control. As a result, such undertakings may not have to be included. A practical alternative is to share the turnover between the parties to the joint venture.

The connection between rules on control and turnover allow the DGCC to move up and down the holding ladder. Since the parties have to list all companies that control them or that they themselves control, they are obliged to disclose the structure of the holding groups.

V. The substantive test

Although it can be said that the system is inherently biased towards granting the approval of concentrations, and practice certainly supports this conclusion, the fact is that Article 10 contains a general rule of prohibition: concentrations that create or reinforce a dominant position in the relevant market in such a way as to prevent, distort or restrict competition are prohibited. Thus, the authorities must (i) assess whether there is the creation or reinforcement of a dominant position, and (ii) whether this dominant position restricts competition.

However, there are two very broad clauses that allow authorisation even if there is a restrictive dominant position: the positive economic balance and reinforcement of the international competitiveness of the participating undertakings.

This second possibility was certainly conceived for the benefit of the typical Portuguese company. Although it has been recognised that this does not apply only to exporting companies, it was clearly devised either to allow the reinforcement of export-oriented undertakings or undertakings that have to face international competition in the national market[15].

The other possibility is the positive economic balance. This concept allows concentrations to be authorised if they contribute to improvements in production or distribution of goods or services or economic and technical development. Moreover, they must cumulatively:
- allow consumers a fair share of the resulting benefits;
- not impose restrictions on the undertakings concerned that are not indispensable to achieve these objectives;
- not give the undertakings the possibility to eliminate competition.

It is obviously difficult to assess whether such conditions are met. Although it may be easy to judge whether improvements in technical and economic matters are present, the conditions pertaining to consumers and the dispensable nature of the restrictions imposed seem quite difficult to assess. On the other hand, these conditions are so broad that they can easily be interpreted with a pro-merger bias. Only time and development of the decisions and opinions of the competent authorities will give clearer indications.

The Minister can impose conditions on the approval of the concentration. The law allows these conditions to take all forms, as long as they are adequate to maintain effective competition.

VI. Sanctions

There are two types of sanction in concentration control. The first are legal sanctions against the non-notified concentrations or the concentrations concluded against the decision of the Minister (either a prohibition or an authorisation under conditions). Non-notified concentrations are, as explained above, not effective. All transactions that pertain to prohibited concentrations or that violate the conditions imposed on the authorisation of concentrations are void.

The second group of sanctions are fines that can be imposed on violating undertakings. Thus, the non-notification of a concentration is punished with a fine of between Esc 100,000 and Esc 100 million (€ 500 to 500,000). The same amounts apply to the violation of a decision of the Minister. Thus, concluding a concentration against such a decision is not only legally void but can also be punished by a fine.

The parties are obliged to fully co-operate with the authorities and to provide all information required. If an approval is based on false information, the DGCC will initiate a proceeding aiming at declaring the concentration illegal. Providing false or inaccurate information can be punished with a fine of the up to Esc 100 million (€ 500,000).

It is disputable whether there are any sanctions if a concentration takes place after the notification but before the authorisation. As explained above, all legal transactions are ineffective before the approval. This puts the concentration in a rather undefined situation until the approval. However, the law does not apply any fine if the parties conclude the merger and, since violations to antitrust law have a quasi-criminal nature, the powers of the DGCC must be strictly construed.

The fact of notifying puts the concentration under the control of the authorities and it can be argued that this is enough, since the DGCC can follow the evolution of the relationship between the parties. Besides, if they proceed, the parties face the risk of eventually being obliged to divest. This explains why there is no clear sanction for the companies that do not wait for the clearing.

Notes

1 There were, however, some attempts to introduce antitrust laws during this period, although the aim was not the protection of competition but rather the interests of small undertakings. See M. Gorjão-Henriques, *Da Restrição da Concorrência na Comunidade Europeia*, Coimbra, 1998, p. 35; A. Robalo Cordeiro, *As Coligações de Empresas e os Direitos Português e Comunitário da Concorrência*, Revista de Direito e Estudos Sociais, 1987, p. 81 e ss.; and Victor Calvete, "Da Relevância das Considerações de Eficiência no Controlo das Concentrações em Portugal", in: *Ab Uno Ad Omnes*, Coimbra, 1998, p. 305, at p. 341.
2 Article 7, paragraph 3 of Decree Law No. 371/93.
3 The fine for non-notification can be up to Esc 100 million; see Article 37, paragraph 3.
4 Direcção Geral do Comercio e Concorrência, which is part of the Ministry for Economic Affairs.

5   See Article 9, paragraph 1 under a), b) and c), respectively, of the Competition Law
6   See Decision 2/96, Seita, 28 November 1996, Annual Report, p. 127, especially at page 130; Decision 3/96, Urex Inversiones, Annual Report, cit., p. 133, especially 137; compare with Decision 4/96, PMM, annual report, cit., p. 141, where the DGCC raised doubts concerning the planned concentration.
7   These rules are defined by the Codigo de Procedimento Administrativo Gracioso, Decree Law No. 442/91, of 15 November. In what concerns the right to be heard, see in particular Articles 8 and 100.
8   See Calvete, *op. cit.*, p. 355, according to whom the nature of competition law precludes that any sort of *locus standi* can be recognised outside Article 35 of the law.
9   In a decision of 4/12/1991, the Council declared national competition law (at that time it was Decree Law No. 422/83, which, on this point, was identical to the present law) applicable to a situation where a French tool maker, which did not have any representative in Portugal and sold directly to local shops, imposed prices on its products. Although it recognised that the violation of the law had taken place in France, the Council quoted the effects doctrine to support its finding. See *Relatório de Actividade do Conselho da Concorrência*, 1991, p. 71 ss., at page 76.
10 Article 1, paragraph 2, Decree Law No. 371/93.
11 The unpublished decision, of December 1998, concerned the change from joint to single control by one of the shareholders of Siderurgia Nacional Longos SA. The Commission had previously declared that the acquisition was covered by a decision of 7 December 1995 on the privatisation of the Portuguese company.
12 See Article 35º of Decree Law No. 298/92. This act is the main regulation on banking and financial activities.
13 See Article 211º d) of Decree Law No. 298/92.
14 Parecer de 28/11/1996, Urex Inversiones, in: *Conselho da Concorrência*, Relatório de Actividade de 1996, p. 133, at p. 138.
15 See Opinion of 6 December 1995, in *Relatório de Actividade*, 1995, p. 99. In this case the Competition Council cleared a merger of all main milk producers, whose market share was between 44% and 75% according to the several markets considered, insisting *inter alia*, on the fact that the market was open to large foreign producers.

Spain

Fernando Pombo

Emiliano Garayar

Contents

1. Introduction 369
2. Merger control in Spain: Law 16/1989, of 17 July, on the
   Defence of Competition 369
   2.1. Competition authorities 370
   2.2. Definition of "concentration" 370
   2.3. Scope of Chapter II of Law 16/1989 on the Control of
        Concentrations 376
   2.4. Notification 383
   2.5. Procedure 385
3. Special Provisions regulating Concentrations carried out
   through Public Bids: Royal Decree 1197/1991, of 26 July 394
   3.1. Voluntary notification by the bidder 395
   3.2. Referral of the operation to the Service for the Defence of
        Competition by the National Stock Exchange Commission 397
   3.3. Publicity 397
4. Requests and referrals to the European Commission under the
   EC Merger Regulation 398
   4.1. Referrals under Article 9 of the EC Merger Regulation 398
   4.2. Requests under Article 22(3) of the EC Merger Regulation 398
5. Setting proposals for a future reform 399
6. Summary 399
Addendum 401
The New Merger Control Procedure in Spain 403
   1. Main Changes in the Merger Control Procedure Introduced
      by Royal Decree-Law 6/1999, of April 16 ("RDL") 403
   2. Mergers subject to Notification 403
   3. Characteristics of the Procedure 403
   4. Termination of the Procedure 404
   5. Fines 404
   Notes 405

1. Introduction

Spanish Competition Law follows the principles and guidelines set out by the Treaty of Rome, in particular Articles 85 and 86 and implementing regulations.

On 17 July 1989, Law 16/1989 on the "Defence of Competition"[1] (referred hereafter as the "Spanish Regulation") was adopted. The Spanish Regulation introduced on a national level the principles laid down in Articles 85 and 86 of the EC Treaty and in Council Regulation 4064/89/EEC on the control of concentrations (the "EC Merger Regulation")[2]. Although the Spanish Regulation was adopted before the EC Merger Regulation was enacted, its principles were clearly inspired by those included in the draft of the EC Merger Regulation then in circulation. Since 1989, the Spanish Regulation has been modified by Royal Legislative Decree 7/1996[3], of 7 June, which introduced some precise rules in line with previous decisions of the Spanish Competition Authority.

The main provisions of merger control in Spain are contained in Title I, Chapter II, Articles 14 to 17 of the Spanish Regulation. These provisions have been developed by Royal Decree 1080/1992[4], of 11 September, which lays down the rules regarding notifications and procedural matters. Special provisions apply to concentrations carried out through Public Take-over Bids, according to Chapter VI, Articles 37 and 38 of Royal Decree 1197/1991[5], of 26 July, on Public Bids. Law 11/1998[6], of 24 April, on Telecommunications, includes a specific provision regarding concentrations in the telecommunications market.

Lastly, Royal Decree 295/1998[7], of 27 February, regulates the action of the Spanish Authorities under Articles 9 and 22.3 of the EC Merger Regulation.

2. Merger control in Spain: Law 16/1989, of 17 July, on the Defence of Competition

The Spanish Regulation intends to ensure the maintenance of undistorted competition in the market as a fundamental element of the economic system enshrined in Article 38 of the Spanish Constitution. Therefore, its first recital emphasises the importance of competition and free market enterprise within a market economy such as Spain, as well as it links the duty of public authorities to protect competition with the mentioned Constitutional provision.

The third recital of the Spanish Regulation states that its principles are inspired by EU competition rules and policy, which are fundamental to the common market. Besides merger control, the Spanish Regulation repeals and replaces the law that previously dealt with restrictive trade practices (Law 110/1963, of 20 July, on the Repression of Restrictive Practices[8]).

2.1. Competition authorities

The control of concentrations under the Spanish Regulation is entrusted to several authorities and bodies with different participation in the procedure.

Notifications and complaints are addressed to the Service for the Defence of Competition, a body integrated in the Ministry of Economy and Finance which is responsible for the first assessment of concentrations, among other tasks. The Minister may then submit the cases of concentrations that threaten to affect competition to the opinion of the Tribunal for the Defence of Competition, an independent administrative authority, even if organically integrated in the Ministry. The Tribunal produces a report analysing the transaction and proposing a decision on the concentration to the Government. This report is merely advisory and does not bind the Government, which is the ultimate authority exercising the control on concentrations. If a concentration takes place between telecommunications operators, the Commission for the Market of Telecommunications will also submit a report to the Government.

The basic provisions regulating the composition and functioning of the Service for the Defence of Competition and the Tribunal for the Defence of Competition are contained in Title II of Law 16/1989. Royal Decrees 538/1965[9], of 4 March, and 422/1970[10], of 5 February, lay down more detailed rules for the Tribunal and the Service, respectively. Lastly, Royal Decree 755/1991[11], of 10 May, adapted the internal structure of the Ministry of Economy and Finance to the needs of the system of control set up by the Spanish Regulation.

The different roles of each of the institutions involved in merger control will be further explained in section 2.5.

2.2. Definition of "concentration"

Article 14 of the Spanish Regulation delineating the scope of provisions regulating merger control states that:

"All projects of concentration or concentrations between undertakings or any acquisition of control of one or more undertakings by another person, undertaking or group of undertakings, where it affects or may affect the Spanish market and in particular where it creates or strengthens a dominant position, may be submitted by the Minister of Economy and Finance to the opinion of the Tribunal for the Defence of Competition...".

First of all, it must be emphasised that under the Spanish Regulation there is no specific definition of the terms "concentration" or "acquisition of control", unlike Article 3 of the EC Regulation that provides several examples of what constitutes a concentration and the criteria defining the "acquisition of control".

However, the underlying principles of the Spanish Regulation require that special emphasis be placed on the economic effects of the operation and Chapter VI of the Regulation refers to "economic concentrations". The definitions of "concentration" and "acquisition of control" laid down by the EC Merger Regulation could in principle be applied by way of analogy for the purpose of the Spanish Regulation, but in some cases there will be substantial differences.

Sometimes, the European Commission and the Spanish Competition Authorities may qualify transactions in different ways. To a certain extent this happened in *Cablevisión*[12], one of the leading cases in the field of merger control, involving the joint acquisition of an undertaking, and the conclusion of a strategic agreement. The Tribunal for the Defence of Competition said that, under Spanish Law, the notified operation should be analysed as a whole in light of Article 1 of the Spanish Regulation (the equivalent of Article 85 of the EC Treaty) rather than under Article 14. On the other hand, the Commission held that the transaction at issue amounted to a concentration with Community dimension[13]. Nevertheless, the Commission's control was to cover only the concentrative aspects of the operation, leaving the co-operation agreement for an ulterior analysis.

Finally, the Spanish Government did not follow the suggestions of the Tribunal for the Defence of Competition and it cleared the operation as a *concentration* of national dimension, thus departing from the opinion that the European Commission had communicated to it only a few weeks before[14].

Cases such as *Cablevisión* show that the treatment of certain concentrations may not always be the same at Community and national level. The Tribunal for the Defence of Competition may feel concerned about the fact that in

Spain, unlike the system in the EU, the instances that decide on concentrations on the one hand, and on restrictive practices on the other, are different, as well as the nature of the control. Therefore, a decision qualifying a given operation as a concentration or otherwise as a co-operative agreement is a crucial one. We will refer again to these questions below[15].

2.2.1. Persons, undertakings or groups of undertakings.

(i) Concept of undertaking
The question "what constitutes an undertaking?" must be answered by reference to two different sets of criteria.

Economic criteria. In the economic sense, an undertaking is an entity engaged in economic or commercial activities such as production, distribution or the supply of services and ranging from small shops run by an individual to large industrial companies. Therefore, the economic sense of undertaking covers any legal or natural person carrying out activities of an economic or commercial nature.

Legal criteria. In the legal sense, the term undertaking is to be identified with the Spanish legal concept of "company". Under Spanish law, a company may be of a civil or commercial nature. Article 1.665 of the Civil Code defines civil companies. According to Article 1.970 paragraph 1 of the Civil Code, a civil company can be incorporated in any of the legal forms provided for in the Code of Commerce. Public limited companies and private limited companies are always of a commercial nature and they are, therefore, subject to the provisions of the Code of Commerce and Laws of 17 July 1951 and of 17 July 1953, amended by Law of 25 July 1989. Under the Code of Commerce (Art. 122), a company can be incorporated as:
- public limited liability company;
- private limited liability company;
- unlimited liability partnership;
- limited liability partnership.

(ii) Groups of undertakings
There is no Spanish law that directly defines what constitutes a "group of undertakings".

By means of implementation of the Seventh EEC Directive on Consolidated Accounts, Spain introduced in the Code of Commerce the Section 3 on Presentation of Consolidated Accounts. This Section refers, for the first time in Spanish law, to the notion of "groups of companies".

The main criterion to be applied in order to determine the existence of a group of undertakings is the "control" exercised by one undertaking on others. According to Article 42 of the Code of Commerce, satisfaction of any one of the following criteria constitutes a controlling undertaking, and therefore annual consolidated accounts must be presented:
 a) The undertaking holds the majority of voting rights in the other undertaking(s).
 b) The undertaking has the right to appoint or dismiss the majority of the members of the board of the other undertaking.
 c) The undertaking is able by virtue of an agreement concluded with other shareholders to control the exercise of the majority of voting rights.
 d) The undertaking has appointed, exercising exclusively its own voting rights, the majority of the members of the board during the current and the two previous financial years.

(iii) Individuals
According to Article 14 of the Spanish Regulation, a "person" may acquire control of one or more undertakings. Given that the Spanish Regulation distinguishes between "undertaking", "groups of undertakings" and "persons", it is submitted that the term "person" is to be understood as connoting individuals or natural persons as distinct from undertakings or groups of undertakings.

The person in question must enjoy legal capacity to act under Spanish law[16].

2.2.2. Categories of transactions involved in a concentration.

Under Spanish commercial regulations, a concentration may be legally effected by a number of different means.

(i) Merger
Mergers are regulated in Spain under Chapter VIII, Section 2, Articles 233 to 251 of the Public Limited Liability Companies Act[17]. The aforesaid provisions implement in Spanish Law Third Council Directive of 9 October 1978, concerning mergers of public limited liability companies.

The Spanish Regulation distinguishes between two different sorts of merger: mergers by acquisition of one or more companies by another, and mergers by the formation of a new company.

"Merger by acquisition"[18] means the operation whereby one or more companies are wound up without going into liquidation, and transfer all their assets and liabilities to another in exchange[19] for the issue of shares in the acquiring company to the shareholders of the company or companies being acquired and a cash payment, if any, not exceeding 10% of the nominal value of the shares so issued[20].

"Merger by the formation of a new company"[21] means the operation whereby several companies are wound up without going into liquidation and transfer all their assets and liabilities to a company that they set up in exchange for the issue of shares in the new company to the shareholders and a cash payment, if any, not exceeding 10% of the nominal value of the shares so issued.

Under Article 251 of the Spanish Public Limited Liability Companies Act, both "merger by acquisition" and "merger by the formation of a new company" may also be effected where one or more of the companies which cease to exist are in liquidation, provided that these companies have not yet begun to distribute their assets to the shareholders.

The Spanish Regulation covers these categories of merger between public limited liability companies, as well as any other transactions between any type of companies that amount to an equivalent effect from an economic point of view.

(ii) Division

Division of public liability companies is regulated in Chapter VIII, Section 3, Articles 252 to 259 of the Spanish Public Limited Liability Companies Act[22], voluntarily implementing the provisions laid down in Sixth Council Directive concerning the division of public limited liability companies.

The Spanish Regulations distinguish between two types of division: the operation whereby a company, going into liquidation, transfers all its assets and liabilities to more than one newly formed or existing company[23]; and the operation whereby a company, without going into liquidation, transfers part of its assets and liabilities to one or more newly-formed or existing company[24].

Both types of division shall be carried out in exchange for the allocation to the shareholders of company being divided of shares in the companies receiving contributions as a result of the division[25].

Under Article 254, the provision governing mergers shall apply to division in so far as they are compatible.

(iii) Concentrative joint venture
Recently, Regulation 1310/97/EEC has introduced an important change in the treatment to accord to so-called full function joint ventures. According to this Regulation, all those joint ventures will be analysed following the procedures set out for merger control, whether they are qualified as co-operative or concentrative. The substantial test for clearance will be different, since co-operative joint ventures are to be analysed under Article 85 of the EC Treaty, but the notification, procedure and decision will be those provided for by the Merger Regulation.

It is submitted that this approach cannot be reproduced under Spanish law. Since the systems of control for restrictive practices and concentrations differ widely, with different bodies taking the final decision in each case, co-operative and concentrative joint ventures must be subject to strictly separate procedures, under Article 1 and Article 14 of the Spanish Regulation respectively. The importance of the distinction between the scopes of application of both Articles will be explained in depth in section 2.3.6 below. Here, it should be said that the definition of concentrative joint venture found in the former version of the EC Regulation[26] can be applied by analogy for the purpose of the Spanish Regulation.

(iv) Acquisition of control
According to the Spanish Regulation, an "acquisition of control of one or more undertakings by another person, undertaking or group of undertakings" may be subject to control by the competition authorities.

As to the meaning of "acquisition of control", Article 87 of the Spanish Public Company Act provides that the controlling undertaking is an undertaking which meets any one of the criteria established in Article 42 of the Commerce Code which deals with the cases where consolidated group annual accounts must be filed, (as explained in section 2.2.1.ii).

2.2.3. Proposed or implemented concentrations

Under Article 14, not only concentrations which have already been implemented but also proposed concentrations fall within the scope of the Spanish Regulation.

It is submitted that the Spanish Regulation does not apply to a mere speculative idea for a future concentration but only to a firm project of concentration.

2.3. Scope of Chapter II of Law 16/1989 on the Control of Concentrations

2.3.1. Jurisdictional thresholds

The Spanish Regulation provides that the Minister of Economy and Finance may refer a concentration which falls within that general scope of Article 14 (i.e. affects or may affect the Spanish market and in particular where it creates or strengthens a dominant position) to the Tribunal for the Defence of Competition in the following circumstances:
  a) where the concentration results in the creation of or strengthens an existing market share of 25% or higher either of the Spanish market as a whole, or of a substantial part of it in a given product or service; or
  b) where the aggregate Spanish turnover of all the undertakings concerned is more than Pta 20 billion in the last financial year.

It must be noted that these are alternative and not cumulative conditions. These thresholds are quite high, because when they were enacted, the Spanish economy needed those mergers to increase its performance to be able to face the challenges of global economy.

2.3.2. Dimension of the concentration: Calculation of turnover

Article 2 paragraph 1 of Royal Decree 1080/1992 establishes the method for the calculation of turnover, and it reproduces almost integrally the text of the first paragraph of Article 5 of the EC Merger Regulation. Therefore, for the purposes of Article 14 b) of the Spanish Regulation, laying down the jurisdictional thresholds, the Spanish turnover "shall comprise the amounts derived by the undertakings concerned in the preceding financial year from the sale of products and the provision of services falling within the undertakings' ordinary activities after deduction of sales rebates and of value added tax and other taxes directly related to turnover".

SPAIN

Specific rules are laid down in paragraph 2 of Article 2 for the determination of aggregate turnover of groups of companies, credit institutions and insurance companies.

(i) Groups of companies
With regards to groups of companies, within the terms of Article 42 of the Spanish Commercial Code, the turnover taken into account must be that from the company involved in the transaction and:
- the turnover of the undertakings controlled by it;
- the turnover of the undertakings exercising control over it;
- and the turnover of all the companies in which one or more of the aforesaid hold rights making control possible.

Only the turnover resulting from the same activities as the one affected by the concentration is relevant for this calculation. Account shall not be taken of intra-group sales or of any sales of the group outside Spain.

(ii) Credit institutions
Turnover of credit institutions shall be substituted by one-tenth of their total assets. This rule is inspired in the previous wording of Article 5.3 a) of the EC Merger Regulation, which has been modified by Regulation 1310/97 that lays down the current system for calculation of turnover of credit institutions. Also in accordance with the former text, Article 2.2 of Royal Decree 1080/1992 defines Spanish turnover as one-tenth of total assets by the ratio between loans to credit institutions and customers in transactions with residents in Spain and the total sum of those loans.

(iii) Insurance companies
The calculation of turnover of insurance companies is to be done in the same way as established in Article 5.3 b) of the EC Merger Regulation, this is, turnover shall be substituted by the value of gross premiums written which shall comprise all amounts received and receivable in respect of insurance contracts issued by or on behalf of the insurance undertakings, including also outgoing reinsurance premiums, and after deduction of any taxes or contributions charged by reference to the amounts of individual premiums or the total volume of premiums, taking only into account gross premiums received from residents in Spain.

2.3.3. "Affects or may affect the Spanish market".

In order to determine whether or not a given concentration affects or may affect the Spanish market or some substantial part thereof it is necessary to clarify two concepts: what constitutes an "effect" for this purpose and how is the "Spanish Market" to be defined.

(i) Effect on the Spanish market
It is generally understood that "effect" in this context does not necessarily imply a prevention, restriction or distortion of competition but simply an effect on the normal conditions of competition within the relevant product and geographic market.

Moreover, Article 14 clearly provides that either an actual or a potential effect on competition is to be taken into account.

(ii) "Spanish market"
The Spanish Regulation does not specify any criteria to be used in the definition of the "Spanish Market". Nevertheless, the practice of the Tribunal for the Defence of Competition helps us to identify some guidelines in this regard.

Relevant product market. The decisive test for defining whether products belong to the same market or not is the criterion of interchangeability. Products that are only to a limited extent interchangeable with other products are arguably not part of the same relevant market.

Interchangeability must also be considered from the point of view of the consumer. To judge whether or not goods are interchangeable, the nature of the goods, their price and use should be taken into consideration. However, not only the objective characteristics of the goods in question must be taken into account but also the consumer's perception.

Data concerning the cross-elasticity of demand can be useful for the inquiry into whether goods are interchangeable. Where there is a high cross-elasticity of demand between certain products, a slight increase in the price of one product causes a considerable number of customers to switch to other products, thereby tending to indicate that the products compete in the same relevant market.

Sometimes the Tribunal for the Defence of Competition has identified very precise markets, after analysing the different segments of demand for one generic product. For instance, in its report on the acquisition of Conelsa and Cofralim (two frozen food and ice cream producers) by Nestlé[27], the Tribunal examined the effect of the transaction on the ice cream market and distinguished the markets for take-home ice cream and for impulse-bought ice cream as distinct, further defining three sub-markets within the latter[28]. In that case, the Tribunal found limited risks for competition only with regard to the sub-market for differentiated products for impulse consumption, recommending the clearance of the merger under conditions.

The *Nestlé* concentration is not only relevant as an example of very detailed (narrow) definition of the market, but also as an example of how Spanish competition authorities take into account the findings made by the European Commission. Indeed, the Tribunal for the Defence of Competition founded its assessment of the relevant market on previous Commission decisions in *Nestlé/Italgel*[29] and *Unilever France/Ortíz Miko*[30].

Other product markets as defined by the Tribunal for the Defence of Competition range from spare parts for cars[31] and beer[32] to rigid plastic PVC materials[33], radio advertising[34] and packages for cosmetic products[35].

Relevant geographic market. Contrary to the Spanish Regulation, the EC Merger Regulation contains a definition of geographic market in Article 9 paragraph 7: "The geographic reference market shall consist of the area in which the undertakings concerned are involved in the supply of products or services, in which conditions of competition are sufficiently homogeneous and which can be distinguished from neighbouring areas because, in particular, conditions of competition are appreciably different in those areas. This assessment should take account in particular the nature and characteristics of the products or services concerned, of the existence of entry barriers or of consumer preferences, of appreciable differences of the undertakings' market shares between neighbouring areas or of substantial price differences."

This definition is intended to assess the existence of "distinct markets", different from the economic point of view. The Spanish Regulation, on the other hand, just refers to the "Spanish market" in Article 14, stating that any concentration that affects or may affect the Spanish market may be submitted to the opinion of the Tribunal for the Defence of Competition.

Besides, when Article 16 lays down the criteria for the evaluation of concentrations, it mentions "external competition" as a point to take into account in the assessment of competitive effects. Indeed, the openness of the

Spanish market to foreign competition may justify the authorisation of concentrations involving high market shares in the national market, as it was held by the Tribunal for the Defence of Competition in cases such as *Procter & Gamble-Ausonia*[36]. But in those cases it would seem appropriate to define the relevant geographic market as European or global, as the case may be.

Sometimes, large geographic markets have been said to exist. For instance, in *Hoesch/Krupp*[37] the concentration was authorised because the relevant market was larger than the Spanish market, and serious competitive restraints were not likely to appear. In *Techpack*[38] the market was said to be wider than the Spanish market and, possibly, wider even than the European market. In such cases, the Tribunal will study the effects of the concentration in the Spanish market alone.

For that purpose, the Tribunal may distinguish between different economic stages for the appraisal of the concentrations submitted to its opinion. In *Sensormatic/Knogo*[39] the Tribunal stated that from a manufacturing point of view, the relevant geographic market for electronic article surveillance systems was European, but from the point of view of distribution and sales the market was national. It went on to examine distribution contracts of the products in the Spanish market and concluded that competitors could access distribution channels as easily as before. Had there been important long-term exclusive distribution contracts for the products of the concentrated undertakings, the positive conclusion on the operation reached by the Tribunal may have been different.

In *Plasgom/Elf Atochem* the Tribunal drew the same distinction between manufacturing and marketing of PVC products.

2.3.4. Creation or strengthening of a dominant position

(i) Dominant position
The specific reference criteria laid down by Article 14 of the Spanish Regulation may perhaps be taken to imply that dominance will be presumptively present where an undertaking holds, at least, a 25% market share in the national market of relevant products or services, or in a substantial part of it.

However, the Spanish Regulation does not rule out the possibility of taking into account other criteria for the determination of a dominant position.

(ii) Creation or strengthening

The Spanish Regulation does not contemplate the existence of a dominant position (i.e. company A, dominant, acquires company B which operates in a different market) but its creation or strengthening (i.e. company A with a modest market share acquires company B, similarly positioned: the combined market share confers dominance).

2.3.5. Application to foreign parties

The Spanish Regulation applies to all concentrations that affect or may affect the Spanish market and that fall above the thresholds set in Article 14. These are two requirements that define the scope of application of the Spanish Regulation, as explained before. Therefore, they obviously limit the number of concentrations that fall under Spanish jurisdiction and in which foreign parties are involved. For foreign-to-foreign mergers to be caught, the undertakings concerned must develop significant activities on Spanish territory.

2.3.6. Control of concentrations and restrictive practices

The relationship of Chapter II of Law 16/1989 with the provisions concerning collusion and abuse of dominant position is one of the points that has caused more difficulties in the interpretation and application of the Spanish Regulation than any other.

Article 1 of Law 16/1989 is the equivalent in the Spanish legal system of Article 85, paragraphs 1 and 2, of the EC Treaty. Article 1 prohibits all kind of agreements and concerted practices between undertakings that may affect competition in the Spanish market, unless they benefit from an exemption granted in accordance with the Law[40].

Article 6 of the Spanish Regulation is intended to prevent the abuses of undertakings enjoying a dominant position on the market.

The distinction between the scope of application of these provisions and the scope of Article 14 of the Spanish Regulation is of crucial importance since procedures, substantive rules and, in the last instance, the institution called to adopt a decision in each case are different. The original version of the Regulation did not address this question. In *Mölnlycke*[41], the Tribunal for the Defence of Competition declared that the application of Article 14 excludes recourse to Articles 1 and 6 of Law 16/1989. In that case, the complainant wanted to challenge the concentration of activities of Procter & Gamble, FINAF and Arbora Holding in their Spanish joint venture Ausonia Higiene, S.L., claiming that the agreement between the companies constituted illegal collusion and, moreover, an abuse of dominant position. As the Government had already approved the concentration following notification by the undertakings[42], the Tribunal pointed out that the complainant should have brought an action of annulment against the Government's decision instead of introducing a new claim before the Service for the Defence of Competition, which rightly dismissed the complaint.

The same issue arose in a more complicated form in *Cablevisión*[43]. In this case, concerning the acquisition by Telefónica and Sogecable/Canal Plus of joint control over Cablevisión (a company operating in the field of cable telecommunications), a complaint based on Articles 1 and 6 of the Spanish Regulation had already been presented and a preliminary investigation had started when the parties to the agreement decided to notify it as a concentration[44]. As we have explained before (section 2.2), the matter was sent to the Tribunal for the Defence of Competition, which qualified the transaction as strategic alliance of co-operative nature, therefore out of the scope of Article 14 of the Spanish Regulation[45]. The Tribunal underlined that, under Spanish law, it is impossible to sever the concentrative and co-operative aspects of a given transaction, and being so it should be for the Tribunal to decide the case on the basis of Articles 1 and 6 of Law 16/1989[46].

The final outcome in *Cablevisión* was rather different from the opinion of the Tribunal for the Defence of Competition. The Government received the report of the Tribunal and it decided to treat the transaction as a concentration, which was approved under conditions by Ministry Order of 14 March 1996.

In 1996, the Spanish Regulation was modified in order to regulate these sorts of problem cases, where the qualification of the operation under scrutiny must be determined as a *prius* of any further action. Royal Legislative Decree 7/1996, of June 7, introduced the fifth paragraph of Article 15, which states:

> "When the Service for the Defence of Competition considers that a voluntary notification of agreements, covenants or alliances between undertakings does not fall within the notion of economic concentration, it shall decide within one month that the transaction be treated as a request for an exemption of an agreement between undertakings, in conformity with Article 3, without the benefit of tacit authorisation.

When a voluntary notification of a concentration is presented after a complaint relating to restrictive practices with regard to similar facts, the Service for the Defence of Competition shall, within one month, join both proceedings and decide whether the transaction is to be regarded as an agreement falling under Article 1 or as an economic concentration.

The decisions adopted by the Service for the Defence of Competition may be reviewed on appeal by the Tribunal for the Defence of Competition in conformity with Article 47."

2.4. Notification

Article 15 paragraph 1 of the Spanish Regulation provides that any actual or proposed concentration between undertakings or any acquisition of control meeting the control criteria may be voluntarily notified to the Service for the Defence of Competition by one or more of the undertakings concerned, prior to or within three months after the concentration.

2.4.1. Obligation to notify

There is no obligation to notify a concentration under the Spanish Regulation. The wording of Article 15 paragraph 1 is clear, "any proposed or actual concentration ... or any acquisition of control may be voluntarily notified". Therefore, no duty to notify exists, even if the concentration meets the control criteria laid down in Article 14.

No negative legal consequences derive from non-notification although only notified concentrations can benefit from the deemed authorisation provided for under Article 15. In any case, in many mergers notification is not submitted, due to the absence of immediate consequences for the non-compliance of the wording of the Law. Even though the concentration would go beyond the limits mentioned above, the effects on the relevant market have to be very important to imply an *ex officio* investigation of the Spanish authorities.

Notifications shall be addressed to the Service for the Defence of Competition.

2.4.2. Time-limits for notification

Article 15 paragraph 1 of the Spanish Regulation requires any notification to be filed either before the concentration takes place or within the three months following the concentration.

Therefore, under Spanish law control of concentrations may have *"a priori"* or *"a posteriori"* nature.

2.4.3. Who should notify?

Article 15 paragraph 1 of the Spanish Regulation provides simply that a concentration may be notified by "one or more of the undertakings concerned".

Article 3 of Royal Decree 1080/1992 gives more precise indications as to the responsible for submitting notifications in each case. According to paragraph 2, when the concentration consists in a merger or a joint acquisition of control, all the undertakings involved in the transaction shall present a joint notification. In the case of an acquisition of control of one or several undertakings by one person or undertaking, paragraph 3 states that the notification is to be done by the acquiror.

2.4.4. Information to be included in the notification

Notification shall be done in an Official Form that can be found in Annex to Royal Decree 1080/1992, which lists in detail all the information that must be provided to the Competition Authorities. The data to be enclosed with the notification include: the identity of the parties concerned, the three latest annual accounts of the undertakings and/or groups of undertakings and their respective relevant turnovers and market shares, legal form and structure of the operation, information on the economic sector affected by the concentration (including external trade) and an assessment of the economic and legal situation resulting from the concentration, underlining pro-competitive and anti-competitive effects of the transaction. Detailed rules on each of these points are found in the aforementioned Annex. All the information will be provided as separate documents together with the Official Form for Notifications.

The undertakings concerned may state in the notification which data should be regarded as confidential, either between the parties in the transaction or as regards third parties. That information will thus be treated according to the rules on confidentiality (see below 2.5.5 and 2.5.6).

2.4.5. Effects of the notification

The prior notification of a concentration does not imply the suspension of the operation until it is authorised. Only notified concentrations can benefit from deemed authorisation of the Administration and from the time-limits provided for in Article 15.

However, the time-limit of one month for tacit authorisation is suspended if the information provided in the notification is not complete. In this case, the Service for the Defence of Competition shall require the undertaking(s) responsible for notification to supplement the documents already given with more information within ten days. If there is no answer, the benefit of tacit authorisation is lost[47].

Surprisingly, there is no provision for express authorisation of notified concentrations at this stage.

2.4.6. Confidentiality of the notification

Contrary to the practice under EC Law[48], there is no publicity of the notifications received by the Service for the Defence of Competition. Confidentiality is always kept except when the Minister of Economy and Finance decides to submit a case to the opinion of the Tribunal for the Defence of Competition[49]. This means that third parties may be prevented from presenting observations on their own motion if they do not know the project of concentration. In those cases, third parties may well see their possibilities to intervene at the initial stage of the procedure reduced to a possible call for co-operation under Article 32 of the Spanish Regulation (see section 2.5.1.i).

2.5. Procedure

The merger control procedure may be initiated either with a notification of the operation by the parties concerned or with an investigation undertaken *ex officio* by the Service for the Defence of Competition. In either case, the Service will investigate the effects on competition of the concentration and it will submit its opinion to the Minister of Economy and Finance. With these elements, only if the Minister considers that as a result of the concentration effective competition may be impeded in the relevant market (and this is a discretionary decision), he shall refer the concentration to the Tribunal for the Defence of Competition. The Tribunal for the Defence of Competition must then consider whether as a result of the referred proposed or actual concentration or acquisition of control effective competition would be impeded in the relevant market. Then, the Tribunal shall refer its opinion to the Minister of Economy and Finance which will refer it to the Government. The Government will take the final decision.

Since 1992, the provisions of the Spanish Regulation concerning the procedure for merger control are developed by Royal Decree 1080/1992.

2.5.1. Procedure before the Service for the Defence of Competition

The Service is the body that is responsible for the initial consideration of the transaction.

The Service is competent to undertake an investigation of a given concentration either where it has been previously notified or, in the absence of prior notification, *ex officio*. The Service will refer appropriate cases to the Tribunal for the Defence of Competition for further investigation.

(i) Service for the Defence of Competition
The Service is responsible for: a) opening and conducting proceedings in respect of concentrations meeting its criteria; b) monitoring the implementation of and compliance with the decisions adopted under its provisions; c) maintaining the Register for the Defence of Competition; d) studying and investigating economic sectors, analysing their situation and conditions of competition as well as the possible existence of restrictive practices; e) informing, advising, and proposing, in relation to agreements and restrictive practices, concentrations and associations of undertakings, the conditions of competition in the internal and external market, comparing them with those prevailing in the former.

For the purpose of carrying out the duties assigned to it, the Service may obtain all necessary information and undertake investigation:

Co-operation and information[50]. Any natural or legal person is under the duty to collaborate with the Service for the Defence of Competition providing at the request of the Service any information relevant for the implementation of this Regulation. The breach of this obligation will entail fines ranging from Pta 50,000 to 1 million.

Investigation and inspection[51]. The officials of the Service duly authorised by the Director of the Service shall be empowered to examine books or other business records, to take or demand copies of or extracts from the books and business records, to ask for oral explanations on the spot, to enter any premises[52], and to withhold copies of or extracts from the books and business records. The officials may keep any of those documents for a period not exceeding ten days. The information produced can only be used for the purposes of the Regulation.

In the event that the undertakings or persons concerned oppose the investigation, the Director of the Service can impose periodic penalty payments of up to Pta 150,000 for each day of the delay calculated from the date set in the decision, in order to compel them to facilitate the investigation.

(ii) Proceedings
As already mentioned, the Service may investigate a concentration meeting the control criteria regardless of whether or not such concentration has been previously notified.

Notified concentrations. Once the Service receives a notification, it must consider whether the notified transaction could impede effective competition in the relevant market, i.e. the "Spanish market or a substantial part of it"[53].

The Service may require the parties to complete the information included in the notification, as explained in 2.4.5. The Service may also require additional information from any natural or legal person, according to its prerogatives under Law 16/1989[54]. Once the information is complete, the Service submits a confidential note to the Minister of Economy and Finance expressing its opinion about the possible risks for competition of the concentration[55]. The Minister will decide whether it will refer the matter to the Tribunal for the Defence of Competition.

Opening of the procedure ex officio. The Service may open *ex officio* the procedure of control of concentrations whenever it gets to know of any project or accomplished concentration that may affect the maintenance of effective competition in the market, provided that the concentration is above the thresholds fixed by Article 14. In such case, the Service may demand any relevant information to the parties in the transaction, under the conditions explained above in 2.5.1.i.

When an investigation has been opened *ex officio*, the parties to the concentration do not benefit from the strict time-limits imposed on the competition authorities, so there will be no tacit authorisation[56].

The Minister of Economy and Finance may submit the cases investigated to the Tribunal for the Defence of Competition, but never later than five years from the date when the concentration was implemented[57]. In the event of referral to the Tribunal (of either a notified or a non-notified concentration), the Service shall notify the parties concerned of the date of reference[58].

In practice, proceedings very seldom begin *ex officio*, as results from the activity of the Service since the adoption of the Spanish Regulation in 1989 show. Sometimes the Service has initiated an investigation on its own motion and the undertakings have immediately notified their concentration as a reply to the requests for information, doing so within the time limit of three months and thus benefiting from the effects of voluntary notification[59].

Complainants. The Service may open an investigation of a given concentration following a complaint by a competitor, but there is no legal duty for it to do so. Complainants may have an interest to inform the Service about the foreseen effects of the concentration on the market in order to defend their competitive positions.

Given the nature of the Spanish system of control of concentrations, complainants cannot demand the annulment of a decision of the Director General for Competition to close an investigation. Indeed, according to the wording of Article 14 of the Spanish Regulation, it is only the Ministry of Economy and Finance who may send a case to the Tribunal for the Defence of Competition for further study, previous to a Government decision on the concentration. Hence, complainants do not have the right to demand a report by the Tribunal and a decision of the Government on any case of concentrations[60].

If a case arrives at the Tribunal for the Defence of Competition, complainants and interested parties may participate in the proceedings as explained below (2.5.2.ii).

2.5.2. Procedure before the Tribunal for the Defence of Competition

As mentioned above, in cases posing significant competition issues, the Minister of Economy and Finance may refer the file to the Tribunal for the Defence of Competition. The Tribunal then carries out a further inquiry and issues an opinion.

SPAIN

(i) The Tribunal for the Defence of Competition
The Tribunal for the Defence of Competition is an independent body with jurisdiction throughout Spain. It is situated in Madrid.

The Tribunal is composed of a president and eight members, nominated by the Minister of Economy and Finance and appointed by the Government for a six-year term. The Tribunal may act by committee or panel and its opinions shall be approved by the majority of voting members[61].

The Tribunal is competent: a) to decide on the matters determined in the Spanish Regulation; b) to institute investigations on reference from the Service; c) to authorise agreements, decisions, recommendations and practices referred to in Article 1 of the Spanish Regulation, in the cases and under the conditions provided for in Article 3; d) to carry out arbitration procedures[62].

(ii) Tribunal procedure
Upon reference from the Minister of Economy and Finance, the Tribunal must initiate an inquiry to determine whether or not the proposed or actual concentration or acquisition of control may impede effective competition in the Spanish market or in a substantial part of it.

In the case of notified concentrations, if the Tribunal fails to issue an opinion within three months from the date of reference, the transaction will be deemed not to impede competition.

Requests for information[63]. The Tribunal may consider it necessary to obtain additional data on the structure of the market, the economic and legal context of the concentration, the opinion of other operators in the market or any other relevant information. For this purpose, the Tribunal may require any administrative body to provide documents or reports.

It may also call any natural or legal person to co-operate in the evaluation of the concentration by providing information. There is a legal duty to co-operate with the Tribunal, which in case of infringement may impose fines of up to Pta 1 million[64].

Apart from competitors of the undertakings involved in the concentration and other undertakings that may be affected by the operation, Royal Decree 1080/1992 enables the Tribunal to hear the Council of Consumer Associations. In these cases there will be reduced access to the file, justified by the need to protect business secrecy: both undertakings affected by the concentration and the Council of Consumer Associations will present their views on the basis of a brief summary of the facts of the operation, avoiding any reference to confidential information.

It is important to underline that natural or legal persons co-operating in the proceedings following a request by the Tribunal for the Defence of Competition cannot be considered as interested parties in the meaning of Article 13 of Royal Decree 1080/1992, examined here below.

Interested parties and hearings[65]. The parties to the concentration are entitled to an oral hearing before the Tribunal before it submits its final opinion to the Government. However, they do not have the opportunity to review the report that is finally sent to the Government. They will only be told when the report was sent. The Tribunal may call the undertakings that voluntarily notified a concentration as many times as it considers necessary to obtain sufficient details and explanations on the nature of the transaction. When the procedure is started *ex officio*, the concerned undertakings also have the right to be heard before the issuing of the final report.

Regarding interested parties, the Tribunal must hear them after ten days from the receipt of the files but not later than 15 days after that date, so that they can submit their observations.

Although Article 13 paragraph 2 refers to "other organs" (meaning administrative bodies) and "other undertakings and associations of consumers" whose reports or observations have been incorporated to the file, the notion of "interested party" is narrower in this context than in cases concerning collusion or abuse of dominant position. The reason is, again, the difference between the legal provisions on restrictive practices on the one hand, and the system of control of concentrations on the other: while the former attributes to the Tribunal for the Defence of Competition the power to make final decisions, the latter entails a procedure where the Tribunal has only an advisory role and the final decision remains under the discretion of the Government. Besides, the protection of confidentiality in procedures for merger control is stricter than in other cases, so access of third parties to the information is limited.

The Tribunal may consider natural or legal persons as interested parties by Order, entitling them to take part in the proceedings[66].

Complainants are not automatically considered as interested parties in the proceedings before the Tribunal for the Defence of Competition. They are subject to the same tests as any other persons who wish to intervene in the procedure. Therefore, they will have to prove a special interest in the case, possibly flowing from their competitive position in the market. For a competitor, it is enough to show the existence of substantial competition between the parties to the concentration and itself. In *Sensormatic/Knogo*, the Tribunal admitted the intervention of another undertaking (*Esselte*) as interested party in the procedure since it was "an important competitor, even though not the main one"[67].

Substantive test for clearance. The Tribunal's opinion must be a reasoned opinion and take into account the restrictive effects, actual or potential, of the concentration and must in particular take account of the following circumstances:
- definition of the relevant market;
- analysis of the structure of the market;
- availability of suppliers, distributors and consumers;
- economic and financial power of the undertakings concerned;
- evolution of supply and demand;
- external competition.

The Spanish Regulation includes an express provision analogous to Article 85(3) of the EC Treaty. According to Article 16 paragraph 2, in the assessment of the restrictive effects of any concentration, the Tribunal may take into account the contribution of the concentration or the acquisition of control to improving the production or distribution of goods, to promoting technical or economic progress, to the international competitiveness of the national industry or to the interests of the consumers where such contribution is important enough to match the restrictive effects on competition.

Therefore, even if the concentration or acquisition of control has restrictive effects on competition, the Tribunal may adopt a favourable decision on the grounds that it contributes, to a significant extent, to improving production or distribution of goods, to promoting technical or economic progress, to the international competitiveness of the national industry or to the interests of the consumers.

The opinion adopted by the Tribunal is presented to the Minister of Economy and Finance.

2.5.3. Final decision

The Minister of Economy and Finance must submit the opinion of the Tribunal to the Government. Within three months, the Government must issue its final decision on the transaction.

The Government is not bound to follow the opinion of the Tribunal. However, its opinion is naturally to be taken into account.

When the concentration involves two or several telecommunication operators, the Government shall also take into account the opinion of the Commission for the Telecommunications Market[68].

The Government's decision may take one of three forms:
a) not to oppose the transaction;
b) to approve the transaction subject to conditions;
c) to declare that the concentration is incompatible with the market and either prohibit the implementation of a proposed concentration or, in the case of a completed transaction, order appropriate measures to restore effective competition, including in particular divestment of assets or shares.

Usually the Government follows the opinion of the Tribunal for the Defence of Competition, but this must not necessarily be the case. The decision of the Government is ultimately a matter of discretion. Sometimes the Government has departed from the opinion of the Tribunal: for instance, in *Nestlé ice creams*[69] the Tribunal had proposed conditional clearance, but the Government approved the concentration without conditions. More strikingly, in *Cablevisión*[70] the Tribunal had warned the Government about the pernicious effects of the notified concentration on the markets of cable TV, decoders, TV contents and services for cable operators, therefore proposing not to authorise the concentration[71]. However, the Government decided to clear the operation under conditions[72].

2.5.4. Fines

If the undertakings concerned do not comply with the decision adopted by the government, the government may impose fines of up to 10% of the total Spanish turnover of each undertaking concerned[73].

The collection of the fines shall be effected according to the provision laid down by the "Reglamento General de Recaudación"[74].

2.5.5. Professional secrecy

Officials and other servants shall not disclose information they have acquired through the application of the Spanish Regulation of a kind covered by the obligation of professional secrecy (privileged information)[75].

Any person infringing this obligation will be liable to civil and criminal responsibility.

2.5.6. Business secrets

The Service and the Tribunal have the competence to decide, at any stage of proceedings, that confidential information is to be kept secret. The parties concerned are entitled to determine which information constitutes business secrets and, therefore to demand that the Service or Tribunal, as the case may be, record such information in a separate file[76].

The Tribunal has laid down the criteria in order to determine in which cases confidentiality is to be safeguarded[77]. The Tribunal stresses the need to strike a balance between the need to disclose information that enables interested parties to defend their views and the need to protect confidential information that was costly to produce and may affect the conditions of competition. Therefore, Spanish Competition Authorities will take into account the effects that the disclosure of business information would have on the market, in terms of competitive advantages gained and lost, and they will then decide on demands of confidentiality or access to the file.

Precautions regarding business secrets start from the moment of notification. The Annex to Royal Decree 1080/1992 states that the undertaking or undertakings notifying the transaction to the Service for the Defence of Competition will state for which part of the information provided they wish to maintain confidentiality[78]. The reserved nature of the procedure goes until the final stage: only the Government's decision is published, and the report of the Tribunal is not made available to the parties or the public in general[79]. Contrary to other activities under Law 16/1989, only limited information is found in the Registry of Competition, namely the names of the parties involved in the transaction, the nature of the operation, the date of authorisation and the Government's decision[80].

The Tribunal publishes summaries of its reports in its Annual Report[81].

2.5.7. Subsidiarity of the Administrative Proceedings Law

According to Article 50 of the Spanish Regulation, the provisions of the Administrative Proceedings Law[82] ("Ley de Procedimiento Administrativo") will regulate the conduct of the Service for the Defence of Competition and the Tribunal insofar as it has not been specifically regulated by special provisions.

2.5.8. Judicial review

As a result of the special legal nature of administrative acts and decisions, under Spanish Law it is necessary to lodge an appeal before the administrative authority prior to judicial review. Only after the Administrative authority has dismissed the appeal or the time limit to do so has expired are individuals entitled to bring an action for annulment before the courts.

Individuals or companies directly affected by the Government decision may challenge such decision in the Courts provided that they comply with the Administrative Proceedings Law (LPA) and the Law regulating the Administrative Jurisdiction ("Ley de la Jurisdicción Contencioso-Administrativa"). The Government's decision can be challenged before the *Audiencia Nacional*, in Madrid, and the decision of this court may be reviewed by the Spanish Supreme Court.

3. Special Provisions regulating Concentrations carried out through Public Bids: Royal Decree 1197/1991, of 26 July

Article 15 paragraph 3 of the Spanish Regulation contains a reference to a special procedure for the notification of acquisitions of listed shares pursuant to a mandatory public bid under Article 60 of Law 24/1988 on the Stock Exchange Market.

Royal Decree 1197/1991, of 26 July implementing Law 24/1988[83], of 28 July on National Stock Exchange Market (Ley del Mercado de Valores), and Article 15 paragraph 3 of Law 16/1989, establishes a special regime of control on concentrations carried out through public bids.

According to Article 12 of Royal Decree 1197/1991, any individual or legal person seeking to launch a public bid intended to acquire shares must apply for authorisation before the National Stock Exchange Commission (Comisión Nacional del Mercado de Valores).

Article 1 of Royal Decree 1167/1991 establishes that any individual or legal person intending to acquire shares of a listed company is under a duty to launch a public bid if, as a result of the acquisition, the person reaches a shareholding of 25% or more, or of 50% or more. The same applies to the case where the purchaser already holds a shareholding between 25% and 50% and seeks to increase it by 6% or more within a 12-month period.

Chapter IV, Articles 37 and 38 of Royal Decree 1197/1991 lay down the provisions regulating specific procedures on the control of concentrations carried out through public bids.

Article 37 refers to concentrations falling within the scope of competence of the Spanish authorities whereas Article 38 contemplates the case of concentrations with Community dimension, acknowledging the exclusive competence of the Community in accordance to Council Regulation 4064/1989/EEC on the control of concentrations.

Within Article 37 two different cases are to be distinguished: on the one hand, the case of voluntary notification by the bidder; on the other, referral to the Service for the Defence of Competition by the National Stock Exchange Commission (CNMV).

3.1. Voluntary notification by the bidder

Article 37 of Royal Decree 1197/1911 deals with voluntary notification by the bidder and provides that the bidder may notify the concentration to the Service for the Defence of Competition either before or after applying for authorisation of the public bid to the National Stock Exchange Commission ("CNMV").

The bidder is not however, legally bound to notify the concentration[84].

3.1.1. Notification of the concentration before seeking authorisation of the public bid before the National Stock Exchange Commission (CNMV)

If the bidder notifies the concentration before seeking authorisation of the public bid before the National Stock Exchange Commission (CNMV), the general regime established in Title I, Chapter II, Articles 14 to 17 of the Spanish Regulation applies. However, proceedings under the Spanish Regulation carry consequences for the bid and the bidder. We will refer to those consequences below.

3.1.2. Notification of the concentration after seeking authorisation of the public bid before the National Stock Exchange Commission (CNMV)

Under Article 12 of Royal Decree 1197/1991, the bidder is bound to seek authorisation of the public bid before the National Stock Exchange Commission.
Within five days after the presentation of such application, the bidder may voluntarily notify the public bid to the Service for the Defence of Competition, according to the provisions laid down in Article 15 of the Spanish Regulation[85].

3.1.3. Effects of voluntary notification

Article 37 paragraph 2 deals with the impact of voluntary notification on a public bid.

Deemed authorisation. If within one month of notification the Service neither opposes the transaction nor refers it to the Tribunal for the Defence of Competition or if the Tribunal fails to issue an opinion within three months of the reference to it by the Service of the case, the merger shall be deemed to be authorised[86].

Government decision. The Government may adopt a decision before the expiry of the time-limit established for the acceptance of the bid:
- If the government does not object to the concentration, the bid will be fully enforceable. The same applies in case the Minister of Economy and Finance decides within a month after the voluntary notification not to refer the file to the Tribunal for the Defence of Competition.
- If the Government opposes the proposed merger the bidder must withdraw the public bid.
- If the Government approves the merger subject to certain conditions, the bidder is entitled with the consent of the National Stock Exchange Commission (CNMV) to withdraw the bid but such consent will not be given if the conditions imposed by the Government are not considered to be sufficiently significant.

Withdrawal of bid pending outcome. If, before the expiry of the time-limit established for the acceptance of the bid, no deemed or express decision has been taken, the bidder is entitled to withdraw the bid.

3.2. Referral of the operation to the Service for the Defence of Competition by the National Stock Exchange Commission

If the National Stock Exchange Commission (CNMV) considers that the bid may meet the criteria specified for in Article 14 of the Spanish Regulation, it may refer the bid to the Service for the Defence of Competition. Any such reference must be made within five days after the application by the bidder for authorisation of the public bid under Article 12 of Royal Decree 1197/1991. Upon any such reference to it of a public bid, the Service for the Defence of Competition may advise the Minister for the Economy and Finance to refer the case to the Tribunal for the Defence of Competition under Article 14 of the Spanish Regulation in the usual way.

If the Minister of Economy and Finance refers the file to the Tribunal for the Defence of Competition, the Service must immediately notify the bidder. If the bidder decides to withdraw the bid it must inform the National Stock Exchange Commission within one day after receiving the notification of reference.

The impact of the proceedings before the Tribunal for the Defence of Competition has been mentioned above (section 2.4.5), but the bidder will not benefit from the deemed authorisation procedure under Article 37 paragraph 2 a) of Royal Decree 1197/1991 and Article 15 paragraph 4 of the Spanish Regulation.

3.3. Publicity

The consequences derived from the proceedings before the Competition Authorities and the withdrawal of the public bid by the bidder shall be published according to Article 18 of Royal Decree 1197/1991 within two days after the expiry of the time-limit established for acceptance of the bid, prior communication to the National Stock Exchange Commission (CNMV)[87].

4. Requests and referrals to the European Commission under the EC Merger Regulation

Article 9 of the EC Merger Regulation allows the European Commission to refer a concentration of Community dimension to the competition authorities of a Member State, under certain conditions. This provision intends to give back to the Member States the power of control in cases where the effects of the envisaged concentration, even if falling above the Merger Regulation thresholds, would nevertheless be mainly felt in a distinct market within one Member State.

Article 22, third paragraph, of the Merger Regulation, on the other hand, allows the Commission to deal with concentrations with no Community dimension, but which affect trade between Member States, if one or several Member States submit a request in this sense.

Royal Decree 295/1998[88] is the rule designed to regulate the competence of the different Spanish competition authorities when Articles 9 or 22(3) are applied.

4.1. Referrals under Article 9 of the EC Merger Regulation

According to Article 3 of Royal Decree 295/1998, the Service for the Defence of Competition is the competent authority for submitting a request for referral to the Commission. The Service will also receive the files if the Commission decides to leave the case to the national authorities.

The Tribunal for the Defence of Competition keeps its consultative role in these cases, producing a report that will be taken into account by the Government before making the final decision on the concentration at issue[89].

4.2. Requests under Article 22(3) of the EC Merger Regulation

For cases of concentration with no Community dimension to be referred to the Commission, there must be a previous opinion of the Tribunal for the Defence of Competition on the convenience of the application of Article 22, third paragraph, of the EC Merger Regulation[90].

SPAIN

The Service for the Defence of Competition will be the responsible for sending a request to the European Commission in order to apply Article 22(3), and it will send the file if the Commission decides to take over the case[91].

5. Setting proposals for a future reform

The Spanish trend based on voluntary notification, although enjoying the advantages of its flexible approach, has been lately criticised, specially because the European position on these grounds has developed to a stronger control of mergers, by virtue of more fixed thresholds and a compulsory notification.

Quite recently, a previous, compulsory and suspensive notification has been proposed in Spain, joined by the maintenance or slightly raising of the actual thresholds. But, even though the Government is considering such change to be introduced in the expected reform of the Law on the Defence of Competition, no legal actions aiming said reform have been arranged yet.

On the other hand, sometimes the merger procedure becomes too obscure to third parties, giving way to discretionary decisions, based on a wide range of concerns apart from strictly legal ones. A new procedure increasing transparency of these operations and of the reasons to give clearance or refuse them should be developed in the following years, taking advantage of an hypothetical reform of the current Law.

6. Summary

Chapter II of the Spanish Law 16/1989 of Defence of Competition establishes the principles for the system of control of concentrations. If a transaction falls under the scope of that chapter, it cannot be subject to examination under other provisions of the Law.

Mergers, divisions of companies, acquisitions of control and concentrative joint ventures constitute concentrations within the meaning of Law 16/1989. All of them bring about a lasting change in the structure of the undertakings concerned, and they involve either the amalgamation of economic activities in a single entity or the acquisition of the power to exercise decisive influence on the behaviour of a separate entity.

As regards co-operative joint ventures, the creation of a new entity entails the risk of co-ordination of the competitive behaviour between the parent companies, which remain active in the same or a neighbouring market as independent undertakings. These cases must be dealt with, both substantially and procedurally, under the rules on agreements between undertakings.

Concentrations between any Spanish or foreign parties that fall above one (or both) of the following thresholds may be subject to control by the Spanish authorities: i) creation or strengthening of a existing market share of 25% of higher of the Spanish market as a whole, or of a substantial part of it; ii) or an aggregate Spanish turnover of the undertakings concerned of more than Pta 20 billion pesetas (€ 125 million) in the last financial year.

Notification of concentrations above the thresholds is not compulsory, but it avoids the risks of an *ex-post* control and it enables the parties to the transaction to obtain the benefit of tacit authorisation. Transactions can be notified either before the concentration takes place or within the three following months. There is no suspension requirement.

Notified concentrations must be first examined by the Service for the Defence of Competition, and the Minister of Economy and Finance may submit trouble cases to the opinion of the Tribunal for the Defence of Competition within one month from the receipt of the notification. Otherwise, the concentration is deemed authorised ("tacit authorisation"). If the Tribunal is called upon to study a given case, it must do so within three months. The Spanish Government receives the Tribunal's report on the case, of a merely advisory nature, and it has a further three-month period to make a decision. Therefore, the procedure for notified concentrations lasts a minimum of one month and a maximum of seven months from the date of notification.

The substantial test for clearance is based on economic considerations on the future degree of competition in the market if the concentration takes place. Political intervention should not be excluded, since the Government has the final word and the procedure is confidential.

Concentrations that involve acquisition of shares in the Stock Exchange Markets are subject to a special procedure that may involve the participation of the National Stock Exchange Commission (CNMV).

Addendum

The Spanish Defense of Competition Act (Law 16/1989) already provided for the control of economic concentrations. However, until the recent reform introduced by Royal Decree Law 6/1999 notification of concentrations was not compulsory, unless so requested by the Competition Authorities.

This situation has radically changed with the last reform of April 16, 1999. According to the new wording of Article 14 of the Competition Act:

> *"Any project of concentration or operation of concentration shall be notified to the Service for the Defense of Competition where one or more of the undertakings concerned:*
>
> *a) As a result of the operation acquire or increase a market share of 25% or more of the National market, or of a defined regional market, of a relevant product or service.*
>
> *b) The overall turnover in Spain of the undertakings concerned exceed for the last fiscal year 40,000 million Spanish Pesetas, provided that at least two of the undertakings concerned have an individual turnover in Spain of more than 10,000 million Spanish Pesetas."*

Concentrations of a Community dimension do not obviously fall within the scope of the relevant Spanish provisions on merger control.

Unlike the Community merger control system, the Spanish regulation does not contemplate the suspension of the concentration until clearance is obtained from the Competition Authorities. The time limit for the notification of the operation is longer, since concentrations may be notified within one month. Projects of concentrations may also be the object of a notification. Another interesting difference is the one affording the parties to the concentration the possibility to submit to the Competition Authorities a consultation on whether or not a given operation fulfills the thresholds set forth in Article 14 paragraph 1. Said consultation suspends the one-month time limit for compulsory notification.

As to the procedure, notification is to be filed with the Service for the Defense of Competition ("Servicio de Defensa de la Competencia", hereinafter "SDC") through a form, which is an abridged version of Form CO. The concentration is deemed cleared if within one month from notification the operation has not been referred to the Competition Tribunal ("Tribunal de Defensa de la Competencia", hereinafter "TDC") by the Minister of Finance, following a proposal of the SDC. The parties to the concentration may offer undertakings before the operation is referred to the TDC. The Minister of Finance, having heard the SDC, may then authorize the concentration.

When the concentration is referred to the TDC, the competence to decide upon passes on to the government. The TDC shall issue a legal opinion on the concentration within three months. Then the government shall adopt a decision within an additional three-month time limit. The government may decide then, either not to oppose the concentration; or subject approval to the fulfillment of certain conditions contributing to the economic or social progress; or oppose the concentration ordering not to implement it or its unbundling. If the three-month time limit has elapsed and the government has not issued a decision thereon, the concentration shall be deemed authorized.

Ancillary restrictions may be covered by the final decision not opposing the concentration.

Whenever the notified operation does not qualify as a "concentration", it may be analyzed in the light of the provisions applicable to agreements between undertakings.

Given that hardly one month has elapsed since the coming into force of this new merger control procedure there are no statistics as to the number of operations falling within the scope of compulsory notification and subsequent scrutiny by the Competition Authorities. However, we may already anticipate a very significant number of concentrations reaching the thresholds set forth in Art. 14 of the Competition Act and, hence, subject to compulsory notification. A substantial reinforcement of the Competition Authorities is probably necessary in order to avoid a risk of collapse. It seems that the government envisages a Pta 1,000,000 (€ 12,000) duty, payable by the parties at the time the concentration is notified.

The introduction of an obligation to notify concentrations of a National dimension is certainly an important step forward. In particular, if due account is taken of the fact that many concentrations escaped any control since operations between major Spanish corporations did not have a Community dimension because of the two-thirds rule of the European Merger Control Regulation.

The New Merger Control Procedure in Spain

1. Main Changes in the Merger Control Procedure Introduced by Royal Decree-Law 6/1999, of April 16 ("RDL")

- Mandatory notification if compliance with the established thresholds (see 2).
- Increase in the threshold on the turnover of the parties.
- Formal threshold inquiry procedure to the Service for the Defence of Competition ("SDC").
- Possibility of conventional procedure termination.
- More transparency in the procedure.

2. Mergers subject to Notification

- Thresholds: mergers are subject to mandatory notification when the aggregate market share of the undertakings is more than 25% of the national relevant market; or when their aggregate turnover is more than € 240 million and the individual turnover of at least two of the undertakings is more than € 60 million each.
- Dimension: the operation must not have European Community dimension according to EC Regulation 4064/89, as amended by EC regulation 1310/97.

3. Characteristics of the Procedure

General
- Notification period: before the operation and within 1 month of the same.
- Non suspension: the operation may still go on after notification.
- Transparency: publication of the notification, of the Court for the Defence of Competition ("CDC") report and of the final decision.

Special
- Previous consultation to the SDC: suspension of the notification time period.

- SDC may formally require the parties to notify with a period of 5 years.
- Public bids are subject to a special procedure (RD 1197/1991).

4. Termination of the Procedure

Formal
- Government Decision: approval, approval subject to remedies or rejection.

Tacit
- No submission to the CDC within 1 month since notification.
- No Government decision within 7 months since notification.

Conventional
- Prior submission to CDC.
- Negotiation between parties and the Ministry of Economy and Finance ("MEF"): compromises.
- MEF: approval or submission to the CDC within 1 month.

5. Fines

Fines of up to € 30,000 for lack of mandatory notification, and of € 12,000 per day for lack of notification 20 days after formal request from SDC.

Notes

1. BOE 17/07/1989.
2. OJ 1989 L395. Modified by Council Regulation 1310/97/EEC, OJ 1997 L180.
3. BOE 8/06/1996; revised in BOE 18/06/1996.
4. BOE 27/10/1992.
5. BOE 2/08/1991.
6. BOE 25/4/98.
7. BOE 7/03/1998.
8. The Spanish Regulation repeals and replaces: Decree 538/1965 of 4 March, regulating the Court for the Defence of Competition; Decree 422/1970 of 5 February, regulating the basis, functioning and procedure of the Service for the Defence of Competition; Decree 3564/1972 of 23 December, amending regulations on the Service for the Defence of Competition; Ministry Order of 28 September 1973, implementing Article 9 of Decree 538/1965; Article 4 of Royal Decree-Law 18/1976 of 8 October, concerning economic measures, and Royal Decrees 2574/1982 of 24 September and 1936/1985 are also repealed insofar as they may be inconsistent with the Spanish Regulation.
9. BOE 15/03/1965.
10. BOE 24/02/1970.
11. BOE 14/05/1991.
12. Cablevisión: C 21/95. Approval published in Ministry Order of 14 March 1996 (BOE 29/03/1996). See also R-183/1996, Decision of the Tribunal for the Defence of Competition of 23 July 1996.
13. See Press Release IP/96/677.
14. The Spanish Government approved the concentration in its meeting on 1 March 1996. The European Commission had communicated to the Government, on February 7, that it considered the concentration to be of Community dimension, thus under its exclusive competence. Indeed, after receiving a statement of objections from the Commission, the parties to the agreement notified the concentration in Brussels on 31 May 1996.
15. Sections 2.2.2 and 2.3.6.
16. Foreigners' legal capacity to undertake commercial activities is determined by their national law according to Article 15 of the Spanish Code of Commerce and Article 9.1 of the Spanish Civil Code.
17. Royal Legislative Decree 1564/1989, of 22 December; BOE 27/12/1989, revised in BOE 1/02/1990. Article 94 of Law 2/1995, of 23 March (BOE 24/03/1998), on Limited Liability Companies refers back to the aforementioned Act for the regulation of mergers.
18. See Article 233 paragraph 2 of the Spanish Public Limited Liability Companies Act.
19. See Article 247 paragraph 1 of the aforementioned Regulation.
20. Limit set forth in Article 247 paragraph 2 of the aforesaid Regulation.
21. See Article 233 paragraph 1 and Article 247 paragraphs 1 and 2 of the aforesaid Regulation.
22. See also Article 94 of Law 2/1995, of 23 March (BOE 24/03/1998), on Limited Liability Companies.
23. See Article 252 paragraph 1(a) of the Spanish Public Limited Liability Companies Act.
24. See Article 252 paragraph 1(b) of the aforementioned Regulation.

25 Article 252 paragraph 2 of the aforementioned Regulation.
26 In Article 3.2: "The creation of a joint venture performing on a lasting basis all the functions of an autonomous economic entity, which does not give rise to co-ordination of the competitive behaviour of the parties amongst themselves or between them and the joint venture, shall constitute a concentration…".
27 Concentration C 15/94 ("ice cream"). Approved by the Government by Ministry Order of April 3, 1995, BOE 17/05/1995.
28 The three sub-markets were: bulk ice cream and big blocks for resale in portions; differentiated ice creams for impulse consumption; and catering ice cream.
29 Commission Decision of 15 September 1993 (Case No IV/M.362).
30 Commission Decision of 15 March 1994 (Case No IV/M.422).
31 Hoesch/Krupp: Concentration C 11/93.
32 Compañía Cervecera de Canarias/Sical : Concentration C 12/93.
33 Plasgom/Elf: Concentration C 20/95.
34 A3/SER: Concentration C 13/93.
35 Techpack: Concentration C 14/93.
36 Ausonia Higiene – Procter & Gamble/FINAF/Arbora Holding: C 10/92. It should be pointed out that the Tribunal referred to the openness of the Spanish market for hygienic products, whilst the European Commission said later in *Procter & Gamble/Schickedanz* (Case No.IV/M.430; decision of 21 June 1994) that external trade from and towards Spain was of very modest importance.
37 Concentration C 11/93.
38 Concentration C 14/93.
39 Concentration C 19/95.
40 The conditions for exemption are laid down in Article 3 of Law 19/1986. Individual exemptions granted by the Tribunal for the Defence of Competition are regulated by Article 4, and block exemptions are foreseen by Article 5. Agreements, decisions, recommendations and concerted practices which conclusion is required by law or implementing decrees are also excluded from the prohibition of Article 1, according to Article 2.
41 Decision of the Tribunal for the Defence of Competition on appeal against the dismissal of a complaint by the Service for the Defence of Competition (Expte. A 51/93 Mölnlycke AB).
42 Ausonia Higiene : C 10/92. Ministry Order of 21 May 1993.
43 *Supra* n. 12.
44 Later, two more complaints based on Articles 1 and 6 were presented by local cable operators.
45 According to the Tribunal, there was only one concentrative element (the setting up of a joint venture operating in the market for cable services), and several co-operative elements, such as the following: an agreement for joint action in the market for telecommunications and for satellite TV, pacts concerning local cable operators, reserve of exclusive rights for Cablevisión of the encrypted TV contents of Canal Plus, and a compromise not to affect the business of Canal Plus in any way.
46 However, this was not a unanimous decision. Mr. Bermejo Zofio, member of the Tribunal, explained in his dissenting opinion that severability was possible under Spanish law in the same way as under EC law. He summarised his point of view in a later public decision:

SPAIN

see Decision of 23 July 1996, in File R 183/1996.
47 Article 5 of Royal Decree 1080/1992.
48 See Article 4 paragraph 3 of the EC Merger Regulation: the European Commission publishes the notifications of concentrations as soon as it verifies that the operation is to be studied under the Regulation.
49 Article 8 of Royal Decree 1080/1992.
50 See Article 32 of the Spanish Regulation.
51 See Articles 33 and 34 of the Spanish Regulation.
52 According to Article 34, access to the premises requires the consent of their occupants or a judicial order.
53 As defined in Article 14 of the Spanish Regulation.
54 Article 6 paragraph 2 of Royal Decree 1080/1992; see above point 2.5.1.i.
55 Article 6 paragraph 1 of Royal Decree 1080/1992.
56 See Article 15 paragraph 4 of the Spanish Regulation, and Article 10 paragraph 2 of Royal Decree 1080/1992.
57 Article 11 of Royal Decree 1080/1992.
58 Articles 7 paragraph 1, and 10 paragraph 1 of Royal Decree 1080/1992.
59 See cases *Sensormatic/Knogo* (C 19/95) and *Cablevisión* (C 21/95).
60 Although in the field of State Aids, the decision of the Tribunal for the Defence of Competition in case A 25/92 ("verificaciones industriales en Andalucía") can be applied to merger control since, as the Tribunal recognises, in both merger and state aid control the Tribunal has a merely advisory role and it is the Government who decides to refer a case to it and who takes the final decision.
61 See Articles 12 paragraph 1, and 14 paragraph 1 of Royal Decree 1080/1992.
62 See Article 25 of the Spanish Regulation. For other functions assigned to the Tribunal see Articles 26 and 27 of the Spanish Regulation.
63 See Article 12 paragraph 2 of Royal Decree 1080/1992.
64 Article 29 of the Spanish Regulation.
65 See Article 13 of Royal Decree 1080/1992.
66 See Decree 538/1965, Articles 65-68, for the rules concerning legal representation and communications.
67 Order of the Tribunal of June 16, 1995, in C 19/95.
68 Article 17.2 of Law 11/1998, of 24 April, on Telecommunications. BOE 25/4/1998
69 *Supra* n. 27.
70 *Supra* n. 43.
71 Nevertheless, it is worth noting that there were three dissenting opinions in the report of the Tribunal for the Defence of Competition submitted to the Government.
72 The decision was taken on 1 March 1996, and it was embodied in Ministry Order of 14 March 1996 (BOE March 29, 1996).
73 Article 18 of the Spanish Regulation.
74 See Article 54 of the Spanish Regulation.
75 Article 52 of the Spanish Regulation.
76 Article 53 of the Spanish Regulation.
77 See specially *Sensormatic/Knogo*: C 19/95.
78 Note 5 to the Annex of Royal Decree 1080/1992.

79 Article 14 paragraph 3 of Royal Decree 1080/1992.
80 Article 22 of Royal Decree 157/1992, of 21 February, on individual and block exemptions, and the Registry of Competition.
81 See the 1st Additional provision of Royal Decree 1080/1992, which states that the Tribunal may publish the reports or parts of them six months after the official publication of the Government's decision.
82 Law 30/1992, of 26 November. BOE 27/11/1992.
83 BOE 29/07/1988; recently modified by Law 37/1998 of 16 November, BOE 17/11/1998.
84 See Article 15 paragraph 1 of the Spanish Regulation and Article 37 of Royal Decree 1197/1991.
85 See Article 37 paragraph 1 of Royal Decree 1197/1991.
86 See Article 37 paragraph 2 of Royal Decree 1197/1991.
87 See Article 37 paragraph 4 of Royal Decree 1197/1991.
88 *Supra* n. 7.
89 Article 1 paragraphs 2 and 3 of Royal Decree 295/1998.
90 Article 1 paragraph 2 of Royal Decree 295/1998.
91 Article 3 of Royal Decree 295/1998.

Sweden

Johan Coyet

Anna Malin Persson

Contents

1. Introduction 411
2. The substantive rules 412
   2.1. Criteria for application: Existing rules 412
   2.2. Criteria for application: Expected amendments 418
   2.3. Test for clearance: Existing rules 420
   2.4. Test for clearance: Expected amendments 424
3. The procedural rules 424
   3.1. Notification matters 424
   3.2. Enforcement agencies and adjucative bodies 427
   3.3. Confidentiality, trade secrets and disclosure 429
   3.4. Expected amendments to the procedural rules 429
4. Special rules 430
   Notes 430

1. Introduction

Sweden's first merger control rules were enacted in 1983. The agency entrusted with enforcement at that time was the Antitrust Ombudsman (Näringsfrihets-ombudsmannen). The Antitrust Ombudsman and the Price and Cartel Authority were merged into the new Competition Authority, Konkurrensverket (the Competition Authority), 1 July 1992.

The Competition Act (the Act)[1] came into force 1 July 1993 and governs all aspects of Swedish competition law. The object of the Act is to eliminate and counteract obstacles to effective competition in the production of and trade in goods and services. In addition to the merger regime, it contains two general prohibitions, one against anti-competitive co-operation between undertakings (Article 6)[2] and a second against abuse of a dominant position (Article 19)[3]. The Act provides that the elements of an agreement or a practice violating the law are void and unenforceable under civil law.[4]

The Act's provisions on anti-competitive co-operation between undertakings and abuse of a dominant position are modelled on Articles 85 and 86 of the EC Treaty. The preparatory works of the Act provide that the Act should be interpreted in line with EC law, including future case-law of the EC Court of Justice.[5] Individual exemption may be granted by the Competition Authority and block exemptions have been adopted in the form of separate regulations most of which correspond to the equivalent EC group exemptions.[6] As under EC law, negative clearance can be obtained in relation to the prohibition of anti-competitive co-operation between undertakings and the prohibition of abuse of a dominant position. Fines may be imposed if the Act is infringed and damages can be claimed.

Although the purpose of the Act is to obtain a national competition law regime that differs from the EC regime as little as possible, the merger control rules are substantially different from the rules in the EC regulation on the control of concentrations between undertakings (the EC merger regulation).[7] As regards merger control, the Act includes provisions on the definition of the acquisition of an undertaking (§ 4), when an acquisition is to be prohibited and the consequences of a prohibition (§§ 34-36), rules on notification of an acquisition (§ 37), second stage investigation rules (§ 38), procedural rules on the prohibition of an acquisition (§§ 39, 40), interim measures to postpone the completion awaiting a final decision (§ 41), time-limits for the procedure (§ 42) and rules on reconsideration of a negative decision (§§ 43, 44).

Under the Act's merger control rules, acquisitions of undertakings that carry out some form of commercial activity in Sweden and attain two sets of thresholds are subject to mandatory notification to the Competition Authority and – under certain conditions – possible prohibition by the Stockholm City Court or on appeal by the Market Court.

A recent committee report (the Committee Report)[8] proposes significant amendments to the Act's merger control rules to align the rules with the regime under the EC Merger Regulation. As for the general rules of the Act, the Committee Report suggests to "base the legislation on the concept of concentration" and to abandon the concept of "acquisition of an undertaking" (see sections 2.1 and 2.2 below). The purpose of these amendments is to increase harmonisation with EC law. More specifically, to modify the scope of the merger regime as suggested aims at resolving the application problems that now exists in connection with examination under the Act of joint ventures and ancillary restraints and to improve the co-operation between the Competition Authority and the Community authorities.

Additionally, the Committee Report proposes raising the turnover thresholds for mandatory notification and the introduction of notification deadlines.

Finally, the Committee Report recognises that it would be appropriate to increase the scope for informal processing in merger cases and suggests that the Competition Authority should design such, using the EC merger law's pre-notification procedure as a model.

The Committee Report has been sent out to intended parties for comments and a Government Bill is expected to be presented sometime during spring 1999 with the aim that new merger control rules should enter into force by 1 July 2000. Since the Government Bill had not been presented when completing this chapter, anything said about the new merger control rules refers to the Committee Report which might not correspond with the final text.

2. The substantive rules

2.1. Criteria for application: Existing rules

The Act is not based on the concept of "mergers" or "concentration" as defined by the EC merger rules, but on "acquisitions of undertakings". Thus, for the applicability of the law, a transfer of ownership is presupposed. This explains some of the material differences between the Act and the EC merger rules.

For the purpose of the Act, the acquisition of an undertaking is defined as the acquisition of an undertaking which is engaged in business activities in Sweden.

2.1.1. Acquisition of an undertaking

2.1.1.1. Definition of an undertaking

Article 3 of the Act defines an undertaking as a legal or a natural person that is engaged in activity of an economic or commercial nature. The term undertaking must be viewed in the broadest sense and be interpreted in the same way as under EC competition law.[9] Virtually every natural or legal person participating in the economic process will qualify as an undertaking.[10] The term covers any activity directed at the trade in goods or services irrespective of the legal form of the undertaking and regardless of whether or not it is intended to earn profits.[11] The Market Court has defined undertakings as including natural persons that classify as "potential undertakings", in the case *Norsk Hydro*.[12] The case in question concerned an acquisition agreement that included a non-competition clause that obliged the sellers of a company to refrain from competing with the buyer. *Norsk Hydro* claimed that the non-competition clause did not fall under the Act since the sellers were natural persons. The Market Court did not follow *Norsk Hydro*'s interpretation of an "undertaking". In its judgment, the Market Court stated that the assessment of whether a natural person is to be considered as a natural person depends on the circumstances of the individual case. According to the Market Court, a natural person cannot be regarded as an undertaking by the mere fact that he is a shareholder, but only if he is active in the undertaking's activities for his own account and not merely as an employee. Natural persons that have sold a business activity that made them qualify as undertakings, may under certain circumstances remain "potential undertakings". Under such circumstances, the Act should be applicable on them as undertakings.

Public authorities can also fall under the definition of undertaking and their activities be covered by the Act, although not to the extent such activity is considered to be exercise of public governance.[13]

2.1.1.2. Acquisition of a decisive influence

The Act applies to acquisitions of undertakings. The acquisition of an undertaking in accordance with the Act, includes the acquisition of a business as well as a merger.[14]

An acquisition where the ownership of an undertaking or a business is not transferred in its entirety, shall be deemed to fall under the Act only if the acquisition enables a decisive influence to be exercised over the undertaking or business.[15] Decisive influence has been defined in accordance with the EC merger rules on acquisition of control. The definition depends on a number of legal and/or factual elements.[16] An acquisition of the majority of the voting rights is an acquisition of a decisive influence according to the Act. An acquisition of a minority shareholding may also be deemed to fall under the Act. If the acquired minority shareholding is by far the largest and it is likely that the shareholder has a possibility to influence strategically important decisions of the undertaking, it is likely for the Act to apply.[17]

In the case *Efthor Holdings*[18], the Competition Authority found that the acquisition of as little as less than 10% of the shares was an acquisition of decisive influence in accordance with the Act. In that particular case, *Efthor Holdings* had an option to buy up to 50% of the shares. Additionally, the acquisition agreement gave *Efthor Holdings* veto power over strategically important decisions concerning the target's business.

The acquisition of joint control also falls under the law, as well as the transfer from joint control to sole control.[19]

Acquisitions within the same group of companies, i.e. the same "economic unit" do not fall under the Act's merger control rules and do not need to be notified.[20] Economic unity should be defined in accordance with EC law. Undertakings are considered to belong to the same economic unit if there is a relation of economic control between them. A minority shareholding is not sufficient to create an economic unit. Joint control by two undertakings, e.g. in the form of a joint venture, normally does not constitute an economic unit.[21]

Provided a de-merger includes transfer of assets, i.e. acquisitions of an undertaking or a business, as provided by the law, such an operation falls under the Act's merger control rules.

2.1.1.3. Jurisdictional issues

For the purpose of the Act, the acquisition of an undertaking is defined as the acquisition of an undertaking which is engaged in business activities in Sweden, irrespective of whether or not the undertaking is established under Swedish law.

This means that the Act applies an effects test in jurisdictional matters. Foreign-to-foreign mergers and acquisitions are, in the view of the Competition

Authority caught by the Act only to the extent that the acquired company carries out some form of commercial activity in Sweden. Consequently, it is important to define the notion "commercial activities in Sweden", a notion that from time to time has been applied in a rather broad manner. However, it seems clear that the acquisition of an undertaking which merely sells its products directly into the Swedish market without having a subsidiary, a branch, a factory, office nor any employees in Sweden, does not fall under the merger control rules.[22]

2.1.2. Joint ventures

Since the decisive criteria for the applicability of the Act is not the "concentrative" or "full function" nature of the operation, but whether an acquisition gives the purchaser decisive influence, the Act does not contain any distinction between concentrative and co-operative joint ventures. This means that a joint venture falls under the Act only to the extent that it *de facto* constitutes an acquisition in the terms of the Act.[23] Both concentrative as well as co-operative joint ventures, whether full functional or not, may fall within the ambit of the rules and for the same reasons, they may as well fall outside the rules.

2.1.3. Notification thresholds

2.1.3.1. Two thresholds
The Act's merger control rules do not apply where the acquisition has an EC or an EFTA-dimension.

The Act's merger control regime provides for mandatory notifications when two sets of turnover thresholds are met. First, the purchaser and the target company, together with the purchaser's affiliates, subsidiaries etc., must have a world-wide turnover of at least SEK 4 billion (approximately € 450 million [24]). Second, there is a *de minimis* rule stipulating that there is no requirement to notify provided that the total (world-wide) turnover of the target company falls below SEK 100 million (approximately € 11 million[25]).

The second threshold was introduced to limit the notification duty to acquisitions that could have an impact on the market, but this failed to a large extent to fulfil its purpose since the threshold does not refer to the target company's Swedish turnover. A large number of acquisitions that fall under

415

the Act involve undertakings with a large turnover world-wide but only limited sales in Sweden. Such acquisitions have continued to be caught by the Swedish notification requirement even after the introduction in 1997 of the *de minimis* rule. This inconvenience has attracted much attention and the Committee Report proposes that the *de minimis* threshold be changed (see section 2.2.3 below).

The parties are free to notify an acquisition that does not attain the second threshold. This can under certain circumstances be advisable since the Competition Authority may, regardless of whether the second threshold is attained or not, on its own initiative require the parties to notify should "particular circumstances" so warrant. Particular circumstances would occur if the acquisition is liable to create or strengthen a dominant position.

If the parties concerned do not fulfil the first threshold requirement of a turnover of SEK 4 billion (approx. € 450 million), the operation falls outside the merger control rules. Such acquisition cannot be reviewed under the Act.[26]

2.1.3.2. Criteria for calculation of turnover

The concept of turnover within the meaning of the Act refers to the amounts derived from the sale of products and the provision of services. Hence, the sale figures of the undertakings concerned is the essential criterion for calculating turnover.[27] The turnover refers to the total world-wide figures and does not include VAT and other taxes that directly relate to turnover. Internal turnover, i.e. the sale of products or the provision of services between undertakings that belong to the same economic unit, should not be included in the calculation.[28]

If the purchaser is a member of a group consisting of several undertakings that are jointly controlled or otherwise related, the aggregate turnover of the group shall be deemed to be the purchaser's turnover for the purposes of calculating turnover under the Act's merger rules.[29] Only the target's turnover, and not that of its group, is included in the calculation of turnover under the merger rules.[30]

The specific nature of banking and insurance activities is formally recognised by the Competition Authority and the methods of calculation of turnover for credit institutions as well as for insurance undertakings are described in the Annex to the Competition Authority's regulation on notification of acquisition of an undertaking[31] and regulations from the Finance Inspection Authority.[32]

The turnover of a credit institution should consist of the total of operating income sales with the addition of interest expenses. In case of leasing, depreciation "according to plan" should be added to the total of operating income sales.

The turnover of life insurance and damage insurance undertakings should consist of the value of gross premiums. The turnover of benevolent societies should consist of fees and grants in accordance with the Insurance Inspection Authority regulation on annual accounts of benevolent societies.[33]

When converting annual turnover figures into Swedish kronor the average currency rate for the twelve months concerned should be used. This average can be obtained from the Competition Authority that uses the figures calculated by the Swedish Central Bank (Sveriges Riksbank).

2.1.4. Ancillary restrictions

The Act does not contain any provision corresponding to Article 8.2 of the EC Merger Regulation requiring the Competition Authority to consider ancillary restrictions as part of the decision on the acquisition. Consequently, an ancillary restriction can never constitute an obstacle against clearing the acquisition.

In practice, standard ancillary restrictions are reviewed by the Competition Authority in the context of merger control if so requested by the notifying parties. Since the procedure for obtaining individual exemptions is often lengthy and complicated, it may be advisable to try to obtain acceptance of ancillary restrictions in connection with the decision on the acquisition.

A finding that a non-competition clause or another restriction is excessive will not affect the decision regarding the acquisition. Instead, the Competition Authority will, for example, state in its decision regarding the acquisition, that it cannot exclude that the restriction in question may be contrary to the prohibition of anti-competitive co-operation between undertakings. In such a case, to obtain legal security, the restriction must be notified separately in order to seek an exemption or a negative clearance. Otherwise the Competition Authority may, although approving the acquisition, start proceedings against the parties under the Act's other prohibitions.

The Competition Authority does a case-by-case assessment of ancillary restraints. However, it is normally prepared to accept as ancillary the same kind of restrictions as those considered ancillary by the European Commission. For example, in the event of an acquisition, a non-competition clause obligating the seller not to compete with the buyer for a duration of five years or less where the transfer of an undertaking includes both goodwill and substantial know-how, will be accepted if the purchaser did not have any know-how prior to the acquisition on the relevant market.[34] If the acquisition only includes goodwill, the Competition Authority normally does not accept competition clauses with a duration of more than two years.[35]

Reversed competition clauses, where the purchaser accepts not to compete with the seller, will normally not be accepted.[36]

The Competition Authority will normally accept as ancillary a supply or purchase contract between the purchaser and the seller of a limited duration.[37] Exclusive supply and purchase contracts will normally not be accepted, although the Competition Authority in the case *Folksam ömsesidig sakförsäkring*[38] accepted an exclusive purchase agreement for a duration of five years, since the supplier in question depended to a large extent on *Folksam* as a customer. Additional guidance as to the assessment of the Competition Authority can be obtained from EC law concerning other types of ancillary restraints, *inter alia* secrecy clauses and ancillary restraints in the context of the establishment of joint ventures.[39]

2.2. Criteria for application: Expected amendments

The Committee Report suggests abandoning the concept of "acquisition of undertakings" and to "base the legislation on the concept of concentration". Additionally, the Committee Report suggests changes as to the threshold requirements.

2.2.1. Concentration

It is proposed that the new merger control rules be based on the concept of concentration. The Committee Report suggests defining the applicability of the merger rules in a general way so as to allow a dynamic interpretation in line with EC law, including future case-law of the EC Court of Justice. Hence, the concept of concentration will closely follow the definition given by the EC Commission Notice on the concept of concentration under Council Regulation (EEC) No. 4064/89 on the control of concentrations between undertakings.[40]

2.2.2. Joint ventures

The new Act will be applicable to concentrative as well as full function joint ventures.[41] The Committee Report suggests that the new merger control rules should include a provision modelled on Article 2.4 of the EC Merger Regulation. This article provides that to the extent the creation of a concentrative joint venture has as its object or effect the co-ordination of the competitive behaviour of undertakings that remain independent, such co-ordination shall be appraised in accordance with the criteria of the provisions on anti-competitive co-operation between undertakings, i.e. Article 85(1) and (3) of the EC Treaty. Additionally, the EC merger regulation provides in Article 8.3 that the Commission should block a concentration where such co-ordination cannot be accepted under Article 85(3). The Committee Report however, does not include a provision modelled on Article 8.3. Under the new merger control rules, only the Stockholm District Court – or on appeal the Market Court – will be able to block a concentration. If a joint venture would be considered to have restrictive effects, it may be blocked on the basis of the provisions on anti-competitive co-operation between undertakings, by these courts only. This has been criticised by the Competition Authority, which does not favour such a procedure under the merger rules for the provisions on anti-competitive co-operation between undertakings.[42]

2.2.3. Thresholds

The Committee Report includes proposed amendments to the threshold requirements and it suggests to introduce a *de minimis* rule that refer to turnover of the target's commercial activities in Sweden.

The Committee Report suggests that the new merger control rules should provide for mandatory notifications when the undertakings concerned by the concentration attain a combined global turnover of more than SEK 4 billion (approx. € 450 million), provided that each of at least two of the undertakings concerned carries out commercial activities in Sweden and in those activities each undertaking has a turnover exceeding SEK 200 million (approx. € 22 million).

The Competition Authority has opposed to this in its published opinion on the Committee Report and proposes that the *de minimis* requirement should not be linked to the criteria "commercial activities", but instead cover any turnover of two of the undertakings concerned that is realised in Sweden, e.g. through independent retailers.[43]

2.2.4. Ancillary restraints

The Committee Report provides that ancillary restrictions should be considered as part of the concentration, in accordance with EC law, including future case-law of the EC Court of Justice.[44] However, no material amendments or additions to the Act have been suggested. This has been criticised by the Competition Authority in its published opinion on the Committee Report. Accordingly, the Competition Authority proposes that the final text of the amended merger regime includes an explicit rule of that nature.[45]

2.3. Test for clearance: Existing rules

The Act provides that an acquisition be prohibited subject to two cumulative conditions. First, the acquisition must create or strengthen a dominant position which significantly impedes, or is liable to impede, the existence or development of effective competition in the Swedish market as a whole or in a substantial part thereof. This is what is referred to as the dominance test. Secondly, even if the acquisition fulfils the dominance test, the Act requires that it takes place in a manner that is detrimental to the public interest. The second condition is referred to as the public interest test.

2.3.1. The dominance test

The dominance test for clearance is identical with that employed under EC Merger Regulation. In order to assess whether dominance is created or strengthened as a result of an acquisition, both the relevant product or service market and the relevant geographic market must be defined.

Among other criteria, the substitutability test is used to define a product or a service market. As is the case under EC law, products or services which are considered substitutes having regard *inter alia* to their properties, price and use are normally considered to belong to the same product or service market. Account is also taken to potential competition and supply side substitutability.[46]

The geographical market is the area within which the conditions of competition are sufficiently homogenous. Under the Act, the relevant geographical market is defined as Sweden or a smaller part thereof, for example Stockholm or the southern region of Sweden. However, this does not exclude maintaining, when arguing for the acquisition to be cleared, that the relevant market should be regarded as larger than Sweden. The costs of and possibilities to transport are relevant factors when determining the relevant geographic market.[47]

As under EC law, dominance under the Act is an objective concept implying a position of economic strength enjoyed by an undertaking which enables it to hinder the maintenance of effective competition in the relevant market by allowing it to behave, to an appreciable extent, independently of its competitors and customers. The number of factors that will be taken into account in assessing dominance include the market shares of the affected parties, their economic and financial power, alternative available to suppliers and users, legal and other barriers to entry, buying power, supply and demand trends for the relevant goods or services.

As for the market shares of the resulting entity, a market share of less than 25% will constitute an almost irrefutable presumption against dominance. A 50% market share will indicate dominance, but the presumption can be rebutted, whilst a market share exceeding 65% similarly provides an almost irrefutable presumption of dominance.[48] Nonetheless, even acquisitions resulting in market share in excess of 65% have been cleared (see section 2.3.4 below).

2.3.2. The public interest test

As for the second stage of the test for clearance, i.e. the requirement that there is a detrimental effect on the public interest, this criterion is based on the notion that an acquisition, whilst creating a dominant position on the market which significantly impedes, or is liable to impede, the existence or development of effective competition, might still have beneficial effect from the public point of view. This means that the effects of the acquisition on competition must be balanced against other considerations which may justify the acquisition. The factors that should be balanced against the competition effects include positive long-term socio-economic effects, rationalised production, restructuring and increased competitiveness of Swedish undertakings on the international markets or the protection of national security interests. The Competition Authority has interpreted this as including consumer interests. In the *Optiroc* case [49], the Market Court has given significant importance to this criterion (see section 2.3.4 below).

2.3.3. Sanctions

The Stockholm District Court may on application of the Competition Authority grant an injunction prohibiting the acquisition of an undertaking which is subject to notification under the Act.[50]

Acquisitions effected on a Swedish or foreign stock exchange, a recognised market or any other market regulated by a recognised authority, or a bid at a compulsory auction, will not be blocked. Instead, the undertaking may be ordered to divest assets acquired.[51]

Provided that it is sufficient to avoid the adverse effects of an acquisition, the purchaser may be ordered to divest itself of an undertaking or a business or to adopt some other measure having a favourable effect on competition.[52]

It can be noted that there are no pecuniary sanctions for not notifying (see section 3.1 below).

2.3.4. Decisions and case-law regarding the test for clearance

In the period between 1 July 1993 and 30 June 1997, a total of 963 acquisitions where notified to the Competition Authority. Of these, 33 required in-depth investigation and in ten cases the Competition Authority cleared the acquisitions subject to undertakings of the parties.[53]

To date [54], the Competition Authority has sought the prohibition of a total of three notified mergers and acquisitions, *Skandinaviska Filmlaboratoriet Holding AB* [55], *Selecta AB* [56] and the *Optiroc* [57] case. Two of these were finally cleared by the courts and the third (*Selecta AB*) was settled out of court. The *Optiroc* case was the first case where the Market Court delivered a judgment under the Act's merger rules.

The Market Court's judgment is of great relevance when assessing the substantive test for clearance of a merger. In the *Optiroc* case, the Market Court refused the Competition Authority's request to prohibit a merger in the construction materials business and set high criteria for prohibiting an acquisition. The Market Court, in its assessment, found that the acquisition formed part of a continuous restructuring process and that a number of strong international actors were present on the market, which would necessitate a restructuring of the Swedish construction materials industry. Additionally, the Market Court found that entry to the Swedish market was relatively easy and that there was considerable purchasing side power. On this basis, the Market Court concluded that the merger in question, even if it should create or reinforce a dominant position, would not be contrary to the public interest. The merger was thus cleared.

There are a number of decisions from the Competition Authority that exemplify what kind of undertaking may be imposed on parties of an acquisition.

In the *Partek/Sisu* case [58], the Competition Authority requested continued supplies of certain machinery to competitors following a merger between manufacturers of forestry machinery. Partek, a manufacturer of forestry machinery, purchased one of its competitors, Sisu. The acquisition would strengthen Partek's position on the market for such machinery. In particular, smaller competitors were dependent on supplies from Partek and Sisu of certain machinery, in particular mobile cranes. Partek therefore undertook to supply third parties with cranes on the same terms and conditions as it applied to its own subsidiaries. Subject to this undertaking, the Competition Authority cleared the merger.

In the *NCC/Siab* case [59], a merger in the construction field was cleared by the Competition Authority subject to extensive undertakings. The construction company NCC acquired one of its main competitors, Siab. This acquisition lead to an increased concentration of the Swedish construction sector. The Competition Authority found that the merger would create strong positions in the markets for primary materials such as landfill and concrete as well as in the building contracting business, and would leave only three major actors on the market. Moreover, NCC was a party to a number of joint ventures with another major player, Skanska. NCC agreed to divest its and Siab's shares in a number of joint ventures as well as asphalt production facilities in a number of local markets.

The Competition Authority cleared a merger in the float glass business after an in-depth investigation, when *Pilkington Floatglas AB* acquired a flat glass manufacturer Combiglas AB.[60] The Competition Authority found that the merger would give Pilkington a 40% share of the isolating glass market. Since this in itself was not sufficient to find that Pilkington held a dominant position on the market, the Competition Authority argued that Pilkington was jointly dominant together with its main competitor, Saint-Gobain, which also held around 40% of the market. The Competition Authority's view was based *inter alia* on the concentrated nature of the market, the absence of other large competitors, the structural similarities between Pilkington and Saint-Gobain and the flow of information on the market. The merger was cleared, subject to undertakings of a structural nature submitted by Pilkington.

Following objections by the Competition Authority in the *Bergman & Beving Tools & Equipment* case [61], a transaction whereby the company Bergman & Beving Tools & Equipment, a wholesaler in the hardware sector, would acquire the competing wholesaler HDF-Paulsson AB, was abandoned. The Competition Authority found that, save the parties to the transaction, there was only one major competitor on the Swedish market. Through the notified operation, the parties would reach market shares in excess of 80%. Moreover, the Competition Authority considered there to be a strong vertical link between Bergman & Beving and one of the largest hardware distributor chains in Sweden.

2.4. Test for clearance: Expected amendments

The Committee Report proposes to keep the existing substantive test and does not suggest any changes to the public interest test. However, the Competition Authority has opposed to this in its published opinion on the Committee Report. The Competition Authority wants to abolish the public interest test to further align the rules with the EC regime and to reinforce the legal certainty since the criterion is much too vague to give any indication as to what is its practical meaning.[62]

3. The procedural rules

3.1. Notification matters

3.1.1. Mandatory notification

Provided the transaction falls within the ambit of the Act, notification is mandatory. However, there are no penalties involved in not notifying, although the Competition Authority may issue an injunction for the parties to file. This injunction may be linked to a fine. The Competition Authority can also request the Stockholm District Court to take interim measures in order to postpone the completion of a non-notified acquisition. Further, ignoring an obligation to notify of course entails the risk of the acquisition being prohibited at a later stage. There is also a risk of loss of goodwill when failing to abide by a legal obligation to notify.

3.1.2. Investigatory process

The notification may be made by any party to the transaction, jointly or separately. No legal effects are attached to which party is notifying.[63] In the absence of penalties for not notifying, there are no formal time-limits for notifying. Nonetheless, there is a practical benefit from early contact with the Competition Authority, as it may then commence an informal investigation prior to formal notification.

Formal notification may be undertaken at the time of signature. An unsigned copy of the agreement or a letter of intent may form the basis of a notification, provided that the notification is submitted jointly by the seller and the purchaser. The Competition Authority does not accept anonymous notifications.

Upon notification, the Competition Authority has 30 days in which to decide whether or not to carry out a special in-depth investigation of the acquisition. During that period allocated for preliminary examination, no party to the agreement may take any steps to complete the transaction. This is what is referred to as the 30-day standstill period. If by the end of that time the Competition Authority has not decided that an in-depth investigation shall be initiated, the acquisition shall be deemed to have been cleared. Notwithstanding the fact that there are no penalties involved with not notifying, nor any formal time-limits for notifying, any completion action during the standstill period would be contrary to the law. The standstill requirement ceases at the expiry of the 30-day period.[64]

Should a second stage investigation be initiated, the Competition Authority shall, within three months, either clear the acquisition or file an application with the Stockholm District Court requesting that the acquisition be prohibited. The three-month period may be extended by consecutive one-month periods with the parties' consent or otherwise if special reasons exist. Should the Competition Authority make an application to the Court, the Court must make a decision within six months. This period may also be extended with the parties' consent or otherwise if special reasons exist.[65]

In addition to the above, the Competition Authority may lodge an application with the Stockholm District Court for an interim order prohibiting the parties from completing the acquisition even after the expiry of the 30-day limit, to prevent completion of the acquisition pending an in-depth investigation.[66]

No measures may be imposed in relation to an acquisition later than two years after the date of conclusion of the contract resulting in the acquisition.[67]

If an order or an injunction has been imposed against an undertaking, the matter may be re-heard in circumstances where revocation or the imposition of a less restrictive injunction or order is justified.[68]

A clearance decision by the Stockholm District Court or the Market Court may only be re-heard where a party to the acquisition agreement has given incorrect information which has been of substantial importance to the decision.[69]

3.1.3. Notification process

On authorisation from the Government, the Competition Authority has issued a regulation on the information to accompany notification of an acquisition.[70] This regulation requires a special form for notification, known as the Form K2. The notification must be made in Swedish. However, the Competition Authority normally accepts that certain documentation (*inter alia* agreements or other contracts linked with the acquisition, reports or analyses prepared for the purposes of the acquisition) is submitted in English, Norwegian and Danish.

At present, no official English translation of the Form K2 is available.

The form requires the provision of the following principal types of information:
(a) details of the notifying party and the parties to the acquisition;
(b) a brief description of the nature of the acquisition, its legal form, the economic sectors involved, and the economic and financial details of the acquisition, including the parties, financial statements for the last three financial years;
(c) full details of the pre-acquisition structure of ownership and control, of the parent, and its subsidiaries and sister companies;
(d) details of personal and financial links between each party concerned and all undertakings belonging to the same group;
(e) data on each of the relevant product markets affected by the acquisition including market shares, turnover, prices, value, imports, exports, and the most important aspects of business strategy;
(f) information on the general conditions in each of the relevant markets, including barriers to entry, vertical integration of the parties, research and development, distribution and service systems, the competitive

environment, co-operative agreements, trade associations, and the world-wide context of the acquisition; and

(g) a description of the expected effects of the acquisition on consumers and technical progress.

3.2. Enforcement agencies and adjucative bodies

3.2.1. Enforcement agencies

The Competition Authority has primary responsibility for the administration of the Act.

It is charged with the implementation and administration of all Swedish competition rules and regulations. Apart from notifications of acquisitions under the Act, it also administers applications for negative clearance and notifications for individual exemptions. The Competition Authority also issues general guidelines on the application of the Act.[71]

In addition to the implementation and administration of competition matters, the Competition Authority is also charged with the administration of some rules on public procurement.

Under the Act's rules on anti-competitive co-operation between undertakings and abuse of a dominant position, the Competition Authority has rather far-reaching powers. It can order an undertaking to terminate an infringement and apply to the Stockholm District Court for a fine to be imposed on an undertaking for an infringement. However, as regards the assessment of the anti-competitiveness of an acquisition as well as orders for divestiture and other sanctions, the powers of the Competition Authority is rather limited. Such decisions and orders may be made only by the Stockholm District Court or on appeal by the Market Court.[72] Should the Competition Authority consider that an acquisition ought to be prohibited, it will have to file an application to this effect with the Stockholm District Court, which will decide the issue.

The office of the Competition Authority is located in Stockholm. The Competition Authority has three departments specialised in various sectors of the economy that are responsible for investigating infringements of the Act and applications for exemptions. There is a separate merger control department and a department responsible for competition policy issues. Moreover, a department for administrative matters is responsible for external information matters. There is one legal and economic secretariat and one secretariat for international matters. The Competition Authority has around 120 employees which gives it considerable resources.

Although the Competition Authority has no power to block an acquisition or to order divestiture, it has extensive investigatory powers. These include requiring any person to supply the Competition Authority with information, documents or other material; or to order persons who are likely to be in a position to provide relevant information to appear at a hearing at a time and place decided by the Competition Authority.

The obligation to supply information does not extend to documents whose content can be expected to be covered by a lawyer's professional secrecy and which are held by him or by the beneficiary of the secrecy. These documents are privileged in relation to the Competition Authority's investigations and orders to disclose information. Moreover, there is no obligation to disclose trade secrets of a technical nature in the context of such investigations and orders.

Upon application by the Competition Authority, fines may be imposed by the Stockholm District Court for the failure to comply with a proper information request from the Competition Authority. There is no set limit as to the fine which may be imposed, but the Fines Act[73] specifies that fines should be set at an amount to ensure future compliance.

3.2.2. Adjucative bodies

Under the Act's merger control rules, the Stockholm City Court is the Court of first instance and the Market Court, the court of appeal.[74]

The Stockholm City Court has a special chamber which hears all cases brought before it under the Act. In these matters, the Court consists of two judges and two economic experts, with one of the judges acting as chairman with the decisive vote.

Every decision by the Stockholm District Court that falls under the merger control rules may be appealed to the Market Court. The appeal may deal with alleged errors of both fact and law. In all matters relating to the Act, the Market Court consists of one chairman, a deputy chairman and five additional members. The chairman, the deputy chairman and one of the other members must be lawyers and have experience as judges. The other members are economic experts. The courts may block an acquisition or take other appropriate measures. Such measures include orders to divest or for the parties to take other steps designed to have a positive effect on competition. Any undertakings may be linked to a fine. Acquisitions effected on a stock exchange or any other recognised market or by auction will not be blocked. Instead the disposal of assets acquired may be ordered.

3.3. Confidentiality, trade secrets and disclosure

As a general rule of Swedish law, all documents which belong to a file of a public body (such as the Competition Authority, the Stockholm District Court or the Market Court) are public. The Secrecy Act[75], however, lists a number of different situations in which documents are to be treated as confidential. In the context of the Competition Authority's case files, information on an undertaking's business, operation, inventions and research results must be treated as confidential, if the undertaking in question may be expected to suffer damage if the information is disclosed. However, this normally does not prevent a *party* to have access to the documents and other material in the case. The same rules apply before the Stockholm District Court and the Market Court. Confidentiality may be requested by a party. However, the Competition Authority or the courts may also refuse to disclose information even in the absence of such request.

3.4. Expected amendments to the procedural rules

The general obligation of notification is retained. However, the Committee Report suggests introducing a procedure which enables more informal contacts with the Competition Authority. It is left to the Competition Authority to consider the detailed design and application of such procedures, but the Committee Report indicates that the procedure should be modelled on the rules for the so-called pre-notification procedure allowed under the EC merger regime. This is the procedure that gives the parties an opportunity "before notification to discuss [with the Commission] the intended concentration informally and in strict confidence".[76]

As for the time-limits for notification of the concentration, the Committee Report suggests the introduction of a rule providing that concentrations that fall under the new merger rules shall be notified to the Competition Authority not more than a week after the conclusion of the agreement, or the announcement of the public bid, or the acquisition of a controlling interest. The week shall begin when the first of those events occurs. There will be a standstill period of 25 working days during which no party to the concentration may take any steps to complete the transaction.

A concentration which consists of a merger or the acquisition of joint control shall be notified jointly by the parties to the merger or by those acquiring joint control as the case may be. In all other cases, the notification shall be effected by the person or undertaking acquiring control of the whole or parts of one or more undertakings.

4. Special rules

The Act's merger rules contain no specific rules regarding particular fields.

Notes

1. Konkurrenslag (1993:20)
2. "6 (1) Without prejudice to decisions adopted pursuant to Articles 8, 13, 15 or 17, agreements between undertakings are prohibited if they have, as their object or effect, to an appreciable extent, the prevention, restriction or distortion of competition within the Swedish market.
   (2) This shall apply, in particular, to agreements which:
      (a) directly or indirectly fix purchase or selling prices or any other trading conditions;
      (b) limit or control production, markets, technical development, or investment;
      (c) share markets or sources of supply;
      (d) apply dissimilar conditions to equivalent transactions with other trading parties, thereby placing them at a competitive disadvantage; or
      (e) make the conclusion of contracts subject to acceptance by the other parties of supplementary obligation which, by their nature or according to commercial usage, have no connection with the subject of such contracts."
3. "19 (1) Any abuse by one or more undertakings of a dominant position in the Swedish market is prohibited.
   (2) Such an abuse may, in particular, consist of:
      (a) directly or indirectly imposing unfair purchase or selling prices or other unfair trading conditions;
      (b) limiting production, markets or technical development to the prejudice of customers;
      (c) applying dissimilar conditions to equivalent transactions with other trading parties, thereby placing them at a competitive disadvantage; or
      (d) making the conclusion of contracts subject to acceptance by the other parties of supplementary obligatory which, by their nature or according to commercial usage, have no connection with the subject of such contracts."

SWEDEN

4   Article 7 of the Act.
5   Prop. 1992/93:56, p. 21.
6   The existing Swedish group exemption regulations concern specialisation agreements (SFS 1998:119), research and development agreements (SFS 1998:120), franchise agreements (SFS 1998:121), exclusive distribution agreements (SFS 1997:842), exclusive purchasing agreements (SFS 1997:843), selective distribution and service agreements for motor vehicles (SFS 1996:65), agreements within the insurance sector (SFS 1996:1368), technology transfer agreements (SFS 1996:345), co-operation agreements between retail chain businesses (1997:155).
7   Council Regulation (EEC) No. 4064/89 on the control of concentration between undertakings, OJ (1990) L257/14, as amended by Council Regulation (EC) No. 1310/97 of 30 June 1997, OJ (1997) L180/1.
8   SOU:1998:98
9   Prop. 1992/93:56, p. 66. As for the EC case-law, see *inter alia* Case C-41/90 *Höfner & Elser v Macroton* [1991] ECR I-1979, Case T-61/89 *Dansk Pelsdyravlerforening v Commission* [1992] ECR II-1931; Case T-6/89 *Enichem v Commission* [1991] ECR II-1623.
10 Competition Authority decision *Asea Brown Boveri* (dnr 1317/93) and Market Court judgment *Norsk Hydro*, MD 1996:33.
11 Prop. 1992/93:56, pp. 66. As for the EC definition, see Commission decision *Film purchases by German television stations*, OJ 1989 L284/36.
12 Market Court judgment *Norsk Hydro*, MD 1996:33.
13 Prop. 1992/93:56, p. 66; Market Court judgment *Konkurrensverket mot Statens Järnvägar*, MD 1997:17.
14 Article 4(1) of the Act.
15 Article 4(2) of the Act.
16 Cf. Commission notice on the concept of concentration under Council Regulation (EEC) No. 4064/89 on the control of concentrations between undertakings, OJ (1998) C66/5.
17 Prop. 1992/93:56, p. 67.
18 Competition Authority decision (dnr 127/94) of 1 March 1994.
19 Competition Authority decision *Texaco/OK Petroleum* (dnr 1046/94) of 9 August 1994.
20 Competition Authority decision *Handelsbanken/Fastighetsbolagen Blasieholmen och Filia* (dnr 829/93) of 8 November 1993.
21 Prop. 1992/93:56, p. 72.
22 See *inter alia* Competition Authority decision *Mannheimer Swartling Advokatbyrå* (dnr 697/1998) of 10 September 1998; cf. Competition Authority decision *Bayer Delia* (dnr 312/96) of 3 April 1996.
23 Competition Authority decision *Statoil Europarts AB/Fuji Kiko Co. Ltd.* (dnr 454/94) of 19 April 1994.
24 With a currency rate of 9.3 and rounded up to the closest one million.
25 With a currency rate of 9.3 and rounded up to the closest one million.
26 Competition Authority decision *FASAB Fastighetssystem AB* (dnr 1103/97) of 20 February 1998.
27 Prop. 1992/93:56, p. 102.
28 Competition Authority regulation on notification of acquisition of an undertaking, KKVFS 1996:2.

29 Article 37(2).
30 Prop. 1992/93:56, p. 102.
31 Annex to Competition Authority regulation on notification of acquisition of an undertaking, KKVFS 1996:2.
32 See Finance Inspection Authority regulation (FFFS 1995:54) on annual accounts of credit institutions and securities companies and Financial Authority Regulation (FFFS 1995:55) on annual accounts of insurance companies, as well as Insurance Inspection Authority regulation (1988:28) on annual accounts of benevolent societies.
33 Insurance Inspection Authority regulation (1988:28) on annual accounts of benevolent societies.
34 *Inter alia* Competition Authority decision *NCC International AB* (dnr 44/95) of 2 February 1995.
35 *Inter alia* Competition Authority decisions *GE Lighting AB* (dnr 806/93) of 8 November 1993; *Canteen Holding AB* (dnr 1578/94) of 17 January 1995.
36 *Inter alia* Competition Authority decision *BalkongGruppen i Sverige AB* (dnr 1518/93) of 17 March 1994.
37 *Inter alia* Competition Authority decision *GE Lighting AB* (dnr 806/93) of 8 November 1993.
38 Competition Authority decision (dnr 1873/93) of 30 May 1994.
39 Cf. Commission notice regarding restrictions ancillary to concentrations, OJ (1990) C203/5.
40 OJ (1998) C66/5.
41 Cf. Commission notice on the concept of full function joint ventures under Council Regulation (EEC) No. 4064/89 on the control of concentration between undertakings, OJ (1998) C66/1.
42 Competition Authority opinion (dnr 673/19) of 2 November 1998.
43 Competition Authority opinion (dnr 673/19) of 2 November 1998.
44 Cf. Commission notice regarding restrictions ancillary to concentrations, OJ (1990) C203/5.
45 Competition Authority opinion (dnr 673/19) of 2 November 1998, cf. SOU 1997:20, p. 426, 40§.
46 Prop. 1992/93:56, p. 85.
47 Prop. 1992/93:56, p. 85.
48 Prop. 1992/93:56, pp. 85-86.
49 Market Court judgment *Konkurrensverket vs. Optiroc Group AB and NCC AB* (MD 1998:10) of 3 July 1998.
50 Article 34 of the Act.
51 Article 35 of the Act.
52 Article 36 of the Act.
53 SOU 1998:98, p. 226.
54 7 December 1998.
55 Judgment of Stockholm District Court (T-8-669-96) of 18 December 1996.
56 Judgment of Stockholm District Court (T-8-537-97) of 18 November 1997.
57 Market Court judgment *Konkurrensverket vs. Optiroc Group AB and NCC AB* (MD 1998:10) of 3 July 1998.

SWEDEN

58 Competition Authority decision (dnr 686/97) of 5 November 1997.
59 Competition Authority decision (dnr 292/97) of 22 July 1997.
60 Competition Authority decision (dnr 961/96) of 13 February 1997.
61 Competition Authority file (dnr 269/98) radiated 23 June 1998.
62 Competition Authority opinion (dnr 673/19) of 2 November 1998.
63 Article 37(1) of the Act, prop. 1992/93:56, p. 102.
64 Article 38(2) of the Act, prop. 1992/93:56, p. 103.
65 Article 39, prop. 1992/93:56, p. 104.
66 Article 41(1), prop. 1992/93:56, p. 105.
67 Article 42(1), prop. 1992/93:56, p. 106.
68 Article 43(1), prop. 1992/93:56, p. 106.
69 Article 43(2), prop. 1992/93:56, p. 106.
70 Competition Authority regulation on notification of acquisition of an undertaking, KKVFS 1996:2.
71 The existing general guidelines on the application of the Act concern agreements of minor importance (KKVFS 1993:2), exclusive sales and exclusive purchasing agreements (KKVFS 1993:4), subcontracting agreements (KKVFS 1993:5), co-operation between undertakings not covered by the Act (KKVFS 1993:7) and co-operation between small and medium sized lorry hauliers (KKVFS 1997:1).
72 Article 34 of the Act.
73 Lag om viten, SFS 1985:206.
74 As of 1 July 1998 the general Competition procedure includes two instances instead of three as was the case earlier. The Stockholm District Court is no longer court of appeal over decisions from the Competition Authority. Such appeals are instead to be addressed directly to the Market Court. These amendments to the Competition procedure do not however affect the cases where the Competition Authority has no competence to adopt decisions (oppositions to mergers and imposition of fines) where Stockholm District Court will still be the forum and the Market Court the Court of Appeal.
75 Sekretesslagen, SFS 1980:100.
76 Recital 8 of the EC Merger Regulation.

United Kingdom

Laura Carstensen

Contents

1. Introduction 437
2. The institutions 439
   2.1. Director General of Fair Trading 439
   2.2. Secretary of State for Trade and Industry 440
   2.3. Competition Commission 441
3. Law 441
   3.1. Qualifying merger 441
   3.2. "Enterprise" 442
   3.3. "Ceasing to be distinct" 442
   3.4. The "assets" test 445
   3.5. The "share of supply" test 445
   3.6. Time limits for reference 447
   3.7. Competition Act 1998 448
4. Merger Reference Policy 449
5. Procedure 450
   5.1. "Standard" OFT clearance procedure 452
   5.2. Merger Notice procedure 454
   5.3. Confidential guidance 455
   5.4. Undertakings in lieu of reference to the CC 457
   5.5. Merger fees 459
6. Reference to the CC 460
   6.1. Interim measures 460
   6.2. Period of reference 462
   6.3. CC procedure 462
   6.4. Powers of the CC to compel evidence 463
   6.5. Confidentiality 463
   6.6. Assessment criteria 464
7. Remedies 464
   Notes 467

1. Introduction

Statutory control of mergers was first introduced in the United Kingdom in 1965[1]. Today, the general law of the UK regulating mergers is contained in the Fair Trading Act 1973, as amended (in particular, by the Companies Act 1989 and the Deregulation and Contracting Out Act 1994) (the "FTA"). This Memorandum deals only with the regulation under the FTA of mergers other than newspaper mergers (in relation to which the FTA applies different rules). Moreover, it does not discuss the systems of merger control – in addition to the general regime under the FTA – to which undertakings engaged in certain special sectors (such as water supply and broadcasting) are subject, or the specific sectoral regulation to which the telecommunications and utilities sectors are subject, which may, in practice, have material implications in a merger situation.

The UK system of merger control is, essentially, predisposed in favour of mergers. In contrast to the position under the EC Merger Regulation (the "ECMR"), there is no system of mandatory notification of mergers[2] (although, in practice, many are notified on a voluntary basis, usually prior to completion), and no penalties for taking part in a non-notified merger. Thus, although the Secretary of State for Trade and Industry (the "Secretary of State") – who has overall responsibility for merger control in the UK – has a very wide discretion to refer "qualifying mergers" (that is, mergers which appear to meet the jurisdictional tests set by the FTA – themselves broad – and which are not within the exclusive jurisdiction of the EC Commission[3]) for investigation into their effect on the public interest, he refers only a small percentage of such mergers. For example, in 1997, of 396 qualifying mergers which were considered by the Secretary of State, only ten – less than 3% – were referred for investigation. Of mergers which have been referred for investigation since the FTA came into force, only about one quarter have been found to be contrary to the public interest. About half have been found to have no adverse public interest effect and the Secretary of State accordingly has had no jurisdiction to take any action in relation to them[4].

Although it is exclusively the Secretary of State who has power of action in relation to qualifying mergers, the scheme established by the FTA provides for the involvement of two further bodies – the Director General of Fair Trading (the "DGFT") and the Competition Commission (the "CC") – in the merger control process.

The DGFT, supported and advised by the Office of Fair Trading (the "OFT"), in particular by the OFT Mergers Secretariat, has a monitoring and advisory role. He has a duty to keep under review merger activity in the UK and, in each case which appears to give rise to a qualifying merger, will conduct an initial assessment and advise the Secretary of State as to whether he considers the merger should be referred for detailed investigation.

Where the Secretary of State decides to refer a merger for investigation, it is the task of the CC to carry that out, and to report back to the Secretary of State with its conclusions and, if it finds that the merger does (or is likely to) adversely affect the public interest, its recommendations.

If the CC finds that a merger is not likely to operate against the public interest, the Secretary of State may not overrule that finding. If, however, the CC finds that a merger does (or is likely to) operate against the public interest, it (and the DGFT) will make recommendations for the remedying of the adverse effects. It then falls to the Secretary of State to decide what action to take in relation to that merger – whether to prohibit it, to order divestment, to permit the merger only on certain conditions (for example, subject to certain restrictions on future conduct) or, in theory, to clear it (although this has hardly ever happened in practice). The Secretary of State may implement his chosen remedy by making an order. More usually, however, he will be content to accept undertakings.

In placing overall responsibility for merger policy with a politician, the UK system of merger control is very much an anomaly. The Government has recently initiated a comprehensive review of the UK merger control process, looking in particular, at the role played by the Secretary of State. A Government paper on the case for reform of merger control is due to be published for consultation in July 1999 and the outcome of the review to be announced in May 2000 [6]. It is anticipated that the consultation paper will propose that merger decisions should, generally, be taken by independent competition authorities against a competition-based test, the Secretary of State continuing to take such decisions only in relation to the small minority of cases which raise important wider public interest issues (such as defence) [7].

That, then, is a brief introduction. Below are explained in more detail: the different roles and functions of the institutions responsible for merger control in the UK (The Institutions, section 2), the law relating to mergers in the UK (Law, section 3), merger policy in the UK (Merger Reference Policy, section 4), the procedure for the initial assessment of a qualifying merger by the OFT

(Procedure, section 5), the implications of a reference to the CC (Reference to the CC, section 6), and finally, the possible consequences which flow from an adverse public interest finding by the CC (Remedies, section 7).

The aim of this chapter is to serve as a practical guide to the principal legal and procedural issues under UK merger law. It is necessarily an abridged account of the relevant law.

The law and practice is stated as at April 1999.

2. The institutions

Under the FTA, each of the DGFT, the Secretary of State and the CC has distinct functions. It is essential to an appreciation of the merger control system within the UK to be aware of the existence and different roles of these three separate institutions.

2.1. Director General of Fair Trading

The DGFT (currently John Bridgeman), supported by the OFT and, in particular, by its Mergers Secretariat, has a variety of responsibilities with regard to merger control. Although appointed by the Secretary of State, his is an independent office; he is not a member of the Government nor is the OFT part of the Department of Trade and Industry (the "DTI", the Government Department supporting the Secretary of State), though it is funded by it. Traditionally, however, the DGFT has discharged his function in accordance with current merger policy as expressed by the Secretary of State.

The DGFT's duties are largely advisory, although he does also have certain monitoring functions, as well as a role in advising on, and responsibility for the procurement of, undertakings to remedy the adverse effects of a merger (whether those undertakings are given in lieu of a reference to the CC, or following an adverse report on a merger by the CC). These various duties are outlined below.

The DGFT has a duty under the FTA to inform himself about actual or prospective arrangements or transactions which may constitute or result in qualifying merger situations and to make recommendations to the Secretary of State as to whether to refer such mergers to the CC (Section 76 FTA) (see sections 5.1 and 5.2 below).

The DGFT has a similar advisory role in relation to the giving of confidential guidance, a non-statutory process whereby parties to a prospective merger not yet in the public domain may, if they request it, be given guidance as to whether or not the proposed transaction is likely to be referred to the CC (see section 5.3 below).

Following a finding by the CC that a merger referred to it is against the public interest, the DGFT will provide further advice to the Secretary of State, as to what action he might like to take. If so requested by the Secretary of State, he must consult with the relevant parties with a view to obtaining from them undertakings for the purpose of remedying the adverse effects specified in the CC's report (Section 88(1) FTA). If the DGFT becomes satisfied, during the course of those negotiations, that no appropriate undertakings will be forthcoming, he is required to advise the Secretary of State as to the exercise of his order-making powers under the FTA (Section 88(3) FTA).

The DGFT also has responsibility for advising on the case for, and negotiating the terms of, undertakings in lieu of a reference to the CC (see section 5.4 below).

Where undertakings are given, or an order made, the DGFT must keep those under review, both with a view to ensuring that they are complied with and that they continue to be appropriate, and he is under a duty to advise the Secretary of State as necessary with regard to these matters (Sections 88(4) and (5) FTA).

2.2. Secretary of State for Trade and Industry

The Secretary of State is a politician, a member of the Prime Minister's Cabinet and head of the DTI. It is through the Secretary of State that UK merger policy is expressed and he has the exclusive power to make a merger reference.

After considering the DGFT's advice, the Secretary of State decides whether to permit a merger, to refer it to the CC, or to accept undertakings in lieu of reference. In the event that he makes a reference to the CC and the CC finds the merger situation may be expected to operate against the public interest, the Secretary of State is vested with extensive powers to take action to remedy, or prevent, the adverse effects of the merger.

2.3. Competition Commission

The CC investigates mergers referred to it by the Secretary of State. It has no power itself to initiate an inquiry. Headed by a full-time Chairman (currently Dr. Derek Morris), it has up to 50 part-time members (including three deputy Chairs), comprising private individuals drawn from the professions, the field of economics, the trade unions movement, academia and industry. While the Chairman and members are appointed by the Secretary of State, and the CC is funded by the DTI, it is independent and guards that independence jealously.

Upon reference of a merger, the CC investigates two questions: first, whether it is a merger which qualifies for investigation (that is, whether it meets the jurisdictional tests set by the FTA); secondly, if so, whether the merger operates, or is likely to operate, against the public interest.

Following its investigation, the CC makes its report to the Secretary of State. Where it finds that a merger does, or is likely to, adversely affect the public interest, it may (and usually does) recommend remedial action. That is, however, the limit of its function; it has no power itself to take remedial action.

3. Law

3.1. Qualifying merger

A merger situation qualifying to be referred by the Secretary of State for investigation by the CC arises when it appears to the Secretary of State that it is, or *may be,* the case that:
- two or more formerly distinct enterprises,
- at least one of which is carried on in the UK or by or under the control of a company incorporated in the UK,
- cease to be distinct, or there are arrangements in progress or in contemplation which, if carried into effect, will lead to enterprises ceasing to be distinct, and *either*
- the gross assets taken over exceed £70 million in value (the "assets test") *or*
- the merger creates or strengthens a share of supply or purchasing of a given description of goods or services of 25% or more in the whole or any substantial part of the UK (the "share of supply" test)[8].

Note that is it open to the Secretary of State to refer *proposed*, as well as completed, mergers. In practice, most references are of proposed mergers – a natural result of the tendency to seek prior clearance in difficult cases coupled with the fact that news of impending mergers frequently precedes their implementation (because, for example, of the need to obtain shareholders' consent or an announcement of talks being made), thus giving the OFT time to act before the planned merger is effected.

Note also that the assets and share of supply tests are a*lternative*, rather than cumulative, jurisdictional requirements.

3.2. "Enterprise"

An "enterprise" for this purpose is defined by the FTA as "the activities, or part of the activities, of a business" (Section 63(2) FTA). In principle, therefore, a "bare" acquisition of assets (that is, without goodwill) could not give rise to a qualifying merger, since no merger of "enterprises" would be involved.

In practice, however, it is necessary to proceed with caution before concluding that no business activities attach to the assets in question, and attempts to dress up a merger as nothing more than an acquisition of assets may attract close scrutiny, particularly if there are articulate complainants. The FTA is designed to catch mergers based on the economic reality of a particular transaction and not its form; the MMC (the predecessor of the CC) has repeatedly stated that, in considering this question, it will look to the commercial realities and results, rather than the legal form, of the transaction[9]. If the net result of a particular manoeuvre is that certain business activities which were once carried on independently end up under common control with other business activities then enterprises have ceased to be distinct.

3.3. "Ceasing to be distinct"

The FTA recognises two distinct cases of enterprises "ceasing to be distinct":
- enterprises coming under common ownership or common control; and
- an enterprise ceasing to be carried on at all in consequence of "any arrangements or transaction entered into to prevent competition between" that enterprise and one or more other enterprises (Section 65 FTA).

UNITED KINGDOM

Cases falling into the latter category crop up comparatively rarely (in part, no doubt, because such transactions more easily escape regulatory notice or defy proof). There has to date been no reference to the CC (or its predecessor, the MMC) of such a case.

The concept of coming under common ownership is self-explanatory. A owns enterprise X and then acquires from B enterprise Y; A then owns both enterprises (X and Y), which have accordingly come under common ownership and thus ceased to be distinct.

As to coming under common control, the FTA recognises three degrees of control, acquisition of each of which can (assuming that all the other FTA criteria are satisfied) give rise to a qualifying merger.

The three degrees of control are normally referred to as:
- *de iure* or legal control (that is, a controlling interest);
- *de facto* control (that is, control of commercial policy);
- material influence (that is, ability materially to influence commercial policy).

Note that it is the *ability* to control, rather than the exercise (or intended exercise) of control which is relevant.

A staged acquisition may pass through each degree of control in turn: moving from acquisition of ability materially to influence, to ability to control commercial policy, to a controlling interest. Assuming that all the other criteria for a qualifying merger are fulfilled, each such acquisition could in theory be referred to the CC (Section 65(4) FTA). Further acquisitions of a company's shares by a person already holding a controlling interest will not, however, give rise to a new qualifying merger[10].

3.3.1. *De iure* control

A controlling interest normally means anything over 50% of the voting rights in general meeting.

3.3.2. *De facto* control

The ability to control commercial policy is not defined in the FTA and there are no precise criteria for determining at what point a shareholding gives its holder *de facto* control. In the usual way of English law, the determination whether that point has been reached will depend upon a close examination of the particular facts in a given case.

In practice, if the existing influence of enterprise A over the commercial policy of enterprise B is "material" (see section 3.3.3 below), then any increase in A's position short of attaining outright control has potential to involve the acquisition of *de facto* control.

3.3.3. Material influence

The lowest degree of relationship that can cause the enterprise affected to cease to be distinct is the possession by another of the ability materially to influence the policy of that enterprise. The FTA is silent as to what constitutes material influence, and there are no precise criteria for determining the point at which a person acquires the ability materially to influence policy. As with *de facto* control, it is a matter that has to be decided on a case-by-case basis by reference to the detailed facts.

Ability materially to influence commercial policy may arise from a significant shareholding, or from a combination of factors which will normally – but need not – include an equity shareholding; other relevant matters are board representation, contractual relationships and financial links.

As to the size of equity shareholding capable of conferring material influence, that again will depend to some degree on the facts – the identity of the shareholder, the way in which the other shares are dispersed, whether any special rights attach to the holding, whether there are restrictions on voting rights and so on.

As a rule of thumb, however, material influence will be regarded as being conferred by a 25% shareholding since a shareholding of that size enables the holder to block a special resolution[11] and so to exert negative influence. Qualifying mergers have, however, in many cases been found to exist on the basis of a shareholding of around 20%. Depending on the particular facts of the case, material influence may very occasionally be obtained in circumstances where a shareholding as low as 10% is held.

Only in wholly exceptional circumstances will material influence be considered present in the absence of an equity shareholding conferring voting rights; indeed, to date there has been only one such instance referred to the CC[12].

The two fundamental questions in determining whether material influence exists are:

UNITED KINGDOM

- Does the acquirer have board representation and, if not, would it be able to force the target company's board to agree representation?
- Is the acquiror in a position to cause the target company's board to adopt, abandon or change any policy?

If the answer to both questions is "No", then clearly there is no ability materially to influence. In less clear-cut cases a judgment must be made on the detailed facts and it may be prudent to seek the OFT's advice.

3.4. The "assets" test

Where an enterprise is taken over by another, the relevant criterion is the value at which the world-wide gross assets of the enterprise that is taken over stand in its books at the date it is taken over (or, if it is a merger in contemplation, at the date of reference to the CC) (Section 67(2) FTA). Where none of the enterprises concerned remains under the same ownership and control, the assets of all the enterprises ceasing to be distinct *except* the enterprise with the highest value assets fall to be taken into account. In each case, if the figure exceeds £70 million, the test is met. (The figure is periodically increased).

Gross assets comprise fixed and current assets (both tangible and intangible, including goodwill), cash and investments. The only permissible deductions are provisions for depreciation, renewals or diminutions in value. In particular, note that current liabilities are not to be deducted.

Normally, the OFT will be satisfied to rely on the latest statutory accounts. Exceptionally, account may need to be taken of post balance sheet adjustments.

3.5. The "share of supply" test

The share of supply test is satisfied if, *as a result* of the merger, a monopoly or monopsony[13] situation is created or intensified either in the UK as a whole or in some "substantial part" thereof.

A monopoly (or, as the case may be, monopsony) situation for this purpose exists when at least 25% of the goods or services of a particular description are supplied by (or to) one and the same person, or by (or to) the persons by whom the relevant enterprises are carried on (Sections 64(2) and (3) FTA). While commonly referred to as the "market share" test, that is a misnomer, for the jurisdiction is framed not in terms of a share of a "market" (in an economic sense), but rather in terms of a share of supply or purchase of a particular description of goods or services. This is a point which is often overlooked.

3.5.1. Measuring share of supply

The FTA accords a very wide discretion to the Secretary of State and the CC in determining the appropriate criterion for measuring share of supply for the purposes of establishing jurisdiction over a merger: they "shall apply such criterion (whether it be value or cost or price or quantity or capacity or number of workers employed or some other criterion, of whatever nature) or such combination of criteria as may appear ... to be most suitable in all the circumstances" (Section 68(3) FTA).

In practice, the OFT usually conducts its initial assessment on the basis of previous year sales volumes and/or values. It should be remembered, however, that this is simply a jurisdictional test. Once within the ambit of the FTA, market power is likely to be gauged by reference to a range of indicators.

3.5.2. Description of goods or services: Market definition

The Secretary of State and CC have a wide jurisdiction under the FTA in relation to determining the appropriate market definition for the purposes of establishing jurisdiction. For example, the market may be defined by reference to particular forms of supply (wholesale, retail etc.), all forms of supply taken together, or to forms of supply taken in groups (Section 68(1) FTA). So far as concerns product market definition, the criteria applied "shall be such as in any particular case the Secretary of State or, as the case may be, the Commission thinks most suitable in the circumstances of that case" (Section 68(4) FTA). On occasion, very narrow market definitions have been employed where mergers in niche markets have been looked at (for example, commission wool scouring[14], metal rainwear products[15] and the supply of organoclays for use in the manufacture (i) of solvent-based paints and coatings; and (ii) of oil-based drilling muds[16]).

Again, it is to be remembered that this is simply a jurisdictional test; the relevant market by reference to which the economic effects of the merger must be assessed may not always coincide with the "market definition" used for the purpose of establishing jurisdiction.

3.5.3. "Substantial part of the United Kingdom"

The FTA does not define a "substantial part of the United Kingdom". The House of Lords has, however, glossed the wording, indicating[17] that the question is whether the particular area is of such size, character and importance as to make it worth consideration for the purposes of the FTA. It is clear that relative size and importance (i.e. relative to the UK as a whole), as well as absolute size and importance, must be weighed.

In the House of Lords case referred to, the reference area accounted for just 4.04% of the total UK relevant economic activity (passenger bus transport); by area and population, it accounted for an even smaller percentage of the total. In all the circumstances, however, despite this relative insignificance, the House of Lords considered that the MMC had not erred or been unreasonable in finding the reference area to be a "substantial part" of the UK.

3.6. Time limits for reference

The general rule is that a qualifying merger may not be referred to the CC following the expiry of four months after the date when the enterprises in question ceased to be distinct (i.e. merged) (Section 64(4)(a) FTA), or, in relation to mergers which have been formally pre-notified to the OFT using the Merger Notice procedure (see section 5.2 below), following the expiry of a maximum of 35 working days after the date of notification (Section 75B(3) FTA).

However, in relation to mergers which have not been formally pre-notified, the four-month period does not begin to run until notice of any "material fact" about the merger is notified to the Secretary of State or to the DGFT or "made public" (Section 64(4)(b) FTA). In this context, "made public" is defined as meaning "so publicised as to be generally known or readily ascertainable" (Section 64(9) FTA), a question of fact.

One important exception to the four-month rule is where there has been a "creeping merger", by which a person has obtained control of an enterprise through a series of transactions over a period of two years (for example, by a series of small share purchases from different sources). In such cases, the Secretary of State, or CC, may treat them as a single event taking place on the date of the last transaction in the series. Thus, a reference may be made despite the fact that it may be unclear at the date of reference when the "trigger" degree of control was obtained (Section 66A FTA)[18].

A reference out of time is also possible in cases where the reference could not be made within the four months by reason of the ECMR or anything done under or in accordance with it – for example, where the merger is notified to the EC Commission but the latter decides the case falls outside the Merger Regulation criteria or accedes to an Article 9 request by the UK[19].

In all cases, in coming to a decision whether or not to refer, the Secretary of State must "have regard, with a view to the prevention or removal of uncertainty, to the need for making a determination as soon as is reasonably practicable" (Section 64(5) FTA).

3.7. Competition Act 1998

Arrangements which result in mergers within the meaning of the FTA (that is, arrangements whereby enterprises cease to be distinct, regardless of whether or not they meet the "assets" or "share of supply" tests) are, as a general rule, excluded from the regime for the control of anti-competitive market behaviours established by the newly enacted Competition Act 1998. Exceptionally, however, and subject to procedural safeguards, the DGFT may "claw back" arrangements into the Competition Act regime (namely, the prohibition on agreements between undertakings, decisions by associations of undertakings, or concerted practices, which may affect trade within the UK, and have as their object or effect the prevention, restriction or distortion of competition within the UK). The limited categories of arrangement vulnerable to clawback in this way are:
- qualifying mergers (in the sense discussed at Section 3.1 above) based on less than the acquisition of a controlling interest, which have not been cleared by the Secretary of State. These may be clawed back notwithstanding the expiry of the four-month review period applicable to mergers under the FTA. (Mergers which the Secretary of State has decided not to refer to the CC and referred mergers, which the CC has concluded are within the FTA, cannot be clawed back);
- non-qualifying mergers based on less than the acquisition of a controlling interest.

The OFT has given no indication of when these powers may be used.

4. Merger Reference Policy

In determining whether a merger operates, or is likely to operate, against the public interest, the CC is bound to take account of all matters which in the particular circumstances appear to it to be relevant and, in particular, is to have regard to the desirability:

"(a) of maintaining and promoting effective competition between persons supplying goods and services in the United Kingdom;

(b) of promoting the interests of consumers, purchasers and other users of goods and services in the United Kingdom in respect of the prices charged for them and in respect of their quality and the variety of goods and services supplied;

(c) of promoting, through competition, the reduction of costs and the development and use of new techniques and new products, and of facilitating the entry of new competitors into existing markets;

(d) of maintaining and promoting the balanced distribution of industry and employment in the United Kingdom; and

(e) of maintaining and promoting competitive activity in markets outside the United Kingdom on the part of producers of goods, and of suppliers of goods and services, in the United Kingdom" (Section 84 FTA).

In practice, the DGFT, in making his initial assessment of a qualifying merger, and the Secretary of State, in deciding whether or not to make a reference, also give particular weight to these factors.

While Section 84 FTA refers to a rather wider range of public interest matters, UK merger reference policy is, and has for over a decade been, based on a statement made by a former Conservative Secretary of State, Norman Tebbit, in July 1984 ("the Tebbit statement"), the key part of which reads:

"I regard mergers policy as an important part of the Government's general policy of promoting competition within the economy in the interests of the customer and of efficiency and hence of growth and jobs. Accordingly, my policy has been and will continue to be to make references primarily on competition grounds."

Exceptionally, however, atypical references occur. For example, when the acquisition by the Kuwait Investment Office of a material stake in BP was referred to the MMC in 1988, considerations of industrial policy and the national interest were to the fore. In referring the competing bids by the Hong Kong and Shanghai Bank and Standard Chartered Bank for Royal Bank of Scotland, regional issues, including the effects of merger on the Scottish economy, were prominent. Other examples of cases that have represented "hiccups" in the predictability of the policy have involved highly leveraged bids [20]. More recently, the Secretary of State has referred the proposed acquisition by British Sky Broadcasting of Manchester United, citing "concerns for the wider public interest", as well as competition issues, as reasons for the reference [21].

In the past, the so-called "Lilley doctrine" (named after Peter Lilley, a former Secretary of State) has been a subject of controversy. Concerned about "back door" nationalisations – the acquisition by state-owned enterprises of private sector enterprises – a series of references was made during late 1989 and 1990 (several contrary to the DGFT's advice – in itself most unusual) all of which [22] bar one [23] (which in any event presented significant competition problems on an orthodox analysis) were held by the MMC not to be likely to operate against the public interest.

The Lilley doctrine survives in theory, though in a highly diluted form. Where the acquiror is a state-controlled entity the competition issues will be assessed taking into account all the enterprises controlled by the state; where there is on that basis a significant competition issue it may be (depending on the facts of the particular case) that state control would be seen as an exacerbatory factor.

5. Procedure

As mentioned, there is no mandatory notification requirement under UK law, whether ante- or post-merger (though a merger fee will be payable in relevant cases, whether or not the parties elect to notify: see section 5.5 below).

In fact, there are a number of practical reasons which may operate to persuade parties to a qualifying merger to seek clearance, and to do so prior to completion of the transaction. Probably the most compelling is the risk of ultimately being ordered to divest in the event that a CC reference is made and the outcome of the investigation is adverse.

Even if the parties to a transaction do not choose to approach the OFT, it is possible that a third party will. (Under Section 76(2) FTA, the DGFT, in formulating his advice on reference to the Secretary of State, is bound to take account of third party comments where the third party in question appears to the DGFT either to be a person with a "substantial interest" in the qualifying merger under investigation or to be a body representing "substantial numbers" of such persons).

Further, as part of keeping itself informed about merger activity in the UK, the OFT does monitor media and other sources of information such as Stock Exchange announcements and trade journals, and, in every case where it identifies a potential qualifying merger, it will issue a standard letter requesting from the apparent parties the basic information required in order to decide whether it does in fact have jurisdiction and whether any material issue arises.

Finally, in the case of take-over bids subject to the City Code on Take-overs and Mergers [24], if the merger that would result from the success of the bid would be a qualifying merger (or indeed, fall within the ECMR), Rule 12 of the City Code requires that it be a condition of the offer that it lapse should reference to the CC be made before the first closing date of the offer (21 days after posting of the offer) or the date the offer goes unconditional as to acceptances, whichever is the later [25].

The question whether in a particular case prior clearance should be actively sought is one for the parties – and, in particular, the acquiror – to consider with their advisers. Normally, it will be wise to do so where a material competition issue is involved and, indeed, merger clearance is commonly a contractual precondition to completion of a transaction that, when implemented, would constitute a qualifying merger. That is, however, a matter of private contract between the parties and not a requirement of the general law.

If a prior approach to the OFT is to be made in a particular case, the best method for seeking clearance is again something that requires to be properly considered with the company's legal advisers. By comparison with the ECMR (under which there is a single standard procedure which must be followed in all cases), there are basically two methods by which clearance may be sought and the suitability of each to a particular case will vary.

The "standard" method of seeking clearance has long been by means of a written submission describing the merger, the parties to it and their activities, and addressing any competition or other public interest issues that may be raised by it. Where a proposed merger has been publicly announced, the formal pre-notification Merger Notice procedure may alternatively be used.

In addition, although it is not the same as clearance, there is a non-statutory procedure – the confidential guidance procedure – whereby one or more of the parties to a prospective merger which is still confidential may seek an indication, in confidence, from the Secretary of State as to whether the transaction would be likely to be referred to the CC if it were to proceed.

5.1. "Standard" OFT clearance procedure

This procedure – which does not involve any prescribed form or process – is still the preferred method of dealing in many cases.

In assessing qualifying mergers, the OFT works within current UK merger policy (see section 4 above), but adopting a non-dogmatic, case-by-case approach whereby each merger is looked at on its facts. The OFT's primary task is to determine by analysis whether it is reasonably likely that serious adverse effects on the public interest – notably on competition – will be produced as a result of the proposed merger.

The process is not a mechanistic one of aggregating market shares or calculating concentration ratios (though such exercises may form part of it). Rather, the OFT undertakes "an analysis of all aspects of market structure and behaviour and an assessment of whether the merger creates a power to raise prices or reduce choice"[26]. The OFT aims to analyse the effects in a dynamic rather than a static way and, though the consideration will focus on the effects in the UK, the role of international competition will be taken into account[27].

In order to be able to perform such an analysis, the OFT requires a considerable amount of hard factual information for which it will rely upon the parties themselves, its own researches and third party views.

Normally, therefore, the acquiror (or, if it is an agreed deal, probably the parties jointly) will prepare and submit to the OFT's Mergers Secretariat a reasonably concise memorandum (with relevant supporting documentation) explaining who the parties are, the nature of the transaction, why it is a qualifying merger, what the likely effects on competition are and why the parties believe a CC reference would not be appropriate[28].

In cases which raise material issues, however, the submission to the OFT is an exercise in written advocacy and the preparation and drafting of such a document is commonly the responsibility of antitrust counsel. It should be emphasised that the OFT is less impressed by style than by content – that is, hard and sufficient information, cogently organised and properly analysed.

Parties and their advisers must note that it is a criminal offence knowingly or recklessly to supply false or materially misleading information to the OFT.

A case officer, responsible for day-to-day management of the case, will be appointed. Normally, further questions will be put – maybe several series of further questions if the case is complicated or third party complaints are received. Quite often, the OFT will want a meeting with the parties and, in difficult cases, supplementary submissions may be made. It is a flexible procedure which takes on its own momentum to a large extent. In cases where there do appear to be competition, or other public interest, issues, the OFT will usually solicit the views of third parties likely to have an interest. It will also often receive a good deal of unsolicited opinion and material. Given that the DGFT is required to take third party views into account where they have "sufficient interest", this can cause considerable delay.

In cases giving rise to significant issues, the papers prepared by the Mergers Secretariat on the case (describing and analysing the issues) will usually be discussed at an *ad hoc* meeting of a non-statutory body known as the Mergers Panel[29]. It is through the Mergers Panel that Government departments may channel any views they may have into the OFT's thinking.

In cases which the OFT considers do not give rise to significant public interest issues, the Mergers Secretariat will circulate a paper to members of the Merger Panel recommending clearance. Where other departments disagree with the OFT's analysis, they can seek a Panel meeting.

When the process is complete the DGFT will send a formal submission containing his recommendations, together with a confidential paper containing the supporting facts and reasons, to the Secretary of State.

The DGFT aims to advise the Secretary of State in these cases within 39 working days of receipt of satisfactory information from the parties, and the Secretary of State to take a decision within 45 working days of its receipt, in 90% of cases[30]. At present, a typical period for a decision to be obtained from the Secretary of State (assuming a cogent and adequately substantiated case has been put forward) would be four to six weeks, but, depending on the complexity of the case and the OFT's workload, it can be considerably longer, particularly if intelligent opposition is raised.

The DGFT's advice may recommend either that the merger be permitted, or referred to the CC. If, having recommended reference, he specifies particular adverse public interest effects which he considers might follow from the merger, it is open to the Secretary of State to accept from the parties, in lieu of reference, undertakings to remedy those adverse effects.

After considering the DGFT's advice, the Secretary of State decides whether or not to make a reference. His decision is published by way of a press release and will disclose whether the reference or clearance is in accordance with or contrary to the DGFT's advice. Although it has, in the past, been rare for the Secretary of State to act contrary to the DGFT's advice, in recent years there have been a number of instances.

5.2. Merger Notice procedure

The Companies Act 1989, which amended the FTA, introduced into the UK merger control regime, on an optional basis, a formal pre-notification procedure by way of a prescribed form "Merger Notice", service of which sets running a timetable[31] within which the Secretary of State's decision on reference must be made. Save for certain exceptions, a merger pre-notified under this procedure will be automatically cleared if it has not been referred within the maximum period allowed to the Secretary of State for its consideration (the "consideration period"). This procedure is only available in cases where the merger proposal has been made public, and it does not apply to completed mergers.

Given that it has, since introduction of the FTA, been normal practice in cases presenting points of difficulty to seek clearance in advance of completion of a merger from the Secretary of State, from the point of view of being a *prior* notification, the Merger Notice offers nothing new. Also, like any prescribed form, the Merger Notice may not be best suited to presenting complex material. In straightforward cases, without extensive derogations, complying with the form may be unduly burdensome.

Further, there may be no timing advantage in use of the Merger Notice procedure since experience indicates that the OFT avails itself of the available extension of time[32] in a substantial proportion of cases so that the timetable under the Merger Notice is often comparable to the typical timetable under the "standard" clearance procedure.

The question of using a Merger Notice in a particular merger situation should therefore be considered by the company with its legal advisers.

The exceptions to the basic "deemed clearance" rule are:
- if the Merger Notice is rejected during the consideration period (see below for grounds);
- if the merger is implemented during the consideration period;
- if any material information known (or which ought to be known) to the notifying person or any connected person[33], whether or not of a kind required

UNITED KINGDOM

by the Merger Notice, is not disclosed to the Secretary of State at least five working days before the end of the consideration period;
- if during the consideration period any of the enterprises in question merge with some third party enterprise (i.e. an enterprise not covered by the Merger Notice);
- if the notified merger does not take place within six months of the end of the consideration period;
- if the Merger Notice is withdrawn; or
- if any information given in relation to the pre-notified Merger by the notifying person or any connected person, whether or not of a kind required by the Merger Notice, turns out to be false or misleading in a material respect.

The DGFT may only reject a Merger Notice on certain specified grounds. These include the fact that the merger appears to fall within the ECMR (and so within the exclusive jurisdiction of the EC Commission)[34]. The DGFT is empowered to request by notice the provision of further specified information by the notifying person (Section 75B(4) FTA). Failure to comply is a further ground for rejection of the Merger Notice.

Once the Merger Notice period begins, the DGFT publishes the fact of the pre-notification and the expiry date of the consideration period by whatever means are regarded as suiting the case (for example, TOPIC screen, trade press) and invites third party comments[35].

If the case is one where the Secretary of State is minded to seek undertakings in lieu of reference (see section 5.4 below) and the DGFT serves a notice to that effect on the notifying person, where the notifying person responds by notice to the DGFT that no such undertakings will be given and the DGFT does not act within ten days of receipt thereof, the basic "deemed clearance" rule will apply to prevent reference following expiry of the consideration period.

5.3. Confidential guidance

As its name suggests, confidential guidance that a merger is unlikely to be referred cannot be taken as a *guarantee* that no reference will be made following its public announcement. This is a reflection of the fact that, because of its confidential nature, the OFT necessarily cannot consult with third parties. Nonetheless – and although confidential guidance is, from time to time, perceived as being more or less reliable – in the absence of a material change in the circumstances or the emergence of a material new fact, the final decision by the Secretary of State after public announcement of the merger should, generally, follow the guidance.

Under the confidential guidance procedure, the OFT will consider evidence and argument put to it by the parties and formulate an opinion as to whether, on the basis of the facts then known, the Secretary of State would be likely or unlikely to refer the merger to the CC. In some cases, the OFT concludes that without wider consultation it is not possible to give either positive or negative guidance (so called "neutral" guidance).

The Mergers Panel will be consulted where the OFT considers that there are significant competition, or other public interest, issues.

The OFT's advice is put up to the Secretary of State for approval and authority to release it, again on a confidential basis, to the party seeking guidance. The OFT aims to advise the Secretary of State in confidential guidance cases within 19 working days of receipt of satisfactory information from the parties, and the Secretary of State to take a decision within 25 working days of its receipt, in 90% of cases.

The OFT considers absolute confidentiality to be crucial to the operation of the confidential guidance procedure. It requires any company seeking guidance not only to keep secret the advice given, but also the fact that such guidance was sought. This requirement applies even after the proposals become public. The OFT will take a dim view of any "breach of trust" with respect to the confidentiality requirement, and has stated that confidentiality lapses, whether by companies or by their advisers, may lead it to take the view that it could not offer those responsible any such guidance in the future. There have recently been a number of cases where confidential guidance has been leaked to the press, and consequently the OFT is taking an increasingly firm line on this issue.

The recipient of negative confidential guidance (that is, an indication that reference to the CC would be likely) remains entirely free to proceed with the transaction and to take the associated risks of reference. This is sometimes done – for example, because the complex issues raised are considered likely to succeed in securing eventual clearance at the CC, with the possibility for detailed consideration over a longer period of time that a reference allows.

Whether it is worth seeking confidential guidance in a particular case is a matter for discussion with the company's legal advisers. Note, in particular, that from application to receipt of guidance the process generally takes as long as a formal clearance procedure.

5.4. Undertakings in lieu of reference to the CC

The Companies Act 1989 amended the FTA so as to allow for the possibility of giving undertakings to the Secretary of State to divest following acquisition ("structural undertakings in lieu") and thereby avert a CC reference (Sections 75G-75K FTA). The Deregulation and Contracting Out Act 1994 extended the procedure to encompass the possibility of giving "behavioural undertakings in lieu" – undertakings to do or not do certain things. Prior to these amendments, the Secretary of State had no power in law to accept such undertakings save following an adverse CC reference. It had been recognised for some time that a system requiring that the costs – in terms both of time and money – of a reference be incurred in cases where the parties were all along willing to give appropriate undertakings was unsatisfactory.

The structural undertakings in lieu procedure is designed for those cases where there is an identifiable market overlap between the merging enterprises which gives rise to a serious competition issue, whether national, regional, or local. In some such cases, it may be that the disposal of certain assets (for example, sales outlets) or shareholdings can provide a clean cut solution to the competition problem. The procedure has been used in the context of contested public take-over bids[36] and in the context of completed deals[37]. The more recently introduced power to accept behavioural undertakings in lieu has been much less used.

The undertakings in lieu procedure is available to the Secretary of State only where the DGFT has recommended reference of a qualifying merger and has specified (whether as part of that recommendation or subsequently) particular effects adverse to the public interest which, in the DGFT's opinion, the implementation of the merger may or might be expected to have (Section 75G(1) FTA).

If the OFT considers that the giving of undertakings in lieu would be appropriate, it will ask the parties if they would be prepared to give such undertakings. It is, however, always open to the parties to suggest undertakings if they consider them appropriate to remedy perceived competition concerns.

The Secretary of State may accept from such of the parties concerned as he considers appropriate (to date, always the acquiror) such undertakings as he regards as apt to remedy or prevent the adverse public interest effects specified in the DGFT's advice. (Note that the Secretary of State's power to accept undertakings is limited by the "mischief" identified by the *DGFT*; the Secretary of State is not entitled to accept statutory undertakings designed to remedy any other adverse effects which may have been identified). In practice, the Secretary of State issues a press notice stating that he is minded to refer absent appropriate undertakings; a text of the type of undertakings sought is normally attached for third party comment. The DGFT will set about negotiating the undertakings with the party concerned; these are then put to the Secretary of State for review and approval. The procedure, should they be acceptable, is as described below.

In the context of a public take-over bid, the undertakings in lieu procedure may well impact upon the bid timetable and extensions may have to be sought from the Take-over Panel.

Once undertakings in lieu have been accepted, the merger in question is immune from CC reference unless it emerges that any material fact relating to the merger was neither disclosed to the DGFT or Secretary of State nor made public [38] (Sections 75G(4) and (5) FTA) before the acceptance of the undertakings.

Once accepted, undertakings in lieu together with the DGFT's original advice identifying the anticipated adverse effects of the merger are published (Section 75H FTA). The practice is for this to be done by way of a press release by the DTI. Any subsequent variation or release of the undertakings must also be published. There is, however, the opportunity to request the exclusion of certain matters from the published form of the DGFT's advice. The Secretary of State must exclude three distinct categories of information:

- *individuals:* any matter (i) which relates to the private affairs of an individual where publication would or might, in the opinion of the DGFT or the Secretary of State, as the case may be, seriously and prejudicially affect the interests of that individual and (ii) in relation to which the Secretary of State is satisfied that publication would not be in the public interest;
- *others:* any matter (i) which relates specifically to the affairs of a particular body of persons (whether corporate or unincorporated) where publication would or might, in the opinion of the DGFT or the Secretary of State, as the case may be, seriously and prejudicially affect the interests of that body, unless in his opinion the inclusion of that matter relating specifically to that body is necessary for the purposes of the advice and (ii) in relation to which

UNITED KINGDOM

the Secretary of Sate is satisfied that publication would not be in the public interest;
- any other matter in relation to which the Secretary of State is satisfied that its publication would be against the public interest (Sections 75H(3) and (4) FTA).

The implementation and continuing appropriateness of undertakings in lieu are kept under review by the DGFT, who must advise the Secretary of State accordingly (Section 75J FTA). The Secretary of State may, in light of this advice, vary or replace the undertakings or, indeed, release one or more of the parties. Where, however, it appears to the Secretary of State that an undertaking in lieu that has been accepted is not being or will not be fulfilled, he has wide order-making powers available [39] to remedy the anticipated adverse effects, including the power to prohibit a particular acquisition, to require the separate conduct of specified business activities, to prohibit the exercise of voting rights and to require disposals to be made. Third parties also have the right to take action in the Courts (Section 93A FTA) where undertakings have been breached.

5.5. Merger fees

Fees are payable on a sliding scale by the parties to a qualifying merger where at least a controlling interest is acquired.
The applicable fee will be payable:
- in cases where the formal pre-notification procedure is used, upon the filing of the Merger Notice. Payment has to accompany the Notice. (Until it is received, the period for considering the Notice is not triggered);
- in cases where no Merger Notice is filed, either upon the making by the Secretary of State of a merger reference or upon the announcement by the Secretary of State of his decision not to refer the merger to the CC. An invoice is issued; payment must be made within 30 days of the date of the invoice.

There are three bands of merger fees which apply according to the value of the gross assets which are to be taken over. Where the merger qualifies for investigation solely on the basis of the market share test, the minimum fee will be payable.

The current scale is as follows:

Gross Asset Value	Merger Fee
£30 million or less	£5,000
Over £30 million, but not over £100 million	£10,000
Over £100 million	£15,000

6. Reference to the CC

Merger references (and indeed merger clearances) are normally announced at 11.00 a.m. to the London Stock Exchange. The parties to the referred merger are, if possible, given very short advance notice by telephone call. The announcement of a reference is made by way of a press release from the DTI to which the formal terms of reference are appended, together, normally, with some brief explanation of the reasons for the reference (that is, the particular competition concerns which have motivated the Secretary of State to refer).

6.1. Interim measures

Upon the making of a CC reference, there are a number of consequences for the transaction – some arising automatically, some relevant only if invoked by the authorities.

6.1.1. Temporary restriction on share dealings

Upon the making of a merger reference, Section 75(4A) FTA automatically applies to prohibit (in broad terms) the parties from acquiring interests in each other's shares (except with the specific consent of the Secretary of State). The prohibition applies until the report of the CC is laid before Parliament (in effect, the publication date) and, in the case of a finding that the merger may be expected to operate against the public interest, for a further 40 days thereafter.

In detail, Section 75(4A) prohibits any person carrying on or having control of an enterprise to which the reference relates (or any subsidiary of or person associated with[40] such person) from directly or indirectly acquiring, at any time during the course of the reference[41], an interest in shares in a company which carries on or controls another enterprise to which the reference relates, save that the prohibition does not extend to the acquisition of such an interest pursuant to an obligation to purchase, including a conditional obligation to purchase, which pre-dates the CC reference (Sections 75(4F) and (4G) FTA).

One general consent disapplying the Section 75(4A) prohibition has been made[42] in respect of intra-group transactions.

6.1.2. Interim undertakings and orders

The Secretary of State also has available a wide range of interim order-making powers (Section 74 FTA) including, for example, the power to order enterprises to be held separate, to prohibit the acquisition of certain assets and to suspend the exercise of voting rights. The purpose of these is to "hold the ring" – that is, to prevent the parties from taking any steps which might prejudice, or make it difficult for the Secretary of State to implement, any remedies which might prove ultimately necessary such as divestment (for example, by the inextricable "scrambling" of the two enterprises).

An interim order may be made at any time from the date of reference to the 40th day following the date of publication of the report (inclusive). An interim order expires on the latter date unless revoked earlier.

In practice, the parties normally give appropriate undertakings to the OFT and the Secretary of State will be content to rely on those.

6.1.3. Lapse of public take-over bid

As mentioned, under Rule 12 of the City Code on Take-overs (see section 5 above), a bid subject to the Code is required to be made subject to a condition that the bid will lapse if a CC reference is made before the later of the first closing date and the date the bid goes unconditional as to acceptances. In these circumstances, Rule 35 of the Code provides, in broad terms, that the bidder may not bid again for the target for a period of 12 months following the date the bid lapses although, if the bid is cleared by the CC, the Take-over Panel will normally permit a fresh bid to be made provided it is made within 21 days of the CC's clearance being announced.

6.2. Period of reference

The terms of reference given to the CC by the Secretary of State specify the period within which it must report. The reference period may not be more than six months but it may be extended, should the CC so request, for a single further period of up to three months. Current practice, however, is for references to be completed within an initial reference period of just three months.

The parties should be aware, however, that they will not know the outcome of the CC's report until it is laid before Parliament (that is, in practice, published). That will not happen until the Secretary of State has considered the report and its recommendations and reached a determination as to his course of action. Typically, this adds a further two to six weeks to the timetable.

6.3. CC procedure

Particular merger references are allocated by the Chairman of the CC to groups of members (the "panel"), each group being chaired by the Chairman himself or by one of his three deputy chairmen. For mergers, the groups have traditionally consisted of a chairman and five other members (though, latterly, smaller panels have on occasion been used due to pressure of work). The panel is supported by a team of CC staff (economists, accountants, lawyers, clerical staff and so on) and may, on occasion, use external advisers.

The CC in effect sets its own procedures. It must take into account representations made by persons appearing to have a "substantial interest" in the subject matter of the reference or bodies appearing to represent "substantial numbers" of such persons (Section 81(1)(a) FTA) and normally such persons or bodies must be given the opportunity of an oral hearing. Subject to that (and to generally applicable principles of English administrative law) "the [CC] may determine their own procedure" (Section 81(2) FTA).

CC hearings are by convention held in private, although the CC could in theory, in an appropriate case, decide that a hearing (or part of a hearing) be held in public (Section 81(2) FTA). Although neither the CC nor its predecessor the MMC have, to date, held a public hearing, it is making moves towards greater transparency. It recently published, for the first time in a merger inquiry, the "issues letter" sent to the main parties, highlighting those matters identified by the investigating group for further consideration[43].

Traditionally, a CC investigation has had two main phases – the inquiry into the facts and the inquiry into the public interest issues. Finally, possible remedies are considered (on the hypothetical basis of an adverse finding and without prejudicing the conclusion on public interest either way).

The modern practice of having a three-month reference period rather than the traditional six-month period means that the phases of the reference are, in practice, telescoped and the period is a hectic one for those responsible for the conduct of the reference. There will be regular – even daily – contact between CC staff and the parties' representatives, in correspondence, telephone conversations, and at formal and informal meetings.

6.4. Powers of the CC to compel evidence

The CC has wide statutory powers (Section 85 FTA) for the purpose of an investigation to compel by formal notice any person to attend and give evidence or to produce any document specified or described in the notice which is in that person's control. In addition, the CC can require any person carrying on a business to furnish such estimates, returns or other information as may be specified or described in the notice for the purposes of the investigation.

However, it should be noted that the CC has no greater powers of compulsion than the Court would have in civil proceedings. Accordingly, the English rules on privilege apply as if the proceedings were civil proceedings before the Court.

It is an offence punishable by fine and/or imprisonment for any person wilfully to alter, suppress or destroy a document required by the CC or to furnish information to the CC (or to another person in the knowledge that it will be furnished to the CC at a later stage) knowing it to be materially false or misleading.

In practice, CC references proceed on a basis of polite but firm request and voluntary compliance and it is rare for the CC to use its statutory powers. Derogations from supplying certain items of information may be able to be negotiated depending on whether the information in question is regarded by the panel as absolutely necessary for an understanding of the issues.

6.5. Confidentiality

It is important for parties to be aware that the CC has no power to guarantee in advance that information furnished to it will be kept confidential and not feature in the published report. However, there are two stages at which there is an opportunity to put the case for confidentiality.

The first such opportunity occurs when the parties are sent for review the draft chapters of the CC's report. The CC is statutorily bound to include in its report to the Secretary of State such matters as in its opinion are necessary to facilitate a proper understanding by the Secretary of State of the questions put in the terms of reference. The CC must reconcile this duty of inclusion with the power which it has to exclude matters which relate specifically to the affairs of a particular person, or of a particular body, and which it considers could seriously and prejudicially affect that person's interest. The CC normally informs the parties which confidentiality claims have been accepted and which have been rejected.

Secondly, there is an opportunity to argue for the confidentiality of certain items of information with the DTI. The test for inclusion of material in the published report is more favourable to the subjects of investigation since exclusion may be obtained by persuading the Secretary of State that the material in question relates specifically to the affairs of a person whose interests would be seriously and prejudicially affected by the publication and that it would not be positively in the public interest to disclose the material in question.

6.6. Assessment criteria

The CC is bound by the FTA to take into account all matters which appear to it to be relevant to the assessment of the referred merger and particularly those public interest matters specified in Section 84(1) FTA (see section 4 above).

The best way of understanding how the CC reaches its conclusions is to read a selection of the recent reports. In general, the reports are remarkable for their lucidity, detail and scope, particularly given the short time available for absorption of a vast amount of factual data, analysis of that data and then formulation of conclusions and recommendations.

7. Remedies

If the CC determines that a merger may be expected not to operate against the public interest then the Secretary of State has no power to block or impose conditions upon the merger. The CC's favourable determination is final.

If, however, the CC determines that the merger may be expected to operate against the public interest, it may make recommendations to remedy or prevent the adverse effects identified. It may for example, recommend prohibition (or, if the merger has taken place, disposal) or other conditions, for example, that the buyer should sell off part of its business or other assets, or conditions as to future behaviour.

The Secretary of State is free either to accept or to reject an adverse public interest finding. If the Secretary of State accepts the CC's conclusion on the public interest, he may nonetheless decide to pursue different remedies to those recommended.

It is very rare for the Secretary of State to overturn the CC's finding that a merger may be expected to operate against the public interest. Indeed, there have only been a couple of such instances[44]. It is also rare for the Secretary of State not to accept the CC's recommendation that, although the merger might be expected to operate against the public interest, appropriate remedies can be framed which would allow the merger to proceed. This happened, however, in 1996 in the case of two bids by electricity generators for electricity distributors[45], when the Secretary of State prohibited mergers which the MMC – though again with a split panel – had recommended be allowed to proceed subject to conditions. Another example, from 1997, was the prohibition of the proposed acquisition by Bass of Carlsberg[46]. A majority of the MMC had considered that the merger be allowed to proceed, although subject, again, to conditions.

Schedule 8 FTA contains the order-making powers of the Secretary of State upon an adverse merger report. The most serious orders that can be made are an order prohibiting the implementation of a proposed merger and an order to divest shares, assets etc. in the case of a completed merger. The Secretary of State's order-making powers are wide ranging and flexible so as to equip him to deal with whatever adverse effects are anticipated in any particular situation he faces.

In practice, the Secretary of State (having indicated at the time the CC report is published the course of action he proposes to take) asks the DGFT to consult the parties with a view to settling appropriate undertakings which the parties are prepared to give to the Secretary of State in lieu of being made subject to orders. Undertakings mirror in their subject matter the sorts of matters covered by Schedule 8 FTA.

Any such undertakings are published by the Secretary of State, as are any variations to the original undertakings. The DGFT keeps the undertakings under review and is required under the FTA (Section 88(4)) from time to time to consider whether the undertakings should be varied, replaced by new undertakings or, indeed, released. Where the DGFT fails to settle appropriate undertakings with the party (or parties) concerned, or if, for any reason, the Secretary of State is unwilling to rely upon such undertakings, the order-making powers of the Secretary of State come into play (Section 73 FTA)[47].

It used to be the case that divestment was imposed exceedingly rarely. This is no longer the case. There is a detectable preference for structural over behavioural remedies where there are serious competition issues at stake and what was once perceived to be a disinclination to seek divestment (whether by undertakings or orders) is evaporating.

Where the Secretary of State intends to make a remedial order he is required (Section 91(2) FTA) to publish his intention indicating the proposed nature of the order and inviting representations from those likely to be affected. A minimum of 30 days must be given for such representations to be made and any that are made must be taken into consideration by the Secretary of State before the order is made. In the case of an order for divestment, a special procedure applies culminating in a draft of the proposed divestment order being laid before Parliament for approval by a resolution of both the House of Commons and the House of Lords (Section 91(1) and Schedule 9 FTA).

Pending the making of a final order (and assuming that any interim order has expired or is insufficient for the Secretary of State's purpose) the Secretary of State may by order made by statutory instrument – a speedy process – make an interim order of a kind which is in his opinion necessary to prevent any matters arising which would prejudice the making or operation of the principal order (Section 89 FTA).

Laura Carstensen is a partner within the EU/Competition Group at Slaughter and May, based in London. She would like to thank Helen Slade for her contribution to this paper.

UNITED KINGDOM

Notes

1 Monopolies and Mergers Act 1965.
2 Except for newspaper mergers, in relation to which, as said, different rules apply.
3 That is, are not within the ECMR nor coal or steel mergers within the scope of the ECSC Treaty.
4 The remaining one quarter of mergers referred for investigation were abandoned.
5 Established as of 1 April 1999 by the Competition Act 1998. The functions of the CC in relation to mergers were, prior to its establishment, carried out by the Monopolies and Mergers Commission (the "MMC"). The MMC was dissolved on 1 April 1999 and its functions transferred to the CC.
6 See the Government White Paper "Our Competitive Future: Building the Knowledge Driven Economy" Cm 4176 (December 1998), para. 4.7 and Competitiveness White Paper Implementation Plan (10 March 1999).
7 DTI press release P/99/226, 10 March 1999 and Secretary of State's Statement to the House of Commons, 10 March 1999.
8 Section 64 FTA (Merger situation qualifying for investigation); section 75 FTA (Reference in anticipation of merger).
9 See, for example, *AAH Holdings PLC/Medicopharma NV*, Cm 1950 (May 1992) and *Stagecoach Holdings PLC/Lancaster City Transport Ltd*, Cm 2423 (December 1993).
10 OFT publication: "Mergers: A guide to procedures under the Fair Trading Act 1973", para. 2.9.
11 A special resolution requires 75% of the votes passed in a general meeting and is required for important matters such as a change in the company's objectives.
12 *Stora Kopparbergs AB/Swedish Match NV and Stora Kopparbergs Bergslags AB/The Gillette Company*, Cm 1473 (March 1991).
13 A "monopsonist" is, as it were, a "monopoly buyer".
14 *Enterprises controlled by Alan J. Lewis/Jarmain & Son Ltd*, Cm 1612 (August 1991).
15 *Glynwed International/Alumasc* (1990); abandoned.
16 *Vahli Inc./Akzo NV* Cm 1387 (January 1991).
17 *R. v MMC ex parte South Yorkshire Transport Ltd*. [HL] [1993] 1 WLR 23. The MMC Report in question was *South Yorkshire Transport, Acquisitions* Cm 1166 (August 1990).
18 Section 66 contains a more limited version of this power, available only where the staged acquisition is made from a single person or corporate group where each stage represents the acquisition of a distinct degree of control (i.e. is in itself a "trigger" for reference).
19 For a further example of where mergers may be subjected to regulatory control, notwithstanding the expiry of the four-month period, see the discussion on "clawback" into the Competition Act regime, at Section 3.7 below.
20 *Elders IXL Ltd./Allied Lyons PLC* Cm 9892 (September 1986), *Goodman Fielder Wattie/ Rank Hovis MacDougall* (1988) (abandoned), *Pacificorp/The Energy Group plc* Cm 3816 (December 1997).
21 DTI press release P/98/835, 29 October 1998.
22 *Credit Lyonnais S.A./Woodchester Investments plc* Cm 1404 (January 1991); *Thomson-CSF S.A./British Aerospace plc* Cm 1416 (January 1991); *Kemira Oy/ICI PLC* Cm 1406 (January 1991); *Societe Nationale Elf Aquitaine/Amoco Corporation* Cm 1521 (May 1991);

467

Signet Limited/Sligos S.A. Cm 1450 (February 1991).
23 *Kemira Oy/ICI PLC.*
24 The City Code, commonly referred to as the "Blue Book", applies as a rule to all take-overs of, or mergers with, listed and unlisted UK public companies and to certain limited categories of acquisition of private companies. Although it does not have the force of law, and so is not legally enforceable, the City Code – which operates principally to secure fair and equal treatment of shareholders in relation to take-overs and mergers to which it applies – forms the basis for the structure and conduct of take-over and merger activity in the UK.
25 Note that some qualifying mergers may also be subject to Rule 5 of the City Code, which applies to prevent the acquisition, until the first closing date of the offer has passed and the Secretary of State has announced that the offer is not to be referred to the CC, of further shares (or rights over shares) which would, together with shares already held, carry 30% or more of the voting rights at general meeting or, in the case of a party holding between 30% and 50% of the voting rights, would, together with shares acquired in the previous 12 months, carry more than 1% of the voting rights. Rule 5 does not apply in the case of an agreed or publicly recommended offer.
26 Dr. Martin Howe, Head of Competition Policy, OFT (1990).
27 See the February 1992 Research Paper by National Economic Research Associates for the Office of Fair Trading "Market Definition in UK Competition Policy".
28 See the OFT publication "Mergers: The Content of Submissions".
29 An inter-departmental Committee to which senior civil servants from the principal Government departments are deputed; its meetings are normally chaired by the DGFT. Which departments attend any given meeting depends on the particular cases under consideration at that meeting.
30 See "The OFT Code of Practice on Enforcement" (January 1994).
31 The initial Merger Notice period is 20 working days beginning with the first day after two preconditions are satisfied: (i) the Merger Notice is received by the DGFT and (ii) the applicable merger fee (see section 5.5 below) has been paid.
32 The initial Merger Notice period of 20 working days may be further extended by 15 working days. The maximum Merger Notice period is, therefore, 35 working days.
33 In relation to the notifying person "connected person" means any person associated with him ("associated person" as defined by Section 77 FTA) or any subsidiary of a person associated with a subsidiary of the notifying person.
34 The other grounds for rejection by the DGFT are: suspicion that the information given in the Merger Notice, or subsequently, is materially false or misleading; suspicion that the pre-notified merger is not intended to be implemented; that any information specified in the Merger Notice, or supplementary information requested, has not been duly provided.
35 Under Section 76(2) FTA, the DGFT is bound to take account of certain third party views.
36 For example, *Williams Holdings/Racal Electronics*, undertakings given 2 December 1991.
37 For example, *Bowater/DRG Packaging*, undertakings given 15 September 1992.
38 As in relation to the four-month rule, "made public" means "so publicised as to be generally known or readily ascertainable" (Section 64(9) FTA).
39 Paragraphs 9A, 12, 12A, 12B and 12C of Part I and the whole of Part II of Schedule 8 to the FTA.
40 Section 77 FTA definition applies.

41 Calculated as specified in Section 75(4B) FTA.
42 DTI Press Notice 89/792.
43 MMC press release 16/98, 9 December 1998, *BSkyB/Manchester United* merger inquiry. The purpose of publishing the issues letter was to inform other parties interested in making submissions and to enable them to tell the MMC if they think any important points have been missed.
44 *Charter Consolidated/Anderson Strathclyde* Cm 7881 (December 1982) and, more recently, *The General Electric Company plc/VSEL plc* Cm 2582 (May 1995).
45 *National Power/Southern Electric*, Cm 3230 (April 1996) and *PowerGen/Midlands Electricity*, Cm 3231 (April 1996).
46 *Bass PLC, Carlsberg A/S and Carlsberg-Tetley PLC* Cm 3662 (June 1997).
47 The Secretary of State is not entitled to exercise his order-making powers in respect of any conclusion in the CC report as to adverse public interest effects which may be expected to result where the conclusion has been adopted by less than two-thirds of the members of the CC panel responsible for the report (Schedule 3, para 16(2) FTA). In such circumstances, the conclusion in question is to be disregarded.

Survey of mergers and acquisitions

European Union

1. Definition of concentrations	A change of control over one or more undertakings, including: * mergers; * purchase of securities and assets; * joint ventures.
2. Joint ventures	Joint ventures exercising on a lasting basis all the functions of an autonomous economic entity.
3. Notification thresholds	Basic rule: * aggregate world-wide turnover > € 5 billion; * aggregate Community-wide turnover of at least two undertakings > € 250 million; * unless all undertakings concerned achieve more than two-thirds of their Community-wide turnover within one and the same Member State. Additional rule: * aggregate world-wide turnover > € 2.5 billion; * aggregate Community-wide turnover of at least two undertakings > € 100 million; * aggregate turnover in at least 3 Member States > € 100 million; * in those 3 Member States at least two undertakings should achieve a turnover > € 25 million; * unless all undertakings concerned achieve more than two-thirds of their Community-wide turnover within one and the same Member State
4. Mandatory or optional notification and sanctions	* Mandatory notification before implementation of concentration. * Fines up to € 50,000 and penalty payments up to € 25,000 for failure to notify.
5. Time-limits for notification	Within one week after the conclusion of the agreement, the publication of the bid or the acquisition of control, whichever takes place first.

6. Procedural time-frame and suspension requirements	* First phase of one month. * Second phase of four month. * Implementation prohibited prior to clearance; fines up to 10% of world-wide turnover.
7. Substantive test	* Dominance test for concentrations. * Restriction of competition test for joint ventures leading to co-ordination of competitive behaviour between parent undertakings.
8. Competent authorities	* European Commission. * Appeal to EC Court of First Instance.

Austria

1. Definition of concentrations	The definition of concentrations covers the following situations: * acquisition of an entire business or of a major devision thereof; * acquisition of shares in an undertaking if the shareholding held after the acquisition is or exceeds 25% or 50%; * creation of personal identities between at least half of the members of the management and/or the supervisory board of two or more undertakings (interlocking boards); * transactions which confer management rights to or direct/indirect controlling influence over another undertaking; * formation of concentrative joint ventures.
2. Joint ventures	Joint ventures, which perform on a lasting basis all functions of an autonomous economic entity but do not give rise to coordination of competitive behaviour among the participants, are caught by the merger control regime

3. Notification thresholds	Large concentrations:
	* aggregate (consolidated) turnover of all undertakings involved is or exceeds ATS 3.5 billion (€ 254.4 million) and
	* turnover of at least two of the undertakings involved is or exceeds ATS 5 million (€ 0.4 million)
	Medium-sized concentrations:
	* aggregate (consolidated) turnover of all undertakings involved is or exceeds ATS 150 million (€ 10.9 million). Special rules apply to certain financial institutions and the media sector.
	Special rules:
	for certain financial institutions and the media sector.
	99 Amendment:
	* abolishment of notification requirement for medium-sized concentrations
	* new turnover thresholds for large concentrations
	   - aggregate (consolidated) world-wide turnover of all involved undertakings is or exceeds ATS 4,200 million (€ 300 million),
	   - aggregate (consolidated) turnover of all involved undertakings in Austria is or exceeds ATS 210 million (€ 15 million), and
	   - world-wide turnover of at least two of the involved undertakings is or exceeds ATS 28 million (€ 2 million).

4. Mandatory or optional notification and sanctions	Large concentrations: mandatory pre-merger notification; implementation prohibited prior to clearance; agreements to the contrary are void; violation of prohibition a criminal offence on pre-clearance implementation is which may lead to fines. Medium-sized concentrations: mandatory post-merger notification; failure to file in time may lead to administrative fines. 99 Amendment: abolishment of post-merger notification requirement and sanctions relating thereto.

SURVEY OF MERGERS AND ACQUISITIONS

5. Time-limits for notification	Large concentrations: no time-limits but implementation must await clearance. Medium-sized concentrations: within one month from implementation. 99 Amendment: abolishment of post-merger notification requirement.
6. Procedural time-frame and suspension requirements	Large concentrations: * if no investigation is required: clearance within 6 weeks of filing; * if investigation is required: maximum period for clearance or prohibition 5-8 months from filing; * mandatory suspension until clearance. Medium-sized concentrations: no suspension requirement.
7. Substantive test	Large concentrations: * Dominance test for concentrations (media concentrations also prohibited if impairment of media diversity is to be expected). * As an exception a concentration which expectedly creates or strenghtens a dominant position (or expectedly impairs media diversity) will escape prohibition if: 1. expected improvements in competition outweigh the disadvantages of market domination, or 2. the concentration is indispensable to maintain or improve the international competitiveness of the undertakings involved and is furthermore justified from a national economic point of view (also applicable in case of a foreseeable reduction of media diversity).

8. Competent authorities	* Official Parties (in particular the Social Partners) as bodies entitled to (i) submit requests for investigation of large concentrations and (ii) take appeals against the decisions of the Cartel Court. * Joint Committee for Cartel Matters as body giving expert opinions on the circumstances relevant for clearance or prohibition of large concentrations. * Cartel Court (i.e. the Appellate Court of Vienna) as court of first instance. * Superior Cartel Court (i.e. the Austrian Supreme Court) as appellate court. * Criminal Courts. * Competition Authority with the Federal Ministry of Commerce.

Belgium

1. Definition of concentrations	A change of control over one or more undertakings, relating to: * mergers; * acquisitions of securities and/or assets; * concentrative joint ventures. Obligation to notify cooperative full function joint venture.
2. Joint ventures	Concentrative joint ventures are caught by definitions of concentration.
3. Notification thresholds	* Aggregate turnover of undertakings concerned in Belgium higher than BFr 1 billion (€ 25 million) and * at least two of those undertakings should each achieve a Belgian turnover of at least BFr 4,000 million (€ 10 million).

4. Mandatory or optional notification and sanctions	* Mandatory notification before implementation of concentration. * Fines from BFr 20,000 to 1 million (€ 500 to € 25,000) may be imposed for late or absence of notification.
5. Time-limits for notification	Within one week after the conclusion of the agreement, the publication of the bid or the acquisition of control, whichever takes place first.
6. Procedural time-frame and suspension requirements	* First phase examination: one month. * Possible second phase investigation: 75 days. * Prohibition to make concentration irreversible before approval.
7. Substantive test	* Market dominance; and * general economic interest
8. Competent authorities	* Competition Service acting as investigation body. * Competition Council as decision making body. * Appeal possible for Brussels Court of Appeal.

Denmark

1. Definition of concentrations	* Mergers * Acquisitions * Amalgamations
2. Joint ventures	Agreements for the establishment of joint ventures are not covered by the duty to notify concentrations. However, anti-competitive clauses in a joint venture agreement must be notified according to the rules on anti-competitive agreements in Section 6 of the Danish Competition Act (which is similar to EC Treaty Article 81).

3. Notification thresholds	* Combined turnover of the participating companies in excess of DKr 50 million (€ 6.7 million). * Exception: the annual turnover of one of the participating companies is below DKr 10 million (€ 1.3 million).
4. Mandatory or optional notification and sanctions	* Duty to notify is mandatory. * Failure to comply may result in the imposition of fines.
5. Time-limits for notification	Notifications must be filed within four weeks after the transaction has been completed.
6. Procedural time-frame and suspension requirements	As there is no review connected to the notification, the procedure is terminated upon the submission of a complete notification.
7. Substantive test	None, there is no review and/or approval connected to the notification. Notifications may subsequently reviewed under the Danish competition rules which are similar to EC Treaty Article 82.
8. Competent authorities	* Competition Authority: notifications must be filed at the secretariat. * Competition Council: official body established to enforce the Competition Act. * Ministry of Economic Affairs and the Danish Supervisory Authority of Financial Affairs: certain financial businesses (such as banks and insurance companies) must notify to these bodies.

Finland

1. Definition of concentrations	* Merger * An acquisition of control in another company * An acquisition of the whole business of another company, or a part thereof * Joint venture

2. Joint ventures	Joint ventures exercising on a lasting basis all the functions of an autonomous economic entity are caught by the merger control rules.
3. Notification thresholds	* Combined aggregate world-wide turnover must exceed FIM 2 billion (€ 335 million). * Aggregate world-wide turnover of at least 2 of the parties must exceed FIM 150 million (€ 25 million). * The target company, or a company controlled by it, must be engaged in business activities in Finland.
4. Mandatory or optional notification and sanctions	Mandatory notification. Failure to notify may lead to fines.
5. Time-limits for notification	Notification must be filed within one week from the signing of the binding acquisition agreement, the publication of a public bid, the merger decision or the constitutives meeting of a joint venture, whichever event is earlier * First stage of one month: the Finnish Competition Authority clears the concentration or decides to initiate an in-depth investigation. * Second stage of three month: the Finnish Competition Authority clears the concentration or requests the Competition Council to prohibit it. * Third stage of three months: the Competition Council clears or prohibits the concentration.
6. Procedural time-frame and suspension requirements	Suspension until clearance. Failure to comply may lead to fines.
7. Substantive test	* Dominance test. * A concentration which leads to 25% share of the electricity transmitted in a network with a capacity of 400V can be prohibited.
8. Competent authorities	* Finnish Competition Authority. * Competition Council.

France

1. Definition of concentrations	* Mergers by: 1. acquisition of assets; 2. acquisition of shares * Obtaining of "decisive influence" * Joint ventures
2. Joint ventures	Joint ventures may come within the scope of French merger control.
3. Notification thresholds	Undertakings have: * either realised together more than 25% of the sales, purchases or other transactions in a national market for substitutable goods, products or services or in a substantial part of such market, or * have realised together in France a total annual before-tax turnover of more than FFr 7 billion, provided that at least two of the undertakings concerned have each obtained in France a turnover of at least FFr 2 billion.
4. Mandatory or optional notification and sanctions	Optional notification.
5. Time-limits for notification	Where there is notification, it must be made either before or within three months of the transaction.
6. Procedural time-frame and suspension requirements	* Notification and/or control procedures do not entail suspension of transaction. * Where there is no notification: Minister of the Economy may initiate control proceedings without time-limit. * Where there is notification: Minister of the Economy has two months (as from receipt of complete notification file) to either approve (express approval or tacit approval) the concentration or refer the matter to the Competiton Council for opinion.

SURVEY OF MERGERS AND ACQUISITIONS

6. *Procedural time-frame and suspension requirements* (cont.)	Where referral, time-limit for decision by Minister of the Economy (acting, where applicable, with other Government Ministers) extended to six months (as from receipt of complete notification file).
7. *Substantive test*	Criteria used for determining whether a concentration is admissible under French law: * consequences of the concentration on the competitive market situation; * economic and social benefits/disadvantages analysis; * prohibitions and partial divestment.
8. *Competent authorities*	* Minister of the Economy (decision making power). * General Office of Competition, Consumption, and Repression of Fraud (Direction generale de la concurrence, de la consommation et de la repression des fraudes; Government office under the authority of the Minister of Economy). * Competition Council (Conseil de la Concurrence) (opinion).

Germany

1. *Definition of concentrations*	* Mergers by: 1. acquisition of assets 2. acquisition of shares (resulting in a 25% or 50% shareholding) 3. acquisition of control 4. influence which is substantial as regards competition * Joint ventures
2. *Joint ventures*	Joint ventures may come within the scope of German merger control.

481

3. Notification thresholds	German merger control is triggered if: * the companies participating in a merger have combined world-wide sales of more than DM 1 billion (€ 510 million); and * if at least one participating company has sales of more than DM 50 million (€ 25.5 million) in Germany.
4. Mandatory or optional notification and sanctions	Notification is mandatory (pre-merger notification).
5. Time-limits for notification	No time-limit for the filing of a notification is stipulated. However, a merger must not be completed before the Bundeskartellamt has carried out its investigation (which may take up to four months).
6. Procedural time-frame and suspension requirements	* First phase: Bundeskartellamt may prohibit a merger only if it informs the notifying parties within one month of receipt of the notification. * Second phase: Bundeskartellamt may start an in-depth investigation, which must be terminated within four months of receipt of notification.
7. Substantive test	The Bundeskartellamt must prohibit any merger which leads to: * the creation of a dominant market position; or * the strengthening of an already existing dominant market position. The largest geographical market possible taken into account by the Bundeskartellamt when it assesses market shares is Germany. However, when it assesses market dominance (e.g. due to the absence of competition) it takes into account foreign competition. There is a (rebuttable) presumption that a company with a market dominance will be presumed, if three or fewer companies together have an aggregate market share of at least 50% or if five of fewer companies together have an aggregate market share of at least two-thirds.

SURVEY OF MERGERS AND ACQUISITIONS

8. Competent authorities	* Federal Cartel Office (Bundeskartellamt): exclusive competence to deal with merger notifications; * Federal Minster of Economics: parties may apply for approval to set aside Federal Cartel Office prohibition; * Higher Regional Court: judicial review of decisions of Federal Cartel Office by a way of complaint; * the Federal Supreme Court (Bundesgerichtshof): an appeal against the decision of the Higher Regional Court.

Greece

1. Definition of concentrations	* Mergers * Acquisitions * Concentrative joint ventures
2. Joint ventures	Concentrative joint ventures fall within the scope of merger control.
3. Notification thresholds	Post-merger notification: * the market share represents at least 10% of the combined aggregate turnover of products or services which are regarded as substitutable; or * the combined aggregate turnover of all the undertakings concerned is at least € 10 million. Pre-merger notification: * the market share represents at least 25% of the combined aggregate turnover of products or services which are regarded as substitutable, or * the combined aggregate turnover of all the undertakings concerned is at least € 50 million, and the aggregate national turnover of each of at least two of the undertakings concerned is more than € 5 million.

4. Mandatory or optional notification and sanctions	* Mandatory notification – fine not exceeding 5% (in case of mandatory post-merger notification) or 7% (in case of mandatory pre-merger notification) of the undertakings aggregate turnover.
5. Time-limits for notification	* Within one month as from the realisation of the concentration in case of mandatory post-notification; * within ten working days as from the conclusion of the agreement, or the announcement of the public bid, or the acquisition of a controlling interest in case of mandatory pre-merger notification.
6. Procedural time-frame and suspension requirements	* First phase examination: the Competition Committee examines whether the concentration falls within the scope of mandatory prior notification – within one month it must either issue a negative decision or inform the notifying parties that the case is introduced for examination on the substance. * Second phase examination: substantive test: two months time-limit to issue a decision. * Suspension of a concentration until thee Competition Committee has reached a decision – fine not exceeding 15% of the aggregate turnover of the undertakings concerned.
7. Substantive test	* Significant restriction of competition (e.g. market dominance).
8. Competent authorities	* Competition Committee. * Minister of National Economy and Commerce.

Ireland

1. Definition of concentrations	Two or more enterprises, one of which carries on business in Ireland, coming under 'common control': * mergers; * take-overs; * asset acquisitions; * acquisitions of more than 25% of shares with voting rights.
2. Joint ventures	* Mergers Act may apply to acquisition of joint control of existing enterprises. * Competition Act may apply to joint venture arrangements which prevent, restrict or distort competition.
3. Notification thresholds	Notification required where two or more enterprises to be involved in the proposed transaction have either: * gross asset in excess of IR£ 10 million (€ 12.69 million); * turnover in excess of IR£ 20 million (€ 25.39 million). In transactions involving non-Irish parties which exceed the thresholds on a world-wide basis, full notification is required only if the business over which control will change exceeds one of the thresholds in Ireland.
4. Mandatory or optional notification and sanctions	* Mandatory notification. * Criminal sanctions for failure to notify. * Invalidation of unnotified transfers of shares and assets.
5. Time-limits for notification	Within one month of the making of an offer capable of acceptance.

6. Procedural time-frame and suspension requirements	* First stage: one month (may be extended by information request). * Second stage: up to three months from date of notification (or date of supply of information requested during first stage). * Effective suspension due to invalidation of title transfer prior to clearance.
7. Substantive test	* Prevent or restrict competition or restrain trade in goods or services in Ireland. * Otherwise operate against the common good by reference to defined criteria (including level of employment, regional development, R&D, consumer interest).
8. Competent authorities	* The Minister for Enterprise, Trade and Employment. * The Competition Authority. * Appeal to High Court on point of law.

Italy

1. Definition of concentrations	* Mergers * Acquisition of shares * Acquisition of assets * Contractual control * Joint ventures
2. Joint ventures	Same distinction between concentrative and co-operative joint ventures as laid down in Commission Notice 94/C 385/01 shall apply.
3. Notification thresholds	Thresholds beyond which notification is compulsory are: * L 710 billion (€ 366.684 million) for the national total turnover of all the undertakings concerned and; * L 71 billion (€ 36.688 million) for the acquired undertaking.

SURVEY OF MERGERS AND ACQUISITIONS

4. Mandatory or optional notification and sanctions	Concentrations must be notified in advance of their implementation. Failure involves a fine of up to 1% of turnover of previous year.
5. Time-limits for notification	* Merger: to be notified before the execution of the notarial deed of merger. * Acquisition: the notification is deemed to be validly filed in advance, if the performance of the acquisition is conditional upon the approval of the Authority. * Joint venture: to be notified before the enrolment of the new company in het company register.
6. Procedural time-frame and suspension requirements	* First phase: preliminary assessment (30 days). * Second phase: investigation (45 days, plus additional 30 days in case of supplement of investigation due to failure to supply sufficient information). During the second phase the Authority may order the parties not to proceed with the concentration.
7. Substantive test	The concentration is forbidden if it creates or strengthens a dominant position on the domestic market.
8. Competent authorities	* Italian competition authority (Autorita garante della concorrenza e del maercato). * Bank of Italy (Banca d'Italia) in the banking sector. Appeals: Regional Administrative Court of the Latium Region.

The Netherlands

1. Definition of concentrations	A concentration is deemed to arise where: * two or more undertakings merge; * one or more undertakings acquire control of the whole or parts of one or more other undertakings; * a joint venture which performs on a lasting bases all the functions of an autonomous economic entity and which does not result in a coordination of the competitive behaviour of the parents.

MERGER CONTROL IN THE EU

2. Joint ventures	Concentrative joint ventures are caught.
3. Notification thresholds	* The combined aggregate world wide annual turnover of the undertakings concerned exceeds NLG 250 million; and * at least two of the undertakings concerned each has an annual turnover within the Netherlands of not less than NLG 30 million.
4. Mandatory or optional notification and sanctions	Mandatory notification prior to the completion of the transaction.
5. Time-limits for notification	The date of filing is left to the discretion of the parties. A two-phase filing procedure is applicable.
6. Procedural time-frame and suspension requirements	First phase examination of four weeks. Second phase examination of 13 weeks. The relevant periods can be suspended by a request for supplementary information. Implementation of the concentration is prohibited during the first phase and second phase examination.
7. Substantive test	Market dominance tests. A positive second phase decision may be subject to conditions and obligations.
8. Competent authorities	The director-general of the Dutch Competition Authority.

Portugal

1. Definition of concentrations	* Merger * Acquisition * Joint venture
2. Joint ventures	Only concentrative joint ventures are caught by the law. Co-operative joint ventures are caught by the general competition law regime.

SURVEY OF MERGERS AND ACQUISITIONS

3. Notification thresholds	* Combined turnover of participating undertakings of more than Esc 30 billion (€ 150 million) in Portugal, net of turnover related taxes, in the preceding year, or; * the merger involves the creation or strengthening of a market share greater than 30% in the national market or in a substantial part thereof.
4. Mandatory or optional notification and sanctions	In practice, notifications are mandatory. The sanctions for violation of the duty to notify are as follows: * the participating undertakings are subject to a fine of Esc 100,000 (€ 500) to Esc 100 million (€ 500,000); * transaction does not produce any legal effects until tacit or express clearance is given.
5. Time-limits for notification	Notification prior to transaction.
6. Procedural time-frame and suspension requirements	* Notification is addressed to General Directorate of Trade and Competition. Within 40 days the file is submitted to the Minister in charge of trade. * The General Directorate may require further information, which causes a delay (until the participating undertakings provide it). * The Minister sends a letter within 50 days of the notification, if there is no negative assessment of the merger. * The Ministers requires within 50 days an opinion from the Competition Council if there is a negative assessment. Within 15 days after receiving the opinion, the Minister issues the final decision. * The General Directorate may initiate a merger control procedure on its own initiative. The enquiry period is extended to 90 days.
7. Substantive test	Concentrations are forbidden if they would result in the creation or strengthening of a dominant position in the national market which would prevent, distort or restrict competition.

489

8. Competent authorities	* General Directorate of Trade and Competition (Direccao Geral do Comercai e da Concorrencia, Conselho da Concorrencia). * Trade Minister.

Spain

1. Definition of concentrations	* Mergers * Divisions of companies * Acquisitions of control * Concentrative joint ventures
2. Joint ventures	Only concentrative joint ventures are subject to the rules on merger control (co-operative joint ventures fall under a different set of rules).
3. Notification thresholds	Concentrations between any Spanish or foreign parties that are above one of the following thresholds: 1. aggregate Spanish turnover of the undertaking concerned of more than Pta 20 billion (€ 125 million) in the last financial year; 2. the creation or strengthening of an existing market share of 25% of higher of the Spanish market as a whole, or of a substantial part of it.
4. Mandatory or optional notification and sanctions	Notification is not compulsory. There is no suspension requirement.
5. Time-limits for notification	Notification must be filed either before the concentration takes place or within three months following the concentration.
6. Procedural time-frame and suspension requirements	* One month before the Service for the Defence of Competition (tacit authorisation if the matter is not sent to the Tribunal for the Defence of Competition). * Three month (maximum) before the Tribunal for the Defence of Competition which produces a report.

6. Procedural time-frame and suspension requirements (cont.)	* Three months for the Government to study and decide on the case on the basis of the report of the Tribunal.
7. Substantive test	The substantive test for clearance is based on economic considerations on the future degree of competition in the market in which the concentration takes place (for example 25% or higher market share of the Spanish market as a whole, or of a substantial part of it).
8. Competent authorities	* Service for the Defence of Competition. * Minister of Economy and Finance. * Tribunal for the Defence of Competition.

Sweden

1. Definition of concentrations	*Present Act* The Act is applicable to "acquisitions of undertakings". *Proposed new merger regime* The proposed new merger rules are based on the concept of concentration and define the applicability of the merger rules in line with EC Merger Control Regulation.
2. Joint ventures	*Present Act* The Act is applicable to joint ventures (concentrative as well as co-operative) only to the extent that the operation includes the acquisition of an undertaking, which gives the purchaser "decisive influence". *Proposed new merger regime* Under the new law concentrative as well as full function joint ventures will be caught by the law.

3. Notification thresholds	*Present Act* Combined global turnover of more than SKr 4 billion (€ 450 million) unless turnover of target is less than SKr 100 million (€ 11 million). Only acquisitions of an undertaking that carries out some form of commercial activity in Sweden are caught by the Act. *Proposed new merger regime* Combined global turnover of more than SKr 4 billion (€ 450 million) provided that each of at least two of the undertakings concerned carries out commercial activity in Sweden and in those activities each undertaking has a turnover exceeding SKr 200 million (€ 22 million).
4. Mandatory or optional notification and sanctions	*Present Act and proposed new merger regime* Mandatory system, no pecuniary sanctions for not notifying.
5. Time-limits for notification	*Present Act* No formal time-limits under the law. *Proposed new merger regime* Concentrations that fall under the new merger rules must be notified to the Competition Authority not more than a week after: * the conclusion of the agreement; * the announcement of the public bid; * the acquisition of a controlling interest. The week begins when the first of these occurs.
6. Procedural time-frame and suspension requirements	*Present Act* There is a 30-day standstill period during which no party to the agreement may take any steps to complete the transaction. *Proposed new merger regime* There will be a standstill period of 25 working days during which no party to the concentration may take any steps to complete the transaction.

SURVEY OF MERGERS AND ACQUISITIONS

7. Substantive test	*Present act and proposed new merger regime* A merger may be prohibited subject to two cumulative conditions: 1. a dominance test that resembles that employed under EC Merger Control Regulation; 2. the requirement that there is a detrimental effect on the public interest.
8. Competent authorities	*Present Act and new merger regime* Konkurrensverket (the Swedish Competition Authority).

United Kingdom

1. Definition of concentrations	* Mergers * Acquisitions of legal and *de facto* control or of material influence * Joint ventures
2. Joint ventures	Joint ventures will fall within the concentrations criteria and thus qualify to be referred for investigation if they involve the coming under common control of previously distinct business activities.
3. Notification thresholds	* Assets test: the worldwide gross assets taken over must exceed £70 million, in value. * Share of supply test: the merger creates or strengthens a share of supply or purchasing of 25% or more in the UK or a substantial part of the UK.
4. Mandatory or optional notification and sanctions	Voluntary notification (although, in practice, very many deals are pre-notified).
5. Time-limits for notification	There is no requirement to notify and so no time-limit for notification.

6. Procedural time-frame and suspension requirements	* Decision takes 4-6 weeks typically. If Merger Notice form used, max. 35 working days. * No automatic suspension though if merger referred to the Competition Commission for second stage inquiry pre-closing automatic prohibition on further share purchases (subject to some exceptions) and order to prohibit asset deal may be made.
7. Substantive test	The Competition Commission may find that a merger does operate against the public interest and make recommendations for the remedying of the adverse effects. It then falls to the Secretary of State to decide what action to take (to prohibit, to order divestment and/or restrictions on future conduct or to clear it). If the Competition Commission clears, that is the end of the matter.
8. Competent authorities	* Secretary of State for Trade and Industry: overall responsibility for merger control; * Director General of Fair Trading: advisory and monitoring functions; * Competition Commission: investigative and advisory functions.

Addresses of contributors

Editor:
Peter Verloop
Nauta Dutilh
Prinses Irenestraat 59, 1077 WV Amsterdam, The Netherlands
Tel no: 00 31 20 5414646
Fax no: 00 31 20 6612827

European Union:
Marc van der Woude
Aymeric Dumas-Eymard
Nauta Dutilh
Terhulpsesteenweg 177/6, 1170 Brussels, Belgium
Tel no: 00 32 2 663 2974
Fax no: 00 32 2 663 2993

Austria:
Dr. Michael Kutschera
Binder, Grösswang & Partner
Sterngasse 13, A-1010 Wien, Austria
Tel no: 00 431 534 80
Fax no: 00 431 534 808

Belgium:
Marc van der Woude
Thomas Chellingsworth
Nauta Dutilh
Terhulpsesteenweg 177/6, 1170 Brussels, Belgium
Tel no: 00 32 2 663 2974
Fax no: 00 32 2 663 2993

Denmark:
Jan Holgersen
Lett, Vilstrup & Partners
Bredgade 3, 1260 Copenhagen K, Denmark
Tel no: 00 4533 154800
Fax no: 00 4533 155995

Finland:
Christian Wik
Ms. Satu Relander
Roschier-Holmberg & Waselius Attorneys Ltd.
Keskuskatu 7A, 00100 Helsinki, Finland
Tel no: 00 358 9 228 551
Fax no: 00 358 9 175 451

France:
Pierre Kirch
Moquet Borde et Associés
Avenue de Messine 30, 75008 Paris, France
Tel no: 00 33 1 42990450
Fax no: 00 33 1 45639149

Germany:
Dr. Thomas Jestaedt
Boesebeck Droste
Gallierslaan 9, B-1040 Brussels, Belgium
Tel no: 00 32 2 735 8945
Fax no: 00 32 2 735 2251

Dr. Martin Sura
Boesebeck Droste
Berliner Allee 48, D-40212 Düsseldorf, Germany
Tel no: 00 49 211 13680
Fax no: 00 49 211 324439

Greece:
Nikolaos Korogiannakis
G.S. Kostakopoulos & Associates
Place Jean Jacobs 7, B-1000 Brussels, Belgium
Tel no: 00 32 2 502 71 88
Fax no: 00 32 2 502 07 54

Italy:
　　Giovanni De Berti
　　Studio Legale De Berti, Jacchia, Perno & Associati
　　Foro Buonaparte 20, I-20121 Milan, Italy
　　Tel no: 00 39 02 725 541
　　Fax no: 00 39 02 725 54600

　　Federico Regaldo
　　Morano & Associati
　　Via Magenta 25, 10128 Torino, Italy
　　Tel no: 00 39 2 76011939
　　Fax no: 00 39 2 76011940

Ireland:
　　Gerald FitzGerald
　　McCann FitzGerald
　　2 Harbourmaster Place, Custom House Dock,
　　Dublin 1, Ireland
　　Tel no: 00 353 1 829 0000
　　Fax no: 00 353 1 829 0010

　　Damian Collins
　　McCann FitzGerald
　　Rue de la Loi 99, B-1040 Brussels, Belgium
　　Tel no: 00 32 2 230 3634
　　Fax no: 00 32 2 230 2562

The Netherlands:
　　Winfred Knibbeler
　　Ms. Willemijn Jurgens
　　Nauta Dutilh
　　Prinses Irenestraat 59, 1077 WV Amsterdam, The Netherlands
　　Tel no: 00 31 20 5414646
　　Fax no: 00 31 20 6612827

Portugal:
Carlos Pinto Correia
Morais Leitão & J. Galvão Teles
Rua Castillio 75-I, Lisboa 1250-068, Portugal
Tel no: 00 351 1 381 7400
Fax no: 00 351 1 381 7496

Spain:
Fernando Pombo
Gomez-Acebo & Pombo
Castellana 164, 28046 Madrid, Spain
Tel no: 00 34 91 582 9100
Fax no: 00 34 91 3508292/345 3679

Emiliano Garayar
Gomez-Acebo & Pombo
Rue de la Loi 99/101, B-1040 Brussels, Belgium
Tel no: 00 32 2 231 1220
Fax no: 00 32 2 230 8035

Sweden:
Johan Coyet
Ms. Louise Widen
Mannheimer Swartling
Norrmalmstorg 4, S-11187 Stockholm, Sweden
Tel no: 00 468 613 5500
Fax no: 00 468 613 5501

Ms. Anna Malin Persson
Mannheimer Swartling
Avenue de Tervueren 13 B, B-1040 Brussels, Belgium
Tel no: 00 32 2 732 2222
Fax no: 00 32 2 736 9652

United Kingdom:
Laura Carstensen
Slaughter and May
35 Basinghall Street, London EC2V 5DB, England
Tel no: 00 44 171 600 1200/dir: 00 44 171 710 4265
Fax no: 00 44 171 726 0038/dir: 00 44 171 600 0289